THE URBAN NATION
1920 – 1960

The Making of America

The Formative Years: 1607–1763 by Clarence L. Ver Steeg

Fabric of Freedom: 1763–1800 by Esmond Wright

The New Nation: 1800–1845 by Charles M. Wiltse

The Stakes of Power: 1845–1877 by Roy F. Nichols

The Search for Order: 1877–1920 by Robert H. Wiebe

The Urban Nation: 1920–1960 by George E. Mowry

THE
URBAN NATION

1920–1960

By

GEORGE E. MOWRY

The Making of America

GENERAL EDITOR: DAVID DONALD

American Century Series

HILL AND WANG   *New York*

N. H. TECH. INST.

For LaVerne

Copyright © 1965 by George E. Mowry
All rights reserved

Library of Congress catalog card number: 65–17423

Manufactured in the United States of America

FIRST EDITION MAY 1965
SECOND PRINTING AUGUST 1967
THIRD PRINTING (FIRST AMERICAN CENTURY SERIES EDITION)
JUNE 1968

Foreword

GRAVE ARE the dangers confronting the historian who attempts to write the history of his own time. He writes before passions have cooled and of events in which he himself often played a part. Since only incomplete records are yet available to him, he knows that he runs the risk of having his most carefully qualified statement refuted. Even more serious is his problem of perspective, for events that loom large in the minds of his contemporaries will often seem relatively inconsequential to subsequent generations, while underlying trends and patterns are obscured among the daily, overdramatized happenings.

Dean George E. Mowry, of the University of California at Los Angeles, has, therefore, exhibited no little daring in writing not a chronicle but an interpretation of the last four decades of American history. Resisting the easy temptation to tell the American story from the end of World War I to the beginning of the Kennedy Administration as a familiar tale of crises at home and abroad, he has endeavored to look at the period as if from the perspective of a remote point in time and to see its significance less in the day-by-day occurrences which have occupied the headlines than in the broad changes wrought in the very nature of American society. His theme is the transformation of American life during the past generation through urbanization and the mass-production-consumption economy. He shows how, stimulated by two World Wars and the Great Depression, these forces have brought about a threefold revolution in the United States,

changing the center of social and economic, if not always of political, power from the country to the city, weakening local and
state governments to the aggrandizement of national authority,
and turning our foreign policy from isolationism to worldwide
involvement in the affairs of other nations.

These changes Mr. Mowry traces with great skill and subtlety,
drawing both upon the formal historical studies of these decades
and upon a broad range of research in demography, economic
theory, sociology, and social psychology. All these sources he uses
with the care and discrimination that readers have come to expect
from the author of *Theodore Roosevelt and the Progressive Movement, The California Progressives, The Era of Theodore Roosevelt,* and other distinguished historical writings.

This in itself is a considerable achievement, but Mr. Mowry
has gone further to analyze another and even more interesting
consequence of the urban revolution in America, the transformation of the minds and the mores of the American people. Equally
at home in discussing the molding of the popular mind through
the mass communication media and in tracing the alienation felt
by many American intellectuals in an age of too rapid social
change, he has made his book an important contribution to
American intellectual history and a profound and challenging
commentary on the dangers which face our democratic society
today.

For all these reasons *The Urban Nation* precisely fulfills the
purposes of The Making of America series, a six-volume series
designed not only to make the best of historical scholarship available to the general reader but to suggest new and basic reinterpre-
tations of the American past.

DAVID DONALD

The Johns Hopkins University

Contents

Maps

Preface

THE RATE of change in American society has always been rapid compared to that in older cultures. The evolution of a settled agricultural society, the creation of a separate nationality, the forging of distinctive political institutions that matured in a few centuries were social processes that elsewhere had taken millennia.

But though for historical reasons American tolerance to social alteration should have been high, perhaps no people, no matter how conditioned to rapid change, could have lived through the forty years after 1920 without being significantly and perhaps permanently marked. The four decades were an age of great crises following one another with frightening speed. These social cataclysms—World War I, the scarifying results of which were just barely discernible in 1920, the Great Depression, the rise of the totalitarian states, World War II, and finally the cold war, hideously illumined by the threat of universal atomic destruction —are all well known. Their origins, nature, and some of their results have been carefully studied in innumerable works. Another historical survey resting upon such a crisis framework might be difficult to defend. But throughout these years two other significant social forces were at work, more slowly to be sure, but in their entirety perhaps just as productive of social change as any of the more spectacular convulsions. These were urbanization and the evolution of a mass-production-consumption economy.

The history of individual cities, the appearance of urban social problems, and the development of distinctive urban services and technology have been the subject of numerous studies, both historical and sociological. But relatively little work has been done on the rise of the modern American urban mind and its influence in changing basic American values and institutions. And although appreciably more studies have been made of the "mass ad" culture resulting from the new consumer economy, most of them have been focussed upon the fine and related arts, and few, if any, on the impact of the "mass ad" mentality upon other social institutions, in particular upon politics, both domestic and foreign. These are the twin themes of this volume: the rise of the urban mind and of the mentality developing from a mass-production-consumption economy; their conflict with the older rubrics of thought, and their impact upon institutions in an age of continuous crises.

The author is as acutely aware of how much this volume owes to the work of other scholars as he is of the number of distressing gaps to be found in it. Most of the facts and much of the interpretation have been borrowed from more diligent workers in the period. Where previous research is thin or nonexistent, as for example in state and urban developments during the New Deal and later periods, the volume is characterized by an eloquent silence. The demands of space have also meant that many important occurrences have been scantily treated. This little book then makes no pretense of treating the period comprehensively, but if it should act as a stimulus to a new way of interpreting the years between 1920 and 1960, it will have served its purpose.

GEORGE E. MOWRY

1

Rise of the Urban Mass Mind

THE CENSUS of 1920 was just as evocative of a new America as that of 1880 had been. The older census figures had marked statistically the end of the American frontier; the more recent ones the dominance of the agricultural way of life. Sometime between 1915 and 1920 the old rural majority living on the producing land, or close to it in small towns and villages, became a minority. The changes resulting from this transformation from a rural to an urban nation were to be just as momentous as those that had accompanied the conversion of the frontier into a settled land.

Despite their many superficial differences and their occasional sharp disagreements—on the slavery question, for example—the once-dominant white rural classes had been remarkably of one kind, and also of one mind on many of the broader questions of social import, no matter what section of the country they lived in, north or south of the Ohio River, or east or west of the tree line in the nation's center. By origin the great majority of them were from Northern Europe, by occupation they were farmers or small businessmen; by religion, Protestants of either Calvinist or Evangelical persuasion. Although parochial and racially conscious, they were on the whole inclined toward an equalitarianism among their own kind. In social and economical matters they believed in self-help, hard work, thrift, and personal sobriety. They disliked bigness, diversity, the exotic, leisure, elegance, and personal indulgence. Restraint and moderation marked most aspects of their lives. And if individually they often violated various aspects of their credo, as a group they lived by it to a remarkable degree and were even more intense in their conviction that other people should also conform to it.

Life in the commercial city, even in Colonial times, had offered significant variations in this provincial pattern, and rural complaints against the city as the home of the irreligious, the amoral, and the unproductive were standard. This rural criticism grew steadily in the nineteenth century as the population centers were increasingly industrialized and became increasingly the home of the new immigrant groups from Southern and Eastern Europe. The sharp class stratification of the cities with conspicuous luxury on the one hand and slums, unemployment, and bread lines on the other, the growth of unions and industrial warfare, the increasingly Jewish and Roman Catholic character of the urban centers, and the rise in crime and political corruption all strengthened the hand of the rural critic. By the end of the nineteenth century the agrarian assumption that the countryside in some mysterious way bred character and patriotism while the city fostered opposing vices was entrenched in American social lore, politics, and literature. Since it was much easier to quit the countryside for the city's opportunities than it was to slough off deeply ingrained rural attitudes, and since in the late nineteenth and early twentieth centuries it was convenient politically for America's ruling economic classes to foster the rural virtues, the agrarian myth died hard, even among city dwellers generations removed from the farm. Social nostalgia, more of a historical force than is generally recognized, also explains the tenacious grip that the rural bias still had on many Americans in 1920 and the decades thereafter, when the nation had become predominantly urban.

Although the 1920 census merely recorded a historical fact, its publication sharpened the alertness of Americans to the increasing urban tilt of the country. Simultaneously another complex revolutionary development was rapidly assaulting many of the cherished values of the rural-minded both in the city and on the farm. The rapid evolution during the twenties of the "ad mass," or the mass-production-consumption society, tied together big business and the masses in a symbiotic relationship so close that the health of one was the health of the other. By developing new techniques and institutions necessary to bind the consuming crowd to the corporate board room this new type of economic society also sapped and destroyed in daily practice much of the content of the rural creed, though verbal and emotional commitment to the old values continued to be celebrated in many social rites. The stage was thus set for a clash between rural beliefs and the actualities of the new urban pursuits, a clash which many individuals could not even logically resolve for themselves. On a more general level the conflict was between the urban and the rural mentality, between the countryside and the city; still more generally between the Middle West and the South as proponents of the old views, and the East and eventually the Pacific Coast as patrons of the cosmopolitan outlook. This ideological schism, quite apparent during the twenties, was to penetrate most aspects of American life during the next forty years and to give a marked quality to both foreign and domestic politics.

The rise of the new mass-production-consumption economy was a logical, but not inevitable, evolution of the historic industrial combination movement. The concentration of heavy and extractive industries into a relatively few large nationwide firms was already an old story by 1920. But prior to World War I the average man, except for purchasing a few products, rarely stood in a face-to-face relationship with the agents of big business. It was during the twenties that the combination movement vigorously breached the service and retail fields. By 1930 ten holding companies controlled over 70 per cent of the nation's supply of electric power, branch banking had been so extended that 1 per cent of the nation's banks controlled 46 per cent of its banking resources, and chain stores were doing 37 per cent of the country's retail drug business, while similar figures in notions and groceries were even higher. But of all the industrial developments contributing to the growing interdependence of the large corporations and the masses, those in the new field of mass entertainment and in household appliances and automobiles were the most important.

Without the film and radio industries it is doubtful that the mass-production-consumption culture could have fastened itself on the country as rapidly as it did. By 1922 40 million cinema tickets were being sold weekly, and the sound waves were carrying news and advertising into 3 million homes. By the end of the twenties the weekly movie audience had more than doubled, and few people in the country were long out of earshot of a radio receiver. In 1929 $852 million worth of receiving sets were sold, the profits from which, when added to the millions the broadcasting industry received in advertising revenues, bulked significantly in the total corporate income of the country. In the same year multimillion-dollar returns from a single film were not exceptional. Profits of such an order generated within the two industries the same consolidating forces that were at work in traditional business fields. By 1930 most of the nation's films were made by five or six large companies producing in Hollywood and New York. Within the following decade over seven hundred of the nation's nine hundred radio stations had been organized into four privately owned networks, two of which were pre-eminent.

Although the national radio-broadcasting industry subsisted entirely upon revenue from advertisers, more politely called sponsors, while movies had to be sold directly to the consumer, the two industries had this in common: they were both hawking a strictly nonuseful product, entertainment for leisure time, the popularity of which rested upon the relatively free choice of the public uninfluenced by utilitarian or other social considerations. In each industry, internal forces led to an assiduous search for the largest possible audience. Since advertisers wanted to know exactly what they were buying on a national broadcast, the radio networks developed a telephone polling system, which indicated to the sponsor what share of the national audience was listening to the production through which his appeals for consumer patronage were liberally sprinkled. It is true that not all advertisers adjusted their programs to conform to the taste of the greatest number. Some, who sold their products to industries or to a special clientele, and others, usually great national companies, who labelled their efforts "public service"—the very name said volumes about the normal radio fare—supported programs of limited appeal. But overwhelmingly the radio listings were governed as strictly as possible by a dollars-and-cents-per-listening-head standard.

The film industry became even more obsessed by the desire to cultivate the greatest number of customers. The ever-rising salaries paid to writers, directors, and actors, and especially the enormous sums paid to the leading actors after the development of the "star system," forced the budgets of films constantly upward. In 1920 the cost of an exceptionally expensive Hollywood production amounted to perhaps a few hundred thousand dollars; by 1929 the comparable figure was in the millions. Such rocketing costs constrained the producing companies to reach for the widest possible audience and therefore to tailor the product as closely as possible to the taste of the masses.

Aside from purely cultural considerations, the radio-broadcasting and film industries played a significant part in forming the mass consumer society, contributing immeasurably to the so-called revolution in the expectations of the common man. Because the majority of the movie audience had no desire to be reminded of their shabby homes and their dreary, monotonous work, most pictures dealt with carefree individuals engaged in exciting adventures and surrounded by frivolous luxuries. The typical heroine wore expensive clothes, furs, and elegant jewels, and either lived in a stately mansion or flitted between the de luxe hotels of the world; the hero, usually without visible means of support, was as splendidly accoutred, drove the fanciest automobile, and pursued the most attractive young women. Since the movies set the constantly changing standards in manners, hairdos, and fashions for village maiden and city working girl alike, there is reason to assume that they changed the nation's attitudes toward more important and permanent values as well. Hollywood, with "its great bargain sale of five and ten cent lusts and dreams," John Dos Passos commented, had become the goal-inspiring source of the masses. The movie credo was one of sustained consumption, not production. And continually reiterating this theme, the industry became midwife to the birth of the leisure-seeking, pleasure-demanding, materialistic consumer society of modern America.

Lacking visual impact, radio broadcasting probably had much less effect upon mass aspirations and habits than the films. But significantly the cost of the entire industry was carried by advertising, the first such development in the evolution of modern business. The advertising industry was well established by 1920, but its proliferation in the next decade was enormous. Atlhough records are uncertain, it has been estimated that the sums spent on advertising during the twenties more than doubled and probably tripled, a result to which the broadcasting industry significantly contributed. Before the advent of radio the advertising industry was silent; it now assaulted the ears of the nation day and night, and the air was charged with the strident plea to consume.

No matter how tempted the average American was to follow the Hollywood example or to heed the pitchmen of radio and indulge himself in an orgy of purchasing, formidable obstacles to action existed at the start of the decade. Among the relatively few citizens with substantial savings old habits of thrift had to be broken down, and for many others the basic wherewithal had to be found. Real wages and salaries had been relatively constant from 1900 to 1915, and much of the wartime increase had been wiped away by the price inflation of 1919–1920 and the depression of 1921. Either wages had to be raised or some other means found to increase mass consuming power. One of the answers was consumer credit, a device not unknown before the war, but one which had been used individually, informally, and with rather rigid discrimination based upon the purpose of the loan. With the advent of the twenties the industry was rapidly organized by so-called finance companies, and retail credit associations sprang up in practically every sizable town and city. No accurate figures exist on the amount of consumer credit extended during the decade, and a history of credit is badly needed, but it is clear from what records do exist that a forcible impetus was given to the expansion by the automobile industry. Soon home appliances, radio sets, furniture, and even such luxuries as jewelry were being sold on the installment plan. By 1929, when apparently over 75 per cent of the automobiles and probably more than half of all major household appliances were sold on time payments, total consumer credit, it has been estimated, had reached a peak of about $7 billion. A large fraction of consumers had learned to live on the philosophy of "a dollar down and a dollar forever," as the lighthearted phrase of the day described installment buying. With the erosion of the old American tradition which considered personal debt akin to sin, it was perhaps reasonable to expect the public to view public debt with something of the same complacency. Possibly private industry's consumer-credit operations during the twenties conditioned the American people to accept the New Deal's deficit financing a decade later.

The sum of the economic results flowing from the bewildering technological advances, the rapidly rising expectations of the masses, and the widespread application of consumer credit still does not explain the replacement of the old business system by a new one based upon mass production and consumption. One vital factor was still missing: the will on the part of corporate managers greatly to expand facilities and production while encouraging higher consumption by stabilizing or lowering prices and raising wages. A safer course would have been the one generally pursued by European industrialists. The Europeans, in effect, established a policy of maintaining low wage rates and high product prices, while limiting facilities, credit, and production to the size of the existing market. Why American corporate managers took the other course is not explained entirely either by the complex economic forces of the moment or the hope for profit in the future. Such long-time social forces as the tradition of competition, the American veneration of bigness and growth, the dislike of immobility, and the willingness to take risks all played a part in their decision. So did an important factor not too much discussed by historians heretofore: a remarkable change in the socioeconomic outlook of the industrial leadership.

Especially when contrasted with his European counterpart, the often and sometimes justly criticized American businessman had never been as asocial as some of his bitterest native critics claimed. But even during the prewar period of progressivism, the standard business answers to charges that the country's productive institutions were unmindful of the common good were often couched in the old brutal language of classical economics. If prewar reformers pointed out that unbridled competition meant the destruction of thousands of small employers and the growth of monopolies, if they decried huge fortunes for the few and poverty for the many, if they assailed the conditions under which food and drugs were prepared, if they criticized high prices and low wages and proposed that political solutions be found for such social blights as unemployment and industrial accidents, the standard business answer was to the effect that that was the way the industrial machine operated most efficiently, and any attempt to interfere with it by restrictive legislation would intensify the social calamities the reformers were trying to obliterate. The inference was plain: the economic machinery was necessarily impervious to finer human feelings and lay outside the moral claims of the state. Occasionally during those prewar years the economic institutions were described not only as existing of necessity, but also as deserving to exist, and even as having been blessed with divine sanction.

Compared to those prewar expressions, many business statements of the twenties contained almost revolutionary phrases. True, the old "root hog or die" spirit still cropped up. But it is surprising how much social and ethical content there was in the postwar business jargon. Instead of presenting themselves as strictly private, large corporations now often described themselves as "public institutions" in which, according to one of the managers of the United States Rubber Company, "the rights of all must be accorded proper recognition." Even such an individualist as Henry Ford was, as presented by his public relations experts, at least, ready to qualify his sense of ownership. "A machine," he wrote, "belongs neither to the man who purchased it nor to the worker who operated it, but to the public. . . . It advantages the worker and the proprietor only as they use it to the advantage of the public." Although organized business was probably more devoted to the open shop than it had been before the war, nevertheless significant changes occurred in the vocabulary, and to a perhaps lesser degree in the actualities, of labor relations. In the rhetoric accompanying the campaign to organize company unions the "harmony of interest" doctrine frequently appeared, and not all the activities of such captive organizations were debits to labor's interests. During the early years of the twenties strike-breaking agencies such as the one owned by Pearl Berghoff prospered, and the use of labor spies and company police was common. But so was the employment of industrial relations experts and the institution of profit-sharing plans and shop medical schemes. Such welfare measures were often described in the business press as an indication not of the benevolence of the managers but of their hard business sense, since "the loyalties of the working men" were an unseen but very real capital asset.

Significant verbal changes occurred in the prevailing attitude toward wages. Before World War I Henry Ford had been almost the only industrialist to advocate high wages. By 1928 *Manufacturing Industries* was editorializing that under modern circumstances "high wages and low labor costs go together." During the same year the editors of *Factory and Industrial Management* argued that "American industries are now geared to a pace of production that cannot be sustained without high wages. . . ." In attempting to describe corporation labor and wage policies during the twenties, one recent labor historian, whose prolabor sympathies are rather obvious, characterizes them as "uncertain and ambivalent."

If one is to judge by business rhetoric alone relations between the seller and the consumer were also substantially modified. The old rule of the market place, let the buyer beware, was no longer a proper or desirable principle, according to the magazine *System*: "Boiled down, *caveat emptor* was merely an attempt to get something for nothing." A like-minded magazine argued that henceforth the buyer must have equal rights with the seller. The president of one large New York merchandising house went even further. He assured the public that his firm considered itself an agent of the consumers, bound not only by the legalities but also by the "ethics of the law of agency." The traditional concepts of price and profit were undergoing redefinition by some business theoreticians. Increasingly the classic definition of price was being modified by the significant words "legitimate" and "fair." Since industry had no other excuse for being, the president of the General Electric Corporation wrote, profit should be "the acknowledged payment for service to society." Even Wall Street, that old haunt of unmodified free market doctrine, was somewhat changing its vocabulary. While the Street made no boast of charity or brotherly kindness, the *Wall Street Journal* declared, if the American people supported progress the financial and business leaders must and would see to it that the masses were furnished with "libraries, galleries and museums."

From the viewpoint of the Depression years, it was easy to ridicule these statements as myths spun by less-than-sincere capitalists or as inventions of the public relations men paid to delude the public. But prior to the Depression they were taken by some responsible people as indications that big business had reformed. As one commentator pointed out, whatever the actuality the rhetoric had changed and the majority of men in the long run were often as much prisoners of their talk as of their acts. In discussing the reason for the change Glenn Frank, editor of the *Century* and soon to be president of the University of Wisconsin, argued that twenty years of progressivism had instilled into businessmen "a sense of social responsibility." Some saw the development as an outgrowth of the business luncheon clubs with their insistent chorus of service to the community, while others felt that the rise of the business schools in the nation's colleges and universities was instrumental in bringing about "a new type of business leader."

One might also argue that the changing corporate structure had an important effect upon the social attitudes of its governing class. As A. A. Berle, Jr. and Gardiner Means pointed out in the thirties in their book *The Modern Corporation and Private Property* (1932), the gigantic size of modern business enterprise had forced changes both in its organic nature and in the character of its control. The one-man corporation dominated by a capitalist-owner had practically disappeared, to be replaced by a managerial group. Because of profits generated internally and changes in the nation's banking structure, the old finance control of Wall Street, while still evident, was being weakened. Ownership through stockholding was so diluted because of the gigantic size of corporate business that any consistent owner control was almost impossible. Sheltered from Wall Street direction, insulated from the demands of stockholders, and almost totally free from significant governmental regulation, the ruling corporate oligarchy, even in the twenties showing signs of being self-perpetuating, had much more room for maneuver of corporation policy.

A mountain of evidence culled from the Depression-born investigating committees of Congress indicates that many corporate managers during the twenties used their new-found freedom to enrich themselves by grossly despoiling the public. Admittedly, many of the activities of the petroleum and electric power industries, and especially those of the suprafinancial community, were reprehensible. But the total record of increasing production and a stable price level also indicates that the great bulk of American industry was dedicated to a program of mass production and consumption. Perhaps as important as any other reason for this continued devotion to the "gospel of production" was the startling fact that by the end of the twenties big industry and the big crowd had formed a face-to-face relationship from which they neither could nor cared to withdraw. In 1920 only one among the twenty largest corporations made products for direct consumer use. By 1929 there were nine, headed by the automobile industry, whose retail dealers were franchised directly by the parent producing corporations. Small wonder then that in the late years of the decade the public was inundated with repeated surveys of consumer tastes and desires. As Henry Ford never tired of pointing out, the consumer had become the real "dictator" of success or failure.

The career of Henry Ford is almost indistinguishable from the evolution of the automotive industry. Both the man and the industry constituted major forces in the great changes that the large-scale mass consumer industries were making in American society. Ford was something of an anachronism in the twenties, and perhaps he really belonged to the nineteenth-century era of industrial tycoons. He was a briary sort of person, a dictator who demanded agreement from his employees, even from his supervising executives. He hated unions, which he fought with labor spies and company police, and he was intensely opposed to government regulation. As late as the 1940's he threatened to close down his factories rather than accept national-defense orders from the government. At one time in his career he was an outspoken anti-Semite and distinctly disliked intellectuals. Books "messed up" his mind, and he preferred Napoleon to Christ because the former was a "hustler." Though he changed the face of America as possibly no other man in his period, he had a deep-seated nostalgia for the past. Outspoken in praise of what he fancied were the institutions and virtues of the past, he collected old furniture, implements, and vehicles for his "pioneer museum." He characterized reform as "trouble-making," and warned that the destruction of old institutions was "a tricky business." Yet as much as any man of his day Henry Ford helped to destroy the social values of nineteenth-century America.

After experimenting with many shapes and types of motor cars, for most of which the basic engineering had already been developed in Europe, Ford settled on his basic Model T in 1909 and continued to make it until 1927 with only minor modifications. Its function and design were in spirit a utilitarian creation of rural America. It was black, sober-looking, innocent of sophistication or adornment, and without much provision for the comfort of its passengers. Its purpose was transportation. It was cheap, and its not too numerous parts were susceptible of simplification and standardization. In 1913 Ford introduced into his factory the moving production line along which the parts of his automobile were meshed together by stationary workmen whose function, more and more, was to perform a single repetitious task. Within a few years Ford could boast that 90 per cent of his workmen could learn their allotted tasks within a few hours.

Despite the revolutionary nature of the production line, Ford's most significant social contributions were perhaps in his wage, price, and selling policies. His avowed aim was to sell an automobile to every family in the country, an objective only possible, he insisted, if wages were high and the selling price low. It is futile to ask whether the man was sincere in his preachment that a factory machine was a public servant and industrial production a social function. The fact is that he lowered the price of his automobile from $950 in 1909 to $290 in 1924, at the same time raising the wages of his workers well above and reducing the working time below the standards for the industry. Though he did not succeed in placing a car with every family, he sold an enormous number. By 1927 the automobile industry had manufactured a total of 20 million cars, of which the Model T accounted for one-half.

Ford's mania for cutting costs—in the early days he spent hours walking through his factory eliminating an unnecessary operation here, consolidating another there—was spurred as much perhaps by his competitors as by his social doctrines. By 1927 the competitive process in the automotive industry had reduced the number of significant producers in the field from at least twenty before the war to three: Ford, General Motors, and Chrysler. As the competitive race tightened, inexorable forces were set loose which changed the social nature of the industry. As prices were cut to meet each competitor's thrust, the necessity to maintain profit by mass volume was imperious. Consequently, increasing attention had to be paid to sales techniques and to consumer preferences, an evolution which ended in the sales and design organizations becoming as important as those devoted to engineering, production, and costs. The nation was divided into sales regions, regions into districts, and districts among franchised retail distributors. A yearly quota of automobiles was assigned to each dealer, which he had to dispose of or risk losing his franchise. When the system developed, as much pressure was put upon the local distributors and their individual salesmen as was placed upon the workmen on the production line. Abetting this sales organization was a nationwide campaign of advertising to persuade the consumer to buy. Even with such an elaborate organization the industry found itself in periodic difficulties. It was attempting to sell what for many people was still a high-priced luxury, the initial cost of which could not possibly be met from the average man's current income. The obvious answer was installment buying, the terms of which became increasingly more lax as hard-pressed dealers sought to fulfill their factory quotas. By 1929, when some dealers were offering an automobile on the initial payment of 10 per cent of the value, 75 per cent of the vehicles were sold on credit. Total sales for that year amounted to over $2 billion, on which consumers paid interest charges running up to 15 per cent.

The urge to sell en masse, which a visiting minister remarked had become "the new religion of Detroit," led to other radical changes in the industry. By 1927 the ownership of a late luxury model automobile had become for many Americans a status symbol to display before envious neighbors. In deference to consumer taste and preference the Ford Company, much against its owner's will, had to abandon its cheap, Spartan type of vehicle. Replacing the Model T, Ford brought out the Model A, incorporating a few of the luxuries but more of the engineering advances of competing vehicles. This was but the first step in the ardent wooing of the consumer by means other than price. Before Ford's death his company had added to its line six- and eight-cylinder cars, resplendent in a rainbow of colors and equipped with many of the gadgets of the year. The company also joined the rest of the industry in bringing out a new model every year, not so much to incorporate engineering advances as to hasten obsolescence. In 1932 the Ford Company cooperated with its competitors in buying old cars for purposes of demolition in order to add to the diminishing market for new ones. Well before the Depression Ford had had to relinquish many of his original ideas, which came straight from old America. With the death of the Model T, a part of the tradition of thrift, the pioneer sense of utility, and the nineteenth-century air of sobriety was buried.

In his novel *Main Street,* Sinclair Lewis observed that his hero, Will Kennicott, had four loves, his wife, his automobile, his medical practice, and hunting. Adding that he would not have known how to rate these in order of preference, Lewis gave vivid testimony to the joyful and hungry mass appetite for the automobile. Fed by a national demand, the industry waxed until it became the key factor in the American economy. During the twenties General Motors passed the once-awesome United States Steel Corporation in earning power, and the total industry, including subsidiary manufacturers of rubber, petroleum, glass, and highway-construction items, employed more men and utilized more raw and semifinished materials than any other industrial cluster in the nation.

The automotive industry made so many economic, political, and social changes that a thick volume would be required to discuss them comprehensively. Of all the major alterations that the industry made, possibly none was more important than its part in ushering in and acting as a talisman for the mass-production-consumption economy by which an increasing portion of the major industries was directly tied to the desires, fads and fancies, and purchasing ability of the masses.

The tale told by the gross industrial statistics for the twenties is an amazing one. Efficiency per factory man-hour rose by over 70 per cent. Total industrial production went up perhaps 60 per cent, an increase that far outstripped gains in population. Simultaneously real industrial wages, monthly salaries, profits, and dividends rose appreciably. All this was accomplished with little or no increase in factory employment and with a reduction of the number of men working in the mines and forests.

Because of the lack of precise statistics most attempts to break down these national figures into ones indicating the relative welfare of various social groups have probably reflected more ideology than accuracy. But this much is clear. The industrial worker enjoyed a perceptible gain in real income of perhaps 15 to 25 per cent while his hours of labor decreased moderately and working conditions improved rapidly. The six-day, sixty-hour week was normal in 1920; by 1929 the standard was a five-and-a-half-day, 48–54-hour week, and such benefits as shop medical plans, recreational facilities, and paid vacations were not exceptional.

The industrial worker also shared in the rapidly proliferating state and civic services.

The real gains secured by the white-collar classes were even more impressive, although exact supporting figures are impossible to produce. The increases in monthly and yearly salaries apparently were far sharper than those for the weekly worker. And the rapid expansion of new executive positions in corporate, service, and governmental functions provided opportunities for the middle classes that have seldom been equalled in the history of the country. As for the fortunes of the owning classes, again the gross national figures are eloquent, if not exact. Total dividends, interest, and rent payments went up during the decade by almost 30 per cent, and income tax records indicate that the rate of increase rose sharply as one went up the scale toward annual incomes of more than a million dollars. Thus while the poor were slowly increasing their meager competence and the middle classes were making substantial gains, the rich were growing richer at a more than moderate rate.

Though the national economic climate was under the influence of a steadily rising barometer, neither all industry nor the entire population was prosperous. As the source of power and the patterns of production and consumption changed with bewildering speed during the decade, whole industries were in deep trouble. The coal and textile industries, as well as agriculture, were in general distress during most of the period. Producers of such anachronisms as bicycles and wagons were forced to the wall. With the assault of the automobile the national network of electric interurban lines collapsed just a few years after it had been built, leaving a trail of rusted rails and ruined investors. As revealed later by the Temporary National Economic Committee's investigations, the struggle of the independent grocer and pharmacist against the rising chain stores was often a tale of defeated hopes and lost capital. Rapid industrial and commercial changes also meant unemployment for both white-collar and factory workers, as did the introduction of labor-saving and skill-destroying automatic machinery. A Philadelphia survey of April 1929 showed that 10 per cent of the city's wage earners were unemployed, and one authority estimated that national unemployment ran from 5 to 13 per cent of the total labor force. At the close of the extremely prosperous year of 1927 economist Irving Fisher, of Yale University, estimating that four-fifths of the American people were earning a little more than their living expenses, declared that the country was "not as yet prosperous in any absolute sense."

Yet for all the weak spots and imbalances in the economy the average American, measured by his past or the past of any other industrial nation, was a man to be envied. He was better fed and better clothed than any other average man in history. Free schooling was thrust upon his children. Whether by his earning power or by the workings of the credit system, he usually possessed an automobile and a radio. For the first time in world history mass man became the master of a complicated piece of power machinery by which he could annihilate distance. The radio gave another dimension to his rapidly increasing mobility, making it possible for him to flood his house with the world's news of the instant, with music and amusement. If more varied circuses were wanted, the movie house was usually just around the corner and easily within his means. Taken together, the automobile, the movie, and the radio obliterated the village and the farm as islands of isolation from the mass luxury economy, for the entire world of fancy goods had been moved as close to the one-time provincial as the nearest movie screen or loudspeaker. Surveying the national scene in 1929, Lincoln Steffens, the one-time muckraker and semi-Marxist, commented, "Big business in America is producing what the Socialists held up for their goal: food, shelter and clothing for all." Coming from an old-time critic of the big-business system this was a tribute indeed.

As the new mass-production-consumption business system made vast changes in the economic structure, it also had extremely important effects upon American culture. In the early days of the films and radio their potential value in leading the masses of the people toward a new and much higher cultural level was widely heralded. When both became almost purely instruments of entertainment, purveyors of modern fairy tales, the lamentations of critics became loud and unceasing. But under the spur of rising costs and competition the key to profits was the widest possible market among viewers and listeners. Box-office receipts and Hooper's radio ratings were sensitive indices to public taste as well as grim dictators of monetary success or failure. In both industries isolated individuals sporadically attempted to lift the cultural level of their product. But the bitter cry of one movie producer, who had lost over two million dollars on one such attempt, that "from now on art is out" was eloquent. Given the structure of the two industries and their dependence upon the mass market, quality and artistic perfection had to be confined to such matters as techniques. With art "out" the film makers concentrated on what their box office receipts indicated the national and world audience wanted. That, in brief, was sex, sin, and sensation, set in a whipped-cream world of luxury and leisure. As flashing electric bulbs in practically every American town and city advertised movies with the promise of "jazz babies," "red hot mamas," "passionate petting parties," "champagne baths," "fast young men," and "faster automobiles," sex had undoubtedly become, as Eugene O'Neill phrased it in *Strange Interlude*, the "philosopher's stone." But in the hands of the movie alchemists the legendary stone ordinarily turned potentially rare metals into the base or the trivial.

Older cultural institutions also felt the weight of the new mass market. Both the daily and the periodical press eagerly sought new readers, more for the purpose of capturing the burgeoning national advertising than to increase the area of their influence. In 1919 the first tabloid newspaper, the New York *Daily News,* was published, creating a new journalistic style that was soon copied in New York by Macfadden's *Evening Graphic* and Hearst's *Daily Mirror* and in Chicago by the *Daily Illustrated Times.* The *Daily News,* eventually to have the largest circulation of any American paper, was scarcely a newspaper in the conventional sense. As its style matured it carried more pictures than reading material and more advertising than either, more gossip than news, more entertainment than information, and, as one critic declared, "more sex than sense." It and the other tabloids were long on criminal and divorce stories, major disasters, sports, and comic strips, and on personal columns giving advice to its readers on how to meet sex and marriage problems; short on political, economic, and social news of a serious nature; and almost entirely innocent of critical comment on literature, art, music, and the drama.

The tabloids that sponsored the first well-advertised bathing beauty contests also ushered in the practice of "keyhole" journalism replete with alleged intimate details of the great, the notorious, the criminal, and of the gaudy, night-blooming sporting and café crowd. So popular did these intimate reporters become that the most expert among them made their names and writings widely known through nationally syndicated columns. Masters of suggestion and innuendo, this new breed walked a dangerous path between the libidinous and the libellous. Much of their information was almost astrological as they attempted to titillate their readers with predictions of major sensations and scandals to come. Of such reporters Walter Winchell became perhaps the most skilled. Born on the Lower East Side of New York, his education having ended with the sixth grade, Winchell was contemptuous of the learned and the cultured. He defined an economic expert as "a bore running for, or holding office" and a philosopher as "somebody who knows all the platitudes and copies things that are clever out of books." When asked once whether he had ever read a book, he replied that he had, but at the moment he could not think of the name of a single one. Possibly because of his cultural limitations Winchell was an avatar of the new type of mass journalism, which sought to be neither conscience nor instructor for its readers. Instead, the tabloid was a merchandiser of advertising and a conveyor of mass entertainment.

At the start of the century William Dean Howells remarked that much of the better American writing appeared in the popular magazines rather than in books. But by 1930 Edward J. O'Brien's yearly collection of the best short stories was dependent for most of its material upon the so-called little magazines and not upon the mass-circulation journals. Predictably the little magazines had to be subsidized by individual or institutional patrons while the popular publications waxed under the stimulation of mass subscriptions and skyrocketing advertising receipts. Authors profited also—one with four successful novels to his credit reported that he had been paid more by a weekly magazine for a hastily written four-part serial than he had made from all his previous work of twenty-five years. By 1922 ten magazines were each claiming a paid circulation of over 2,500,000, and another dozen claimed circulation of over a million. More than half of this total belonged to the "pulps," magazines printed on cheap wood-pulp paper and devoted mostly to detective, Western, or movie stories. Among the top leaders in circulation were the newly conceived confession-story magazines, full of alleged first-person accounts of moral wrongdoings and inevitable repentance. But perhaps the most significant change had come about in the kinds of material which the better and more traditional magazines chose to print. According to a recent study comparing the nature of magazine material in the twenties with that of twenty years before, the mass-circulation magazines of the decade carried far fewer serious factual articles and many more devoted to sports, fads, and leisure-time pursuits. The great majority of the biographical articles of twenty years before had been devoted to politicians, businessmen, and professional people. By the late twenties and the thirties precedence had shifted to studies of movie stars, sports heroes, and radio "personalities." The significant trend, the author concluded, was away from the heroes of production and culture toward the idols of consumption and leisure.

Even the staid book trade felt the impact of the new mass market. Both the Literary Guild and the Book-of-the-Month Club were organized in the decade with the announced intention of selecting the best books, giving them a national market, and thus retailing them at a cheaper price; exactly the ends of Henry Ford with his Model T. There were prestigious literary names on the boards of editors; nevertheless, as club memberships grew the temptation to choose books that would please the greatest number of patrons was obvious. At the end of the decade a national survey of the book trade indicated that many publishers had in fact adopted many of the new business techniques. Instead of publishing a few quality titles, some admitted to producing many more dubious ones in the hopes of publishing a "best seller" that could be sold en masse and the profits from which would alone insure a successful business year. The best seller, a term given currency in the decade and redolent of its newer values, was often a work of serious literature. But just as often, one critic pointed out, it was a volume seemingly written "to justify a reasonable amount of adultery in the eyes of suburban matrons."

According to a contemporary survey of the book trade many publishers admitted to a sizable amount of "merchandising" in pushing their most popular wares. "Mass advertising," some felt, aided greatly in "putting over" a book, as did "building up an author" and the "placing of reviews." Whether by design or by a surge of charitable instincts the standards of reviewing had become far less critical than those at the turn of the century. Of 6,542 reviews taken at random, 294 were unfavorable, 3,639 favorable, and 2,609 noncommittal. Such excellence, if real, was grounds for congratulation, the survey concluded, but neither the style nor the contents of the books studied warranted such a conclusion.

The contents of both fiction and nonfiction changed significantly during the twenties. One of the marked developments was the rise of a new school of popular biography which so stressed the intimate details of the lives of national heroes, their more questionable activities, and their shortcomings that it was given the name "debunking." After George Washington and Benjamin Franklin had been so debunked, James Truslow Adams complained that the tendency of the age was to see "no difference between the operations of the bowels and those of the brain." When the reading public seemed to tire of such sport with the nation's venerables, some biographers turned their attention to a study of the more sensational characters of the past, a process characterized by one sour critic as a change from "pulling down idols" to "setting up criminals for inspection."

Fiction, too, was busy pulling down idols as well as venerated

ways and ideals of the past. At the start of the century Theodore
Dreiser's *Sister Carrie* was withdrawn from public circulation for
a decade because its heroine became the mistress of two men. But
beginning with the publication of Edgar Lee Master's *Spoon
River Anthology* (1915) and Sherwood Anderson's *Winesburg,
Ohio* (1919), both inquisitorial studies of small Midwestern communities, the attack upon the village and its respected morals and
ethics was heavy and continuous. One of the abler craftsmen of
the prewar years, Ellen Glasgow, had escaped challenge by contemporary bluenose critics, though she had repeatedly dealt with
the moral decay of the old Southern aristocracy. During the
twenties Miss Glasgow wrote four novels, in which two of her
heroines had illegitimate children, a third left her husband for
another man, and the fourth scandalized her Virginia intimates
with her "gutter" ways and talk. Sinclair Lewis, F. Scott Fitzgerald, Ernest Hemingway, and John Dos Passos were even more
explicit, and by the end of the decade what had once been immorality had now become, in the words of one of Hemingway's
characters, "only the things that made you disgusted afterwards."
As for writers of less ability, one can measure the distance they
had departed from the old conventions by the advertising blurbs
describing their works. "As intimate as a boudoir, as amusing as
a peephole and as suggestive as a bill of fare," one such read.

Whether the new moral and ethical climate of the twenties was
brought about more by the ideas disseminated by towering think-
ers like Freud, Bergson, and Einstein, and by those of the lesser
essayists and the creative writers, scholars, and artists, or more by
such mundane and objective factors as urbanization, the rapid
change in technology, and the complex forces let loose by the
creation of the mass-production-consumption society is a historical argument without apparent end. From the days of Plato
idealists have argued that the spirit and the mind are masters of
men's destiny; the materialists have countered with the assertion
that mind and spirit apart from the concrete have no reality. But
from the narrow focus of the twenties it would seem that in the
destruction of old ways and morals the objective factors of urbanization, technology, and the new business system had as much

effect as, if not more than, the so-called seminal ideas. How else is one to explain the fact that the morals of the movies, the tabloids, and the confession magazines, all presumably dictated by the crowd, were almost identical with those conveyed by the more literate novelists and essayists? There was, of course, the difference that sin and evil rarely triumphed in the end on the screen or in the pulps, whereas Hemingway could write that the good and bad perished alike before implacable natural and social forces. But in a way the movie or confession-story heroine who departed from existing conventions only to be absolved ultimately by true love and marriage made the way to transgression easier for palpitating viewers and readers. For the popular heroine had the best of both worlds; she had tasted sin and had her moral cake and security, too.

Whatever the origins of the more important forces in the assault on traditional institutions, morality, and folkways, there is little question that the twenties marked a battleground between the defenders of the old ways and the innovators. During the decade a cultural conflict raged in which almost every existing social institution was questioned and many were modified radically. In Sinclair Lewis' *Main Street,* published in 1920, the heroine and her classmates discuss what business positions they will seek after graduation from college. Twenty years before, few midland girls had even attended college and among this favored few, business was scarcely in the range of their ambition. But by the twenties the feminine employment revolution had reached flood tide. By 1928 the number of women working was five times the figure of ten years before, women at Columbia University outnumbered men for the first time, and women had been elected governors of states and had been appointed to the Federal bench.

Perhaps even more startling than woman's changing occupations were her changing manners and morals. The "flapper," or the new woman of the twenties, imitated men as closely as possible. She cut both her hair and her dresses exceedingly short, de-emphasized the feminine form by throwing away her corsets and by dieting, and participated with gusto in what had hitherto been masculine amusements and sports. Whereas before 1918 she had rarely been seen in a saloon, by 1925 she was a familiar sight in the illegal speakeasy and cocktail bar. She had also become such a consumer of cigarettes that a tobacco company dared to show a woman smoking in an advertisement. One of the favorite subjects of magazines and Sunday supplements was women's changing moral standards. There was much discussion of what "necking" and "petting"—terms used with much vagueness to describe the degree of sexual activity by unmarried couples—meant for the institution of marriage. Fanny Hurst, a popular novelist, created a public scandal in 1923 when she gave an interview describing her "experiment in marriage" since she and her husband had agreed in their marriage contract to live in separate establishments so as better to pursue their individual artistic careers. A storm of opposition met Judge Ben Lindsey's proposal for companionate, or trial, marriage. But few critics met head on his argument that since the sexual part of marriage was generally practiced before the ceremony anyway, society might as well legalize and institutionalize it. Prompted by the almost doubled divorce rate in the decade, five volumes appeared in 1929 on the so-called marriage crisis. At the same time a scholarly survey of urban marriages showed that 50 per cent of the husbands and wives interviewed were "unhappy" with their institutional state, and 15 per cent felt that adultery should not be denounced since it was a normal occurrence in modern marriages. On the basis of such evidence it is not too much to say that modern feminine morality and attitudes toward the institution of marriage date from the twenties.

The movement toward feminine equality had of course started before the Civil War. And the breakdown of the Victorian moral code, with its emphasis upon feminine purity, began in the Bohemian Greenwich Village society of pre-World War I New York, foreshadowing one of the effects of the coming urban revolution. The War itself had much to do with upsetting old standards, and the passage of the Nineteenth Amendment probably inspired the feminine sex to seek greater conquests. The influence of Sigmund Freud and the new psychology, the movement of technology (in particular the development of the automobile), and especially the large-scale movement of women into the business and industrial world all played their part in the enfranchisement of the sex. It is doubtful whether the movement could have been as rapid or as marked in any other society as it was in the hedonistic, mass-producing-consuming society of the twenties. One might argue, indeed, that the developing consumer society and the feminine revolution were closely related. As new careers were offered to women in business and the rising service trades, and as the supply of household servants radically decreased, a revolution occurred in the kitchen and the home. The modern power-appliance industry throve in the twenties with sales of refrigerators, power washers, toasters, mixers, and sweepers describing an ever-mounting curve. By the end of the decade the American kitchen was well on its way to becoming one of the most highly mechanized institutions in the world and the most highly styled. As women increasingly became the ultimate consumers, style became as important a factor in the choice of articles as function and mechanical efficiency. Since it was easier to change exterior design and color than the basic mechanism of the equipment, built-in obsolescence was the watchword for the manufacturer. Shortly after a General Motors executive confessed that his corporation was taking as much care with the design and appearance of its automobiles as with the engineering, the practice of introducing a new model every year became standard in the industry. Soon after, most household-appliance manufacturers followed. And though there were other than the feminine forces at work in this development, just a glance at the advertising trends in the nation's magazines during the late twenties will indicate that manufacturers and their feminine clientele had consummated a lasting and ardent love affair.

Since women had been largely responsible for passing the Eighteenth Amendment and the Volstead Act, one might logically presume that their political and social enfranchisement would have brought added support to the Prohibition cause. Instead, it might be argued that the rising influence of the sex had an opposite effect, at least in some portions of the nation. It is true that during the first month of Prohibition, when violation of the Act was already widespread, the lawbreakers seem to have been overwhelmingly masculine. But with the early advent of the illegal speakeasy, the night club, and the cocktail bar, women appeared more and more frequently as consumers of illegal beverages, if not as producers and merchandisers. By 1925 the New York City Investigating Committee of Fourteen reported that the number of women in illegal establishments devoted to the sale of alcohol was "astounding." Two years before, the state of New York had repealed its prohibition-enforcement act, joining Maryland, which had never been prompted to pass one. In both states the enfranchised women presumably had the opportunity to sustain the dry crusade. Instead, they apparently agreed with the largely feminine-dominated Church Temperance Society of the Protestant Episcopal Church, which in 1926 voted to modify the Volstead Act. Prohibition, the Society declared, had increased drinking "among young people of both sexes," had "brought about disrespect for all laws," and was essentially class legislation since it permitted liquor for the rich and denied it to the poor. Subsequently the W.C.T.U., the Methodist Board of Temperance, and other evangelical religious organizations decried the Episcopalians' action. But by 1929 there was no denying the fact later brought out by the Wickersham Committee that the attempt to enforce Prohibition had not stopped drinking and had possibly increased it among women. In 1929 the Assistant Attorney General admitted before a Congressional committee that liquor could be bought by either sex at almost any time, day or night, in almost any place in the nation.

The defeat of Prohibition by 1929 and its official repeal four years later constituted a devastating and perhaps culminating blow to a whole series of intertwined American traditions. A cynic might argue that Prohibition had been largely the work of the ethically minded middle-class evangelical Protestant American women, their animus largely inspired by their exclusion from the pre-1919 saloon, and that once they had been invited into the cocktail bars of the twenties their ardor for abstinence rapidly cooled. There is much truth to the observation that the socially fettered nineteenth-century woman, intent upon uplifting men to her own strict standards of decorum and morality, started aping them in their sinful ways once she had encountered freedom. But it could be argued that what the nineteenth-century woman wanted was equality as much as masculine reform, and that by the time she achieved it the ethical and moral system that had originally inspirited the dry crusade had been seriously eroded by the new urban-industrial values of the twenties. The hallowed place names of the dry crusade—Churchville, Vermont; Oberlin College; Westerville, Ohio—are redolent of the old American small-town system of values. But by 1920 this venerable tradition was in retreat before the challenge of a new society. In 1919 it had achieved one of its greatest triumphs, in the dry law. Ten years later the flaunting of the law marked its defeat and the erosion of its moral and ethical content.

The defeat of the Prohibition effort also was a setback for the Protestant churches, particularly the Methodist, Baptist, and Presbyterian, which had so zealously supported the dry crusade. Protestantism in general was in grave difficulties during the decade. Its most vigorous manifestation during the first twenty years of the century, the social gospel movement, had lost most of its élan and many of its followers before the materialist challenge of the twenties. As this attempt to reconcile Christian ethics and capitalist economics waned, many of its renowned clerical leaders turned their attention to the causes of Prohibition and world peace, only to see the first defeated and the second become dubious of attainment as the years ground on. By the midtwenties the Methodist missionary societies reported that nourishing funds were diminishing yearly, and the Sunday plaint from the pulpit that the faithful were either in their automobiles or on the golf courses became customary. In 1927 the *Christian Century* reported that the evangelical churches had lost over a half-million members in the preceding twelve months.

On the East Coast a former Lutheran minister from North Dakota, Dr. Frank Buchman, was beginning to attract attention among the upper social and economic classes. Buchman's religious house parties, where in comfortable surroundings the initiates held something like a group confession, appealed particularly to the undergraduates of the Ivy League universities and to their social confreres. Divorced from practically all dogma or ritual, Buchmanism—or the Oxford Movement, or Moral Rearmament as it was subsequently known—stressed the ease with which the individual could secure "God guidance." The chief requirements after a personal "washing out" of sins were faith and a daily time of spiritual silence during which the believer could talk with the Creator directly.

In Los Angeles Aimee Semple McPherson, ex-missionary, ex-schoolteacher, and ex-carnival barker, established her Four Square Gospel Temple, to which in droves came thousands of transplanted Midwesterners and Easterners to witness her "religious productions," replete with scenery, music, and theatricals and, as one unfriendly critic described it, full of sensuality and faith healing. Sister Aimee, like Buchman, made few demands upon her rapidly growing congregation. As dogma, creed, and catechism were overlooked, the way to heaven was not particularly difficult. A "show for the Lord" and "a helping hand" for one's neighbors and friends, including Sister Aimee, was all that was needed. Compared with the most modern of traditional Christian sects, Buchmanism and McPhersonism were miles apart. Their almost complete lack of dogma and theology, their promise of a close and easy companionship with God, and the elegance of one and the sumptuousness of the other removed them far from the spare and hard-oak pew tradition of historic Protestantism. To that extent they reflected the new materialist, mass-consuming, sophisticated, pleasure-loving urban culture.

The defenders of the old traditions and morals, the agrarian-minded social conservatives and the religious orthodox, did not let this complex series of radical innovations in American society go without an angry and persistent challenge. The spate of movies and books in which sex was free, easy, and explicitly shown was met with such a volume of state and local censorship laws that the film industry decided to establish its own control of morals and manners in self-protection. But what the Hays Office, named after the former Postmaster General Will H. Hays, succeeded in doing with its "two feet on the floor" rules for bedroom scenes was to substitute the suggestive for the explicit. By requiring that virtue must triumph it also divorced the average movie from any connection with life. Book censors also took vigorous action, and in cities like Boston, where the new Catholics and the old Puritans were allied in the effort, even acknowledged literary masterpieces were denied a place in libraries or bookstores.

Some state legislatures and local councils, mostly in the West and South, attempted also to stem the tide of the feminine passion for short dresses and scant bathing suits. But police with yardsticks to measure the required minimum coverage were not unknown, at least in the early years of the decade, on the big city beaches of the Eastern shore. Here and there divorce laws were tightened up, mature hostesses were installed in public dance halls to see that the proximity of the partners did not infringe the local standards of propriety, and occasionally local legislation went so far as that in Norphelt, Arkansas, which prohibited "improper and lascivious sexual intercourse," even among married couples.

The leaders of the evangelical Protestant churches, convinced that much of the prevailing immorality was a direct result of the flouting of the Prohibition law, demanded and often obtained, especially in the rural Midwest and the South, stricter enforcement legislation. But Bishop James Cannon, Jr., of the Virginia Methodists, and other prominent Prohibition leaders were handicapped in marshalling their churches against the demon rum because they were opposed on the issue by a large body of Roman Catholic sentiment, and because their own churches were split on a variety of issues centering around the conflict between modern and traditional Christianity.

By mid-decade the battle between the pew and the pulpit over social Christianity had been won largely by the conservatives, who insisted that the ministry confine its attention to theology and avoid involving the church in matters of economics and politics. Perhaps their defeat inspired many of the one-time defenders of social Christianity to the more venturesome theology of the modernist movement. This movement sought to reconcile the new views of science and psychology with traditional religion, an activity which was usually engaged in at the expense of a literal interpretation of the Bible and some of the venerated creedal views of particular Protestant sects. Modernism was met, however, with the same vigorous opposition that social Christianity had encountered. For the first time in years the Episcopal Church held a heresy trial, and the Presbyterians forced the resignation of one of their most popular and influential preachers, Dr. Harry Emerson Fosdick, from his pulpit in New York City.

The most bitter and most publicized clash between the modernists and the fundamentalists, however, came in the rural South. Throughout the Southern states the evangelical churches led a movement during the early twenties to prohibit the teaching of evolution in the public schools as an affront to the true biblical doctrines. The fundamentalists failed in North Carolina, but in Tennessee the state legislature responded and passed an antievolution act. The denouement of the issue came with the famous "monkey trial" at Dayton, Tennessee, where an inconspicuous high school teacher, John Scopes, won for himself a temporary place in the national headlines and an imperishable one in history by being convicted of teaching evolution in his biology class. The trial might not have attracted national attention had not the old "peerless leader," William Jennings Bryan, become the principal prosecuting lawyer and had not a confessed agnostic, Clarence Darrow, of Chicago, the most brilliant criminal lawyer of the day, taken up the defense. The entrance of Nebraska's Bryan, the hero of the prairies, stout Prohibitionist and fundamentalist Christian, into the small-town Southern trial was at once symbolic and prophetic. Stripped of politics, the contesting forces at Dayton were those of 1896, the countryside versus the big city, the West and the South against the East, Anglo-Saxondom against the polyglots, traditional Protestantism versus the nonbelievers and the wrong believers, Prohibitionists against the sybarites, the simple innocents against the sophisticates. Although Bryan won in a technical sense, since the court found Scopes guilty, he lost the national argument in the newspapers by a country mile, and his death a week after the trial portended the eclipse of the cluster of values he so well represented.

From almost every angle the old small-town-countryside Protestant culture was being viciously assaulted in the twenties. The census returns indicated that its numerical superiority was past. Its religious, ethical, and moral values were being flouted at the same time that its economic underpinning was collapsing, with disastrously falling farm prices. Small wonder then that the countryside and its like-minded allies in the city responded to another crusade against its alleged enemies, a crusade growing out of frustration and impending defeat, and consequently one that could easily be perverted from the defense of its own disappearing values to the lynching of others. Historically, such folk movements have often led to bigotry, intolerance, and mass cruelty. The culminating battle of this American cultural struggle was to be no different.

The post-World War I Ku Klux Klan has usually been interpreted by historians as a traditional nativist movement fuelled by the old American intolerance toward the Negro, the Roman Catholic, and the Jew. There is, of course, truth to this point of view that may be documented from a variety of sources. The popularity of such books as Madison Grant's *The Passing of the Great Race* (1916) and Lothrop Stoddard's *The Rising Tide of Color* (1920) clearly indicated the swelling nativist sentiment that resulted in the Immigration Acts of 1917, 1921, and 1924. "America must be kept American," Calvin Coolidge observed as he signed the 1924 Act, which eventually limited all immigration to approximately 150,000 people a year. The numerous race riots in Northern cities and efforts by Southerners to exclude Jewish people record the rising sentiment against the Negro and the Jew. "The time has come," the Secretary of the St. Petersburg, Florida, Chamber of Commerce pronounced openly, "to make this a hundred per cent American and gentile city as free from foreigners as from slums." And one has only to glance at a few symptomatic titles in the *Christian Century*—"Is the Future with the Catholic Church?" "Protestantism Has a Fighting Chance," and "Will Protestantism Destroy Itself?"—to mark the rising sensitivity of the traditional church. These sentiments taken together with the Klan's liturgy of hate directed toward the Jew, the Negro, and the Catholic would seem to indicate that the organization which at one time claimed over 5 million members was just another if not more violent installment of traditional outbursts against minorities and newcomers to the land of freedom.

But for all of their bigotry, excessive language, and violence the anti-Irish Know-Nothing movement, Denis Kearney's California crusade against the Chinese, as well as the Iowa-born, anti-Catholic American Protective Association, all had been excited by economic and social difficulties between majority and minority groups living very close together. The impoverished Irish Paddies fleeing from famine in their homeland swarmed into the Eastern seaboard cities during the fifties and took what jobs they could get at what wages were offered, undercutting the opportunities for native whites. In California, during the seventies, the Chinese presented a similar problem to Kearney's pick handlers. In the nineties the rapid establishment of Catholic elementary schools throughout Iowa and Wisconsin and the subsequent Catholic claims for subvention from the state tax rolls excited local sentiment, as the issue still does wherever it is raised.

But what can be said about the origins of the Klan? The Klan's strength lay largely in the village and rural South, Midwest, and West, where except in Louisiana the Catholic and Jewish populations were small and innocuous. Militant assertions of Negro rights were made after the war by the followers of Marcus Garvey and the members of the National Association for the Advancement of Colored People, founded in 1910, and ugly race riots occurred in a number of Midwestern cities. But the great strength of the Klan in the Midwest lay in such nonurban states as Indiana, Kansas, and Oklahoma. Little evidence has been produced to indicate that a marked postwar increase in Negro militancy took place in the rural South.

That the Klan fed upon intolerant attacks upon minorities is unquestioned. But in a larger sense perhaps this may have been the surface eruption of a much deeper and more widespread twentieth-century social malaise, with the Negro, the Catholic, the Jew, and the immigrant being unfortunate and convenient, if not accurate, symbols of what was troubling small-town and rural America. More research needs to be done on the motivations and origins of the Klan and on those of the more significant, but perhaps not dissimilar, European Fascism. Granted the different historical and cultural conditioning of the two movements, their similarities are striking and not confined to the superficial trappings of uniforms and insignia. Both movements were ideologically grounded in country and village soil, and both called in almost mystical terms for a return to the primitive and virtuous life of the past. Both were highly nationalistic, stressing racial purity. Both vehemently attacked minority groups, considering them to be composed of inferior stock and possessing an inferior culture. Both were adamantly opposed to many of the manifestations of the new urban culture—its polyglot racial mixtures, its intellectuality, its leftist politics, its new standards of ethics and morality, and what was considered its sensual living.

In a long article in which he attempted to describe the nature and the purposes of the Klan, Imperial Wizard Hiram Wesley Evans admitted that the organization's membership was made up of "hicks and rubes and drivers of second-hand Fords," "plain people, very weak in the matter of culture," but representing "the old pioneer stock," the blend of the "Nordic race" which had given the world "almost the whole of modern civilization." They had been first "uncomfortable" and then "deeply distressed" at the dissemination of strange ideas in religion, politics, and morality by liberals and leftists and representatives of minority groups, ideas threatening their homes, their concepts of chastity, the sacredness of their Sabbath, and the right to teach their children in their own schools the "fundamental facts and truths." Economically these pioneers had "outworked" the aliens, but the latter had so far "underlived" them that their patrimony was menaced. Moreover, "the intellectually mongrelized liberals" had convinced the country that the producers—the Nordics—"should carry the unfit and let the unfit rule them." What the Klan demanded, Evans concluded, was the "return of power into the hands of everyday, not highly cultured, not overly intellectualized, but entirely unspoiled and not de-Americanized, average citizen of the old stock." Its object, according to Evans, was to recreate a "native, white, Protestant America."

In the same article Evans spent much time reciting the familiar Klan bill of particulars against the Catholics, the Negroes, the Jews, and the immigrants from Southern and Central Europe. But his description of his own followers and what was troubling them was perhaps even more interesting from a historical point of view than his indictments against the minorities. Obviously the Klan represented a deeply troubled group of Americans, recruited mainly from the countryside, conscious of their growing inferiority, and deeply sensitive to the destruction of their traditional values by the new mass-producing, mass-consuming culture of the burgeoning cities. Like many politicians of the age, like Henry Ford and numerous other industrialists, they readily accepted the technology and the financial and selling techniques upon which the new mass culture rested, but they assailed its social results. Needing a villain, they turned to the convenient Catholic, Negro, and Jew, who together had probably far less to do with the destruction of the ancient rural heritage than their fellow Protestant-Americans caught up with glittering material promises of the great boom. Whatever its irrational qualities, the protest of the tradition-minded American during the twenties left its imprint upon practically every major social and political debate of the decade.

2

The Politics of Nostalgia

IF DURING THE TWENTIES the traditionalists were rapidly
retreating on moral, religious, and social grounds, they at least
won the outward trappings of national political power. As the
decade progressed new forces generated by urban centers became
ever more demanding of attention. But in politics a fear of the
future, a desire to escape present troubles, and the urge to return
to the values of a fancied Golden Age of the past combined to
sound one of the two dominant chords of the decade. The other
was the persistent Republican policy of accelerating the forces
creating the new mass-production-consumption economy. A few
elements of this studied policy were positive, but most were of a
negative sort. Whether positive or negative in character, the
official policy led unerringly to one result: the rapid overturning
of the social values ardently proposed by three Republican presidents.

The almost universal social malaise following World War I
was well calculated to inspire a "retreat to the past." Abroad the
world in 1920 was anything but the peaceful and secure one that
Wilson had promised for his war to end war and his peace with
justice and without victory. In Europe, Ireland was in rebellion
against British rule, Poland was waging a full-scale war against
the Soviets, and Rumania had just ceased her military occupation
of Hungary. With the franc falling disastrously, French cabinets
were made and unmade with alarming regularity. Both the
Communists and Mussolini's newly organized Fascists threat-

ened the Italian government, and in Munich a Nationalist *coup
d'état* had just missed being successful. Elsewhere, as Communist
votes mounted, rightist dictatorships rapidly replaced the democratic governments sponsored by the peace settlements.

In the United States the economic transition from war to peace
had been anything but smooth and had borne exceedingly bitter
fruit. With little or no reconversion plan the government
abruptly terminated war orders, almost before the ink on the
armistice had dried, and rescinded much of the regulation in
effect during hostilities. These actions created first unemployment
and then ballooning prices as the pent-up demand for consumers'
goods established a wild sellers' market. As wages fell behind skyrocketing prices, a wave of strikes further unsettled normal economic processes, the coal strike during the severe winter of 1919
in particular causing severe shortages and actual distress. Seeking
to counter the rapid inflation, the Federal Reserve Board in late
1919 and 1920 tightened credit, an action which brought on a
deflationary cycle. Well before the Presidential election the country was in the first stages of the so-called primary postwar depression. During the summer of 1920 farm prices as well as the
inflated values on agricultural land skidded dangerously, and
by late fall unemployment in the cities was rapidly rising.

For eighteen months before the election of 1920 the industrial
scene had been violently disturbed by a bitter, protracted struggle
for power between organized labor and capital. Attempting to
protect and extend the gains made during the war, labor sought
to organize the mammoth steel industry, as well as scores of
lesser industrial opponents. But labor's challenge was met by a
grim management determined to stop further organization and
intent on returning the country, if possible, to the open-shop
philosophy of the nineteenth century. Exciting the labor-capital
issue almost to the flash point was the baleful threat of the
Russian Revolution and the rise of world radicalism. Despite the
many attacks inspired from the West against the new Soviet
state, its chance for survival appeared to be more than even in the
summer of 1920. No one knew at that time whether the Communist tide might not overwhelm many existing governments of

Eastern and Southern Europe. With the publication of British Labor's 1919 program calling for nationalization of the nation's major industries, even that traditional home of conservatism appeared to be in danger of falling before the radical thrust. To frightened American conservatives it seemed as if the United States was next on the radical timetable. In 1919 the Plumb Plan for modified government ownership of railroads was advanced by the Railroad Brotherhoods and supported by President Wilson's son-in-law, Secretary of the Treasury William G. McAdoo. Almost simultaneously the striking miners voted overwhelmingly for the nationalization of the mines. In 1919 an American Communist party was formally organized. Although not a party member at that date, William Z. Foster, a future Communist leader, was then heading the striking steel workers in their battle against the industry's low rates and its standard twelve-hour day.

Meanwhile a wave of bombing atrocities swept the country, aimed at a score of political and financial leaders. But the most frightening episode of all the year's ominous harvest was the Boston police strike of September. If the police walked out, the question was repeatedly asked, what was to become of private property and of the social order? It was against such a background that Attorney General A. Mitchell Palmer organized his "ship or shoot" campaign against all alien radicals, and that over twenty state legislatures passed criminal syndicalist laws providing for heavy fines and prison sentences for advocating or inciting assaults against public officials, destruction of real or personal property, and the overthrow of government. A committee of the New York legislature solemnly proposed that "every strike is a small revolution and a dress rehearsal for a big one." In such an atmosphere it is small wonder that the leaders of the industrial and financial community were able to convince themselves and much of the public that the labor movement was crowded with agitators advocating the overthrow of the Constitution and asserting that the open shop was a basic ingredient of "the American way."

A good many other developments excited the imagination of the conservative and the timid during the election year of 1920.

After five years of little immigration from abroad over 400,000 immigrants entered the United States, and wild predictions appeared in the press that unless radical restrictions were made from 2 to 5 million refugees from war-torn Europe would descend on the country in the following twelve months. The same stories invariably recalled that Wilson had vetoed a literacy test for immigrants, and that many of the radicals violently disturbing the domestic scene had European backgrounds. Closer to home, a series of ugly race riots broke out on the fringes of the war-born Negro communities in a number of Northern and Western cities. And although in 1920 most of the massive revolt against prewar moral standards was yet to come, the publication of Sherwood Anderson's *Winesburg, Ohio* and F. Scott Fitzgerald's *This Side of Paradise* had ushered in the new jazz age. While the Volstead Act enforcing the Prohibition amendment was but six months old, by midsummer of 1920 it was already being flouted openly. Meanwhile the automobile and the Hollywood movie, both enthusiastically received by the public, were rapidly contributing to the erosion of manners and morals, especially among the young.

Leaving a Republican National Committee meeting in 1919, Boies Penrose, the cynical and outsized Republican Senator from Pennsylvania, predicted that the leading issue in the 1920 elections would be "Americanism." When asked what that meant, Penrose was alleged to have replied, "How in the hell do I know? But it will get a lot of votes." Uncommonly frank at times, Penrose was probably honest in voicing his perplexity over an exact definition of Americanism. But the Senator was unerringly accurate in predicting the public's emotional response to the term and its value in vote getting. Both national parties, in fact, sensed the nostalgic mood of the country, and in their platforms and their choice of candidates they honored Penrose's judgment. Neither party dealt in any realistic way with present or future problems; they contented themselves with arguments about past issues. Only on the League of Nations question was there an attempt to grapple with the future. But by November, when the candidates and their followers were through discussing or avoiding this vital question, no one, whether friend or foe of the League, knew precisely how to vote to obtain the desired result.

Like the party programs, the candidates also had an aura of prewar and even nineteenth-century America. Passing over the strong, prominent, or able men of the party—Newton D. Baker, William G. McAdoo, A. Mitchell Palmer, and the more-than-willing Woodrow Wilson—the Democrats selected the unexceptional James M. Cox, a Dayton newspaper publisher and Governor of Ohio, pale of character and of political convictions. Only the energy and personal charm of the young and rather impetuous Franklin D. Roosevelt, the Vice-Presidential candidate, promised to lift the Democratic campaign above the mediocre. The Republicans likewise avoided choosing one of their party luminaries. Governor Frank O. Lowden of Illinois was passed over, as were General Leonard Wood, Hiram Johnson, and Herbert Hoover. By agreement among the managers of the party, particularly those from the Senatorial wing, who were tired of being upstaged by an able and dominant President, the nomination went to Warren Gamaliel Harding, whose lack of qualification for the office was only surpassed by his ineptitude while serving in it.

Handsome, of imposing stature, modest, affable, kindly, and quite uncritical of his companions (possibly because he had so few standards to judge by), Harding had made his way in the world almost totally by these mundane human qualities and by luck. Failing to graduate from a preparatory school, he managed to become owner and editor of a small country-town weekly newspaper. The Marion, Ohio, *Star* was, under his direction, uninspired, mediocre, and in persistent financial difficulties. His marriage to the daughter of the town's banker, over the opposition of her family, eventually offered financial support and social entree to the community's ruling circle. Harding soon found his proper milieu in Republican machine politics, where he allied himself with Senator Joseph Benson "Fire Alarm" Foraker, the venal George Cox, boss of Cincinnati, and finally with Harry M. Daugherty, shrewd and unscrupulous business lobbyist and political manipulator. Harding was elected to the State Senate, the

Lieutenant Governorship, and, after losing a race for Governor, in 1914 to the United States Senate. He contributed nothing to the Senate other than a reliable party vote on political matters and a bleakly conservative one on economic issues. He voted against war taxes on business because he thought they would weaken the country. But in party organizational affairs his star rose consistently, possibly because of his convivial habits and more certainly due to his ability to make resounding if meaningless speeches. Although few of his colleagues were ever in doubt about his meager intellectual and moral attainments, he made the chief nominating speech for Taft in 1912 and four years later was named Chairman of the Republican National Convention. Eloquent of the existing questions about his character was the tenor of the meeting between him and the party managers just before his nomination. He was required to pledge that nothing in his personal past would stand in the way of his nomination and election to the Presidency.

The Harding campaign was so pitched as to mark the sharp distinction between the character and policies of Woodrow Wilson and those of Harding. And its tone, including those notes imparted to it by the Vice-Presidential candidate, Calvin Coolidge, was such as to evoke the alleged American past with its folksiness, its stability and security, and its prosperity. Harding was kept at home to conduct a front-porch campaign after the fashion of William McKinley. Mrs. Harding described her family as made up of "just folks," and the nominee declared that he was "just a plain fellow," "old-fashioned and even reactionary in matters of faith and morals." One of the advantages of keeping the candidate in Marion, Ohio, Senator Penrose observed, was that he would not be tempted to answer questions on difficult issues. The candidate obliged, confining himself to advocating the Golden Rule as the solution to the labor problem, arguing for the return of natural resources to the citizens, and uttering the hope that every American laborer would eventually become "a small business man." Otherwise Harding was content to offer bromides such as "Stabilize America first, prosper America first, think America first and exalt America first."

The startling conservative Republican victory, by the greatest majority in the party's history, has been explained in a variety of ways. Some have argued that it was the inevitable result of twenty years of reform, since the one-time reform leaders had arrived at the end of their tolerance for change and had been frightened into conservatism by postwar radicalism. The splintering of the reform will by personal rivalries and the sapping of the movement's *élan* by the aging of its leaders may have contributed to the same end. Others saw the results as a vast popular revulsion against the nation's entrance into the war, and against the disparity between the glowing promises held out for it and the realities of the postwar world at home and abroad. The processes of waging modern war, both on the battlefields and at home, it has been argued, are such as to destroy idealism and to engender a consuming spirit of despondent materialism. Practical reasons of politics of course contributed to the result. Wilson's dire sickness, his growing rigidity of mind, and the leaderless state of the Democratic party through the year preceding the election also helped in his defeat. But in the last analysis the voters in 1920 probably responded more to a mood than to specific issues and political stratagems. For all the jests at Harding's prenomination slogan of "back to normalcy," this and the rest of the Republican candidate's liberties with the language—"not heroism but healing, not nostrums but normalcy, not revolution but restoration, not agitation but adjustment, not surgery but serenity . . . not experiment but equipoise, not submergence in internationality but sustainment in triumphant nationality"—expressed precisely what many citizens wanted, or thought they wanted. The country was tired of chasing elusive, newly formulated high ideals on either side of the Atlantic, tired of the wrangling in the Senate over the League and of the leaderless and bad administration given to it in 1919–1920, tired of the sharp price inflation and deflation, and of strikes, riots, and Reds. It was not a little apprehensive of what was happening to its moral standards and social institutions. The handsome and affable man sitting on his front porch in Marion, Ohio, and talking in the backyard language of yesterday seemed to offer an end to all its present troubles.

During the campaign Harding had promised the country to appoint the "best minds of his party" to his official family, as well as to "play square" with the voters, the last a rather gratuitous and ominous pledge. Unquestionably he tried to do both. Charles Evans Hughes, Herbert Hoover, and Andrew Mellon were selected for the Cabinet, and William Howard Taft was appointed Chief Justice of the Supreme Court. The President was in desperate need of expert advice, his own limitations being clearly marked in the tariff debate. "We should," he told a reporter without a trace of guile, "adopt a protective tariff of such character as will help the struggling industries of Europe to get on their feet." Hughes served the administration well in foreign affairs; Hoover supplied most of the ideas for combatting the short depression of 1921. And if Andrew Mellon, of the multimillionaire Pittsburgh aluminum and banking family, ran the Treasury with nineteenth-century ideas, he did run it efficiently. Most of the administrative and legislative successes chalked up came from these men, although the President himself, with his benign and indulgent disposition, helped eradicate some of the rancor built up during the war and the struggle over the peace. He not only commuted Socialist party leader Eugene V. Debs' Federal sentence for antiwar activities, but also met him at the White House with a cordial handshake.

Harding's real troubles came from two sources: his inability to stand firm against Congress, and the friends and cronies he had appointed to a host of important positions. Although supported by some of the strongest and best-informed elements of his party, his recommendation for World Court membership was ignored, and he accepted the harmful Fordney-McCumber Tariff because he would not or could not stand up to small groups of intransigent nationalists and blocs of narrowly self-interested high-tariff partisans in Congress.

Hughes, Hoover, and Mellon, all of whom commanded respect in both the party and the country, were the leaders of his Administration. But it was apparent that Harding's golfing, drinking, and poker-playing companions, his real friends, made up as dubious a group of characters as had been seen in Washington since the Grant Administration. Albert B. Fall, Secretary of the Interior, Harry M. Daugherty, the Attorney General, Edwin Denby, Secretary of the Navy, as well as many lesser appointments, had been selected from the circle of the President's Ohio cronies and national political friends. Most of them were without a shred of qualification for office, and some were simply political innocents. But a great many were old-fashioned spoilsmen, political shysters, and just plain crooks. By the summer of 1923, while the President was on a trip to Alaska, rumors of corruption in the Administration were freely bruited about Washington. Apparently Harding was told the facts during his trip, for he repeatedly asked his companions what a President did when he found that his friends had betrayed him. He died in San Francisco at the close of the trip, fortunately spared the sordid revelation that through the machinations of the Secretary of the Interior the nation had been despoiled of some of its naval oil reserves, that the Veterans' Bureau and the Office of the Alien Property Custodian had been looted, and that some of the money had subsequently appeared in bank accounts controlled by the Attorney General and by the Republican National Chairman. Other revelations followed, Fall went to jail, and the Attorney General of the United States, on trial for fraud, escaped by pleading the Fifth Amendment. Others in the group committed suicide or received long prison sentences.

For a time after Harding died there was apprehension among the country's conservatives that the policies of the government might be given a new direction by Calvin Coolidge, who as Vice-President had been even more of a cipher than the usual incumbent in that somnolent office. But those who knew Coolidge best hastened to assure their fellows that Harding's death was, if anything, a blessing; it would help remove the taint of corruption from the new Administration, which could be counted on to intensify the steady conservative drift of the government. "God is still in His Heaven," the President of the National Association of Manufacturers wrote, and he was precisely right. For if Harding was an amiable standpatter, Coolidge was both in personal life and in political philosophy an American primitive.

On August 2, 1923, Coolidge took the oath of office from his justice-of-peace father in a typical Vermont village dwelling and then proceeded to take much of this provincial and rustic atmosphere with him to the White House. There the whiskey-and-poker-game camaraderie disappeared overnight. So did much of Harding's kindness and feeling for human beings. As for past Administration policies, they were intensified to the point that politically the age of the twenties was the age of Calvin Coolidge. By the things he did, as well as by the many things he did not do, he left his stamp ineradicably on the decade.

A rather small man of 150 pounds, with sandy hair, a high forehead, and a prominent nose turned down at the end, Coolidge was not an impressive figure from any viewpoint. He spoke with a harsh nasal twang and usually what he said was as uninspiring as the way he said it. Walter Lippmann commented that the President had a genius for "deflating interest" in almost any subject. Coolidge had never been out of the United States and indeed seldom out of New England, where he had been raised and schooled and where he had pursued a career in Massachusetts politics characterized by its colorlessness and by good fortune. When he came to Washington he brought with him a set of attitudes and ideas which he had picked up from his early life on a Vermont farm, from the small-town law office in Northampton, Massachusetts, and from Boston politics. Although a graduate of Amherst College, he was almost entirely innocent of either the cultural or the intellectual life of Boston society. His favorite poet, he confessed, was Whittier; his preferred music, martial and patriotic. His was a small-town mind, and if we are to believe his secretary, utterly inflexible. He had never changed his position on a fundamental public issue throughout his whole career, C. Bascom Slemp wrote, in what was meant to be an admiring statement. This rigidity of mind may have come from the man's innate conservatism or it may have been an expression of a basic inclination to conserve his energy. He told a reporter once that he had preserved his composure and his health over the years by avoiding big questions. While in the White House he customarily added a long afternoon nap to the ten or eleven hours of sleep he ordinarily got at night. When leaving the capital on one of his long summer vacations he preferred not to be bothered with governmental reports, especially if they were long ones.

Calvin Coolidge was a man of one piece, his political philosophy harmonizing closely with his basic personal characteristics. The important things in the universe, he felt, never changed much. This was especially true of human nature, which, on the whole, he viewed rather pessimistically. The historic American institutions, he believed, could be subjected to little if any just criticism, and any attempt to change them would probably result in far more harm than good. "Four-fifths of all of our troubles in this life would disappear," he once commented, "if we would only sit down and keep still." By 1920 Coolidge was no friend of direct primaries or any of the other political reforms which had been a part of the progressive creed in the country since 1900. Direct democracy, he feared, might lead to popular excesses and unsound financial legislation resulting in "disorder and the dissolution of society." Neither was the President charitably disposed toward the regulatory state. Some regulation might be necessary, he admitted, but bureaucracy was an abomination—the element in American institutions that "set up the pretense of having authority over everybody and being responsible to nobody." The progressive attempt since 1900 to regulate business in fact had been devoted mainly to "destructive criticism." That was not surprising, for the President believed that human nature, whether operating in government or business, was all of a piece and subject to the same faults. If the American people, he remarked in 1924, could not secure perfection in their own economic life, "it is altogether improbable that the government can secure it for them." Throughout his Presidency, he wrote after he left office, he had attempted to substitute "positive policies" for the negative progressive philosophy.

The essence of Coolidge's positivism can be found in the man's almost mystical devotion, as William Allen White phrased it, to a business system untrammelled by government regulation or legal obstruction, and to the free accumulation of wealth. "Business should be unhampered and free," he reiterated many times, because the prosperity and the ethical and intellectual welfare of the whole nation depended upon its profitable operations. The accumulation of wealth was of prime importance because it not only created large payrolls but also was the chief support "of all science, art, learning and charities. . . ." But there were even more hidden values interconnected with the business system, he told the New York Chamber of Commerce. "It rests squarely on the law of service. It has for its main reliance truth, faith, and justice. In its larger sense it is one of the greatest contributing forces to the moral and spiritual advancement of the race." And as for the private acquisition of wealth, the law of property, the President once observed, was "founded upon the constitution of the universe."

For such a mystical materialist it followed that the proper end of government was to encourage and nurture the business world and to oppose its enemies. Harassing regulation should be mitigated or abolished, labor should be disciplined, critics confounded or silenced. Since income taxes bore most heavily on the wealthy, stringent government economy should be observed and taxes reduced. "Economy," the President said in his inaugural address, "is idealism in its most practical form." To add practice to the preachment, Coolidge subsequently investigated the government's yearly bill for lead pencils, which he found amounted to $125,000, and demanded that it be radically reduced. Government aid to any distressed nonbusiness classes was unthinkable. During the 1914 depression he remarked that the state was not warranted in furnishing employment to anyone, for anyone incapable of supporting himself was "not fit for self-government." During the twenties he told the hard-pressed farmers to find their own way out of their difficulties. He remained unmoved in his position even in the face of national disasters. When the victims of a Mississippi River flood appealed for help he replied, "The Government is not an insurer of its citizens against the hazards of the elements." Coolidge, in fact, was even doubtful about the social utility of many private charities. Just before the election of 1924 he spoke to the Jewish philanthropic societies of New York, urging them to temper their benevolent instincts with sound business caution and business methods, including that of strict

budgeting. "There is an impressive array of testimony," he concluded, "that the average dollar of indiscriminate, well-meaning,
ignorant donation to charity is mostly wasted; many such dollars
are far worse than wasted."

One of the better biographies of Calvin Coolidge spends about
eighty pages on his six years as President, which perhaps is a fair
measurement of his contributions as Chief Executive. Even so, a
good share of those pages is used to describe the activities of
Mellon, Kellogg, and Hoover, his Secretaries of the Treasury,
State, and Commerce. His most trusted adviser was Andrew Mellon, and Mellon's policies of reducing government expenditures,
lowering taxes, and paying off the debt received his enthusiastic
support. By 1928 the highest surtax on incomes had been reduced
from its 1920 level of 65 per cent to 20 per cent, and comparable
reductions had been made in the inheritance tax levels. The Federal levy on gifts was abolished. Meanwhile the wave of prosperity increased income, and as expenditures were curtailed, the total
Federal debt was sharply reduced, even though that of the states
was mounting yearly. Mellon was restrained from further reductions by Congress. But under his direction the Treasury was so
lenient in administering tax rules and so ready to grant refunds to
big taxpayers that the existing rate structure was in effect reduced
further. Mellon and the President together consistently pursued
one other policy that delighted the business expansionists. At least
twice when the Federal Reserve Board was inclined to contract
credit by raising the rediscount rate, the President and his Secretary of the Treasury threw their weight against the move. Thus
the credit supply remained cheap and plentiful, fuelling the ex-
pansionist and speculative boom. Even when it became obvious
early in 1929 that much of the easy money was being used to
speculate in stocks, the President remarked that Wall Street
prices were "not too high." Needless to say, as long as the boom
lasted Mellon was hailed by businessmen as "the greatest Secretary of the Treasury since Alexander Hamilton."

The policy of government by inactivity was further reflected by
the President's unwillingness to recommend to Congress any
major legislation of a positive stamp. This and his zeal for veto-

ing Congressional enactments resulted in the smallest crop of important legislation since the nineteenth century. A soldiers' bonus bill was passed over the President's negative stand by an insistent Congress facing the elections of 1924. Coolidge was sustained, however, in his two vetoes of the McNary-Haugen Bill, which would have granted aid to the hard-pressed farmers. The Immigration Act of 1924, a Federal radio act, and two measures providing very modest financial support for Mississippi flood control and for the merchant marine constituted the major legislative harvest for six years. Without grass growing in the streets of Washington, Federal negativism could scarcely have gone further.

Perhaps the most pervasive influence of the studied policy of inactivity was felt in the areas dominated by the Federal regulatory commissions and by the Federal courts. With almost unerring accuracy Harding and Coolidge appointed men to the commissions who were opposed to strenuous Federal regulation. The 1926 Coolidge appointee to the Federal Trade Commission, for example, announced that the old Commission had been "a publicity bureau to spread Socialist propaganda" and that he intended to remedy that condition. Throughout the decade, consequently, the Interstate Commerce Commission, the Federal Trade Commission, and the Bureau of Corporations, as well as many other less important Federal agencies, ceased to perform some of the functions for which they had been created during the progressive years under Roosevelt, Taft, and Wilson.

Presidential appointments to the Federal courts similarly changed the prevailing judicial attitudes toward the place of government in national life. In a little more than two years Harding appointed four new men to the Supreme Court, all of them, including Chief Justice William Howard Taft, conservatives or reactionaries. During one of the first conferences of the new Court Taft announced that he had "been appointed to reverse a few decisions." The Taft Court then proceeded measurably to narrow the permissible areas in the social and economic fields in which either state or national government could intervene. Within five years the Court had outlawed a national child labor law, declared a District of Columbia minimum wage law for women unconstitutional, and so limited the public utility concept that it all but removed the power of the Federal government to regulate effectively the prices charged by, and the profits accruing to, interstate power monopolies. From its origin until 1925 the Court had found only fifty-three Congressional acts unconstitutional. During the twenties it invalidated twelve such, or nearly one-fourth. Looking at the record of the Taft Court, Senator Norris of Nebraska declared that the Federal government had in name two legislative bodies, the Senate and the House, numbering over 400 members. But in fact another had been recently constituted, the Supreme Court of nine men who were "more powerful than all the others put together."

In the realm of restricting radicals and labor union activity the Court did vest more power in legislative and administrative hands at the expense of traditional civil rights. By following the "clear and present danger" reasoning of Justice Oliver Wendell Holmes in the historic Gitlow case (Gitlow v. New York, 268 U.S. 1925), the Court opened the way for Congress and state legislatures to pass security measures against radicals of all breeds which substantially narrowed the personal freedoms granted in the first ten amendments, provided it could be shown that the security of the state was in danger. The Court's subsequent findings that many of the numerous state "criminal syndicalist" enactments were valid testified to the substantial abridgment of the Bill of Rights, as well as to the amount of apprehension pervading many state legislatures.

The willingness of the Federal courts to grant sweeping labor injunctions also increased the administrative power of the Federal and state governments. In obtaining a series of injunctions against strikes, unparalleled in both number and amplitude during the twentieth century, Attorney General Daugherty assumed massive power to intervene in labor relations and thus in the operations of the market place. On both civil rights and labor cases the Supreme Court usually followed the reasoning of an inferior court that although "governments exist for the protection of life, liberty, and property, the chief of these is property." Aside from these exceptions, however, the whole drift of the Court's decisions during the decade was toward limiting governmental power. Thus it is not too much to say, as one conservative historian has, that during the Harding-Coolidge Administrations American conservatism became almost totally identified with the laissez-faire doctrines of fifty years before.

The retreat of government power under Harding and Coolidge was also evident in foreign policy, although there was nothing near the acceptance of the complete Chinese Wall isolationism that some writers have depicted. Too much unfinished business from the war remained and the world was too intimately connected for a hermitlike program. One important wing of the Republican party had historically never been isolationist in any precise meaning of the term. Instead, it had supported the acquisition of an empire and had tolerated Theodore Roosevelt's foreign ventures. Even during the League of Nations debate the issue for many Republicans had not been isolation as against internationalism, but rather international unilateralism as against collective action. Whenever and wherever the nation's material interests were involved, the party, usually led by its urban Eastern representatives, had vigorously supported an active foreign policy, but one which was apt to be characterized by a "go it alone" quality rather than by international multilateral effort. Only among the party's Western and more rural representatives was there strong "little America" sentiment decrying foreign ventures of any sort. And even this truly isolationist agrarian attitude was compromised by the obvious growing concern of Pacific Coast Republicans with Asia. With but a slight change in emphasis, probably reflecting the anachronistic and rural character of Calvin Coolidge, the party's policy during the twenties remained the same.

True, the United States refused to participate in any outright political discussions of the League of Nations. By 1924 even the Democratic party apparently accepted this position by playing down the League as a campaign issue. Entrance into the World Court, recommended by both Harding and Coolidge, was defeated in the Senate. But the United States did not refrain from political relations with either Europe or Asia. The Washington Armament Conference, in addition to prescribing reductions of naval armament by fixed ratios, which surely involved political decisions of the most important order, also prescribed by a series of treaties between the world's great nations the new power relationships in the Pacific, which in effect diminished America's potential power in East Asia while restricting that of the Japanese in the South Pacific. And the country readily and enthusiastically signed the rather meaningless and completely impotent Pact of Paris, outlawing war. Over these years the United States maintained four or five permanent officials at Geneva to represent the nation's interest and sent special delegates to over forty congresses sponsored by the League. What the United States consistently refused to do was to sign treaties of alliance or international agreements which contained a promise of support with arms.

A hint of the old militancy was conveyed by the Coolidge-Kellogg use of Marines in Nicaragua to re-establish peace and support the claims of the conservative candidate for President against those of the liberals. The Marines, in effect, supported the conservative administration until recalled by President Hoover in 1933. But even in the Western Hemisphere the aptitude for using force when the real interests of the United States were involved was de-emphasized in the twenties. When the Mexican Congress in 1924 acted to implement the nationalization clauses of the 1917 Constitution, threatening vast American holdings, the Coolidge response three years later was to send Dwight W. Morrow to Mexico City with instructions to negotiate. In 1924 the Marines were withdrawn after a decade's stay in the Dominican Republic. And the last of the Coolidge years saw the formulation of the Clark Memorandum by the State Department, a document which in fact repudiated the Roosevelt Corollary to the Monroe Doctrine, and an action that laid the groundwork for the later "Good Neighbor" policy of Hoover and Roosevelt. Calvin Coolidge, as might be expected from his basic attitudes, was neither an imperialist nor an internationalist, but a man who wanted to avoid trouble, maintain peace, and keep the budget low.

The only problem threatening to disturb Coolidge's desire for

composure during his six years arose from the continuing distress
of agriculture. Increasing yields and falling farm prices, coupled
with an overcapitalization of land values, high mortgages, and
sharply increasing local taxes, contributed to the farmers' precarious existence, particularly in wheat and cotton growing areas.
Two farm bills passed during the Harding regime, the Capper-
Volstead Act and the Intermediate Credit Act, failed to grant
substantial relief. In January 1924, the McNary-Haugen Bill, incorporating a radical scheme for government support for farm
prices, introduced an issue that persisted into the Hoover years.
Coolidge's opposition to any major government help to the farmers was adamant, and this attitude helped to spur the political revolt of 1924, which resulted in the formation of the "Progressive"
party, supported by farm and labor groups and led by Senator
Robert M. La Follette of Wisconsin and Senator Burton K.
Wheeler of Montana. The Progressive platform denounced the
Coolidge-Mellon financial program, the Administration's sizable
contributions to the growth of monopoly, and the corruption ram-
pant in Harding's official family. It argued for support for the
farmers and the right of labor to organize freely, and demanded
government ownership of railroads and waterpower resources,
the ratification of a child labor amendment, and the enactment
of curbs on the Supreme Court's power of judicial review.

Since most of the Progressive following presumably would
come from Republican areas, the La Follette challenge looked like
1912 all over again, with a Democratic victory possible. But for a
number of reasons history did not repeat itself. The La Follette
net was not cast nearly as wide as that of Roosevelt's in 1912.
Personal qualities of leadership may have contributed to some of
the difference. The temper of the country had also changed in
the intervening twelve years. For one thing it was an urban
nation in 1924 and many of its major unsolved problems lay in
the cities. And though La Follette tried his best to appeal to the
dissatisfied city voters, he was never able to convince the majority
of them that he was more than an old-style agrarian reformer.
Significantly some of the very labor leaders who had helped or-

ganize the Progressive protest wavered in their support before the campaign was through.

As has been pointed out in recent studies, progressivism persisted throughout the decade and managed to score a number of legislative victories. The majority of these, however, were of a negative sort; for example, the Congressional refusal to concur with Secretary Mellon's radical proposal practically to abolish taxes on wealth or to accept Presidential recommendations to sell the Muscle Shoals Dam and power facilities to private interests. But aside from electric power, the real concerns of most of the Congressional Progressives of the twenties were intimately tied up with agriculture. Senators La Follette, Wheeler, Borah, Brookhart, Magnus Johnson, Shipstead, Norris, Hiram Johnson, and Walsh were all from Western states, and although they sympathized with the few urban radicals in Washington, these Western leaders were unable to command either attention or support from most of the urban masses. Until Progressivism could develop national leaders who were involved in the myriad problems of the nation's cities, it seemed as if it were doomed to a minority existence, and to a dying minority at that.

The Democrats, who ordinarily might have profited from the split in the Republican party, contributed to Coolidge's re-election by engaging in a long and bitter convention struggle between the followers of Governor Alfred E. Smith of New York and William G. McAdoo. Smith was the darling of the Eastern city masses, an anti-Prohibitionist, a Roman Catholic, and a man who was sympathetic to many of the insistent social problems of the great metropolitan areas. McAdoo, born in Tennessee, Protestant, and one of the few remaining leaders of the Bryan-Wilson tradition in the party, evoked the enthusiastic support of the South and the West. After a sectional battle involving the Ku Klux Klan, Catholicism, the farm problem, and the issue of the countryside against the city, all of which were fought through 102 separate ballots, the convention wearily accepted a worthless compromise by nominating John W. Davis. An eminent international lawyer and Morgan partner, Davis was a political unknown, the appeal of whose Jeffersonian principles to the distressed farming regions of the South and West or to the urban masses was almost nil.

In a thoroughly standpat campaign, Coolidge turned most of his attention to La Follette, whom he depicted as a dangerous radical who, were he successful, would turn America into a degraded "communistic and socialistic state." Coolidge's victory margin was impressive, the President polling almost 16 million votes to the 13 million collected by his two adversaries. Elated over the poll, Chief Justice Taft effused that this was no country for radicals but rather "the most conservative country in the world." Whether Taft was right or not, the farm problem would not down, and after being defeated in 1926 the McNary-Haugen Bill was passed by both houses of Congress in 1927 and again in 1928, meeting in each instance a blistering veto by the President on the score that the bill provided for government price fixing and thus would grant special privileges to one group of citizens at the expense of all the others.

Coolidge's vetoes of the McNary-Haugen Bill raised the hopes of the Democrats that in the 1928 Presidential election they might at last reverse the political tide that had been running so strongly against them for ten years. For though the prince of immobility was still in the White House, liberals, progressives, and radicals, long now in the minority, sensed an opportunity for a change in the nation's political temper. It is now obvious that well before the great Wall Street crash of 1929, the mood of the country was changing. Already discernible was a growing dislike for the politics of statics, an increasing distaste for the narrow cultural and social outlook emanating from the White House, and even a faint spirit of rebellion. In the West and the South the hard-pressed farmers were restless. And in 1927 the Sacco-Vanzetti execution had elicited for the first time in the decade, as Malcolm Cowley has pointed out, an explosion of conscience in the ranks of the intellectuals. Most of these rebels, moreover, were urbanites. In opposition to what they held to be a political lynching, hundreds of them collected money, wrote articles, and even marched to the Charleston prison gates to protest against the sentence of execution. Not for years had the intellectuals grouped themselves together for a social cause. Led by John Dewey, Paul Douglas, and Oswald Garrison Villard, they had organized, within eighteen months, the radical League for Independent Political Action, looking toward increased social planning and increased social control. The organization soon had over 2,500 dues-paying members. Organized labor, torpid for long, began to bestir itself. At Gastonia, North Carolina, labor launched one of the most bitter and protracted strikes of the decade. Further to the left, the *New Masses,* an acknowledged Communist magazine, had been founded. Even among the professional politicians there was disquiet, which may have had some relation to Coolidge's enigmatic remark in the summer of 1927 that he did not "choose to run" for the Presidency the following year. So as to quell their fears about a possible invitational quality in the President's remarks, the Senate passed an anti-third-term resolution the following January.

As if to mark further a change in traditional ways, the Democrats, gathering at Houston, Texas, nominated Alfred E. Smith with a minimum of conflict. Born in a tenement house near the wharves of the East River, Smith attended a Catholic school before he became, at the age of 15, a salesman in the Fulton Street fish market. He subsequently joined Tammany Hall and after eight years as a subpoena server was elected to the state Assembly, where he made a reputation by his support of social legislation. In 1918 he was elected Governor, a position which he filled, except for a two-year interval, until 1928. The Smith record over the years was a mildly humanitarian one. Associated with such people as Robert Wagner and Frances Perkins, he was a friend, but perhaps not the advocate, of the immigrants and of the working people of the large cities. He defended civil liberties during the days of the Red hunt, and his civil service reforms gave the state its first efficient bureaucracy. Though Smith advocated but never secured a minimum wage and state ownership of hydroelectric power, he was never an economic radical. In 1927 Walter Lippmann called the Governor of New York "the most powerful conservative in urban America." Smith was important, however, not for the things he was for or against, but rather as a symbol. Although somewhat strait-laced in his personal life and aloof from his fellows, he represented the new gregarious breed from the melting pot of the large Eastern cities. Smith was not the first successful urban politician, as William Allen White wrote, but rather the first from the very bottom of the city who almost went to the top.

The Republican party chose for its nominee in 1928 Herbert Hoover, who was Coolidge's Secretary of Commerce, but who pleased neither Coolidge nor the party's more antediluvian spirits. Hoover was no less a child of fortune than Smith, although he had started life in a Quaker family on an Iowa farm and was soon an orphan. His career was also symbolic, not of a new but of an older breed of Americans. Through hard work, persistence, and help, Hoover had worked his way through high school and an engineering course at Stanford University. Shortly after graduation, he became one of the world's top mining engineers, and much of his early life was spent in Australia and China. The outbreak of World War I found him wealthy and living in London, where he volunteered to supervise the repatriation of Americans from the war-torn continent. He was then asked to head the organization for relief of the Belgians and subsequently called home by President Wilson to administer the wartime food administration. So efficient was his performance in all of these endeavors that by 1919 both parties talked seriously about nominating him as Presidential candidate.

Had Hoover run true to the nineteenth-century model of the self-made man or to the engineering type, he might have been a regular Republican, an ardent advocate of laissez-faire, and a narrow materialist, as suspicious of social theory and the cultivated life as Calvin Coolidge. Instead, he was a Bull Mooser in 1912, later a strong advocate of the League of Nations, and an ardent follower of Woodrow Wilson. As a member of the Harding and Coolidge Cabinets, he was one of the few activists and certainly one of the most liberal-minded. Coolidge was alleged to have said that he was constantly getting gratuitous advice from Hoover, all of it bad. Compared to most American Presidents, Herbert Hoover was also a literate man. He read widely and wrote extensively. Among his books are a translation of a 16th-century text on mining and a volume entitled *American Individualism,* published in 1922, containing the most reasonable statement of political conservatism published in recent years by a politician.

From the timing of Hoover's *American Individualism* one might conjecture that it was an old Bull Mooser's apology for joining the Harding Cabinet. But there is also the possibility that the erstwhile engineer felt that his fellow Republicans in the Administration and Congress needed more than a little missionary effort to introduce them to the modern world. For although the future President felt that progress in historic societies had been achieved by a small group of creative individuals and that any effort to enforce an equality of conditions and rewards would destroy most of these creative impulses, he was by no means an expositor of the economic law of the jungle. He could write that the crowd, compared to the elite, "feels rather than thinks but never creates," and that occasionally, operating on its emotions, the masses could "hate, consume, and destroy." But he balanced those judgments with the acknowledgment that many of the impulses of the elite, impulses accounting in part for their very creativity, their competitive appetites, their demand for adulation, and their desire for power and wealth, were destructive of the social fabric and had to be modulated. "No civilization," he wrote, could be built or can endure "solely upon the groundwork of unrestrained and intelligent self-interest."

Hoover's ideal elite, moreover, was not one selected by inheritance of either name or fortune, but rather a "natural" one based upon ability, in each generation selected after a fair start by "the free running mills of competition." It was the government's job to secure and maintain that equality of opportunity, the state of competition, and the attraction of rewards that would make possible this fluid selective process. To do so, the government would have to place certain restrictions on the strong and dominant. But it followed that if government were to be effective in this task it could not be controlled by the very class it was supposed to regulate. A truly democratic process, therefore, was imperative in

Hoover's ideal state, a democratic process that could not be influenced unduly by organized capital. In a society where the property group controls the state, Hoover wrote, "the individual begins to feel capital as an oppressor."

In looking at contemporary American society, Hoover felt that it had done an effective job of maintaining equality before the law. In fact, the United States had "gone further than any government" in securing an "equality of franchise," an "equality of entrance into public office" and a "government by the adult majority." And it had been far more successful than most other governments "in safeguarding an equality of opportunity through education, public information, and the open channels of free speech and free press." The nation's greatest failure lay strictly in the economic field, where the rise of big industry and big labor was throttling individual initiative and making necessary the increasing role of government, which had become "the most potent force for the maintenance or the destruction of our American individualism." Already, Hoover admitted, industrial concentration and resultant governmental regulation had gone a long way toward the abandonment of Adam Smith's capitalism. Government regulation pointed toward social and economic justice had restrained individualism but it was entirely proper since "a fair division of the product was necessary if we were to keep the modern impulse of production alive." But whatever the quantity of governmental regulation, Hoover concluded, it must all be attuned to the major aim of the American system: "To curb the forces in business which would destroy equality of opportunity and yet maintain the initiative and creative faculties of our people are the twin objects we must obtain."

This was a conservative creed, but it was a reasoned and defensible one, drawing most of its presuppositions and insight from the best hopes of classical liberalism and applying them to the conditions of the day. Given its presuppositions, if Hoover's argument had major faults in its reasoning, they lay in the assumptions that equality of opportunity had not seriously decreased since his own youthful ascent from orphan lad to world-famous engineer, that something like a fair division of the social product was then being made, and that concentrated wealth would not wield inordinate power in government. In the light of the tone and record of the Harding-Coolidge Administrations, these last two assumptions looked especially dubious. But for all of its weaknesses, real or fancied, Mr. Hoover's credo was so far removed from that of most men surrounding him that it marked him as possibly the one positive force in the Coolidge Administration. It is little wonder that Coolidge's most devout followers expressed anxiety at his nomination.

From the party platforms and the speeches of the contending candidates it appeared that the election might be fought over the issues of farm relief, Prohibition, the granting of labor injunctions by the courts, and the interstate regulation of electric power. For although neither party satisfied the more zealous McNary-Haugenites, Smith seemed to promise the farmer more governmental action in solving his problems. And although the Democratic platform supported the Eighteenth Amendment, Smith early made it clear that he was a foe of the Volstead Act, whereas Hoover supported Prohibition as "a noble experiment." At contention, however, were two traditions, which seemed to be personified by the respective candidates. Al Smith, "the Happy Warrior," as Franklin D. Roosevelt had called him, was extremely articulate, and on the platform at least, gave all the appearance of being a sidewalk extrovert. Smith, a Wet and a Roman Catholic, wore a brown derby such as rural America had probably never seen outside a vaudeville act, and pronounced familiar words in the strange accents of Lower East Side New York. Herbert Hoover apparently embodied all the virtues of rural Iowa. He was shy, dour, and slow of speech, wearing high stiff collars that looked as if they had come from the village general store and were somewhat reminiscent of the Puritan Sunday dress. In reality, by training and experience he was much more sophisticated and cosmopolitan than Smith. But when Hoover spoke of "rugged individualism" he conjured up the pioneer past, with its alleged simple McGuffey Reader ethics. Smith, on the other hand, epitomized the teeming multiracial cities, from which, according to many Americans, arose most of the

social problems which bedevilled the decade. "This is the first
time in history during a national political campaign," Senator
Simeon Fess of Ohio remarked, "that we have on one side all of
the loose elements of society and on the other the very highest
and best of morals." Few remarks could have been more unfair
and more partisan. But this one cut deep enough into the irrational attitudes of the old-stock American to evoke positive
response.

Although the candidates strove to keep religion out of the
campaign, it was certainly an issue in both heavily Protestant and
Roman Catholic districts. The most respected Protestant magazine, the *Christian Century,* sharply questioned whether religious
tolerance should be exhibited to the extent that it tolerated an
intolerant religion, and several high Protestant church officials in
the South let it be known publicly that they were supporting
Hoover, although the nominal reason they gave for deserting the
Democrats was Smith's attitude toward Prohibition. But probably an even more influential factor than either the religious or
the alcoholic issue was the prosperity of the country excluding
the agricultural regions. The Republicans naturally took credit
for it, and Hoover promised that if the party was retained in
office, even better things lay ahead. America's "final triumph"
over want and poverty, he proclaimed, lay in sight.

Even with the most attractive and expedient candidate, the
Democrats would have had a difficult time defeating the incumbent. And with religion, Prohibition, and the urban-farm issues
added, the results were rather certain. Hoover marked up 21.4
million votes to Smith's 15 million, maintained a solid Republican supremacy throughout the Middle and Pacific West, and
even won Texas and the upper South. About the only comfort
the Democrats could draw from the election figures was that
Smith had won Massachusetts and Rhode Island and had increased the percentage of Democratic votes both in the Middle
West and in the large cities of the country. If the future should
turn out not so prosperous and if these voting trends should
continue, Republican candidates would obviously be faced with
trouble.

During the first seven months of his administration Hoover made it obvious that he was not content to follow the front-porch-sitting characteristics of his predecessor. Within weeks the new President had reorganized the White House Secretariat, had reversed the Coolidge-Mellon easy-money policy by raising the Federal Reserve Board's rediscount rate, ordered publicity for large income tax returns, and withdrew as many of the Federally-owned oil lands from further leasing to private firms as he was legally empowered to withdraw. True to his promise in the campaign, he also called a special session of Congress to deal with the farm problem and greeted it on April 16 with a proposal for the creation of a Federal Farm Board to secure the orderly marketing of farm products. A second message to Congress asked for higher tariffs on agricultural products. As journalists noted, a new spirit animated Washington: "The age of inactivity was over."

During the campaign Hoover had indicated his opposition to the McNary-Haugen Bill. He now exerted himself to defeat a Congressional proposal to incorporate into the new farm legislation the "export-debenture" principle, which would have granted a bounty on the export of domestic staples in the hope of dumping American surplus production on the already disorganized world market. Instead, the Agricultural Marketing Act of June 2 created a Federal Farm Board with a revolving fund of $500 million which might be used to make loans to cooperative marketing associations and to privately managed stabilization corporations with the power to purchase, process, and store surplus commodities. Since the stabilizing corporations could purchase commodities at whatever price they chose and hold them off the market indefinitely, it was hoped that their operations would reduce the troublesome surpluses and thus raise the price of farm products. Government funds were thus to be indirectly committed to an attempt at price fixing.

The history of the Hoover tariff legislation was much more involved. Called for the purpose of enacting higher rates on agricultural goods, Congress soon busied itself with a general revision which by the traditional means of vote trading produced the Smoot-Hawley Tariff of June 1930, containing the highest rates in

American history. Despite the fact that many American industries, including the automotive trade, and practically all the important academic economists protested against higher tariff schedules, the President did not intervene in the tariff fight until the bill had arrived at the stage of conference between the two Houses. At that point, the President managed to salvage a provision permitting him to reduce the existing rates on recommendation of the Tariff Commission by as much as 50 per cent. The new Tariff Act, as predicted, set off a round of retaliatory increases by foreign countries, thus choking the channels of an already contracting world trade. The most Administration apologists could say for the Act was that Hoover, unlike Coolidge, would use the tariff-cutting provision in a substantial way. Whether in normal times the effects of the Smoot-Hawley Act would have been mitigated, and whether the Agricultural Marketing Act could have substantially helped the farmer, were both academic questions by mid-1930. For in October 1929, the Wall Street crash had triggered the start of a world-girdling depression which effectively ended normal times for at least two generations. From the fall of 1929 on, the entire world was to face one great crisis after another. And Hoover, who had been elected with a mandate to continue the good, fat, and soft days of the twenties, was now to be judged on how he met the first of these catastrophic social movements.

If the President's record could be taken as a basis for prognosticating the future there was to be trouble ahead. Secretary of Commerce Hoover had been engrossed in making the industrial productive system more efficient. In pursuit of this goal he had encouraged industry through trade councils and other types of organizations to cooperate in self-government, a process which inevitably led to the critical diminishing of the individualism he was so fond of talking about. Yet he had evinced little concern for the other necessary half of the new economic system, the masses of consumers. He supported standardized industrial specifications set by the government, but was opposed or indifferent to grade labelling for the consumer. This dichotomy was not very different from the response of most of the American leadership of the day. They were ardently for maintaining the old individualistic social ideals and values among the masses. But for themselves and their fellows, especially in economic matters, they had, to a rather startling degree, become collectivists dependent upon a restricted kind of governmental paternalism. Hoover was the epitome of what many Americans of the twenties wanted: an able exponent of the new business system and a forceful expositor of the old rural social values and ethics. In good times the ambiguities involved were neither so pronounced nor immediately harmful. But under the strain of a major depression these incompatible threads were to produce serious rents in the social fabric.

3

The End of Normalcy

OCTOBER 1929 marked a fateful month for the United States and Western civilization. As a significant milepost along the chaotic road of modern history it deserves to be ranked with August 1914 and September 1939. From the stock market crash flowed an irreversible tide against which men and nations seemed almost helpless. The stock crash triggered a world depression, which in turn upset governments, ignited revolutions and wars, fundamentally changed the nature of the dominant international economy, and ended many famous personal careers. Through the latter part of the 1920's there were numerous indications of ugly economic weather ahead. The so-called Coolidge prosperity was built upon some obviously shaky foundations. Since the collapse of farm prices in June 1920, agriculture and the communities it supported had led a precarious existence spotted with losses, foreclosed mortgages, and bankrupted financial institutions. The coal and textile industries were plainly in distress by 1927. The following year a glut of petroleum products led to a ruinous wholesale price war. By September 1929 the construction and building industry, which had contributed much to the great boom, had slumped 25 per cent under the levels they had recorded during the previous twelve months. In the face of these distressing facts, a few men voiced the prophecy that disaster might be imminent. Noting the extent of installment buying, Roger Babson warned a business conference that a recession was almost inevitable and a panic possible. As 1928 ended, an economist of the National Industrial Conference Board, citing the already "developing depression in basic industries," warned that the existing prosperity rested precariously on "a state of mind" rather than upon basic economic facts.

Most men were unaware of the portents of the rising storm; since the United States had not had an extended depression since 1893, few had personal memories of such a disaster. Besides, they were daily beguiled by the hypnotic figures provided by the booming stock market. The market had not been without its temporary ups and downs throughout 1927 to 1929. In February and again in June of 1928 the market broke violently, Bank of Italy stock dropping, for example, 160 points in one day. After every such break the market rebounded with vigor, as millions of people sought to make quick fortunes on borrowed money. Buoying up confidence was a national chorus of unbridled optimism. Politicians, journalists, businessmen, academic economists, and those who stood to profit most from the great boom—brokers and bankers—joined the refrain. Twice before he left office, President Coolidge stated that stocks were "cheap at current prices" and that the huge amount of brokers' funds loaned to speculators, large and small, were not too high. The owners of *Time* magazine, reflecting the buoyant confidence, chose January 1929 as the time to start *Fortune,* their plush new journal devoted to business. The academic world joined in the yea saying. So as to let the "poor professors get in on the ground floor of financial opportunity" a faculty fund was formed at Columbia University for speculation purposes. Wall Street itself was a bit startled in July 1929 when the news leaked that Bishop James Cannon, Jr., the politically minded churchman, was "playing the market," so as, he later explained, "to make money that it might be an instrument of service."

With the new President talking about the possible abolition of poverty in the foreseeable future, with Secretary of the Treasury Andrew Mellon agreeing with the judgment of an expert economist that the country had reached a "permanent plateau of prosperity," and with the multimillionaire Chairman of the Democratic National Committee publishing an article in the *Ladies' Home*

Journal entitled "Everybody Ought To Be Rich," who could really believe the Cassandra-like voices of the few? Such pessimism, a leading New York banker declared, "was more to be feared than Bolshevism." Consequently, as thousands of new recruits daily invested their savings and all they could borrow, the market swept up to majestic heights. United States Steel finally stood at 250, American Telephone and Telegraph at 300, Montgomery Ward at 439—fantastic prices which bore little relation to the worth of the firms or their existing earning power. By September 19, 1929, when the market stood at the highest point in its history, the paper profits of investors were measured in the billions. But on October 3 and 4 stocks took measurable slides downward. Three weeks later leading industrial issues lost from five to ninety points in one day. And then on "black Thursday," October 29, came chaos. As stocks plummeted by fifty to one hundred points, millions wanted to sell to nonexistent buyers. For the next three years the market ground inexorably downward until 75 per cent of the total value of the nation's listed securities, or some 90 billion dollars, had been wiped out.

The total effect of the great stock slide on the nation's financial structure was ruinous. Since much stock purchasing had rested on credit, the immediate calls for repayment in the plummeting market not only wiped out speculators by the thousands but also so tightened credit generally that business and industry were starving for funds. In the stringent situation banks refused to make loans, business men to extend credit, and the general consumer to make purchases. As the wheels of industry and commerce began to slow down and in some cases came to an almost complete stop, men and women by the millions lost their jobs. The end of an age was written in the little pink slips appearing with the weekly and monthly pay checks, announcing that the services of vice-presidents, managers, engineers, salesgirls, and manual workers were no longer needed.

The effects of the Great Depression were worldwide. Starting in May 1931 with the collapse of Austria's credit system, the contagion swept all over Europe and then to the colonial world. In the aftermath of human suffering and insecurity, democratic governments, including that of Germany, fell before a rash of dictatorships. After Great Britain went off the gold standard in September 1931 the three-century-old world free market was replaced by a state-directed system of mercantilism, replete with exchange controls, export and import quotas, and managed currencies, all manipulated to gain commercial advantage from neighbor states. Unemployment, bankruptcy, and personal deprivation was almost ubiquitous. Peasants wore potato sacks in the Balkans, fresh eggs sold for two cents a dozen in Budapest, and millions of Frenchmen were eating one meal a day in a country long noted for its agricultural self-sufficiency. But in no nation were the economic and industrial effects of the Depression as sharp as they were in the United States. Elsewhere production neither sank so low nor was unemployment so high and recovery so long retarded. Whereas the world trade figures fell by about 25 per cent, American imports and exports in 1933 were only one-third of the 1929 figures. The United States industrial collapse was of terrifying proportions. In 1932 the total wages paid throughout the nation amounted to only 40 per cent of the 1929 figure, dividends to only 43 per cent. It was estimated that American business wound up the year with a net loss of over $5 billion. Meanwhile farm prices had dropped even more disastrously, cotton falling from 17 cents a pound to 6 cents, and wheat from $1.05 a bushel to 35 cents. Before the mid-1930's national unemployment statistics were a matter of guesswork. But estimates in 1932 placed the unemployed figure at 1 million for New York, 600,000 for Chicago. In the following year the Lynds of *Middletown* fame found that only 42 per cent of the workers in Muncie, Indiana, a town of 50,000 population, had regular positions. By March 4, 1933, perhaps 12 to 15 million men, or one-third of the nation's working force, were without jobs.

When it became apparent in late 1930 that the nation was faced with a major industrial depression, President Hoover appealed to employers not to cut wage scales. If the prevailing wage standards were maintained, Hoover predicted, the effects of the Depression would be limited. For a time the nation's manufacturers faithfully tried to meet the President's precedent-making request.

But in the face of mounting deficits and after reducing dividends and white collar salaries, the United States Steel Corporation on October 1, 1931, reduced wages by 10 per cent. The example of the big steel company was soon followed by General Motors and United States Rubber. The rout of existing wage standards was on. By 1932 Pennsylvania reported that men were working for ten cents an hour and children in sweat shops for as little as one dollar for a fifty-five-hour week. Among the want ads in the *Saturday Review of Literature* a request appeared for an English Department head for a "select college preparatory school" near New York. The offer promised room, board, and laundry but no salary. A year later among the emergency workers constructing a reservoir in Hollywood were farmers, ministers, actors, engineers, a school principal, and a pre-Depression president of a Missouri bank. The downgrading of labor skills could scarcely have gone further.

As soon as it became evident that the country was faced with an intense and possibly enduring industrial depression all manner of alleged authorities came forward with cures for the great debacle. Invariably each man's cure reflected his own diagnosis of why the Depression had come about. By 1932 a few conservative spokesmen were advocating basic changes in the existing industrial system and thus repudiating many of the hallowed economic maxims of the twenties. One of the major causes of the Depression, columnist David Lawrence wrote, was "ruthless competition." Gerard Swope, President of the General Electric Corporation, and Owen D. Young agreed, proposing that by a national plan of self-government, business should eliminate such harmful competition and regulate production and pricing. Such self-regulation, Owen D. Young admitted, meant "the voluntary surrender of a certain amount of individual freedom by the majority and the ultimate coercion of the minority . . ."

But by far the great majority of industrial and financial leaders of the country stood rigidly pat on their classic views. The business system was sound, they argued, and without need of basic reform. The decline was simply a product of the business cycle and probably would be productive of good, since it would prune away many of the inefficient elements in the industrial and commercial structure. If government abstained from intervention in the natural business process, the Depression would soon be over, probably within a year or two. Even after more than two years of public suffering most industrialists and financiers had little to offer other than this negative program. They were as much opposed to any reform of the nation's productive and financial machinery as they were to attempts by government to alleviate distress through the dole, public works, or social insurance. During a Senate Banking and Currency Committee hearing of 1933 they still argued that government should reduce its expenditures, balance its budget, and otherwise fold its hands. Expansion of charitable activities at the local level, business leaders argued, would alleviate the distress arising from unemployment. In their home communities most of them contributed handsomely of their time and money to charity. But as the months went by, as unemployment rolls grew ever longer and local contributions tended to dry up, the majority of them still refused to moderate their opposition to public relief supported by taxation. Into their remarks crept bitter statements against the unemployed which revealed a state of growing frustration and anxiety as well as a lack of will to lead. Echoing Henry Ford's sentiment, the President of the National Association of Manufacturers in early 1932 ascribed the Depression and the growing unemployment to mass laziness. Most men without jobs, he said, either did not want to work or were "utilizing the occasion to swell the Communist chorus."

Among the major liquidations of the Great Depression was that of business prestige and influence. From their venerated position during the twenties businessmen fell to objects of public hostility, suspicion, and ridicule, not so much because of the Depression but rather because of their subsequent unwillingness or inability to provide or support new solutions for the pressing problems of unemployment and growing poverty. Their doctrinaire hostility to relief and reform obscured their private charitable activities, fostered the public image of them as cold, indifferent, and greedy, and led to their social bankruptcy.

Organized labor in the early days of the Depression appeared to be almost as barren of ideas and leadership as business. Until 1931 William Green, President of the American Federation of Labor, contented himself with sterile criticism of business, and opposition to any state scheme of dole or compulsory unemployment insurance as sure to turn the worker into a "ward of the state." Somnolent since the stirring days following World War I, organized labor seemed no more able than business to discern the reasons why the productive machine had slowed down or ways by which to accelerate it. Characterized by an almost total lack of leadership and besieged by mass unemployment and a rapidly falling wage scale, unions lost members in droves, and by 1932 the union movement appeared to be on the way to oblivion.

Outside the ranks of organized business and labor not a few individuals made public their own diagnosis of what had happened and their proposed cures. A group of radical economists, anticipating some of the doctrines of John Maynard Keynes, argued that the basic cause of the Depression was the maldistribution of saving and spending under unregulated capitalism. David Cushman Coyle, Marriner Eccles, Rexford Tugwell, and Adolph A. Berle, among others, contended that in the old unplanned mass-production economy dominated by a few great industries and financial institutions, the few had siphoned off too many of the rewards, and the masses of people had obtained far too little. This maldistribution of national wealth had led to oversaving or overinvesment by the few and underspending or underconsumption by the many. The process had resulted in too many factories, producing too many goods, with consumers unable to purchase enough to keep the industrial wheels spinning. This conclusion seemed to be borne out by one of the most influential scholarly studies to appear during the Depression. *America's Capacity to Consume,* published by the Brookings Institution in 1934, drew a picture of the distribution of the national wealth in 1929 which was profoundly disturbing to social conservatives. Eight per cent of the nation's families, it appeared, had earned 42 per cent of the national income, while at the other end of the economic pole 60 per cent of the families had received only 23 per cent.

Since private industry had been unable to preserve a balance of earning and consumption power sufficient to keep the productive machine working, the Keynesians argued, government would have to assume that task in one form or another. The more conservative among them, who desired to maintain capitalistic institutions as little changed as possible (as for example, Eccles), contended that this could be done by a change in taxation policies and by the government's taking up the slack in mass incomes during times of recession by extensive public works and construction programs. Tugwell, to the contrary, believed that the only way to salvage the situation was by a thorough-going system of government planning and control in which the separate indentity of industry and government would tend to disappear. The future, he remarked in 1932, "is visible in Russia." He was joined in this radical outlook by such noted reformers as John Dewey and Charles A. Beard, who supported their positions on philosophic and ethical grounds.

In retrospect there seem to have been many reasons for the stock market crash and the Great Depression. Among the more important were the major economic maldistributions arising out of World War I; a chaotic international financial policy, to which the United States contributed markedly by its insistence upon high tariffs and upon repayment of war debts, after it had become the world's creditor; the speculative urge, which was probably as rabid on the European exchanges as it was in New York; the overextension of credit, which applied to families buying appliances, as well as to businessmen and stock speculators; the downright dishonesty of some financial and business leaders, whose practices in America as elsewhere were little above those of the cardsharp; and the rigidity of the world and national price structure for industrial goods as compared to that for primary goods or raw materials.

But it would seem that basic to the condition of the United States, as to the world, was the fact that some classes of people and some nations were obtaining too much of the rewards of industry and commerce, while others were receiving too little, to keep the highly industrialized machine devoted to mass production and consumption operating. Thus the primary-goods-producing nations were receiving too little to continue purchasing the manufactured goods of the industrially mature nations on a scale sufficient to maintain the vigorous exchange of goods. In the same way, the working masses of the industrialized nations were unable to maintain a level of purchasing sufficient to keep the factories operating on something near the level of full production. Seemingly the new mass-production-consumption economy of the twentieth century required either that men be rewarded more equally by conventional pay checks or that government skim off a portion of the goods produced in order to utilize them for nonproductive pursuits such as armaments or war, or for disposition by gift or by dole. Years after he had left the White House, Herbert Hoover blamed the Depression on two major causes: the "weakness" and "wickedness" in the nation's financial system, and maldistribution of rewards. "A margin of some thousands" of people, he declared, "got too much of the productive pie for the services they performed. . . . Another margin of some 20 per cent got too little."

There is some indication that Hoover appreciated the danger of maldistribution of income even while he was President. One of his first acts in meeting the Depression was to ask the industrial leaders of the country to maintain the existing wage scale. But Hoover did not go beyond requesting. To dictate on such matters was unthinkable. One of Hoover's most cherished ideals was freedom for the individual. Few, if any, of the other freedoms could be maintained if economic liberty was denied, because it supplied "the most nearly universal field for the release of the creative spirit of man." Consequently he relied upon private actions and individual decisions to cure the Depression; and he gave way to government activity reluctantly and only when he believed it was absolutely necessary.

The chief difficulty with the President's program was that business refused to provide the leadership he requested. This was made clear in the autumn of 1931 at a national conference of bankers. During the previous year over 2,000 banks, unable to collect from their debtors or pay their creditors, had closed their doors. The President asked the large banks to form a pool of their common resources to help the weaker institutions over the period of financial stringency. The bankers' reply that this was the government's business so discouraged Hoover that he returned to the White House thoroughly despondent. The growing realization that business would not act and the steadily deteriorating economy finally pushed Hoover to action. Already he had violated his major economic principles by agreeing to the Federal Farm Board's purchase of surplus wheat and cotton, a program given up the following year because it failed to raise agricultural prices. In his annual message to Congress in 1931 the beleaguered President asked for a revival of the World War I War Finance Corporation, with power to loan public money to privately owned banks and corporations. During the next two years the Reconstruction Finance Corporation loaned $1.5 billion to financial institutions. But despite these large loans to private firms, and despite the Administration's attempts to raise agricultural prices, the President was still adamantly against granting relief to individuals, even by indirect means. Perhaps Hoover's willingness to aid agriculture and business but not the urban unemployed was due largely to his reluctance to make any individual a direct grantee of the Federal government. Part of his opposition to unemployment relief may have come from his bias toward rural values and his antipathy to, or ambiguous feelings toward, the urban masses, among whom the need for relief was centered. In his more philosophical writings the President many times scathingly referred to the "mobs" of the French Revolution and of the Paris Commune. Herbert Hoover, like so many of his friends and supporters, was a twentieth-century industrial man, but much of the cast of his social creed was molded by the values of West Branch, Iowa, from which he had come.

Hoover was neither a flint-hearted social Darwinist nor a blind believer in *laissez faire,* even for the city masses. From the first days of the Depression he called for massive private action to alleviate the distress of the unemployed. Repeatedly he asked utilities and railroads to expand their construction and thus afford work to the jobless. Simultaneously he encouraged the increase of private and local charity to provide for the needy. In October 1930 he created the President's Emergency Committee for Unemployment and supported this organization's national campaign to persuade homeowners, block by city block, to create work by repairing and adding to their properties. But beyond encouraging voluntary, local, and private efforts the President refused to go, because, he argued, Federal grants for relief, even of the indirect kind, would be "a step toward a national dole" which would deprive the individual of a sense of responsibility, dry up "the precious charitable instincts" of the people, enfeeble local and state government, and make the unemployed direct and perhaps permanent wards of the national government. Relief in its most direct sense, Hoover reiterated many times, was the responsibility of local individuals and local government.

During 1930 and 1931 the President adhered to his position. He opposed a scheme for national unemployment insurance and rejected a suggestion by William G. McAdoo that the Federal Farm Board release its surplus wheat to the poor. If Federal support were the last alternative to avoid starvation, Hoover would support it. But, he added, "I have faith in the American people that such a day shall not come."

Hoover's solution to the problems of unemployment and poverty might have been successful had the Depression been of short duration. But as grim month succeeded month and all the major economic indexes pointed steadily downward, the size of the problems ballooned while private and local efforts to alleviate suffering dwindled due to a diminishing lack of funds. Private industry, instead of increasing construction of facilities, had little recourse but to cut expenditures. From 1929 to 1932 the total of all private construction in the country fell from $10 billion to $1 billion. Public works followed the same pattern. Even though the Federal government eventually attempted to take up the slack, huge cuts in construction by the states meant fewer jobs. From

1929 on the total spent for public works declined steadily from $3.3 billion to $1.3 billion in 1933. As a consequence work of any kind became more difficult to obtain and the number of families on public relief or on the charity rolls grew steadily. From 40,000 in the winter of 1928–29 the number increased to 500,000 by 1931–32.

Compounding the bleaker aspects of the situation, states and local governments were running out of money. During 1931 and 1932 most states cut their relief appropriations. Michigan, where unemployment in the hard-hit automobile industry was acute, reduced its funds from $2 million in 1931 to $860,000 in 1932. In cities and towns relief funds were as short. Many communities were unable to care for their own citizens, to say nothing of the thousands of drifters looking for jobs or food. By 1933 an estimated million men and women were on the roads without permanent homes. During that year the Southern Pacific Railroad reported that its guards had thrown 683,000 people off its freight trains. As the disparity between local resources and the size of the relief problem grew, the disposition increased to give all strangers short shrift. California first set up labor camps in forests and then posted guards at the state borders to turn indigent people away. Other communities, unable to care for their own citizens, simply escorted the drifters to the next county or city. Atlanta even placed the impoverished wanderers in chain gangs. A national survey by *Fortune* magazine in 1931 reported that the theory of local responsibility for the impoverished had completely broken down, simply because locally organized charity depended upon "contributions of communities no longer able to contribute."

Amidst the growing destitution a number of alternatives were proposed to replace Hoover's reliance upon local and private efforts to alleviate distress. With a view to the elections of 1930 the Democrats were of course bitterly critical of the Administration's program, but though long on criticism, the party as a whole was short on constructive measures. Among party leaders, only Senators Robert Wagner of New York and Hugo L. Black of Alabama advocated radical measures to soften the effect of the Depression. They were joined in 1931 by Governor Franklin D.

Roosevelt of New York and by Democratic mayors like Tony Cermak of Chicago. Roosevelt was signally successful in passing his legislative program of raising income taxes and creating an emergency state relief agency, which was to spend $83 million on relief by 1933. As early as January 1930 Senator Wagner proposed the creation of a Federal employment service, national unemployment insurance, and the expenditure of at least $2 billion on public works. Supporting Wagner's proposals was an important group of Western Senators including Robert La Follette, Jr., George Norris, Bronson Cutting, Edward P. Costigan, William E. Borah, Hiram Johnson, Burton K. Wheeler, and Gerald Nye. The Democratic Congressional victory of 1930 added further bipartisan support for the project. But even in the spring of 1931 the friends of direct Federal relief did not have a majority in Congress.

Except for the radical Westerners most Republicans were still against Federal relief either by a public works program or by grants to the states. As late as May 1932 Secretary of the Treasury Ogden Mills argued that public works were "destructive to the public credit, ineffective in reviving business and wasteful of the national resources." Prominent independents were also opposed to large expenditures of Federal funds for work relief. Walter Lippmann, for example, while he agreed that something had to be done to provide for the armies of unemployed in the big cities, argued that since New York City and Chicago, the two loudest claimants for direct relief, lay in the richest states in the union, the necessary money should be raised by their state legislatures and not by Congress. Even among the Democrats no unanimity existed on what was to be done. In March 1931 the President vetoed the Wagner Bill, which would have created a Federal unemployment agency. Some months later he mobilized a Congressional coalition of Republicans and conservative Democrats to kill the La Follette-Costigan Bill, which provided for distribution of $750 million among the states for either public works or direct relief to the unemployed.

By the late winter and spring of 1932, however, the unemployment and relief situation had further deteriorated, especially in the large cities. In Philadelphia and Pittsburgh one of every three adults was on charity rolls. Toledo had sufficient funds to grant only 2.14 cents a meal for relief applicants. By late February Chicago, with over 700,000 unemployed, had spent all of the relief funds budgeted for the entire year. Pointing out the danger of insurrection, Mayor Cermak demanded that the city get either "Federal relief or Federal troops."

Nineteen thirty-two was also a Presidential election year, and a good many members of Congress, who had previously been opposed to large Federal appropriations, now changed their positions. Consequently they supported a Democratic party proposal to float a $2 billion bond issue, from which the receipts were to be used in self-liquidating public works. Faced with Congressional approval of this and possibly even more radical measures, Hoover capitulated and agreed to approve the compromise 1932 Emergency Relief Act, provided all other relief bills were pigeonholed. The Act extended the lending authority of the Reconstruction Finance Corporation by $300 million, which might be loaned to the states to bolster their relief programs. Considering the extent of the need, the sum was extremely small. Even so, the money would be spent cautiously, the President observed. Grants would be made to states only after evidence of their "financial exhaustion" had been produced and then only on a loan basis. Such monies, with interest, were to be paid back to the RFC by July 1935.

Hoover's reputation and political fortunes foundered on the shoals of the urban relief question. It was not true, as was later charged, that his was a do-nothing, care-nothing Administration. By 1933 Hoover had gone far along the road to governmental intervention in the economic life of the country. With his approval both the Federal Farm Board and the Reconstruction Finance Corporation had spent and lent billions attempting to bolster the sagging economy. Moreover the President had interjected the government into the private mechanisms of costs, wages, and profits to an unheard-of degree. Looking at the Hoover record in 1932, James M. Beck, former Solicitor General, felt that the President was in competition with Russia for the title

of being the more socialistic. Nor could it be said in 1932 that
Hoover was indifferent or callous to the misery around him. The
depths of his concern were written on his face, and few Presidents
have worked harder or spent longer hours at the Presidential
desk. But the very intensity of Hoover's efforts to overcome the
Depression were to be used against him. If so much money and
time had been spent to save banks and corporations, why not, the
jobless man asked, a few pennies for the poor? The President had
come to office with a well-known record as a great humanitarian.
He had fed the Belgians during World War I and the Eastern
Europeans and Russians afterwards. Why not Americans now?
the man on the street asked. Hoover answered with allusions to
spiritual values and talk of freedom and responsibility, thus opening himself to the charge that he was the cold and uncaring
servant of the ruling economic classes, as ready to help business as
he was to sacrifice all other human values.

During the depression of 1921 and 1922 Hoover proposed to
President Harding that an extensive program of public works be
inaugurated to combat unemployment. Why did he not give the
same response in the hours of much greater need? The question
will probably never be answered with certainty until the Hoover
manuscripts are opened, and perhaps not then. But it may be
worthy of note that when many journalists, economists, and politicians were shortening their ideological sails to fit the prevailing
winds, the President continued to talk in the terms of his philosophy expounded in *American Individualism* back in 1922.
Down through history, in times of rapid change and social upheaval, the so-called practical men have often been the real
doctrinaires.

Walter Lippmann noted in 1932 that the greatest problem of
the modern state was "the management of plenty." The motives
responsible for the creation of much of society's productive
machinery—acquisitive instincts, the possibility of enormous
profits, and the overriding desire for personal power—had to be
exchanged for others, Lippmann continued, "more disinterested
and cooperative in their effects." Columnist Elmer Davis was
more blunt: "The profit system as our ancestors knew it is

apparently on the way out." Confirmed radicals agreed with this and were jubilant about the future. A planned society, George Soule wrote, was not only imperative but also desirable, since it would "liberate human energies" hitherto stultified to an unimaginable degree. The Communist party, under the leadership of Earl Browder, was certain that the crack-up portended the end of capitalism and opened the way for the dictatorship of the proletariat. But in the midst of all the distress, the party had been able to recruit only some ten to fifteen thousand dues-paying members by 1932. And despite the manifesto signed by Sherwood Anderson, Theodore Dreiser, John Dos Passos, and Edmund Wilson claiming that Communism was the only political creed able "to save civilization," obviously if a great political shift were to come, it would not be to the Red end of the political spectrum.

More of a danger to established institutions were the individuals and groups demanding a non-Communist dictator. During the twenties much praise had been lavished on Benito Mussolini. The reviews of the dictator's *Diary*, in 1925, and his *Autobiography*, in 1928, were overwhelmingly favorable to both the man and his works. By 1932 all sorts of individuals and organizations were suggesting that the appointment of a dictator with similar views would solve the country's economic dilemmas. On September 8, 1930, the "American Facist [*sic*] Association and Order of Black Shirts" was organized in Atlanta with the hope of federating similar local organizations springing up over the country. A year later the American Legion in its national convention gave encouragement if not precise support to the movement by resolving that the social and economic situation of the country could not "be promptly and efficiently met by existing political methods." In 1932 Lawrence Dennis published *Is Capitalism Doomed?* This volume argued openly for a syndicalist society on the Fascist model. Simultaneously such diverse individuals as Senator David A. Reed of Pennsylvania and publicist Bernarr Macfadden were advocating the appointment of a dictator and the institution of martial law.

Countless other schemes were suggested, including a spate of proposals for a controlled inflation that would stimulate the economy but not overturn society. One of the more interesting was Professor Irving Fisher's program to compel more purchasing and the faster circulation of money by requiring everyone to buy stamps to be placed upon paper money and having the effect of decreasing its value monthly. Louis Bromfield, the novelist, and Henry Seidel Canby, the critic, argued for a retreat from the machine age and a return to the land. On the other hand, the "Technocrats," drawing their inspiration from Thorstein Veblen, urged Americans to make their peace with modern production by junking capitalism and the existing political system and installing the engineer as governor of a new society.

For a short time in 1932 and 1933 the air was full of technocracy's program for "an ordered full production" to be measured by units of energy and divided among all citizens through a new system of exchange based upon "monetary ergs." By 1934 the Los Angeles Utopian Society, a technocratic organization, claimed 750,000 members, some of them unquestionably bemused by the promise of one technocratic speaker to connect the economy with "the mean flow of stellar energy," by which it would rise "higher and higher into the cosmic nebulae of the perturbations of time-space."

The average man without a job, however, preferred to be connected with a pay check, or with groceries and goods, rather than with stellar energy. As the national and state governments either refused or were unable to meet the problems of the unemployed, local organizations, seeking survival for their members, sprang up all over the country. Unemployed Citizens Leagues, Republics of the Penniless, and Cooperative Life groups planted community vegetable gardens, established guild workshops and commissaries, and issued script or exchanged goods among their members by barter. In Dayton and Seattle the unemployed established community workshops to can vegetables, make flour and soap, and manufacture shoes, clothing, and furniture.

Here and there a disregard for private property and constituted authority gave evidence that orderly society was beginning to disintegrate. In Seattle empty lots were gardened with or without their owners' consent. In Pennsylvania and Kentucky individual miners worked company coal seams, bootlegging their product to surrounding towns. In August 1932 Milo Reno's Farmer's Holiday Association barricaded the roads to Sioux City, attempting to prevent the sale of farm goods at the prevailing ruinous prices. In eastern Iowa milk strikers met local authorities head-on in violent clashes, and increasingly throughout the Middle West sheriffs seeking to foreclose farm property encountered ragged lines of determined farmers armed with hunting rifles and shotguns. Meanwhile, thousands of men made "hunger marches" to state capitals and to Washington. Some demonstrations were undoubtedly inspired by Communists hoping to extract political profit from the misery. But newspapers reported that from the 12,000 men led to Washington by a Pittsburgh priest there were few if any political overtones. The men carried crude simple signs asking for bread and jobs. The most significant march started from Portland, Oregon, in May 1932, a march of unemployed World War veterans seeking to pressure Congress into passing a veterans' bonus bill, to which the President had already announced his opposition. By the time the Patman Bill was debated on the floor, 20,000 veterans were camped along Pennsylvania Avenue and later on the mud flats where the Anacostia River meets the Potomac.

Fear was abundant in 1932, the fear of the poor and unemployed that tomorrow would be no better, the fear of the rich that they would lose all they had, and the fear of the government that revolution was imminent. As organized labor cried that they had enough, and the head of the Federal Farm Bureau predicted a revolution in nine months unless something was done, wealth began to panic. Gold was shipped from the country to Switzerland; places of refuge were selected against the day the mob might start marching. A Hollywood director announced that he had gathered some old clothes together so that at the crisis he could "disappear into the crowd."

In the midst of this taut atmosphere the President was confronted with the critical problem of the veterans camped along the Potomac. So far the President and the District of Columbia authority, represented by General Glassford, had treated the veterans with consideration. Hoover had even supplied funds with which to ship the veterans back to their homes and many had taken advantage of the offer. But when the Patman soldiers' bonus bill was defeated in the Senate, the remaining men grew restless. Some talked wildly, and a story circulated of the possibility of organizing the veterans into a khaki army representing the poor of the country. At that juncture, against the advice of Glassford, the President ordered General Douglas MacArthur and the army to remove the men from the capital. Calling the veterans "a mob . . . animated by the essence of revolution," MacArthur quickly accomplished the task. But the act probably sealed the fate of the Hoover Administration. To the unthinking the soldiers' bonus was confused with general relief. Many interpreted the action as a token of the government's intention to provide bullets instead of bread. Had a compelling rabble rouser arisen and had not the coming fall election offered a promise of a change in administration, the action at the Anacostia Flats might have ignited a disastrous social upheaval.

The selection of a Republican candidate and a program for the 1932 elections was little more than a formality. Unless the party wished to repudiate itself it had to renominate Hoover and stand on his record. The Republican program was therefore a cautious document designed, according to one commentator, "to defend what was left of Prohibition and what was left of the country." The Democratic choice was another matter. Here the split between the conservatives and the liberal-minded had been widened by Franklin Roosevelt's speech of April 7, in which he charged the Hoover Administration with neglect of the ordinary American and expressed his sympathies with "the forgotten man at the bottom of the economic pyramid." Alfred E. Smith, who desperately wanted the nomination again, announced after the speech that he was ready to fight any candidate who persisted "in a demagogic appeal to the working classes." Newton D. Baker, an old Wilsonian internationalist, and Speaker of the House John Nance Garner were also conservative or moderate candidates.

On the other side of the political wicket but still not too far from the center, the Governor of New York had rallied most of the liberals to his cause. Roosevelt's record of providing sizable relief funds, his support of public power installations, and his opposition to a national sales tax (which Garner and the conservative Democrats had advanced in Congress) pleased the Democratic left. The forgotten-man speech won their affection. Roosevelt obtained the nomination, but the fact that he won through the support of many conservatives and as a part of the bargain had to accept Speaker Garner as the Vice-Presidential candidate indicated the very fine balance between the factions. The Democratic platform, which Roosevelt told the convention he accepted "100 per cent," also illustrated the relatively equal strength of the contending ideologies. The platform, Walter Lippmann observed, had been written by old Wilsonians and indicated their desire to return to the liberalism of Cleveland and Wilson rather than to point the party toward a new collectivism. Weighing both candidates and platforms, Lippmann wearily observed that they illustrated the truth of John Morley's remark that democratic politics was the "science of the second best."

Whatever Roosevelt's other limitations, he soon showed himself as a superb popular politician who did not fit easily into the ordinary American mold. Although his letters reveal him to be far from a stylist in language, his speeches were political masterpieces. Simple, concrete, and filled with homely analogies, they were understandable and infinitely appealing to the common man. He simplified even the most complex technical questions so that he had the ear, and apparently the understanding, of the masses. Yet Rooosevelt never seemed to talk down to his audience. His warm and vibrant voice carried real conviction and concern. And his superbly confident delivery in a cultivated Eastern accent seemed to lift his efforts far above traditional vote seeking efforts. His personal demeanor contributed to the same effect. He was one of the nation's few really light-hearted leaders, given to quips and cracks, carrying laughter around with him. But he never once demeaned his office or himself by vulgarity or absurdity. Roosevelt achieved that most difficult of public images, a man of immense zest, warmth, and at the same time dignity. With his large distinguished head held at a characteristic angle, his chin forward, a cigarette angled at the sky, and sometimes a cape flowing in the wind from his broad shoulders, the man fairly exuded confidence and vitality. All in all, he was one of the most personable and attractive public figures the twentieth century has produced.

At the start of the critical campaign of 1932 there was little to indicate that Franklin Roosevelt would institute momentous changes in national policy. He had been an efficient Governor of New York, but his accomplishments, except for public relief and an old age security program, could scarcely be distinguished from that of his predecessor, Alfred E. Smith. Except for his "forgotten man" effort and the inevitable attacks against the Hoover Administration, his prenomination campaign was likewise pitched in a low key. At the convention he called for a legislative program which was neither radical nor conservative nor characterized by an "improvised hit-or-miss irresponsible opportunism." During the campaign that followed, many of the respected party leaders talked straight conservatism. Alfred E. Smith advocated a balanced budget and a sales tax as the way to end the Depression. Speaker Garner attacked Hoover's intervention in what should essentially remain nongovernmental affairs, and he trumpeted loudly for states' rights. The 1924 Democratic nominee, John W. Davis, assailed Hoover for "following the road to socialism." In many of his own speeches Roosevelt sang in chorus with the party's conservatives and with the men who were largely responsible for financing his campaign: William Randolph Hearst, Bernard Baruch, John J. Raskob, Vincent Astor, and Joseph Kennedy. In his acceptance speech Roosevelt paid vague tribute to the hallowed phrases—"liberal thought," "planned action," "the greatest good to the greatest number." He promised that the Federal government would "assume" the responsibility for public welfare and "distress relief." But he also assailed Hoover for wasteful expenditures and pledged himself to a sharp reduction in taxes. "For three years," he reminded his audience, "I have been going up and down this country preaching that government—federal, state and local— costs too much. I shall not stop that preaching." From such phrases his conservative friends drew cheer and predicted that his course would be a sound one. James M. Beck, the reactionary Republican lawyer who had attacked Hoover for "going down the road to socialism" at a faster clip than the Communists, predicted that if Roosevelt were elected, he would at once "assure the people that he is very conservative. . . ."

There were two and possibly more Roosevelts during the campaign of 1932: the Roosevelt associated with his financial backers and the Roosevelt who gathered around him as intimates four professors who were later to become the core of the so-called "brain trust," Felix Frankfurter of Harvard and Raymond Moley, Rexford Tugwell, and Adolf Berle of Columbia. Each of these Roosevelts had an eloquent voice. Berle wrote much of the speech Roosevelt gave at the San Francisco Commonwealth Club. Arguing that the nation's industrial plant was probably overbuilt and that the creators of new railroads and factories "were as likely to be a danger as a help," the candidate described the fundamental task for the future as one of distributing the country's wealth more equitably and "of adapting the existing economic organizations to the service of the people." The major task of the government, he continued, was to assist in the development of a new "economic declaration of rights," which should include the right of all to a comfortable living and to own property. To achieve these goals government would have to restrict "the manipulator and even the financier" and to restrain the "lone wolf," "the unethical competitor," and "the reckless promoter." In other speeches during the long campaign Roosevelt promised to restore the farmer's purchasing power and to help save home owners from loss of their properties and small banks from forced liquidation. But the Commonwealth Club speech was the only really radical one Roosevelt made during the campaign. He naturally attacked Hoover for a great many things, and by implication suggested that his own Administration would take the opposite tack. But if one focuses on his positive proposals, one can find little that would have antagonized the conservative voter.

Herbert Hoover was a sad figure during the election contest. Overworked, and bewildered by the persistence of the Depression, he did not campaign until October. Then came real disaster for the man and for his party. In his Des Moines speech he set the theme for the campaign and for the party for the next twenty years. Instead of centering his attack on Roosevelt's inconsistencies, he chose to depict his opponent as a radical who would destroy the American system. In his powerful Madison Square Garden speech he charged that the New Deal would enslave the masses by the creation of a giant bureaucracy, run the government into ruinous debt, debase the currency by a ruthless inflation, undermine the national credit, and destroy the Supreme Court. This was no ordinary political contest, he warned in his parting shot, but rather a decision whether or not to depart from "a hundred and fifty years of American tradition," and one which would determine "the direction our nation will take over a century to come."

In drawing a fixed line where there was in reality little to mark, the President may have unwittingly shoved the New Deal further to the left. Certainly Hoover's campaign tactics were unjust to his past principles and to his own record. In defending something very near *laissez faire* and the "percolator" theory of economics, and in attacking Federal aid to the farmers and the unemployed he departed from many of the principles of his younger years and did scant justice to his Administration's efforts to cure the Depression. By adopting a position of rigid and doctrinaire conservatism, he confirmed his party in the narrow beliefs which were to help make it an impotent, impractical minority for the next two decades and to deprive the majority of a responsible opposition.

The discerning voter in 1932 was faced with a difficult choice. The Socialist party, running Norman Thomas as its candidate, had dropped most of its ideology and had become an ineffective group with only 1,200 dues-paying members. The Communists, despite the country's years of hardship, were little better off. The minor parties, "Coin" Harvey's Liberty Party and Jacob Coxey's Farmer-Labor Party, were more subjects for jokes than for serious consideration. This left the alternative between the two major candidates, between one who smilingly carried varying ideologies on both shoulders and the other who, patently weary and disheartened, seemed to hark back to Adam Smith for his inspiration. It is little wonder that the intellectual was in his usual election-time state of perplexity. But so were groups with hard measurable interests to defend. Organized labor, which had denounced both major party platforms, refused to commit itself. And business, large and small, was more sharply split between the two candidates than it had been in years. The overwhelming Roosevelt victory was thus probably due to the majority's determination to vote against the ins and to cast a ballot for a hope and a very appealing personality. Whatever the cause, the election was a rout. Roosevelt defeated Hoover easily and carried with him sizable Democratic majorities in both houses of Congress, majorities which included a great many new men who would naturally be favorably disposed to the first Democratic leader in sixteen years able to lead the party to victory.

The inconsistencies of Roosevelt's campaign, his appeal both to the right and to the left, presaged trouble for the future. His support ran through a wide section of the political arc, from Tugwell and Berle on the left to Kennedy and Raskob on the far right. Both extremes, as well as the center of the party, claimed him after the election. In fact, he was the first President-elect since William Howard Taft about whom there was so much confusion among his supporters. It was such considerations that led Walter Lippmann to conclude before the campaign that Roosevelt had few if any really deep convictions. He was "not the dangerous enemy of anything," the journalist wrote; he was "too eager to please."

What then was Roosevelt on election day in 1932? Coming from an old, wealthy New York family, he had been given the best education the country offered. But the nonacademic qualities that he thought educational institutions should promote are indicative of the man. Speaking in 1936 he maintained that proper

education should instill first a "sense of fair play among men,"
second "a sense of equality," and finally a devotion to "freedom
in the pursuit of truth." Despite his background and his culture, the President was not a lover of books. He read detective stories and naval history, but otherwise spent his leisure
sailing and collecting stamps. He had little interest in art and
less in music, and, on the whole, was not very conversant with
the world of contemporary ideas. When he was first introduced to Lord Keynes, the President was uncertain who the
renowned British economist was. Another key to the complex
Roosevelt mentality was his practical cast of mind, his love of the
concrete. He had been born and raised close to the Hudson River
soil, and he retained all his life something of the farmer's practical sense, something of the farmer's aversion to the theoretical.
The questions he raised during his Presidency were not what this
or that measure would do to the nation's ideology in the long
run, but how the unemployed could be fed, the homeless housed.
But if Roosevelt always retained something of the cultivator's
practical mind, he also knew the city and its ways intimately. A
good portion of his life had been spent in New York City, and
during his Governorship the problems of the nation's major city
were always among the most pressing he had to face. In the
early part of his life, it is true, Roosevelt had been an urban
aristocrat and something of a snob. But sometime, probably during the period he was so severely struck down with infantile
paralysis that he would never walk unaided again, he acquired a
pervasive sense of sympathy for his fellow beings. He was also a
firm believer in the more optimistic dogmas of Christianity.

Confident of man's power and will to change himself, and
tolerant perhaps to a fault of man's minor vices, he was an incor-
rigible optimist—almost a shallow one, some said. Perhaps this
peculiar neohumanist spirit lay at the base of the New Deal. In
the face of human need or deprivation all other values were
secondary. "The only real capital of the nation," he once said, was
"its natural resources and its human beings." Federal relief to the
masses might lead to corruption and bureaucracy, he acknowledged. It might create a huge Federal deficit and upset the

budget. But these were minor evils compared to the specter of hungry men. No decent democracy could afford "to accumulate a deficit in the books of human fortitude."

As a young man in the 1912 campaign Roosevelt spoke of the necessity of securing a social system in which both competition and cooperation were essential ingredients. How much of each a society needed at any one time depended upon what it had to do to provide a decent living for its citizens. In his 1929 inaugural speech as Governor of New York he said he was prepared to preach the doctrines of *laissez faire* and private enterprise. Two years later he launched the state on a vast relief and social security program. He remained all of his life scornful of social absolutes and theoretical constructs that limited a society's attempt to achieve a good life for its citizens. What economic and social doctrines he stressed at any time depended much upon what was happening. Had a sharp recovery taken place in the fall and winter of 1932-33, the New Deal, as we know it, might never have been conceived. Instead, a banking crisis occurred, bringing the country to the brink of a social abyss. That crisis, widespread unemployment, and increasing personal want created the famous "hundred days," as well as much that came afterward.

4

The New Deal:
The Politics of Urbanism

THE NEW DEAL has often been characterized as a sort of
Santa Claus political movement, able by enormous expenditures
of Federal funds to offer something tangible to almost everyone—
businessman, miner, farmer, laborer—and to almost every section—East, West, urban, rural, big city, and small town. By gross
definition it was all of this. But the New Deal Administration
was also the first one that was intimately concerned with the
spectrum of urban life and city problems. Although it appropriated billions of dollars to aid the rural regions, the weight of
its expenditures and efforts went to the city, and more specifically
to lower economic classes in the city and to minority and recent
immigrant groups that had in the past been spoken of with less
than pride by most politicians. It even helped sustain two very
small minorities, the creative artists and the intellectuals, that
previous to 1933 had been the object of the ordinary politician's
suspicion rather than his cultivation.

Prior to 1933 one wing of the Democratic party had been based
on New York, Boston, and Chicago political machines, which in
turn rested upon racial, religious, and immigrant minorities. But
in Philadelphia, Pittsburgh, Chicago, and elsewhere Republican
machines existed that turned in approximately the same political results. The big-city machines of both parties were built on
local loyalties for favors received locally, were often quite inde-

pendent of the national organizations, and were most often supremely indifferent to any principle other than an obsessive desire to control local court and statehouse. What the sum of New Deal ideology and activities did was to bind the minorities together with middle-class and lower economic groups so as to form an impressive Democratic majority in practically every large city, irrespective of its past political tradition. By 1938 to 1940, despite the continued loyalty of the South, the main support of the New Deal Democratic party lay in the nation's cities. It had become the first political party in the nation's history to be dominated by an urban-oriented ideology, and even as early as 1938 the traditional and rural-minded South was beginning to question its allegiance to it.

The urban emphasis of the New Deal was not clearly revealed in the early days of the Roosevelt years, for a host of more universal problems had to be faced. Among them was the breakdown of the banking system. Despite the improvements made by the Federal Reserve Act, the national banking system during the 1920's remained chaotic compared to those of the major countries of Western Europe. Numerous state banks, weak in resources and relatively unregulated, existed outside the Federal Reserve System. Even within the system there was no effective way to pool regional or national resources so as to aid institutions embarrassed by frozen assets. The London *Economist* characterized the American system as "unregulated, unstable, and unsound." Throughout the twenties the number of banks closing their doors rose steadily, especially in the depressed agricultural regions. By 1929 almost 7,000 banks had closed. After the market crash the pressure on banking institutions increased by the month. In 1931 President Hoover asked the major institutions to pool their resources to aid weaker units. Turned down by the financiers, the President recommended the establishment of the Reconstruction Finance Corporation, creating machinery whereby the government might loan money to distressed banks. Although the RFC acted with dispatch, providing more credit to banks than the President was willing to offer to public relief, the pressure continued to grow. In December 1930 the first important large-city bank, The Bank of the United States, had closed its doors in New York. Thereafter public distrust of banking strength created runs all over the nation. Funds were rapidly withdrawn and either hoarded or sent out of the country in the form of gold for safekeeping. During 1932 a Congressional committee's revelations of widespread fraudulent practices among the nation's financial institutions added to the rapidly growing lack of confidence. In that year failures rose to the rate of forty institutions a day, tying up on the average $2 million of deposits per institution. Before the election in October 1932 the Governor of Nevada instituted a bank holiday to save some of the state's banks from disaster. The holiday movement spread rapidly after Michigan's Governor closed all Detroit banks on February 14, 1933. Within three weeks bank holidays were declared in many states.

Faced with the awesome possibility that the economy's circulatory system would suddenly stop, Hoover tried desperately to avoid impending chaos. But big-city bankers, fearful for the solvency of their own institutions, could only suggest that the government deposit money without security in banks tottering on the brink. The lame-duck Congress, with many of its members already defeated in the election, passed the problem to the President, as did the Federal Reserve Board. Hoover then tried to get an agreement with the incoming Roosevelt, which would have limited Roosevelt's freedom of action to what the Hoover Administration considered sound financial practices. But Roosevelt was not to be entangled with Hoover's troubles until after March 4. Receiving little help from anyone, the President might understandably have acted on his own in an extraconstitutional manner, as Ogden Mills, his Secretary of the Treasury, advised. Instead, the harassed Hoover stuck to his principles to the last and did little or nothing. As a result, on the eve of Inauguration Day more than half of the nation's financial institutions were closed and those remaining open faced the peril of massive runs. By March 3, 1933, the dark cloud of fear gradually smothering the productive resources of the nation had reached continental proportions. Few men knew what the following dawn would bring. Practically the entire nation, including the so-called captains of industry and finance, looked to Washington and the new President as a last resort against total calamity.

In ordinary times, new Presidents in their first week in office are usually freer to make personal decisions than at any other time in their careers. Because the Democratic party had been out of office for so long, Roosevelt was even freer than most of his predecessors. What really liberated the President from ordinary restraints was the depth of the crisis he and the nation faced. In March 1933 the majority of citizens and probably Congress would have followed Roosevelt along any path he chose that gave promise of mitigating their woes and their fears. The common peril stilled criticism, invalidated normal procedures, and even suspended constitutional doubts. Roosevelt soon made it evident that he was aware of the extraordinary situation freeing him from platform and campaign promises, and from normal Congressional opposition.

"The only thing we have to fear," Roosevelt said in his inaugural address, is "fear itself—nameless, unreasonable, unjustified terror which paralyzes needed efforts to convert retreat into advance." Of the many things the new Administration did during those hectic days from March to June, commonly called in retrospect "the hundred days," perhaps the most important was to animate the government and the country with a sense of action, if not of precise purpose. On March 4 Roosevelt boldly told the country that he expected unusual speed and action from Congress, but that if Congress should fail, he was prepared to seek extraordinary emergency powers of a wartime nature to confront the desperate situation. On his first day in office the President closed all the nation's banks without grant of authority. Five days later he presented to Congress a draft banking bill which, when passed in a few hours, went far to preserve banking assets and to restore public confidence in the financial structure. Observing on the following day that many liberal governments had been "wrecked on rocks of loose fiscal policy," he asked for and obtained wide powers to economize on veterans' pensions and to slash pay rates to Federal employees. But within the next six weeks he secured the passage of a spate of measures involving the expenditure of billions of dollars. Half a billion was made available to the states for direct unemployment relief. Three billion was appropriated for a gigantic public works program. The creation of the Civilian Conservation Corps and the farm and home loan policy to rescue distressed mortgages obligated the government for billions more.

The gigantic New Deal relief program, which in its entirety and over an eight-year span touched almost one-third of the nation's workers, was at once the most controversial and the most popular of the Administration's efforts. The conservative and parochial-minded objected, of course, as much to Roosevelt's assumption that to every man was due the opportunity to work as to the Federal government's direct efforts to provide the jobs. They denounced the New Deal reasoning that by such "pump priming" the economy might be restored to something near the normal level, and they even opposed the extensive public works program which Hoover had accepted in a much less generously financed version. The insistence of Secretary of Interior Harold Ickes, director of the Public Works Administration, that the public buildings, dams, schools, and highways to be built be of palpable use and initiated locally and that many be susceptible of self-amortization did little to soften the more conservative criticism, even though the extent to which private contractors and the building industry would profit was obvious.

But far more opposition arose to the many relief projects headed by Harry Hopkins, the former director of social work in New York State, who rapidly became for many Republicans the New Deal bête noire, perhaps because of his single-minded devotion to Roosevelt but perhaps also because his ruthless energy and amazing efficiency were wedded to a bundle of intensely held social convictions. He was, observed a colleague, "a high-minded holy roller in a semi-religious frenzy."

At the very start of the relief program Hopkins became public champion of the "immediate work instead of dole" approach for the unemployed, even though many of the projects amounted only to leaf sweeping and grass cutting. The public ridicule of the relief worker on the Federal Emergency Relief Administration's payroll as a man leaning on a shovel and of the project as "boon-doggling" deterred Hopkins not at all from combining a deep concern for human dignity with the administration of public relief. Embedded in the philosophy of the New Deal's "permanent" relief agency, the Works Progress Administration, was the injunction against downgrading labor. Trained men were not asked to do manual labor if it was possible to arrange for them to pursue their own skills. Out of this approach, as well as Mrs. Franklin D. Roosevelt's concern for the intellectual and for the arts, came projects for writers, artists, musicians, and dancers. The young were provided for by the National Youth Administration, which kept many of them in school and more in pocket money. Such diverse New Deal programs welded the once-alienated urban intellectuals and creative artists to the Administration, at the same time causing consternation and opposition in the rural sections. The farmer was unable to understand why Federal money should be paid to support something called the ballet.

New Deal relief projects were devised for the countryside as well as for the city. But because the great bulk of unemployment was urban, and because many of the more conservative-minded rural places refused to accept Federal grants, a large proportion of relief funds went to the cities. And here the recent immigrants and the racial minorities profited disproportionately from the Federal largesse. Since such people were traditionally the last hired and the first fired, they were natural candidates for relief rolls. The persistent affinity of racial, religious, and national minorities for the New Deal was not all explained by relief checks, but the election slogan in Negro Harlem, New York City, "Ham everyday on the WPA instead of a turkey [on Thanksgiving Day] with Tammany," was eloquent of a new order of politics, and as significant for the urban-rural conflict as it was for the future of the Northern urban-rural Southern alliance in the Democratic party.

The New Deal's legislative program during the hundred days was just as paradoxical as its actions on economy and spending. Although the President had spoken of driving the money changers from the temple and of substituting "social values" for that of "monetary profit," his financial proposals were characteristically far more temperate than his language. The financial acts of 1933 prohibited commercial banks from trading in securities. They gave the Federal Reserve banks far more power over their members in regulating the rate of interest charged and the volume of loans made. They transferred many decision-making powers from the twelve regional banks to the national Federal Reserve Board, and made the latter more responsive to the President. The Securities Act provided for rigorous regulation over what had been a self-governing free market. But though these acts signalized a radical shift of power away from private enterprisers to the government and made possible for the first time a managed currency, they abolished neither private ownership of the nation's basic financial institutions nor monetary gain as the impelling force of the economy.

The Administration's programs for agriculture and business were also radical, when measured by historic standards. Inspiration for the Agricultural Adjustment Act came principally from Henry Agard Wallace, who managed *Wallace's Farmer* after his father left the editorship in 1921 to become Secretary of Agriculture under Harding and Coolidge. Throughout the twenties the younger Wallace preached the doctrine that the farmers would have to manage their production as capital and labor did. During the lean year of 1931, Wallace asked for voluntary crop reduction and government crop insurance, and coined the phrase the "ever-normal granary." Other ideas for the new plan came from the McNary-Haugen proposals, the experience of the Hoover Federal Farm Board, from George N. Peek of the old War Industries Board, and from the agricultural economist John Black, who had studied a scheme of crop control in Germany. The essential idea behind the AAA was to pay farmers for curtailing production of major crops to achieve a balance between supply and demand. Under the scheme production of important staples was to be limited until their prices reached "parity" with nonagricultural prices, "parity" being defined as the price ratio existing during the years 1909-1914. This "ordered harvest," it was hoped, could be secured by an elaborate plan of setting marketing quotas for individual farmers, who would be paid for their reduced output by a tax on the processers of farm goods. The necessity for approval by two-thirds of the farmers involved gave the plan a democratic aura. The AAA abolished neither private holdings nor the profit motive in farming. But it did emphasize group ends and objectives at the expense of the individual. As violations of both the spirit and the letter of the Act grew, so did the necessity for increasing restrictive and coercive measures. Eventually production quotas for some crops were assigned to particular acreage plots, and the right to grow and sell specific produce at the going market price without penalties was frozen to the ownership of particular land parcels. Agricultural planning thus introduced a host of regulations which substantially curtailed the freedom of the individual husbandman.

The New Deal's major hopes for recovery lay in the National Industrial Recovery Act, the essential ideas for which came from organized business. Arguing that unfair and unregulated competition had in part destroyed prosperity, Gerard Swope, President of the General Electric Company, proposed a vast scheme for the self-regulation of business, which he hoped would "stabilize production and prices" and lead to recovery. This idea, supported by the United States Chamber of Commerce, appealed to the planning-minded Administration, which also saw it as a way to stabilize wages and spread existing work among more men, and at the same time as a vehicle to kill off much more radical labor legislation being proposed in Congress. At a press conference on April 12, Roosevelt said the NRA's aims were to spread employment over a large number of people, to prevent any individual from working too many hours, and to stop the drift toward concentration of industrial production. The President described it as a national scheme for "the regulation of production." To achieve these diverse and contradictory ends, the Congressional Act set aside the antitrust laws and provided for the adoption of industrywide codes of business conduct. A national code prohibited the employment of anyone under sixteen years of age, established a minimum wage scale of forty cents an hour and a maximum work week of thirty-five hours.

Hurriedly 557 separate industrial codes were adopted by representatives of various industries, in the making of which small business had some voice, labor had little, and the consumer almost none. Some of the codes, such as in cotton textiles, for example, sought to curtail production by limiting the use of machines, in this case spinning machines, to a maximum number of hours a week. Others sought to establish minimum prices for industrial products by a complicated system of computing production costs. Practically all of them sought to abolish "unfair competition" by regulating the branding of products, the granting of credit terms, rebates for volume buyers, and other discriminatory sales practices. Inherent in the codes was the obvious desire to apportion markets, limit production, and to a degree eliminate price competition. Although the revolutionary scheme was described as one of self-government by industry, it was apparent that the codes were essentially made by the large industries and favorable to them. Hailing the advent of the codes, one Wall Street publication stated that in the long run the "large aggregates of finance capital" stood to benefit from the new regime. But even large business had to pay something for its new freedom from competition and antitrust laws. As will be noted later, Section 7a of the NIRA gave labor the legal right to organize unions, the exploitation of which subsequently resulted in a measurable transfer of power from industry to labor.

The NIRA also introduced the power of government into industrial areas where it had not existed before. Although the Administration hoped that the real enforcement of the Act would come from public pressure, punitive measures were written into it, and eventually Administrator General Hugh S. Johnson and his 4,500 fellow employees used them against violators. Never before in peace time, except in antitrust actions for distinctly different purposes, had the government proceeded against individual businessmen in matters concerning hours of labor, prices, and selling methods.

During the hundred days, the business community had to submit to another great incursion of governmental power into what had been considered an essentially private domain. The Tennes-

THE NEW DEAL: THE POLITICS OF URBANISM

see Valley Authority Act instituted not only regulation but outright government competition in the production and sale of electric power. The rise of the interstate electric power industry had
been one of the amazing business phenomena of the twenties.
Technically American industry led the world, and the spread of
electrical lighting and appliances throughout cities and farm-
steads effected a virtual revolution in American life. The electrical
industry had much to its credit in creating artificial daylight out
of the night and in decreasing immeasurably the amount of human toil. But the industry, essentially unregulated during the
twenties, had become the plaything of corporate manipulators,
who, piling holding company upon holding company, contributed little to efficiency and much to the public cost and the profit
for the few. Led by Senator George W. Norris of Nebraska, a
small band of Congressional reformers sought unsuccessfully in
the twenties to bring the interstate aspects of industry under
effective public control. They did manage to defeat the efforts of
Presidents Coolidge and Hoover to sell the publicly constructed
Wilson Dam on the Tennessee River to private interests. Norris'
long struggle was partially successful in April 1933, when Roosevelt proposed and Congress passed an act creating the Tennessee
Valley Authority, a public corporation with wide powers to plan
for the full development of the natural resources of the Tennessee
River valley, comprising most of the upper South. Ostensibly the
TVA was established to engage in flood control and to further
navigation of the river, tasks in which it succeeded admirably.
But a subsidiary clause in the Act empowered it to sell power,
and within a few years the manufacture, transport, and sale of
electric current from its twenty newly constructed dams became its major concern. In proposing the Act Roosevelt had
spoken of creating a Federal yardstick by which to measure the
costs incurred and profits won by private industry. At the eventual cost of over a billion dollars, the New Deal created a vast
industrial complex publicly owned and publicly operated, competing directly with private enterprise.

In the long run, the greatest New Deal challenge to business
prestige and power came about through Section 7(a) of the NIRA.

The section was neither inspired nor particularly wanted by the Roosevelt Administration. It had been added to the Act by organized labor's friends in Congress as a minimum payment for their support of the industrial measure. Throughout the early days of his Administration the President, in fact, paid scant attention to organized labor as a useful force for recovery. He was gravely concerned about the plight of millions of workingmen out of jobs, but he spent little time and thought on the languishing labor organizations. In fact, the NIRA without Section 7(a) would have probably weakened the unions since it established by government mandate minimum wage and maximum hour regulations, objectives which the unions had been unsuccessful in obtaining for their members. But Section 7(a) asserted that labor had the right to organize and bargain collectively "through representatives of their own choosing." It also outlawed the yellow dog contract and stipulated that men could not be forced to join a company union as a condition of employment. Although these were simply declarations without means of administrative enforcement, the union movement became inspirited and launched so many organizational and wage strikes during the next few months that a National Labor Board was created to mediate strikes in August 1933, with the staunchly prolabor Senator Robert F. Wagner as chairman. Within two years membership in organized labor rose by over 25 per cent.

Toward the end of the hundred days, a perplexed reporter asked the President at the newly reinstituted news conference whether the government was embarked upon an economy or a spending program, on one that would lead to the restoration of capitalism or to nationalization and socialism. Roosevelt's answer that the government was bent upon feeding the hungry and restoring prosperity did not clarify the issue much. But a look at the record of the three months should have supplied the answer. Except for the TVA, there had been nothing really revolutionary so far in the New Deal program. Direct relief and managed agriculture were radical in terms of the past, but the NIRA had been conceived by the business community and on balance, even with its wage and hour controls and Section 7(a), its immediate, if not long run, consequence was to bolster the health of big business.

During 1933 and the early months of the following year the business and conservative community interpreted it that way. The U.S. Chamber of Commerce, the *Magazine of Wall Street,* the *Wall Street Journal,* and independent conservatives like David Lawrence agreed that thus far the New Deal's actions had been "inventive," "courageous," and "fair." During the latter half of the year the most trenchant criticism of the Administration, in fact, came from labor and from those on the left, who demanded real revolutionary action. In good part the remobilization of the defeated and scattered right against the New Deal was a matter of politics. During 1933 Republican leaders agreed that the New Deal program was so popular they could ill afford to be openly critical. But the 1934 Congressional elections, which resulted in the most stunning defeat in history for the Republican party, seemed to indicate that if the party were to survive it had to draw a line of distinction between itself and the New Deal. Herbert Hoover, looking backward as well as forward, led off the attack in 1934 by publishing his *Challenge to Liberty,* the tone of which was indicated in its first few pages. The New Deal, he wrote, represented "the most stupendous invasion of the whole spirit of liberty that the nation has witnessed since the days of Colonial America."

In part the opposition to the New Deal came from a reviving business community. By the opening of 1934, the economy had climbed out of the pit of 1932 to 1933. Industrial production, which had stood at 56 per cent of the preceding five-year average in March 1933, reached upward to 93 per cent in June, and although wavering from that time on, the economy continued to inch forward. Aided by the drought and sizable government subsidies, farm prices were even more responsive to the general upturn, the average by 1935 being 66 per cent higher than that of 1933. Corporation balance sheets looked better, and even the stock market showed signs of optimism. With returning health, the business community regained its confidence and its voice. Relatively docile while desperately sick, it now began to scan the bill

for medical fees and was shocked to realize how much it had
paid and was likely to pay in the future for the New Deal treatment.

Just a few years back, the basic business principles clustering
around such phrases as rugged individualism, competition, private enterprise, the profit motive, sound currency, and the gold
standard had been cardinal tenets of the American faith. Now, if
they had not been swept away most of them were in the process
of being radically modified. From being public heroes, businessmen had become whipping boys, or at least the subjects of
common jest. The once awe-inspiring title "banker" had become
"bankster" in common argot, and the allusion to Al Capone and
his gangsters measured the extent of his fall from grace. The 1934
elections made it apparent that a real shift in social power from
the business to the political community had occurred. Politicians
and bureaucrats were setting rules for the new game and enforcing them. And as if to pour salt on severely wounded vanity,
some publications were advising businessmen to cross the line
and join the enemy. Commenting that the "revolution of 1933"
was the most effective experiment "yet undertaken to reconcile
capitalism and social justice," the *Magazine of Wall Street* urged
capitalists to "give up economic privateering" and enjoy the "new
dignity of serving the state." That was to come in time, but to
expect the master class of the twenties to become the "servants"
of the thirties was a little too much to ask of human feelings.

The once-reigning conservative community's state of extreme
perturbation in 1934 came not only from what had happened so
far but also from its fears for the future. Business anxiety was not
without justification, even though during his first term Roosevelt
usually talked a good deal more radically than his subsequent
actions warranted. In the four years after 1933, the President
proposed at one time or another what amounted to an entire new
bill of rights, which if enacted into law would have insured the
creation of a semisocialist economy. He referred to the right to
work, the right to adequate food, to housing, a decent education,
clothing, and recreation. At other times he suggested expanding
the TVA concept to include all the great river systems of the

country. As businessmen counted the possible cost of these new objectives and considered the intricate regulation of private enterprise involved, they found it a frightening prospect.

Worse yet were the prophetic statements coming from FDR's so-called "brain trusters," who even more than their chief were given to loquacious radicalism. Henry Wallace published a book in 1933 entitled *New Frontiers,* in which he argued that since the days of American expansion were past, the keynote of the new age would be cooperation instead of competition, social inventions instead of mechanical ones, "the worship of beauty and justice and joy of spirit" instead of the worship of "power and wealth." A. A. Berle, in the *Saturday Review of Literature,* claimed that the collapse of private enterprise in 1929 was as significant in human history as the collapse of feudalism, since it inevitably meant a transfer of many individual transactions into "a public process." But of all brain trusters, perhaps Rexford G. Tugwell produced the most fearful hobgoblins for the business community. In his book, *The Industrial Discipline and Government Arts* (1933), Tugwell predicted a great augmentation of "government compulsion" to combine with whatever forces existed in private industry in order to spur industrial production, widen public access to goods, protect wage scales, limit price rises, and direct capital investments. "We need," Tugwell concluded, "some kind of compulsion to efficiency to adhere to a common purpose." Since Wallace, Berle, Tugwell, and Raymond Moley were commonly supposed to be the drafting architects of the New Deal's future—as expressed by a chant going around the country: "Tugwell, Berle, Moley—Holy! Holy! Holy!"—it is small wonder the disciples of private enterprise were shaken by the prospect.

With some justification, conservatives saw the specter of revolution everywhere during the first four years of the New Deal. After their dismal performance in the elections of 1932, the Communists were flexing their muscles, assaulting every political movement to their right. Closely following a party resolution, Browder accused Roosevelt of being more brutal than Hoover in suppressing the living standards of the masses and in exhibiting the "sharpest national chauvinism in foreign relations." On the moderate left a "continental congress of farmers and workers" met in Iowa to demand more action in defense of their homes and living standards. In the following year, a Farmer-Labor Party already in control of the Minnesota statehouse re-elected Henrik Shipstead to the Senate. At Fond du Lac, Wisconsin, a similar group met to form the Wisconsin Progressive party. Meanwhile, California had produced two movements, both of which were far more radical in their aims than the New Dealers. Under the leadership of the old Socialist Upton Sinclair, the "End Poverty in California," or EPIC, organization demanded the flotation of a gigantic bond issue with which to establish state-owned farms and workshops where the unemployed could be put to work in useful production. All workers in the plan were to be paid in scrip or in necessities obtained by barter between the workshops. Sinclair won the Democratic nomination for Governor in 1934, and although beaten in the election, continued to organize the state for a second campaign in 1936. Simultaneously a former Long Beach health official, Dr. Francis E. Townsend, respectable churchgoer and foe of radicalism, organized a movement to give every citizen over sixty years of age a pension of $200 a month, provided the pension scrip was spent in thirty days. His scheme, Townsend argued, would take care of the superannuated workers laid off during the Depression, remove them from the labor market, and restore prosperity. Fuelled by the distress among the aged, the Townsend movement took on some of the character of a religious crusade. In December 1935 twelve thousand people met in a National Townsend convention at Chicago, representing, so they claimed, 2 million voters organized in five thousand local clubs spread across the nation. The radical attempt of the Townsendites to stimulate purchasing power by taxing away the value of government-issued scrip over a short period of time was a device favored by a number of other reformers, including some reputable economists, the Utopians, and the "Ham and Eggers" of California. The appeal of the scheme for the Townsend followers was indicative of the widespread destitution among the older age groups; it was also eloquent of the changing values of the traditionally conservative older generation. The Puritan injunction to work and save had now been transmuted into an injunction to retire and spend, and to do so at the government's expense, all in the national interest. The revolution in popular economic thought initiated by the widespread extension of consumer credit during the twenties had now turned almost full cycle.

Since 1930 Father Charles E. Coughlin, priest of an impoverished parish near Detroit, had been promoting on his radio program a mixture of religion and politics. Son of a poor Irish laborer, who had won a doctor's degree from the University of Toronto at the age of 23, Coughlin developed an impressive radio personality, and by 1931 he was broadcasting every Sunday evening on a national hookup of twenty-two stations to an audience estimated in the millions. Describing himself as a "simple Catholic priest endeavoring to interject Christianity into the fabric of an economic system woven upon the loom of greed. . .," Coughlin blasted Communism, Fascism, the Wall Street millionaires, and the prevailing monetary system. In 1932 he described Morgan, Mellon, Undersecretary of the Treasury Ogden Mills, and Governor of the Federal Reserve Board Eugene Meyer as the four horsemen, and insisted that it was either "Roosevelt or ruin." His contributions to the Roosevelt victory were not inconsequential, but by 1934, disenchanted with Roosevelt's moderate program, he enunciated a sixteen-point program of political action and organized his National Union for Social Justice. Among the more radical elements of the Union's creed were proposals for the nationalization of "important natural resources," the control of private property for the public good, abolition of the Federal Reserve System, establishment of a government-controlled bank, and conscription of wealth as well as men in wartime.

All that was needed in 1935 to bring these diverse groups together in a new radical party was a skillful leader, a master politician of the radical tradition whose desire for power was greater than his regard for consistency and his concern for what was economically feasible. In 1935 it looked as if that man was Senator Huey Long of Louisiana. Long arose out of the poverty and illiteracy of the Southern poor whites. His subsequent political career was rooted in attitudes they could readily understand. As champion of the poor white, but unlike so many of his kind in the South never a Negro-baiter, Long was elected Governor of Louisiana at the age of thirty and United States Senator four years later. Once Governor, he built modern roads into the back country, provided free school books for everyone, handsomely increased the physical resources of the State University, and constructed an impressive state hospital where, he promised, anyone in Louisiana could be treated free of charge. Long paid the bills for his program by income and inheritance measures and by a severance tax on oil. In passing his program, he met bitter opposition from the influential and wealthy elements hitherto controlling the state with an awesome disregard for conventional methods of politics and for the provisions of the state Constitution. He dictated to the state legislature (even resorting to intimidating its individual members), ordered the University to construct buildings though there was no money for them in its budget, and surrounded himself with a bodyguard of gunmen in Al Capone fashion.

When Long left for the United States Senate, he fired the properly elected Lieutenant Governor so that he could place his own man in the Governor's chair. A flabby, pudgy, red-nosed individual, with a vocabulary profane, earthy, and ungrammatical, he impressed his fellow Senators as a man of inordinate energy and ambition. Along with his dietary proposal to extend the consumption of "corn pone" and "pot likker," which he claimed would improve the health of the nation, he initiated the "Share Our Wealth" movement. "There is no rule," he declaimed, "so sure as that the same mill which grinds out fortunes above a certain size, grinds out paupers at the bottom." If the wealth at the top were curtailed and properly distributed, he promised, a republic might be built in which every man was a king but no one wore a crown. Delighting to call himself the Kingfish of the movement, he elaborated his program after 1933 by promising everyone a minimum income of $2,000, a house, an automobile, and a radio, free homesteads, and free education.

With a view to attracting Townsend and Coughlin support, he vigorously attacked Roosevelt. "The New Deal," he roared on the floor of the Senate, was "headed just as straight to hell as a martin ever went to a gourd." He assaulted international bankers and promised a pension to everyone over sixty-five. Townsend and Coughlin responded favorably to these invitations, as did William Lemke, a veteran Non-Partisan League Congressman, who said he hoped the agricultural vote might be combined with that for Long in 1936 "to end wage slavery." In the spring of 1935 James A. Farley, Postmaster General and Roosevelt's able political adviser, took a secret poll which showed that Long might get as many as 4 million votes in 1936 and thus hold the balance of power between the two old parties.

While the radicals were mobilizing in 1935 to imperil the New Deal's tenure in Washington, so was the conservative right. In August 1934, just before the Congressional elections, a bipartisan committee of one hundred met in Miami, Florida, to organize the American Liberty League, whose single-minded purpose, they proclaimed, was to "teach the necessity of respect for the rights of persons and property." From its first days the Liberty League was identified with big money, Wall Street, and large corporations. Among its founders were politicians Al Smith and Jouett Shouse, as well as John W. Davis, John J. Raskob, William S. Knudsen, Pierre du Pont, and Sewell L. Avery. That the League intended to extend its activities beyond simple teaching was evidenced by the remark of John W. Davis in early 1936, justifying the League on the grounds that it was natural for men with property to resent the political control of other men. Not to expect them to try to "capture the seats of decision for themselves is a lotus eater's dream." Simultaneously a group of conservative Democrats including Davis, Al Smith, ex-Governor Albert Ritchie of Maryland, Governor Eugene Talmadge of Georgia, Bainbridge Colby, and William Randolph Hearst organized the Jeffersonian Democrats, whose object, it was rumored, was to found a conservative Democratic party and defeat Roosevelt in 1936 by splitting the Democratic vote. The scheme for a third party was later vetoed by Smith and Raskob, but the organization's unwavering opposition to Roosevelt was clearly and publicly expressed in 1935 and 1936.

The New Deal's difficulties in 1935 included more than political ones. Three years of experience with the AAA indicated that additional regulation, often of a coercive type, was needed to reduce the production of some crops without increasing the supply of others. Between March 1933 and January 1936 the Federal government had appropriated over $3 billion for public works and direct relief. Although many unemployed had been shifted from direct to work relief, in 1935 over 2.7 million people were still on direct relief and over 6 million were receiving some benefits from the government. The relief program, considered in 1933 as a temporary one to meet an emergency situation, now began to look as if it might be permanent. Even some steadfast liberals were disenchanted with the process. Elmer Davis pointed out early in 1936 that one of the most durable "reforms" of the Gracchi in ancient Rome was the free distribution of bread, and he questioned whether the experience was not being duplicated in the United States. If so, he felt there was "something wrong with the economic system or the backbone of the government or both."

Industrial affairs were, if anything, more chaotic than those in agriculture and relief. By 1935 it was obvious that most employers had no intention of honoring the National Industrial Recovery Act's dictum that workers were entitled to unions of their own choice. A wave of strikes broke out in 1934, including some very bloody ones in the Southern textile regions. It was soon apparent that the newly created National Labor Board had insufficient power to cope with industrial disturbances of such magnitude. But of even more significance, the National Industrial Recovery plan, the New Deal's major hope for economic health, was coming apart at the seams. Within a few months after its organization, labor became extremely hostile to the NIRA, branding it as a creator of industrial monopoly and as a foe of the farming and laboring classes. Small business, often ignored in the formation of the industrial codes, rapidly joined the opposition. The inevitable letdown in public enthusiasm forced the Administration into more coercive measures. Eventually, as the economy recovered, even big industry, which had sired the measure, became restive under its restrictive aspects. Moreover many qualified experts decided that the NIRA, instead of helping, was hurting expansion. Where the NIRA was effective, the London *Economist* declared, its inevitable effect was "to raise prices and *pro tanto,* to discourage demand." By May 1935 the NIRA had few friends, and most of the country sighed with relief when the Supreme Court in the famous Schechter chicken case gave it the *coup de grâce* by unanimously declaring the act unconstitutional on the two principal grounds of an improper delegation of legislative power and an unwarranted use of the interstate commerce powers of the Federal government. Of the two, the latter was far more significant, since the distinction the Court made between the direct and indirect effects of intrastate transactions upon interstate commerce seemed to imperil many other important New Deal measures. Conceivably Roosevelt's bitter remark that the Court had returned the country to the "horse and buggy age" was directed more against the Court's refusal to broaden the interstate commerce powers of the Federal government than it was against the killing of the NIRA.

The future of the New Deal was doubtful during the spring of 1935. Many of its major programs were not producing the promised results. The Schechter decision imperilled the constitutional base for others. Politically, it was assailed by both the right and the left, within and without the Democratic Party. With the 1936 elections looming ahead, the New Deal obviously needed a major blood transfusion if it was to remain politically healthy. The revitalization of the New Deal has been called by some historians "the second hundred days."

The second great reform program of the New Deal was not spun out of Roosevelt's head entirely as a matter of economic and social justice. During much of 1934 the President acted as if his major reform work was finished. He called for no crusades and spoke out for few reforms. Some Administration-supported measures granted considerable aid to business; for example, the Corporate Bankruptcy Act, which permitted distressed firms to reorganize without formal bankruptcy, a blessing to a great many corporations. Roosevelt resisted the demands of the inflationist and labor blocs in Congress. Inside the party there was no witch hunt for conservatives. Instead, undercover efforts were made to quell Huey Long by an examination of his personal income tax and by an investigation of Louisiana elections. During the autumn Congressional campaign Roosevelt seldom attacked the business community. He depicted the New Deal's past efforts as directed toward the goal of "unifying American society, rich and poor, manual worker and brain worker, into a voluntary brotherhood of freemen . . . "

But after the elections of 1934 events began to push Roosevelt the politician. The organization of the Liberty League and the Jeffersonian Democrats, the attacks of Long and Coughlin, the threat of Upton Sinclair and Townsend made it appear as if the American electorate were being rapidly divided between antagonistic left and right groups, as had happened in many European countries. Roosevelt was thoroughly aware of the rising discontent among liberal leaders of his own official family and equally sensitive to the hostility of the organized right. In his message of January 1935 opening Congress, he made a verbal attempt to consolidate his leadership of the reformers. He confessed that the New Deal had not as yet "weeded out the overprivileged" or "effectively lifted up the underprivileged." And he hinted strongly as to what course he would likely be following during the coming Presidential election. Americans "must foreswear" the acquisition of great wealth, which had created "undue private power over private affairs and to our misfortune over public affairs as well." During the next four months the President, however, did little to interfere with Congress, where a vicious battle was being conducted between the partisans of what was later to be called the second hundred days and the conservatives. It was during those four months, also, that the Supreme Court killed the NIRA, that organized business for the first time voiced its unequivocal opinions of the New Deal, and that the Liberty League and the Jeffersonian Democrats began to attack the President personally.

Roosevelt consequently shifted sail. In June 1935 he called upon Congress to pass a new tax bill that by raising income and inheritance taxes would stop the transmission of vast fortunes from generation to generation, a process "not consistent with the ideals and sentiments of the American people." The bill also sought to place a graduated tax upon corporations instead of the flat rate they were then paying. Popularly known as the "soak the rich" bill, it was a partial answer to Huey Long's proposed government guaranteed minimum annual income of $2,000, and it obtained support in Congress on that basis. Roosevelt's support of the Wagner Labor Bill, which outlawed company unions and guaranteed labor's right to organize and bargain collectively, was perhaps animated as much by his desire to retain the confidence of the laboring man as it was by his rising antipathy to big business. When the Wagner proposal first came to him in May 1934, he agreed that it might be helpful against "autocratic employers," but he observed that there were people on the labor side who were just as autocratic. Until mid-1935 the President showed little enthusiasm for the Wagner Bill. Irritated then by industry's adamant refusal to cooperate with organized labor, and sensitive to the rising business criticism of his Administration, he called upon Congress to pass the bill, which would prevent the destruction of organized labor's independence and guarantee every worker his just freedom of choice and action. Nevertheless, Roosevelt never became an unreserved admirer of unions. He consistently felt that the National Labor Relations Board was far too prolabor in its administration of the Wagner Act. His 1937 angry "plague on both their houses" expostulation against labor and business indicated his fundamental distrust of any organized private economic group. Several commentators have pointed out that the New Deal significantly contributed to the substitution of the organized for the individual as the potent factor in society. But this came about by consequence of Roosevelt's actions and not his wishes. He continued to think of his fellow citizens as individuals rather than as faceless members of organized groups. His emphasis on the individual worker's "freedom of choice and action" in arguing for the Wagner Bill was eloquent of the temper of his mind.

The President's support of the Social Security Bill was probably a labor of affection and not mainly inspired by politics. As Governor of New York he was heartily in favor of old-age and unemployment insurance. But it should be noted that the Social Security Act dealt a deadly blow to Dr. Townsend's more radical schemes. The Utilities Holding Company Act, requiring interstate power-producing firms to divorce themselves from their nonoperating structures, also contained principles that Roosevelt had previously supported. But his attack on private utility companies at this specific time was extremely useful throughout the South in countering Huey Long's charge that the New Deal had become the creature of private corporations.

In some ways, the second hundred days of the New Deal were almost as significant for the future of the country as the first hundred had been. The gift and inheritance tax features of the "soak the rich" taxation bill probably changed somewhat the future division of wealth. The Wagner Labor Act obviously altered power patterns in the nation's industrial and commercial complex. During the first hundred days, the power of government had been sensibly increased at the expense of the business community. By the operations of the Wagner Act, organized labor was to win a significant portion, though not the lion's share, of the total power remaining to industry and commerce. The Social Security Act removed many economic hazards that once threatened the individual in a traditional capitalist community. And it unquestionably accelerated the change in American loyalties from the old rural nineteenth-century virtues of personal thrift, self-reliance, and individualism toward the new mutual-help and collective goals of the midcentury. The major reforms of the second hundred days enabled Roosevelt to beat back the challenge from the radicals—Long, Coughlin, and Townsend. They also practically predetermined the nature of the 1936 campaign, since it was obviously impossible after 1935 for the President to regain his pre-1935 pose of being above the battle of the left and the right and above the struggle of labor and capital. Roosevelt wrote to Roy Howard, the newspaper-chain owner, that with the passage of the Utilities Holding Company Act, a breathing spell for business was at hand. But by that time conservative opposition had become so virulent that there was no chance of turning back to the moderate center position.

Administrations seeking re-election have always been fair game for unbounded criticism, but few have received such a savage enfilade from so many different quarters as did the Roosevelt regime in 1936. The assassination of Huey Long spared the New Deal his rancorous voice. But Father Coughlin and his farmer labor allies made up in part for the missing Long. The New Deal, Coughlin said in one of his wildest moments, had both of its feet of sordid clay mired, "one in the red mud of Soviet Communism, and the other, in the stinking cesspool of pagan plutocracy." From the right the Liberty League shouted equally fervent denunciations. Roosevelt and the New Deal, it charged, had overturned the Constitution, sacrificed freedom, abolished private enterprise and individual initiative, and destroyed the American way of life. Even more sober conservative voices took up this chorus after ex-president Hoover alleged that the New Deal had introduced into the United States personal government based upon FDR's "collectivist theories" and "the foreign creeds of Regimentation, Socialism and Fascism." The Chicago *Tribune's* attack was less qualified. "The Red New Deal with a Soviet seal, sired in an alien land," was a sample of the poetic efforts of this paper, warning readers daily in a front-page box that they had only so many days in which to save their country.

From the passionate protests of Republican leaders, one might have expected their 1936 national convention to have written a platform and chosen a candidate that would have been palatable to the Old Guard of the eighties and nineties. Actually, it did neither. Bridging the gap between the party's passion and its sense of expediency, the convention borrowed the New Deal program while denouncing its philosophy, promising that the Republicans would provide the same services but with less ideology and much more efficiency. The convention then proceeded to nominate a pair of Theodore Roosevelt progressives, Governor

Alfred M. Landon of Kansas and Frank Knox, the Chicago newspaper owner and publisher. Both men were well to the left of Hoover, who was, or had been, a radical compared to the men of the Liberty League.

Fortune shone on Roosevelt during 1936. It was a good year economically. The volume of industrial production almost doubled that of four years before, farm income rose from $4 billion in 1932 to $7 billion, and unemployment dropped by over 4 million from the figure of the previous Presidential election year. Even the Supreme Court's action in denying the constitutional validity of one important new program after another brought unexpected dividends. When the Court declared the Agricultural Adjustment Act unconstitutional, the Department of Agriculture announced a new subsidy program to stop soil erosion. Almost immediately thereafter a series of violent dust storms, following a persistent spring drought, threatened to blow away most of the topsoil on the Great Plains.

By his 1935 legislative program, Roosevelt had annihilated his radical opposition. The organization of the American Labor Party in New York and of Labor's Non-Partisan League nationwide, both pledged to Roosevelt, were the direct political results of the Wagner Act. Even the American Communists, following the Moscow directive to support popular front governments against the Fascist threat, muted their campaign against the New Deal. Roosevelt was also fortunate in his opposition. Though the opposing candidates were not agents of reaction, many of their vocal supporters resorted to clichés so divorced from reality that the official candidates were overlooked. Roosevelt did not run against Landon and Knox. He ran against Hoover, the Liberty League, the United States Chamber of Commerce, the National Association of Manufacturers, Robert R. McCormick's Chicago Tribune, the Hearst newspapers and most of the American press. In his acceptance speech at Philadelphia, he described his enemies as "economic royalists" who had created "a new despotism," a new "industrial dictatorship" that was depriving the majority of Americans of freedom and the pursuit of happiness. Freedom, he observed, was no half and half affair. The average American, "guaranteed equal opportunity in the polling place . . . must have equal opportunity in the market place." He concluded with a call for his generation of Americans to meet their "rendezvous with destiny" in a great reform crusade. He promised his total enlistment for the duration of the war. In September the President said he hoped to achieve "an ordered economic democracy" in which all would profit and in which all would be secure from faulty economic direction. In his last speech of the campaign, in Madison Square Garden in New York, he went even further in his challenge to the industrial and conservative opposition. Never before, he exclaimed, had these forces been so united in their opposition and in their hatred of a candidate. He welcomed their hatred, he retorted, and if in his first Administration "the forces of selfishness and lust for power met their match," he hoped that during his second they would "meet their master." Pointing out that the New Deal was accused of wanting improved conditions for workers and farmers, increased income for consumers, protection for the crippled and the blind, and food for the poor and the jobless, he admitted to the particulars of every charge and ended with a promise: "For these things too and for a multitude of things like them, we have only just begun to fight . . ."

The election results of 1936 were hardly credible. Roosevelt won by 11 million votes, the largest popular plurality on record up to that time. He carried every state except Maine and Vermont. The Republican delegations in the Senate and the House were reduced to the almost unbelievable figures of 17 and 89 respectively. The elections were notable for other reasons. Never before had the United States been so sharply divided on economic lines. Return after return indicated that wealthy and upper-middle-class neighborhoods were mobilized almost solidly for Landon, the slums and lower-class areas almost solidly for Roosevelt. The important newspapers of the nation, except in the South, almost unanimously supported the Republican candidate. With them were the solid ranks of business magazines and business organizations. Union organizations, on the other hand, were almost all for Roosevelt. A radical shift of power had taken place in the country between 1932 and 1936. Business prestige and the influence of wealth were probably never at a lower ebb than in November 1936. The influence of newspapers was so severely questioned that it was never to be taken for granted again. Predictions were numerous that the Republican party would die. The prestige of Roosevelt, of the reformers, of the planners, and of organized labor was never higher.

New Deal history is full of paradoxes. But possibly none is so striking as the contrast between Roosevelt's campaign promises and the legislative results following each of his canvasses. Although he promised little during the campaign of 1932, Roosevelt then proceeded to harvest one of the most comprehensive reform programs in American history. During the 1936 campaign he predicted that the period of social pioneering under the New Deal aegis had just begun. Since one-third of the nation was still "ill-housed, ill-clad, and ill-nourished," he observed in his second inaugural address on January 20, 1937, the present was no time for pausing on the reform road that lay ahead. Given that statement of intention and the overwhelming New Deal victory of 1936, it was reasonable to expect that Roosevelt's second four years would be punctuated with as many important legislative measures as the first. That exactly the contrary happened was due to many diverse and complex reasons; but admittedly, the first decisive check of the New Deal and the start of its decline lay in the Supreme Court struggle.

The 1933 Court in make-up and legal philosophy was largely the conservative body that it had been during the twenties. Charles Evans Hughes, the one-time progressive, had replaced William Howard Taft as Chief Justice in 1930. But according to an estimate of *Time* magazine, "the pure white flame of Liberalism had burned out in Hughes, to a sultry ash of conservatism." On the liberal side of the bench, Benjamin Cardozo had replaced Oliver Wendell Holmes. Otherwise the Court was identical to the Court of the twenties, dominated by the Harding and Coolidge appointees, with Louis Brandeis, Harlan Stone, and occasionally Owen Roberts as a protesting minority. After the first hundred days of the New Deal, Bertram Snell, the Republican

House leader, talked with Chief Justice Hughes about organizing resistance to the reformers. Hughes apparently cautioned him that the time had not yet arrived when Republican and conservative leaders could safely crusade against the President's program. Subsequently, in 1934, the Chief Justice joined a 5–4 majority of the Court in finding constitutional both a Minnesota act giving courts the right to postpone the foreclosure of mortgages and a New York law setting minimum prices for milk. But Hughes' general dictum in these cases that, while the emergency of the Depression might "furnish the occasion for the exercise of power," it did not create additional powers, gave the conservatives heart; the Court, they hoped, was preparing a position from which to attack the more radical New Deal measures. Even though Justice James McReynolds observed in 1934 that the two decisions "meant the end of the Constitution," conservative leaders were still of the opinion that the Supreme Court was their "last and best hope."

They were not disappointed. By a unanimous decision in May 1935 the Court overturned the NIRA, a finding which few people regretted. The Court found the law unconstitutional because of the Federal government's limited power to regulate interstate commerce. Only those matters that had a direct effect upon interstate commerce, it declared, were susceptible to Federal power. If the Court were to hold that only goods in transit across the state borders fell within their restricted definition of interstate commerce, then as the President pointed out at the time, much of the New Deal legislation was in danger. During the following year of 1936 the Court justified Roosevelt's fears. With either Hughes or Roberts or both joining the majority, the Court struck down the Agricultural Adjustment Act and the Guffey Act regulating the production and hence the price of coal. At the same time, by a 5–4 decision, it invalidated a New York State minimum wage law for women on the grounds that such a law violated the freedom of contract guaranteed by the Fourteenth Amendment. Thus by 1936 it looked as if neither Federal nor state government could regulate the fundamental conditions of labor. If that were so, it was likely that the Wagner Labor Act and even the Social Security Act were threatened.

During its previous 140 years of existence, the Court had held only some sixty Federal laws unconstitutional; now in 1935 and 1936 it found eleven New Deal measures void. Justice Stone, one of the minority, felt that the session ending in June 1936 had been the most disastrous in the history of the Court. Moreover, the lower Federal courts had caused as much devastation to the New Deal program. Within three years Circuit and District courts had issued over fifteen hundred injunctions against administrative officials of the numerous New Deal agencies, injunctions which at times almost brought to a halt important operations of such Federal administrative bodies as the TVA and the National Labor Relations Board. By June 1936 many ardent New Dealers were in full agreement with the judgment of the journalists Drew Pearson and Robert Allen. In their book *Nine Old Men*, they wrote that "no real or lasting progress in reshaping the economic system can be achieved without a fundamental reconsideration of the controlling role held by the Supreme Court."

Roosevelt and the New Deal had a perfect opportunity to challenge the Court before the electorate and utilize the 1936 campaign as a referendum on the issue. But neither the President nor his chief aides spoke out during the campaign. The Democratic platform promised only that if the New Deal were invalidated by judicial action, constitutional means would be found to reverse the decisions. When, on February 3, 1937, Roosevelt submitted his judiciary-reform bill to Congress, he could rightfully be accused of having acted cavalierly toward the democratic process. The bill would have empowered the President to appoint a new Federal judge whenever an incumbent, on reaching the age of seventy, failed to retire within six months; it limited the number of such Supreme Court appointees to six, thus enabling the President to increase the size of the Court to fifteen. The measure was prepared in secrecy. Most of the Cabinet and the Democratic Congressional leaders were unaware of its existence until its presentation. It was accompanied by a justification based principally upon the argument that old and infirm justices were impeding the judicial process and contributing to the crowded dockets. Since it was clear that what Roosevelt wanted was new judges who would agree with the New Deal, the disingenuous explanation hurt the proposal as much as did the secrecy with which it was prepared.

The overwhelming election returns of 1936 would have proved a heady wine for any politician. For Roosevelt, whose love of power and fondness for secret deals sometimes overrode his basic devotion to the democratic process, the very size of the 1936 victory probably led to an entrapment. Dismayed by the President's refusal to consult them on the Court bill and by his later rather brutal use of patronage to gain his ends, many liberals in Congress joined their conservative colleagues in opposition. A similar movement of moderate and liberal opinion stirred throughout the country. From sources that had hitherto either supported the President or had treated him with consideration came sharp judgments of censure. "Lack of good faith," "lawless legality," "political sharp practice," and "intent to deceive," were just a few of the phrases that must have stunned the overconfident Roosevelt.

Within a few weeks it was clear that the President had for the first time lost control of Congress. An intervening stroke of bad luck was the death of the Senate majority leader, Joseph T. Robinson of Arkansas, who, while not liking the bill, had supported it faithfully. But the most devastating blow to the Court-packing scheme was probably delivered by the Court itself. With Hughes and Roberts palpably shifting their constitutional views, the Court on March 29, 1937 (*West Coast Hotel* v. *Parrish*), declared a state of Washington minimum wage statute valid in such broad language that the legality of any reasonable state regulation of wages and hours was assured. Less than a month later, in a series of cases featured by that of *NLRB* v. *Jones and Laughlin Steel Corporation,* the Court agreed to an even more astounding reversal of their recently enunciated doctrine on the interstate commerce power. By viewing commerce as a unified stream from the manufacturing to the selling of goods and not merely the transit over state borders, and by declaring that the Federal power was applicable to all parts of the stream, the Court in a 5-4 decision, with Hughes and Roberts assenting, opened the way for a vast augmentation of Federal power over the nation's economic life. Quickly thereafter the Court upheld the Social Security Act, and in May, Justice Willis Van Devanter, one of the most unreconstructed conservatives, resigned. Almost simultaneously the Senate Judiciary Committee defeated Roosevelt's bill, and eventually a weak compromise was agreed to, denying the President the right to pack the Court but making possible by procedural changes quicker hearings and appeals on actions questioning the legality of administrative regulations.

By its strategic retreat, the Supreme Court had saved much of its prestige, while losing a good deal of power. Roosevelt, on the other hand, had won much of what he was contending for, but at the expense of considerable prestige. Within a short time he was to lose even more. Throughout 1937 the new industrial unions employed the sit-down strike as one of their chief weapons against their more stubborn industrial opponents. This threat against property rights set off choleric spasms of "I told you so" from inveterate opponents of labor. But the sit-down technique also worried a good many moderates. Books with such titles as *When Labor Rules* conjured up ominous specters of the future, and the numerous and prolonged strikes in the automobile, rubber, and steel industries worried even a great many liberals. A more damaging blow to New Deal strength was the depression of 1937 to 1938. Throughout 1937 the President confidently predicted that the budget would be balanced in the following year. Roosevelt had often asserted that the New Deal had planned the nation out of the depression and into a prosperous era in which the danger of radical shifts in the business cycle would no longer exist. But during the fall and winter of 1937-38, the economic climate changed. As the major indices fell off rapidly, the stock market plunged downward. Unemployment reached the 8 million mark. Forgetting the promised balanced budget, the Administration asked for greatly increased relief appropriations. There was to be no turning back to the selfish creed of the twenties, Roosevelt said—"this nation has definitely said yes—with no 'but' about it—to the old Biblical question, 'Am I my brother's keeper?' " Most needy people were provided with relief, and the economists coined the new term "recession" to describe the retrograde movement. But though Roosevelt would never admit to the existence of the economic plunge, the "Roosevelt depression," as it was called by many, undermined many Administration claims at the same time that it dimmed the luster of the word "planning."

Meanwhile, the New Deal was meeting with constantly growing Congressional opposition. At the opening of the 1937 session of Congress, the President outlined a major reform program, along with his historic court plan. Among the measures passed were the important Wagner Housing Act, providing Federal funds for low-cost housing; a bill regulating the production of coal; renewal of a Trade Agreements Act; and a proposal to grant Federal loans to farm tenants. But when Congress adjourned in August, no action had been taken on a bill to create seven regional TVA's, a wage and hour bill, a new farm program to replace the AAA, and an executive-reorganization scheme. All bore Administration tags, and all were reintroduced in 1938. But the conservative opposition, emboldened by the existence of the "recession," was even more vocal and more numerous than in the preceding year. The nature of this new conservative bloc was defined by Representative Martin Dies of Texas. It should not be called a Southern bloc, the Congressman declared, because it had "the support of nearly all small-town and rural Congressmen. . . ." The enemies of the new coalition, he concluded, "are the men from the big cities which . . . are politically controlled by foreigners and transplanted Negroes, and their representatives in Congress have introduced insidious influences into the New Deal." For the first time commentators noted the formation of a lasting alliance between Republicans and conservative Southern Democrats, a combination that was to plague Roosevelt during the rest of his days.

Won from an obviously reluctant Congress was a new AAA act, a reactivation of the WPA and PWA, and a much-amended wage and hour bill. But despite most intense pressure from the

White House the executive-reorganization bill was defeated, and the regional TVA proposal never got beyond the committees. Meanwhile, from the conservative wing of his own party in Congress, Roosevelt heard charges of "executive domination," "tyranny," and even "dictatorship."

The President tried to meet the challenge in the primary elections of 1938, with his famous purge. Singling out a number of the most recalcitrant Democrats, including Senators Walter George of Georgia and Millard Tydings of Maryland, he attempted to defeat them in the primaries. Other conservative Democrats he obviously ignored, giving cheer and comfort to their opponents. The results of the purge, undertaken against the advice of many of the President's friends, were meager. The only marked success Roosevelt scored was in defeating New Yorker John O'Connor, Chairman of the House Rules Committee. Elsewhere his opponents won resounding victories and returned to Washington confident and resentful. The 1938 Congressional elections also proved a turning point in the hitherto dismal fortunes of the Republican party. Republican numbers in the House and the Senate had been regularly decreasing since 1930, and with each election it appeared that the party was headed for extinction. But in 1938 the Republicans almost doubled their numbers in the House, from 88 to 170, and gained 8 seats in the Senate. Among the new Republican Senators was the son of a former President, Robert Taft. The long-prevailing liberal wind turned in 1938, and with it the fortunes of the New Deal. The last important reform measure was the wage-hour bill of 1938. Afterward much brave liberal talk and a few radical proposals were made, including Roosevelt's own of limiting annual incomes to $25,000, during the war. But from 1938 on the liberal forces simply did not have the votes to carry a major reform measure through Congress.

Who killed cock robin? The menacing international situation and the President's increasing involvement in foreign affairs meant a decreasing emphasis upon domestic reform. But Roosevelt also contributed in a more positive way to that end. During the Court fight, his methods were deplored by many people who approved of his general ends. His 1938 intrusion into local politics was resented by others as not playing the traditional game. His growing reluctance to see individual members of Congress, his inclination to put a "must" tag on executive-sponsored legislation, and his hard-fisted use of patronage concerned many citizens. During 1938 an opinion poll showed that an impressive majority of voters still approved of the President personally, and of his program, but a majority also disliked his methods and felt that he had too much power.

The New Deal as a militant reform organization killed itself with its own practical successes. By 1939 business had recovered from the recession of the previous year and was in a relatively healthy state compared to its condition in 1933. The farmers were buoyed by government subsidies. Both groups resented and feared the growing power of labor, especially after the sit-down strikes of 1937 and 1938. Despite the millions still unemployed, the Social Security Act had introduced at least some protection against vicissitude for the laboring classes. As a degree of economic health returned to an increasing number of people, the inclination for further social surgery diminished. A majority was still ready to defend the New Deal's past, but fewer had the incentive for further radical reform. The reforming zeal had so decreased by 1938 and 1939 that the creative part of the New Deal was over, a situation that may have helped prompt the President to search elsewhere for a field of activity.

What had the New Deal accomplished? While it made few, if any, really revolutionary changes, it so accelerated existing trends that the years 1933–1937 can be considered the most eventful in domestic politics since the days of the Civil War. Among its many achievements, perhaps the most noteworthy was saving the nation from chaos in March 1933. Its success in inspiring confidence in the financial structure was a critical act in the history of the country. Only slightly less important was its recognition of the necessity for feeding the needy, supplying work for the jobless, and protecting the owners of homes, farms, and small business from loss of their establishments. For all such relief work the New Deal spent some $8 to $10 billion in nonrecoverable funds, an expenditure which despite the accompanying inefficiency and corruption was one of the best the nation ever made. Had deflation been permitted to run its course, as Secretary of the Treasury Andrew Mellon proposed, much of the middle class might have been wiped out. The New Deal attained what few democratic governments have been able to achieve in such periods of acute social stress. It was creative enough to retain the loyalties of the majority without forcing either the left or the right into violent opposition. Except on the labor-capital front, where the action was often local and almost never pointed toward government, there was less violence from marching men after 1933 than before that date.

By its economic and labor reforms the New Deal shifted power somewhat from the reigning business classes, some of it to the newly inspirited labor unions, but most to the government itself. The prestige of big business took a severe beating during the Depression and New Deal years, a pummelling that accounted for much of its choleric attitude toward the Roosevelt Administration. To a slight degree, the owning classes may have lost a fraction of their inheritance. One study of the gross national product showed that between 1929 and 1939 the proportion going into interests, rents, and corporate dividends decreased by about 3 per cent, while a similar figure appeared as an increase in the sum of wages and salaries. But the most palpable loss of the business classes was the power to make decisions vital to the economy. Previous to 1933 the setting of interest rates, the methods by which securities were sold, the determination of wage and salary scales and the choice of individuals for employment, the prices at which electric power, coal, oil, and even farm goods should be sold, the number of dwelling units to be built in a community, and a host of other questions had been decided either by millions of enterprisers or by an industrial and financial elite. After 1933 such decisions were invariably influenced and sometimes controlled by the Federal government. In many instances, the decisions of the new regime were not made on the grounds of profit and loss, nor were profit and loss the only guiding determinants for others. Often political considerations bulked larger than economic ones. The new state of affairs was summed up by a business periodial, in 1937, as one in which economic life was "arrogantly" dominated by politics, resulting in a system in which the "law of supply and demand" was in shambles, production was "artificially restricted or stimulated," and a horde of unproductive politicians were dominating the banking system and setting prices and wages at "false levels." A more friendly analysis summarized the change in the economy as one in which the front page of the daily newspaper had become "more important to the businessman than the market page, and the White House press conference of vaster import than the closing prices on the New York Stock Exchange."

Economically and socially, the most significant failure of the New Deal was its inability to achieve recovery and a reasonably efficient economy. After six years of reform and spending, 8 to 10 million workers were still unemployed in 1939. Per capita income was still considerably below the 1929 figure. The economy did not recover its 1929 productiveness and did not absorb all the stagnant labor power until the government primed the pumps with billions for preparedness and war. But since the process of achieving prosperity by allocating an increasing amount of the total national energy to producing nonuseful goods was to be the normal one for the next quarter century, perhaps the New Deal should not be judged too harshly for not obtaining what two postwar Administrations failed at.

The New Deal made almost as many substantial changes in the political system of the 1920's as it did in economic life. During its first four years practically all important legislation originated not in Congress but in the executive branch of the government, the Wagner Labor Act constituting the principal exception. Throughout the hundred days, Congress virtually abstained from changing important features in the draft legislation presented to it. Often during this hectic period newly created administrative agencies were empowered to issue their own regulations, which would have the same legality as if enacted by Congress. This tendency to delegate substantial legislative power to executive agencies was somewhat curtailed by the NIRA decision. But by the end of the New Deal, Congress had almost ceased to be a legislation-initiating body in important matters and had become a reviewing, modifying, and negating agency.

Although Roosevelt's contest with the Supreme Court diminished his personal prestige, it also resulted in a substantial loss of power both for the Court and for the several states. By radically broadening the Federal power over interstate commerce, the Court seriously limited its own power to declare Federal economic regulation unconstitutional, as well as that of the state to intervene in economic matters. The residual powers of the states were also steadily reduced by the numerous New Deal subsidies, for along with each subsidy ran the mandate of the Federal government. To help pay the mounting bills the Federal government invaded the traditional sources for state taxes, notably such consumer items as gasoline and automobile tires. But probably the most potent force in the erosion of state power lay in the proliferation of direct beneficial relations between the Federal government and the individual. Before 1933 only a few citizens had had direct beneficial relations with Washington. By 1939 the Federal government and its agencies were making money payments to farmers, to men on relief and Federal works projects, to college and high school students, to the aged, to the unemployed, to widows, to dependent children, and to the needy blind. It was also making loans directly, or guaranteeing them at low interest rates, to home owners, farmers, sharecroppers, and small businessmen. Hundreds of thousands of citizens took advantage of government-financed housing projects, school and college buildings, parks and playgrounds. As these ties became more numerous, and as the national pattern of movement from state to state in search of climatic or economic opportunity was accelerated, state and parochial loyalties withered and Americans became more and more national-minded.

In the realm of pure politics the New Deal scored perhaps its most astounding success. From 1894 to 1930 the Democratic party had been distinctly a minority one, winning only three Congressional elections in the thirty-six years, with two of those occurring in 1912 and 1914, when Theodore Roosevelt had split

Republican unity. But after 1932 the New Deal fashioned a coalition of urban voters, composed largely of the underprivileged classes and minority ethnic groups, which, when tied to the South and other distressed rural areas, produced a majority in six successive Congressional elections and in seven of the following nine. The new majority was, of course, a disparate one, full of conflicting and anomalous elements. By 1937, despite the Administration's extensive aid to agriculture, rural America was obviously alienated by the urban parts of the New Deal program. This was especially true of the South, whose attitude toward the racial and immigrant minorities in the northern cities was intensely colored by its own racial history. But so strong was the people's memory of the Depression, and so vivid the remembered contrast between Republican passivity and New Deal action, that the victorious coalition held together long after its reason for being had disappeared. To that extent post-World War II politics was based upon past memories instead of current issues.

The interaction of the Great Depression and the New Deal left many other marks on American attitudes. Some nineteenth-century folk convictions were badly eroded during the twenties by the mass-consumption society, with its emphasis upon mass sales, mass advertising, and installment buying, and by the hedonistic appeal of the automobile, the movies, and the radio. The Depression and the New Deal rapidly speeded up that process. By the midthirties it could be questioned whether the majority of Americans believed that work was altogether good and idleness or leisure necessarily bad, that any man could really find a job if he looked for one, that a man who worked hard got ahead, that personal security was the responsibility of the individual and not of society, that saving was therefore a good and spending at or beyond one's income an evil. If their votes meant anything, the American people were adopting a new set of individual and social mores, which contradicted many of those the majority had held in the past. Certainly their attitudes toward work and leisure were changing, as was their thinking about their own security. Apparently they were content to accept subsidies, however offered, and most were unworried by large amounts of debt, whether of the governmental or personal variety. They were also acclimated to a bewildering variety of governmental regulations and controls. This process of trading individualism for a collective mentality, of developing social consciousness instead of the individual conscience, for investing in the common security at the expense of individual freedom, was well advanced by 1940. During the following decade, it was to be accelerated by the demands of war and a succession of foreign crises.

5

The Totalitarian Challenge:
Foreign Policy, 1933–1941

IN HIS FIRST and second inaugural addresses, Franklin
Roosevelt scarcely mentioned foreign policy. During March 1933
and January 1937 his mind was preoccupied with domestic problems. Yet within ten months after his second inaugural he declared in a major speech given at Chicago that the peace, freedom, and security of the United States and of the world was
being jeopardized by aggressor nations. He proposed to quarantine such nations from civilized world society. He did not specify
particular nations, but even the most untutored citizen was aware
that he was talking about Japan, Italy, and Germany. Flaunting
the League of Nations' official censure, Japanese armed forces
continued to ravage Manchuria and China, and Mussolini had
invaded and conquered Ethiopia. Hitler's rearmament of Germany, which in 1936 was extended to the Rhineland in clear
violation of the Versailles peace terms, constituted another severe
blow to the tottering prestige of the League and to the concept of
a world ruled by law instead of force. The virulent antidemocratic propaganda emanating from Hitler and Mussolini and the
beginnings of the Rome-Berlin axis in 1936 and 1937 challenged
not only international stability but also world democratic institutions. Hitler's and Mussolini's joint aid to Franco's forces in the
Spanish Civil War indicated that the aggressor nations were
not content to assault their European neighbors with words but

were ready to translate their aggressive vocabulary into armed
deeds. By 1937 international pundits were already predicting that
soon a nationalistic and rearmed Germany, aided by Italy, would
challenge the Versailles settlement and attempt to remake the
map of Europe. In East Asia it was obvious that Japan sought
nothing short of dominance. As the President spoke in Chicago a
second and greater world war was clearly in prospect.

Franklin Roosevelt's 1937 proposal for an international quarantine revived and intensified many slumbering feelings of hostility
and loyalty. Since the defeat of Wilson's League the lines of
cleavage within the country on foreign policy had remained exceedingly complex and had refused to conform to any exact geographical, party, or occupational basis. Because of sentiments of
party fealty there remained perhaps slightly more devotion to the
idea of internationalism among Democrats than Republicans.
And on the whole it was apparent that except for the Democratic
South, more friends of international action were clustered in the
urban areas than in rural regions. The international trading and
financial communities produced more internationally minded
people than the industrial ones. And the rural Midwest was perhaps the center of the most intense isolationism. The President's
suggestion, therefore, was once again calculated to change the
existing political patterns in the country. It certainly was made in
the face of a dominant isolationist majority in both parties and in
all sections of the country. In 1937 the American people were not
only opposed to any new armed adventures outside the Western
Hemisphere but also regretted such episodes in the past. To the
1937 Gallup poll question of whether it had been a mistake for
the United States to enter World War I, 70 per cent of those
queried answered yes. Both the question and the answer were
obviously prompted as much by future possibilities as by past
history, but both also reflected fifteen years in which the American mind had been conditioned against any war save that of
immediate defense. After the turn to isolation in 1920, the number of scholarly and popular books decrying America's participation in the war was far greater than of those defending the
historic venture of 1917 and the following world settlement. Nov-

els, poetry, and most movies and plays of the twenties and thirties were almost unanimous in condemning America's entry into World War I and in questioning whether any modern war was worth fighting. Personal heroism, except the kind displayed by pacifists, was usually depicted as either cheap or useless, patriotism was considered something of a fraud, and the question of whether civilization could survive another war was constantly raised. From Hemingway's *A Farewell to Arms* and Dos Passos' *Three Soldiers* to Maxwell Anderson's *What Price Glory,* one conclusion emerged: peace under almost any circumstances was preferable to war. With the waning popularity of the social gospel, churchmen eager to pursue more fertile fields of Christian endeavor turned to Prohibition and to peace. As late as 1935, Kirby Page declared in the *Christian Century* that since war was sin, no Christian could legitimately engage in it.

Throughout the postwar period much literary and scholarly effort was devoted to ferreting out exactly what had drawn America into the struggle. Wilsonian idealism was blamed, as was British and French propaganda. Some authors insisted that words alone had hoodwinked America into joining the war. In 1939 the *Saturday Review of Literature* editorialized that the causes and the issues of the war were extravagantly and deliberately exaggerated by propaganda and that Americans were thus first beguiled into joining the struggle and then sustained in supporting it. A more popular explanation, especially after the Great Depression, designated the profit motive as the chief villain. International investors, traders, shippers, and the producers of war goods had so committed the country, this argument ran, that intervention was simply the formal acceptance of an already existing fact. For those who wanted to narrow the hunt to even more personal and particular prey, the munitions makers were an obvious quarry. When it became known that certain American steel and munitions firms had attempted to wreck the London Naval and Geneva Disarmament Conferences, both House and Senate committees, the latter under the chairmanship of Senator Gerald P. Nye, began investigations into the profits and the influence of the munitions industry. Casting aside judicial restraint, the Nye Committee proved its preconceptions that the munitions makers, the international bankers, and the businessmen had really been responsible for the nation's participation in World War I. A galaxy of articles and plays pursued the "merchants of death" theme.

In the reforming, antibusiness atmosphere of the thirties the public demanded that the profits be taken out of armaments, confident that this would insure insulation from future wars. As a result, the Pittman Neutrality Resolution passed both houses of Congress and was rather reluctantly signed by the President on August 31, 1935. The resolution prohibited the export of munitions from the United States and the shipment of arms on American vessels to foreign powers engaged in an international war. It also empowered the President on the outbreak of a war to warn American citizens against travelling on ships flying the flags of belligerents. By such action the risk of becoming involved in foreign wars was presumably reduced. But the Act also served notice on the world that the United States would not aid victims of aggression, thus possibly sharpening the appetite of potential aggressors. The Neutrality Resolution also put into place the last arc of an unfortunate circle. United States intervention in World War I upset the power balance of Europe. Allied victory and the Versailles peace were the results of the addition of American power to that of the Western Allies. Already the American withdrawal from Europe during the twenties had made the peace unstable by raising the question whether the defeated countries were not actually stronger than the remaining victors. And America's announcement of her probable neutrality in the event of another European round almost insured a readjustment of the Versailles settlement either by diplomacy or by warfare.

Although Franklin Roosevelt had hedged during the twenties and early thirties on the issue of international cooperation for peace, there was little question where his sympathies lay. He cheered the early Ethiopian successes in the Italo-Ethiopian war and was indignant at the Hoare-Laval Plan to settle the conflict by giving Italy a portion of Ethiopia. When Germany occupied the Rhineland in 1936, he denounced the country's reverting to the "law of the sword" and claiming, by assuming the preposterous title of "master race," to be the arbiters of human destiny. Two years later he protested against the Nazi persecution of the Jews and confessed he could scarcely believe such things could happen in modern civilization. During the Spanish Civil War he privately labelled the actions of Germany and Italy as "armed banditry."

Despite these sentiments, the President was extremely cautious in committing the nation to international action against aggression. But the record indicates that Roosevelt took as many steps toward cooperating with the League of Nations and the Western democracies as he felt would be supported by Congress and the voters. As Coolidge and Hoover had done before him, he urged American membership in the World Court, only to see the proposal again defeated by the Senate. The American representative to the Geneva Disarmament Conference, Norman H. Davis, promised in May 1933 that if a satisfactory disarmament treaty were achieved, the United States would consult with other nations about a threat to world peace, and that if the international organization voted sanctions against an aggressor, this country would refrain from any action tending to defeat such collective effort. Upset by the German rearmament in the spring of 1936, Roosevelt considered the possibility of cooperating with a proposed Anglo-French blockade of Germany. So as not to involve Congress, he suggested that the United States recognize the blockade by executive action.

The President was never happy with the Neutrality Resolution, stating repeatedly that it was "impossible for any nation completely to isolate itself from economic and political upheavals in the rest of the world . . ." Both he and Secretary of State Hull were particularly opposed to an automatic embargo upon all parties to a foreign war. Instead, they supported a measure to give the President an option to impose an embargo on either one or both of the belligerents, thus making it possible to discriminate against a supposed aggressor and to cooperate with the League of Nations' sanctions. But as both Congress and the country were against this tying of America to the League, Roosevelt retreated.

He signed the measure with the observation that the inflexible provisions might precipitate the country into war. Since there was little or no opportunity for America to trade with Ethiopia, the President applied the embargo provisions to arms for Italy with enthusiasm and even wished to extend them to other commodities, including oil, copper, and steel. In September 1935 both the President and Hull supported an amendment including these items, but again, in face of stubborn Congressional opposition, the President backed away from a full-fledged fight. The elections of 1936 were too near to take such a risk. He therefore contented himself with denouncing those who made profits from the Italian war trade and asking for a moral embargo against the shipments to Mussolini's forces, an effort which at least proved that little could be accomplished by such voluntary schemes, as American trade to Italian Africa increased about twenty times.

During the campaign of 1936 Roosevelt was particularly sensitive to the pacifist sentiment in the country. His famous "I hate war" phrase probably allayed the doubts of many voters. But the President had not changed his foreign policy persuasions. In his opening message to the Congress of 1937 he asked for major modifications in the expiring Neutrality Act. Again Congress insisted upon a mandatory embargo and even added provisions barring loans to belligerents and arms to the League of Nations if it should apply sanctions against an aggressor. Almost from the first days of the Spanish Civil War, Roosevelt understood that it was an international contest, and his sympathies were entirely with the Loyalist government. But Hull and the State Department strongly supported cooperation with the British and French Non-Intervention Agreement, which handcuffed the democracies while ignoring Russian aid to the Loyalists and German and Italian aid to Franco. The Anglo-French agreement also violated the long-acknowledged right of all existing governments to import arms with which to put down a rebellion. Since the Spanish war was technically a rebellion, the terms of the Neutrality Resolution did not apply, and Roosevelt's application of the act was probably inspired as much by State Department pressures as by political reasoning. Later, when the Fascist triumph was imminent, Roosevelt thought of lifting the embargo. But he did not act, possibly because he felt such an attempt would cost the Catholic vote in the 1938 elections. American policy, together with that of Britain and France, went a long way to insure increasing Russian Communist influence in the Spanish Loyalist Government and the eventual defeat of the Spanish Republican forces.

The United States had followed the British and French lead on the Spanish question, with disastrous results for the future of democracy and peace. Subsequently Great Britain and France offered to follow the American lead in Asia with approximately the same outcome. The Japanese armed invasion of Manchuria in 1931 had drawn the strongest words of censure both from President Hoover and from his Secretary of State, Henry Stimson. Since Japan had clearly broken the Nine Power Treaty of Washington, Stimson urged collective retaliatory action by the United States and the other signatory nations. But the President, appreciative of Congressional and popular opposition to any warlike actions in the Orient, rejected even a proposed economic embargo and confined his response to words. After it became apparent that the League of Nations was not prepared to offer any more resistance than had the United States, the Japanese turned to the much bigger game of China. Following the Marco Polo Bridge incident near Peiping in July 1937, the Japanese army launched a full-fledged campaign to defeat Chiang Kaishek and conquer North China. In the context of European and Asiatic developments, on October 5, 1937, Roosevelt delivered his famous "quarantine speech," obviously designed to warn Americans of the awful realities of the world, as well as to measure the domestic support he could command for an effort to stop the drift toward chaos. If the "present reign of terror and international lawlessness" were to continue, Roosevelt solemnly warned, even the Western Hemisphere would not be spared armed conflict. Consequently, the "peace-loving nations" had to concert to restore "the belief in the pledged word, in the value of the signed treaty." As a start toward that restoration he proposed to quarantine the aggressor nations as health officials quarantine a virulent plague. If words meant anything, the President sought to impose an international embargo upon Japan, Germany, and Italy.

Twenty-four hours after the quarantine speech, the League of Nations condemned Japan as an aggressor and proposed that the signers of the Nine Power Treaty of 1921 meet and consider collective action. Eager to win American support in Europe, Great Britain and France welcomed the suggestion of a conference and approved Secretary of State Hull's suggestion of Brussels as a meeting place. Before the conference met, British Foreign Minister Anthony Eden informed the American representatives that his country would support the United States in any sanctions against Japan but would not take the initiative, Britain being content to base her actions on American policy. The United States' hand was called on November 3, 1937, the opening day of the conference, when numerous delegates announced they were awaiting the formulation of a positive American policy. This was not forthcoming, simply because Congress and the American people were determined to avoid any international action that might lead the country to war. The response to the quarantine speech was critical. Roosevelt and the State Department were accused of warmongering. A poll taken in Congress indicated that two-thirds of the members were opposed to participating in sanctions against Japan. Against such odds the President felt he had to retreat, and he assured the American people that the Brussels Conference would seek settlement of the Chinese problem by peaceful means. The meeting disbanded with a pious statement of support for the Nine Power Treaty principles. The only American reaction to the Japanese bombing and sinking of the U.S.S. *Panay* and three tankers on the Yangtze River a month later was a demand for an apology and indemnity. A subsequent Gallup poll indicated that over 70 per cent of Americans favored a complete withdrawal from the Far East, an action that would presumably leave even the Philippines to a dire fate.

Despite his humiliating Spanish and Chinese experiences, Roosevelt continued his efforts to secure an international understanding to counter the dominant pattern of aggression. Early in 1938 he proposed to the British Prime Minister, Neville Chamberlain, a plan to change treaties without the use of force and to assure all peoples access to raw materials. Chamberlain replied that a conference for this purpose would obstruct his developing policy to grant "a measure of appeasement" to Italy and Germany. The Prime Minister was prepared to recognize the Italian conquest of Ethiopia. Chamberlain later reversed his stand on recognition after Anthony Eden and Winston Churchill made vigorous protests. But he persevered in his Italian policy and Eden resigned. Although both Roosevelt and Hull felt that the Ethiopian deal was "a corrupt bargain" there was little they could do about it. By the spring of 1938 it was evident that the majority of the people of the United States, Great Britain, and France were prepared neither to go to war nor even to risk war in any cause other than their own immediate national security. Consequently the world policies of the three powers differed only to this extent: Britain and France were willing to bargain with the aggressors, the United States would do nothing either to bargain or seek other means of restraint. Since the attitude of all three was on the public record, the events of 1938 and 1939 were predictable.

In March of 1938 Hitler marched into Austria. That fall and winter he precipitated a world crisis by demanding and obtaining at the Munich Conference the westernmost provinces of Czechoslovakia and the Sudeten Mountain land without which the defense of the country was practically impossible. Faced with the threat of a world war, Britain and France ignored the French treaty with the Czechs, as well as Russia's promise of aid. Excluding the Czech and Russian representatives from the bargaining table at Munich, they agreed to the German acquisition in return for Hitler's promise to respect what was left of Czech territorial integrity.

Though Chamberlain and French Premier Édouard Daladier came home to cheering crowds acclaiming them as men who had secured "peace in our time," the results of Munich were catastrophic for the democracies. Czechoslovakia, with the best army in Central Europe, was alienated from and embittered against the West. What was left of the French position in Central and Eastern Europe was destroyed. Russia was more suspicious and sullen than ever, and nursing the suspicion that Munich opened the way for a German attack eastward with British and French blessing, no longer argued for collective security at Geneva but retreated into an isolationist position. Maxim Litvinov, Russia's most insistent defender of collective security during the thirties, was recalled to Moscow. All of Central and Eastern Europe lay helpless before Hitler. In March 1939 he indicated exactly what his signed word was worth by overrunning and subjugating the rest of Czechoslovakia.

Germany's breaking of the Munich pledge ended all talk of appeasement in Britain. Rearmament was speeded up, defensive alliances were hastily offered to Poland, Turkey, Rumania, and Greece, and as a new German propaganda campaign against Poland was instituted, Britain and France even approached Russia, proposing a defensive alliance against the Nazi menace. Since the first Russian price for an agreement was a guarantee of hegemony over Eastern Europe from the Baltic to the Bosporus, with the further understanding that Russian troops might occupy any or all of the territory in furtherance of the agreement, the negotiations at Moscow understandably went slowly. Additionally, Poland and Rumania feared Russia as much as Hitler. Meanwhile Russia and Germany were negotiating in Berlin, where if good faith in future performance was at a lower premium, the immediate price offered the Soviet seemed to be better. On August 23, 1939, the German and Russian Foreign Ministers signed a treaty of nonaggression, by which both agreed to refrain from attacking the other. They also agreed secretly that if the boundaries of Eastern Europe were changed, Germany was to obtain Lithuania, East Prussia, and Western Poland, and Russia would be compensated by the acquisition of parts of Eastern Poland, Finland, Estonia, Latvia, and Rumanian Bessarabia. Having isolated the Western powers from Eastern Europe, Hitler increased his demands on Poland and on September 1 invaded that stubborn and unhappy country. Two days later Britain and France declared war on Germany.

Although the United States did not participate officially in the Munich negotiations, the President called upon both sides to arrive at a peaceful settlement. Roosevelt had few illusions about the permanence of the Munich agreement. In response to the 1937 revival of Japanese naval construction, he had requested a sizable increase in appropriations to start the construction of a "two-ocean navy" capable of protecting both the Atlantic and Pacific coasts. Immediately after Munich the President increased expenditures for armaments, and in his January 4, 1939, message to Congress he requested a defense budget of almost $2 billion, most of it for the construction of ships and airplanes. Despite the criticisms of pacifists, the money was voted. Congress remained opposed, however, to changing the Neutrality Act, despite Roosevelt's argument that the Act, operating unevenly and at times unfairly, was helping to bring on war instead of stopping it.

During the early spring of 1939 the Administration made its last urgent effort to repeal the neutrality legislation. Roosevelt let it be known that he had given up his intention of purging the Democratic party of its conservative anti-New Dealers. He invited many Congressmen and Senators to the White House, and even made a deal with Senator Key Pittman of Nevada, the Democratic chairman of the Senate Foreign Relations Committee. He met the Senator's price for introducing a repeal bill by promising a raise in the government-supported price of silver. But all his activity was futile. In a direct encounter at the White House, Roosevelt and Hull argued with the foreign-policy leaders of the Senate that an outbreak of European war seemed imminent and that repeal might possibly stop the descent into the world-embracing maelstrom. Apparently relying upon information carried by a news tip sheet, the senior Republican member of the Senate Foreign Relations Committee, Borah of Idaho, replied that he had better information than the State Department. War hysteria, he claimed, had been manufactured. "There is not going to be any war this year," he added. After making a count in the

Senate, Vice-President Garner told the President he did not have the votes, and that was that.

When Hitler marched into Poland, Roosevelt assured the American people that as long as he could prevent it, there would be "no blackout of peace in the United States." "The nation will remain a neutral nation," he further promised, "but I cannot ask that every American remain neutral in thought as well. Even a neutral has the right to take account of the facts. Even a neutral cannot be asked to close his mind or his conscience." The nation was far from neutral, for the American conscience had already moved, as Roosevelt realized. Immediately after Munich American opinion was so fragmented and so torn between a sense of relief that war had been avoided and fear that it might still be on the next leaf of the monthly calendar, anger at the dictators for their brutal demands, and disgust at Britain and France for their weak submission, that it was impossible to speak of a consensus. But Hitler's seizure of Czechoslovakia, his barbarous campaign against the Jews, and his invasion of Poland convinced the majority of Americans that Hitler and Germany were responsible for starting another world war. In the autumn of 1939 a national poll indicated that an overwhelming majority of 96.5 per cent still felt that the United States should stay out of war. But when the same people were asked what countries they blamed most for starting the war, 82 per cent named Germany and only 3 per cent Britain and France.

Immediately after the declaration of war, Roosevelt traded on this strong partiality toward the Western democracies by again asking Congress to revise the Neutrality Act, so that Britain and France might purchase war goods in the United States. The kaleidoscopic events of 1939 revealed the embarrassing position into which neutrality legislation had placed the country. The "cash and carry" provisions of the Act, permitting export of American-made arms provided they were paid for in cash and were shipped on a foreign vessel, expired in 1939, leaving mandatory an embargo against shipments of war goods to Britain and France, whom the country so patently favored. But it permitted such shipments to Russia, whose diplomatic *démarche* of August had helped bring on the war and who was now an alliance partner of the Nazis. The President was acutely aware of the fact that over 90 per cent of the American people wanted to stay at peace. He therefore asked only for a reinstitution of the "cash and carry" provision and supported his appeal by argument that this would mean noninvolvement in the war. The struggle in Congress was long and bitter. Roosevelt's assumption that a British and French victory was essential to save Western civilization and that, therefore, this country, in its own self-interest, should do everything necessary to insure that victory, was well known only to a very few intimate friends. The President therefore kept very quiet during the debate on the Neutrality Act, which became law, as amended, in November. The new act reinstituted the "cash and carry" provisions but barred loans to belligerents, prohibited the arming of American merchant ships, and forbade American citizens from travelling on the ships of belligerents in war zones. The President continued his silent policy after the passage of the Act, only very occasionally reminding the populace that there was a great difference "between keeping out of war and pretending that this war is none of our business."

For the world and for the United States, 1940 was a momentous year. During the early fall of 1939 the German war machine overran Poland, and that country was divided between Germany and Russia. A short time later Russia invaded Finland and eventually dictated a peace. In the following month, Germany invaded neutral Denmark and Norway and occupied Holland. These events helped tumble Neville Chamberlain from power in Britain. But Winston Churchill's new government was powerless to stop the tide of German might. By June the British had achieved their incredible evacuation of Dunkirk, but the army came back to Britain defeated, dispirited, disorganized, and without equipment. France fell, and Mussolini entered the war to grab the jackal's share of the spoils. On August 12, three superb mechanized German armies were poised on the Channel in view of England, while overhead the Luftwaffe of 1,800 planes struck at the Royal Air Force in the Battle of Britain. Against these formidable men and machines, the British fought with an outnumbered air force, the fleet, the indomitable spirit of the people, and the leadership of Winston Churchill.

During those months, when the fate of Western civilization was in balance, the Presidential elections of 1940 were being fought out. Sometime in 1939 Franklin Roosevelt decided that he might run for a third term, despite the fact that every poll showed a majority of voters opposed to breaking the two-term tradition. His fears that the Republicans might nominate and elect a reactionary who would destroy the New Deal, or that continued German success might demand American intervention on a much wider scale, and that a new President would fail to meet the challenge, probably played a part in his determination not to commit himself against running. So, undoubtedly, did his own lively sense of ambition and his fondness for power. Whatever the combination of emotions, fears, facts, and fancy that impelled his course, he let it be known that he did not want the nomination and would not run for the office, but never once said definitely that he would decline it. He encouraged a number of his chief supporters, including Harry Hopkins, Alben Barkley, Paul McNutt, and Cordell Hull, to work for the honor, but he never gave any of them substantial help, and he did intrigue behind the scenes to obstruct the campaigns of Vice-President Garner and James Farley. His unwillingness to announce his intentions kept all candidates in a most awkward position, and by the late spring of 1940 it was evident that the nomination was his for the asking. Since he would not ask, a draft movement was rather clumsily devised, and the Convention nominated him for a third term despite the opposition of the conservatives led by Farley and Garner, the latter being replaced as the Vice Presidential candidate by Henry A. Wallace.

As soon as the Republican party nominated Wendell Willkie, Roosevelt knew that 1940 was not to be another 1936. For the big, broad-faced, tousled-haired Willkie was a difficult man for Roosevelt to attack. Willkie was a Wall Street man and a utility executive who had fought the TVA to the last ditch. But he was no antediluvian business reactionary. Able, literate, and energetic, he had been a Democrat until 1938 and had supported many

New Deal measures. Moreover he was no isolationist; he stood for all possible aid to Britain short of war. He was a committed man arguing, with a hoarse voice that carried conviction, against New Deal regulations that crippled private enterprise and against the third term, with its implications of dictatorial ambitions. Against Willkie, Roosevelt ran on his record and used the mounting Nazi terror in Europe to its utmost, insinuating that any change during these perilous days would necessarily be for the worse. But the great German crisis building up over the English Channel carried with it grave political liabilities as well as opportunities. In June, during the death agonies of France, both French Premier Paul Reynaud and Churchill pleaded for massive aid to shore up the crumbling democratic cause—France for American armed intervention, and Britain for destroyers. Roosevelt promised all the material aid he could muster, but both military intervention and the gift or sale of destroyers were matters for Congress, and it was not a propitious time to ask. With France defeated and Britain tottering on the brink, however, the state of both the home defenses and those of the British Isles became even more critical. In Congress a bill for compulsory military service, the first of its kind in peace time, met intense opposition not only from the Republican leadership but from many Democrats. For a long time the President did not commit himself to "selective service," but on August 2, when it was apparent that without his support the bill would languish for months in debate and perhaps face defeat, Roosevelt publicly defended the selective service measure. The President also desperately wanted to grant Britain fifty overage destroyers, but he was almost certain that Congress would not agree, and he was keenly aware of the great political risk he would take in even broaching the subject. All his political instincts warned him against a destroyer deal immediately before the elections. But on September 3 he announced a bargain with Britain transferring fifty destroyers by Presidential edict in return for the lease of naval bases on British Western Hemisphere possessions. Although the deal could be defended as a measure of national defense, it also made the President vulnerable to a charge of dictatorship in bypassing

Congress and of committing the country in defiance of the Neutrality Act to an unneutral position and possibly to war. But if Roosevelt strained legality in September of 1940, he also acted against his sound political sense. He had momentarily ceased to be a politician, aware that he was risking his re-election for what he considered to be a much greater cause.

The destroyer deal, as Roosevelt predicted, unleashed a tornado of criticism in Congress and throughout the country. Even Willkie characterized the deal as "the most dictatorial and arbitrary" Presidential act in American history. Willkie's supporters and the isolationist press were much less restrained. For the remainder of the 1940 campaign the President was depicted as a would-be tyrant and a warmonger ready to sacrifice the lives of millions of Americans in another futile Wilsonian crusade. In the last week of the canvass, Willkie charged that Roosevelt's re-election would result in the country's entering the war within six months. Under the opposition attack, the New Deal coalition seemed to be dissolving. Isolationist and pacifist criticism appealed especially to liberals and the farming Middle West. Incensed because he felt that the President had not accorded the CIO enough support, John L. Lewis returned to his original Republican allegiance, while labor generally seemed to be wavering. Unemployment was still high and the economy in an uncertain condition. The American Communist Party, slavishly following the Moscow line, depicted Roosevelt as the militarist leader of reactionary capitalism. The charge seemed to carry weight particularly with youth groups, whose male members were obliged to register on October 16 under the Selective Service Act and to stand ready for possible induction into the armed forces by the operation of the first national drawing, scheduled just a week before the election.

In the face of narrowing odds, Roosevelt retreated from the high ground of principle and once again became the politician. During the last week of the campaign he continued to strike out at the opposition Republican leaders who, he said, were playing politics with national defense. But he also reacted perceptibly to the charge of warmongering. Up to that time, he had repeatedly promised that American soldiers would engage in battle only in national defense. On October 30, at Boston, he struck out the qualifying phrase already written into his speech and flatly promised, "Your boys are not going to be sent into any foreign war."

Despite the fact that Willkie carried only eight states, in popular votes the election was the closest one since 1916. Though foreign affairs had bulked large in the campaign oratory, and though New Deal support was radically diminished among Italian and German groups, the nation was obviously still voting in patterns based upon economic and social classes. Roosevelt carried every large city with over 500,000 population, his support there in the main coming from the poorer neighborhoods. But if the New Deal magic was still potent politically, and if Roosevelt was still the hero of the underprivileged groups, his party, as it had in 1938, received something less than unqualified support. The Democrats only succeeded in gaining six seats in the House over their totals of two years before, and in the Senate they lost a total of three.

Once the elections were out of the way, the President returned to the fundamental problem of how to aid the British without antagonizing the majority in Congress. By this time Roosevelt was committed to aiding Britain, even if that meant war and the violation of his pre-election pledge. So were many top army and navy officials and most of the Cabinet, including the two internationally minded Republicans, Secretary of the Navy Frank Knox and Secretary of War Henry Stimson. But the President was mindful also of the grave danger of leading a divided nation so close to war that any untoward event might push it to a decision for peace at any price, the results of which would be a catastrophic blow to his own leadership, to world democracy, and to the eventual security of the United States. Just how close the Administration came to this perilous situation was revealed in August 1941, when the Selective Service Act was extended by the margin of one vote in the House. Roosevelt therefore defended all his openly announced policies with the argument that they would help insure the maintenance of peace, though he was often aware that they were bringing the country closer to participation in the war. Such was his strategy in proposing the Lend-Lease Act.

By the fall of 1940 it was apparent that while Britain would protect her island, she could not much longer protect her empire, to say nothing of mounting a victorious attack against her enemies, without massive assistance from the only available source of such support, the United States. North Africa was endangered, with it Suez, and, as a consequence, most of Asia. Britain was also running out of available funds with which to purchase goods in the United States. Either the "cash and carry" provisions of the Neutrality Act had to be amended or the likelihood of most of the non-American world falling to the Fascists faced. At this grave juncture, Roosevelt proposed that the nation become the "arsenal of democracy." He suggested to Congress that the President be empowered to lend or lease supplies and munitions to those countries whose preservation he considered vital to the continued security of the United States. Since the bill proposed that the United States freely give munitions to one side and deny them to the other, this was a highly unneutral policy, even a quasi-belligerent one. The President was aware of the implications and so were the members of Congress. To placate public sentiment, Roosevelt argued that the proposal would not violate the Neutrality Act but would, instead, tend to insulate the country from actual war.

The lend-lease proposal brought to a showdown the struggle between two large groups of Americans separated by the convenient but very inexact labels of "isolationists" and "interventionists." Like the great foreign policy questions of the past, the issue cut across traditional party lines and basic political and social attitudes, the strangest of bedfellows being found on both sides of the conflict. Supporting the isolationist position were those who disliked anything Roosevelt did (a major group by 1941) and those who feared that lend-lease was a certain step toward war and that war would bring a dictatorship to America, or that it would mean the end of reform and a wave of reaction comparable to that experienced in the twenties, or that it would be used by Roosevelt to embark on all sorts of wild socialist schemes. Bitter-end Republicans, pro-Fascists, and anti-Semitic groups found themselves leagued with the Communists, the ardent pro-Irish group, many socialists, dedicated pacifists, Anglophobes, pro-Germans, and followers of the old Midwestern progressive tradition. On the opposite side were the people ready to support Roosevelt in almost anything he proposed, professional Democrats, convinced internationalists, a majority of the Jewish and Scandinavian peoples, liberal and conservative anti-Fascists, Anglophiles, and many high military officials. Clustered on the membership rolls of the America First Committee, dedicated to keeping America out of war, were the names of Herbert Hoover, historian Charles A. Beard, Robert Wood (president of Sears Roebuck), the two La Follette brothers, Charles A. Lindbergh, and Father Coughlin. Although not members, Earl Browder and Gerald L. K. Smith were also in the opposition. At the opposite pole, supporting the program of the William Allen White Committee to Defend America by Aiding the Allies, was an equally improbable collection of names including General Pershing, Harold Ickes, Owen D. Young, John Dewey, Frank Knox, Henry Stimson, and Harry Hopkins. Throughout the country the issue disrupted old political patterns, while domestic matters were more or less forgotten. But although there were enough exceptions almost to defy analysis, if one ignored the Democratic South wedded to Wilsonian internationalism by historic factors and to Britain by ancestry, opinion polls showed a discernible difference in the geographical roots of the contending positions. On the whole, overlooking the Scandinavian community, the root strength of the isolationists seemed to lie in the rural regions of the country extending from Pittsburgh west to the Pacific Coast. Conversely, again excepting the South and pockets of citizens of Irish extraction, the nucleus of internationalism was in the urban and Eastern areas. In other words, the urban tinge of the New Deal was beginning to show in foreign policy just as it had in domestic issues.

In Congress many Democrats and most Republicans disagreed with Roosevelt's lend-lease proposals. Democratic Senators Clark, McCarran, Wheeler, and Walsh were opposed, as were La Follette and most of the leaders of the opposition, including Senators Taft and Vandenberg. It was perhaps no accident that except for Senator Walsh of Massachusetts, of Irish-Catholic extraction, these Senators all represented states lying west of the Appalachian Mountains. Spurred by such remarks as Senator Wheeler's that the bill represented the Administration's "Triple A foreign policy," and that it would result in plowing under "every fourth American boy" and in giving the President dictatorial power "to conduct undeclared war anywhere in the world," the debate over lend-lease was as bitter as it was protracted. But the majority of Congress and the American people saw in this measure a possible means of reconciling their contradictory desires—of remaining at peace and of preserving the democratic world. By substantial majorities in both Houses, lend-lease became law on March 11, 1941, and very soon a sizable flow of American-made munitions was on its way across the Atlantic.

Roosevelt subsequently pursued his policy of aiding Britain by indirection, by subterfuge, and even by misrepresentation of the Administration's policy to Congress and the country. Damaged British warships were repaired in American harbors. British fighter pilots were trained in the United States, and American technical specialists flew in combat flights against Germany from British air fields. The American and British General staffs met in January 1941 in a secret full-dress conference in Washington. Although the President specifically denied on May 27, 1941, that the United States was convoying merchantmen in the Atlantic, within a few months this was being done. In September 1941 the U.S. destroyer *Greer,* "patrolling off Iceland, discovered and followed a German submarine, meanwhile periodically radioing its position to nearby British forces. When the submarine attacked with two torpedoes, the *Greer* replied with depth charges. Roosevelt reported the incident to the American people as an attack upon an American naval ship, without mentioning the preceding provocation. Within a few days the Navy was ordered to convoy British, American, and neutral ships as far as Iceland and to attack German warships and submarines on sight. We did not want a "shooting war," Roosevelt remarked on October 27, but if such a war should start, the American people could be certain who had begun it. By that time the United States and Great Britain were alliance partners against the Axis, engaged in a shooting war on the North Atlantic.

By October 1941 many high army and navy officials, some of the Cabinet, and perhaps even Roosevelt wanted open participation in the world struggle. But there appeared to be no expedient way to enter it. Germany refused to counter American activities in the Atlantic with a full-scale attack, and the Administration realized that Congress and the American people would only be activated to support an all-out war by a major enemy assault. This attack came, finally, not in the Atlantic but in the Pacific.

After the 1937 Brussels Conference fiasco, Japan continued the invasion of China, checked only by Russia. During the summers of 1938 and 1939 the two powers fought major but inconclusive engagements along the Manchurian-Siberian border. A short-lived peace came to the northern area by virtue of the Russo-German pact of August 1939 and the Japanese-German alliance a year later. Subsequently Japanese attention was momentarily focused on Southeast Asia, where after the fall of France and Holland opportunity beckoned to seize French Indochina and the Dutch East Indies. The June 1941 Nazi invasion of Russia eliminated the Soviets for a time as a major Asiatic power. Consequently only the United States remained as a counterpoise against Japanese ambition to become master of East Asia. After Germany's invasion of Poland American policy was consistently aimed at maintaining an independent China and protecting the French, British, and Dutch empires in East Asia. But such a policy meant rising conflict with Japan and possible war, and war in the Pacific was the last thing the Administration wanted. Time was needed for American rearmament and for supplying of Britain. Moreover the main interest of the United States was in the struggle for Europe, rather than the diverting conflict in the Orient.

Throughout 1940 and 1941 the United States attempted to restrain Japan through diplomatic and economic pressure. In order to be effective this had to be automatically increased as British,

French, and Dutch strength waned and as Russia became totally preoccupied with the German attack. As early as July 1940 the United States embargoed shipments of aviation gasoline and scrap metal to Japan. A month later a loan was made to the hard-pressed Chinese government, and in October 1940, after Churchill had reopened the Burma Road, American supplies began to move across the Himalayas to the forces of Chiang Kai-shek. Facing this potential check to Japan's territorial ambitions, ruling circles of that country divided into contending groups. The first, led by the army leaders, demanded that the Empire expand to its utmost limits, at the risk of war with the United States. Included in their plans were French Indochina; the Dutch East Indies, possession of which would assure Japan of adequate oil, tin, and rubber; and possibly Malaya and Burma. A second group of naval and civilian officials, led by Premier Fumimaro Konoye, were fearful of defeat in a contest with the United States and were more moderate. If the United States were willing to acknowledge the Japanese occupation of China, renounce its embargo, and stop its support of Chiang Kai-shek, they would be ready to accept the continued independent existence of French Indochina and the Philippines. While the two groups jockeyed for control, almost continuous negotiations were conducted with the United States. Matters came to a head in July 1941, when, after the German invasion of Russia, Japanese forces occupied the military bases of French Indochina. In retaliation the United States froze all Japanese funds in this country, closed the Panama Canal to Japanese shipping, and called Philippine reserve forces to active duty. On Roosevelt's return from the Atlantic meeting, both he and Churchill underlined these menacing actions by stating that in the event of further Japanese aggression, the United States would protect its interests by all available means. Only if the Japanese retired from Indochina would the President be willing to continue the discussions.

Prior to Roosevelt's blunt statement, Premier Konoye had proposed a personal meeting with the President to settle by negotiation the growing differences between the two countries. He now redoubled his efforts to persuade his associates that more could be gained by discussions than by war. As an advance tender of good faith, the Japanese government, on August 28, promised that no further advance would be made in South Asia and that it would withdraw its troops from Indochina as soon as the "China Incident" was settled. The Konoye government even hinted that Japan might ignore its treaty arrangements with Germany if the United States should be drawn into "a defensive war" with Hitler. Along with this tempting offer came the unofficial warning through Ambassador Grew that if this overture were turned down, the Konoye government might fall before the demands of the military expansionists.

For a time Roosevelt was inclined to accept the Japanese offer of August 28 as a basis for a personal meeting with Konoye. But upon the State Department's judgment that Japan would again back down if pressed, and would not resort to war, he replied that he would consent to attend such a meeting only if a prior agreement were made about China. On the issue of China the last hope of avoiding war was shattered. During the next six weeks, Premier Konoye repeatedly asked the President for a conference and even proposed to his government that Japan withdraw its troops from China. But his suggestion was overruled by the army chiefs, and on October 18 the Konoye government fell, to be supplanted by a group of militarists headed by General Hideki Tojo. Although negotiations with Washington continued, the new Cabinet, on November 5, won the Emperor's consent to prepare for an attack if the United States refused to change its position on China.

The developments of November and early December were simply an epilogue, for events were already determined. Since neither country would yield on the Chinese question, the special Japanese mission of Saburo Kurusu to Washington, as well as Secretary of State Hull's proposal for a ninety-day truce, were useless. Both governments were well aware of the fact. An intercepted Japanese message indicated on November 21 that war was impending at any time after November 29. On November 24 and again on the 27th, the day after the Japanese fleet had left Japan on its way to Pearl Harbor, American commanders in the Pacific area were warned that a Japanese assault on Guam and the Philippines was probably imminent. But neither the Administration nor the army or navy was convinced that Japan would have the temerity to strike at Hawaii. The President and the State Department were mainly concerned about a possible response to a Japanese attack on British and Dutch possessions in the Pacific. As American commanders had taken few precautions against attack, on Sunday, December 7, their naval and air units were as concentrated and as unprotected as if on parade. Within ninety minutes, the major part of the Pacific fleet, including eight battleships, had been either sunk or disabled while it slept in the warm Hawaiian morning sun. On nearby airfields the remains of American airpower lay shattered and smoking. Hours later, General Douglas MacArthur's bombing squadrons were destroyed in the Philippines.

By the greatest defeat in American military annals, Washington's perplexities about how to answer the Japanese challenge were dissolved. So, eventually, was the problem of how to enter the European war without alienating major segments of the American public. Feeling that they had been ruthlessly attacked for little or no cause, the American people stopped their debate over foreign policy and demanded retaliation. With only one dissenting vote, Congress passed the declaration of war against Japan on December 8.

Nothing official had been said so far in Washington about Germany and Italy, but on December 11, Hitler, committing another of his colossal mistakes, declared war against the United States. Had he not done so, American opinion might have insisted that the nation concentrate its energies in the Pacific, and the President would still have been confronted with the question of how to deploy forces against Germany. Congress answered Hitler's declaration of war on the same day with one of its own, and a thoroughly united nation grimly turned to fighting a global war.

Almost as soon as the shock of the Pearl Harbor debacle had subsided, Congress demanded an investigation of the apparent negligence that had made the disaster possible. Some former isolationists charged that the President himself had been remiss in not warning the armed forces, and the insinuation was clear that Roosevelt had goaded Japan into the attack to achieve his objective of entering the world conflict. After the war not a few writers and historians expanded these insinuations into charges that Roosevelt had secretly committed the nation, despite its obvious will to peace, to the British cause in the Atlantic sector and had contrived by arbitrary and unconstitutional methods to bring on war with Japan in order to achieve his ultimate aims. In most of such writings the conclusion, even if not precisely stated, was that the future would have been far happier had events in Europe and the Pacific been allowed to run their course without American intercession. From the evidence now at hand, it seems reasonably clear that Roosevelt wanted to join and would have joined the war against Germany at a much earlier stage had not public opinion and Congress restrained him. The record also indicates that the President cut his constitutional corners rather close in the destroyer deal. He withheld information from both Congress and the people and at other times even deliberately misinterpreted some of his more warlike actions so as to soften the attack of the isolationists. It is also clear that Roosevelt and Hull never really took either Congress or the people into their confidence in the delicate negotiations with Japan. A pragmatist, Roosevelt was never too concerned about means when he was convinced of the desirability of the end.

It is still, however, difficult or even impossible to say exactly what would have happened if either Roosevelt or his opponents had won an early victory in the prolonged isolationist-interventionist debate. If the United States had gone to war against Hitler before June 1941 Germany might never have invaded Russia, and the Soviet state at peace might have waxed even stronger than it did in war. It was probably to America's interest to keep Japan neutral as long as possible by paying a price in China, at the same time preventing Japan from overrunning all of South Asia. In the light of present developments, a Japanese-occupied China in 1946 might have been preferable to the China that fell before the Communists. But the mistake, if mistake it was, of pushing

Japan too far in 1941 was not Roosevelt's as much as it was the miscalculation of Hull and the State Department. The President was ready to negotiate with Japan in September 1941, and the present world might have been a happier one had he done so. But if a modus vivendi had been arranged in Asia, the question arises how would the United States have intervened in Europe? That intervention came none too soon. Had American participation been further delayed, the critical battles of El Alamein and Stalingrad in the fall of 1942 might both have been lost, with incalculable results, or Russia might possibly have fought its way back from defeat to become the liberator of most of Europe, thus bringing Communism to the shores of the Mediterranean and possibly to the Atlantic. Perhaps the most one can say is that American armed intervention in Europe was a necessity if a relatively free and decent society was to survive there, and that it occurred neither unreasonably early nor too late to preserve traditional European civilization.

6

The Divided World:
Foreign Policy, 1941–1960

THE PROBLEMS of the peacemakers in 1945 and 1946 were far more complex than those confronting the statesmen of Versailles in 1918 and 1919. In 1918 the Western democracies for a few precious moments of history had a virtual monopoly of power. Except for Japan, scarcely any significant organized power existed to contest their judgment. But in 1945 and 1946, Russia bulked ominously, not only because of its major contribution to victory, but also because of its central position in the European-Asiatic land mass, directly confronting the majority of the world's population. Russia also represented a new and as yet relatively untarnished revolutionary faith, whose promises to the impoverished masses were as unlimited as its demand for orthodoxy and its hostility to the underlying social assumptions of the West. Communism in 1918, a serious problem only in Russia and Central Europe, was after 1945 a major force threatening to overturn the entire colonial world and even some of the more enduring governments lying outside the Anglo-American orbit of relative stability.

In 1945 the world was in violent flux. The successive fall of France, Holland, Italy, Germany, and Japan, and the rapid decline of the British Empire, created turbulent changes in the power structures of Europe, Africa, and Asia. As the Europeans withdrew from their vast empires, Asian and African nationalism became quickly identified with both race and color, compounding the confusion.

By the end of the war the United States had mobilized over 16 million men and had extensively deployed them on every populated continent save South America. The total force represented by its land, air, and naval components was staggering. Measured either by its fire power or by its reach, nothing like it had hitherto been experienced.

Since its factories were producing over 45 per cent of the world's total armament, the United States was able to supply impressive amounts of weapons, food, and other equipment to all of her allies. By the end of the war the country had shipped under the Lend-Lease Act some $42 billion worth of material, of which 69 per cent went to Britain and 25 per cent to Russia, material which included locomotives, oil refineries, and rolling mills. Throughout the North African campaign, after the landings in Morocco and Algiers, up the Italian peninsula, on the beachheads of France, and in the Pacific, the weight of both men and material was contributed by America.

Consequently, even though the United States had entered the war almost two years after Great Britain had stubbornly faced the Nazi challenge virtually alone, American opinion weighed heavily at the British-American council tables planning the strategy of the war and the peace to follow. At Casablanca (January 1943), Quebec (August 1943), and Cairo (November 1943), where the United States, the British Empire, the Free French, and other allies had concluded their formal agreements, the judgments of Franklin Roosevelt, his Chief of Staff, George Marshall, and his Secretary of State, Cordell Hull, tended to prevail. Prime Minister Winston Churchill, backed by superb British staff work, was a formidable figure. But on most points of conflict, and there were not a few, the truth of the old saw of "he who pays the piper" was generally observed. One important exception, however, was the decision not to launch the cross-Channel attack that Russia had been pleading for in either 1942 or 1943. Despite the consensus among American military leaders that an attack was necessary to relieve the hard-pressed Russian armies, Roosevelt reluctantly, but probably wisely, agreed with the British leaders that such a gamble before 1944 was too hazardous.

Conversely, one of the more important military decisions affecting the shape of postwar Europe was contrary to British desires. From 1942 on Churchill had argued for a British-American thrust in the Eastern Mediterranean against the "soft underbelly of Europe," in the hope that a victorious campaign through Yugoslavia, Greece, or the Balkans might seal off the territory from the Russians and thus save the entire region from occupation by Communist troops. Upon American insistence that the military objective of destroying the German army was paramount to all other considerations, including the postwar political situation, the plan was dropped. This decision, coupled with the rapid advance of Russian troops in 1944, contributed to the Communist domination of Eastern Europe. As a compromise, partially meeting the Russian demands for relief and Churchill's plans for Southern and Central Europe, the North African and the succeeding Sicilian and Italian campaigns were fought. But as late as 1944 the United States government objected to a British campaign in Greece, a campaign that probably saved the country from a Communist dictatorship.

Despite such conflicts the relations between the two countries were remarkably smooth, partly because of the determination of Roosevelt and Churchill to agree, and partly because their goals for the postwar world were generally similar. No such harmony characterized either the British or the American relations with Russia. After agreeing on January 1, 1942, in Washington, not to make a separate peace with the Axis nations until victory was won, the three powers also pledged their support to the principles of the Atlantic Charter, a document previously signed by Roosevelt and Churchill. Among the first principles of the Charter were those of self-determination for all nations and peoples and a pledge against territorial aggrandizement. Nevertheless, on May 20, 1942, Soviet Foreign Minister Molotov demanded as the price for a British-Soviet alliance Britain's recognition of the Russian conquest of the small Baltic states, as well as large and vaguely defined parts of Poland, Finland, and Rumania. Supported by the

United States, the British refused the demands but still persuaded the Russians to sign the declaration. Regardless of Russia's temporary acquiescence, however, the fact that the Communist power had so promptly entered a territorial bill of demands foreshadowed a stormy future for relations between the partners in the Grand Alliance.

Relations between the three powers continued on an edgy basis as plans for the second front were repeatedly postponed. Stalin was clearly unenthusiastic about both the North African and the Italian campaigns and adamant against the British proposal for a thrust through the Balkans. As plans for a cross-Channel invasion matured, the Russian temper improved perceptibly. At a foreign ministers' meeting in Moscow in October 1943, the three powers apparently saw eye to eye on an American plan for the treatment of postwar Germany—the plan that, apart from precise territorial arrangements, became the basis for future policy. During the first meeting of Roosevelt, Churchill, and Stalin, at Teheran in November 1943, relations continued to improve. A second front was definitely promised for 1944, further conversations were held on Germany with the result that a proposed partition of Germany won informal agreement, and Stalin even seemed to approve of Roosevelt's general plans for a United Nations organization to police the world in the postwar era. The personal relations among the three leaders at Teheran were excellent, and Roosevelt believed that he had won Stalin away from his suspicious and cynical attitudes of the past.

The peak of cooperation between the three allies was reached at the Yalta Conference in February 1945. By that time Western troops were near the Rhine, and Russian forces were only fifty miles east of Berlin. Spring and good campaign weather alone were needed for the final crushing of the Nazi forces. The Yalta Conference was held to make definite arrangements, in anticipation of Germany's early collapse, for occupation zones to separate Russian from Western troops and thus prevent accidental conflict, and for the restoration of order in the occupied territories stretching from the Mediterranean to the Baltic. For eight days in Yalta Roosevelt, Churchill, and Stalin, accompanied by a crowd of diplomatic and military officials, met and worked out a host of agreements which were to go far to settle the future course of European and world affairs.

The three on whom the ultimate decisions rested were a remarkable trio. The affable squire and democratic politician from Hyde Park, upon whose aging features the marks of a final sickness were already etched, was faced by Churchill, the cultured aristocrat, a realist with a long historical memory, and by Joseph Stalin, ruthless revolutionist and dictator, whose mind and personal appearance bore the stamp of the Russian peasantry. Frequent disputes arose during the week at Yalta, but on all sides the spirit of compromise seemed to override the conflicts. The Yalta agreements provided for the division of Germany into three spheres, the eastern half to be occupied by Russia, the western by the United States and Britain. A restored Poland was to share in the division of East Prussia with Russia, and Russia was further to obtain sizable portions of what had been East Poland. Poland was to be compensated by annexations of portions of Eastern Germany, the exact boundaries left unspecified. On all these territorial matters the Russians won a reluctant consent from Roosevelt and Churchill. But Russia did agree, contrary to its previous stand, to permit France to share in the occupation of Germany and to participate in the combined control commission which was to oversee and unify occupation policy. Both Roosevelt and Churchill refused to accept the Soviet proposal that $20 billion be exacted from Germany as reparations, but they consented to use the Russian figure as a start for further negotiations and, indirectly at least, sanctioned the use of German prisoners for forced labor inside Russia and the removal of industrial facilities from Germany to Russia.

On the nature of the new Polish government Russia also retreated. In 1943 Russia had severed relations with the Polish government-in-exile in London, a group made up mainly of representatives of the peasants' party, dedicated to democracy, and had organized their own, Communist-dominated, Lublin provisional government. In the face of Roosevelt's and Churchill's adamant demands, Stalin at first offered to include representatives of the London group and finally to reconstitute the provisional government so that it would reflect "all democratic elements" in Poland and abroad. He coupled this offer with a promise of an early "democratic election" to determine the permanent nature of the Polish government. On the last day of the Yalta Conference, the American delegation made a proposal to extend the principles of the Polish settlement to all the liberated states in Eastern and Central Europe. This formula, promising so much on paper, was accepted without discussion or debate, probably because the Russians had made a prior agreement with the British about Southern Europe at the Moscow Conference of October 1944. The parties had agreed there that as long as the fighting endured Britain was to have the pre-eminent role in ordering Greek affairs, and Russia a similar one in Bulgaria and Rumania. The two powers promised to cooperate in the restoration of Yugoslavia and Hungary. Though Roosevelt had not consented to this division of spheres of influence, he had indicated that the United States would not play an active part in the restoration of Europe since he felt the problem was one largely for British determination.

A separate agreement, not published for over a year, was made between the United States and Russia on the Far East. In addition to the Kurile Islands and the southern half of Sakhalin, Russian influence in Outer Mongolia and Manchuria was assured by the promise to return all the concessions she had lost in the Russo-Japanese War. In return for these bountiful grants, Russia was obligated to recognize Chinese sovereignty in Manchuria and to conclude a treaty of alliance with the Chinese Nationalist Government. But the greatest *quid pro quo* that the United States obtained by the territorial concessions was the Russian promise to join the war against the Japanese within three months after the German surrender.

Returning from the Yalta meeting, Roosevelt and other high American officials were elated at what had been done there. Certain they had obtained a Russian commitment to cooperate in the building of a peaceful, democratic world, Roosevelt remarked on March 1 that never before had "the major allies been more closely united—not only in their war aims but also in their peace aims." Harry Hopkins stated that all the American delegates were "absolutely sure they had won the first great victory of the peace. . . ." "The Russians," he observed, "had proved that they could be reasonable and farseeing. . . ." After a visit to Moscow in April, General Eisenhower wrote: "Nothing guides Russian policy so much as desire for friendship with the United States."

This general jubilation over the Yalta results, however, was remarkably short-lived and was replaced with growing criticism that eventually swelled into a chorus of denunciation. Triggering the first doubts was the secret character of the agreements. When the news of the provision for three Russian votes leaked out, and subsequently the facts of the Far Eastern settlement were published, political opponents of the President asked what other portions of the treaty were still undisclosed. Turning over Chinese territory without Chiang Kai-shek's consent smacked of Munich, it was said. More importantly, Yalta had definitely prescribed the fundamental shape of the postwar settlement both in Europe and East Asia without either the advice or the consent of the Senate. The President and his aides had ignored the constitutional treaty-making powers and presented Congress with a *fait accompli* in much the same way as Woodrow Wilson had. Even so, the deluge of criticism did not appear until after Eastern Europe and China had been lost to the Communists. In 1950 Senator Robert Taft, looking ahead to the Presidential campaign of two years later, wrote that the Yalta Conference "handed Stalin the freedom of Eastern Europe and prepared our present peril."

Some legitimate criticisms can be brought against the Yalta agreement. Admitting that the territorial settlement in the Far East was tied in with military plans that had to be kept secret if they were to be effective, still members of Congress and especially some representatives of the opposition party should have been taken along to Yalta and consulted before commitments were given. The very fact of such consultation might have been of some value in demonstrating democratic ways to the Russians. Roosevelt's approval, implied or otherwise, of the Russian plan to use German prisoners of war as virtual slaves indicated a callousness to democratic-Christian values that was shocking. But as for the remainder of the Yalta pact, it probably gave the West more than could have been reasonably hoped for.

On the surface the Far Eastern arrangements looked like the granting of territory and concessions to the Communists without a proper return. But all the territory, as well as the concessions, had been taken from Russia in the 1905 Peace of Portsmouth. In return for the re-establishment of a Russian naval base at Port Arthur and the joint Chinese-Russian operation of the South Manchurian and the Chinese Eastern Railroads, a Russian alliance with the Chinese Nationalist Government insured that the Soviets would not recognize or support the Chinese Communists, whom, even before Japan's defeat, Chiang considered his major enemy.

As of February 1945 another major advantage accrued from the bargain. Japan had not yet been defeated, and most American intelligence reports indicated that victory in the Pacific would have to be won by an invasion of the Japanese home islands. According to the calculations of Generals Marshall and MacArthur, the American General Staff, and Winston Churchill, the assault on Japan would probably cost a million to a million and a half casualties. (The eighty-three-day battle for the island of Okinawa, which started April 1, 1945, was to result in almost 50,000 American casualties, including 15,520 dead.) It was obvious that if the Russian armies were to engage the Japanese-Manchurian forces, the cost in British and American lives would be materially reduced. Only after Japan's capitulation was it revealed that the submarine campaign had sapped the strength of the island empire to the extent that her early defeat was inevitable, a defeat that was further speeded up by the atomic bomb. But in February 1945 the work on the bomb was known only to a very few high American and British officials, and a good many of those who knew never expected it to materialize. "The bomb will never go off," Admiral Leahy, Chief of Staff, wrote in April, "and I speak as an expert in explosives."

As for the European end of the Yalta bargain, that, too, on a rational basis, was a good deal more than the Western allies could reasonably have hoped for. In February 1945 Russian troops were deployed along a much-indented line running south from Budapest and north to within fifty miles of Berlin; the Allies were still west of the Rhine, three hundred miles from the German capital. American military policy insured that the Russians would reach Berlin first and occupy Prague and Dresden. Since the Nazis were using most of their rapidly dwindling strength in the East, the Russian forces were held up at the Oder River for weeks, and Eisenhower could easily have entered Berlin and occupied Prague. Despite Churchill's plea to take Berlin, General Eisenhower argued that the city was no longer a military objective and chose, without consulting either Roosevelt or Churchill, to send his motorized forces into Bavaria. From there the capture of Prague was still possible before the Russians arrived. But after having first ordered General Patton to proceed to Prague, Eisenhower revoked the command. Ignoring Churchill's reiterated pleas to "shake hands with the Russians as far east as possible," he withdrew his troops to west of the Elbe River, permitting the Soviet forces to liberate Czechoslovakia, all of Eastern Germany, and Berlin. Had Franklin Roosevelt still been alive, the war in Germany might have ended otherwise. But President Truman, who had succeeded Roosevelt on April 12, 1945, apparently agreed with the opinion of the American military that the British were only seeking "to complicate the war," with their political and other nonmilitary objectives. Inexperienced, and with little knowledge of what had gone before, Truman supported his generals and left the Russians in possession of most of Eastern Europe. Such possession was more than nine points of the law; as events turned out in Eastern Europe, it was all the law.

The fact that Russia, supposedly dedicated to the Communist faith which was to wipe out all the old iniquities of capitalistic imperialism, should have been the one major victorious power to have practiced the ancient game of grabbing territory from the defeated, is irony compounded. But on any sort of rational basis it was to be expected that Russia would have a major hand in ordering the destinies of the newly reconstructed states of Eastern Europe. The Soviets had suffered over 6 million battle deaths compared to a total of a little over 650,000 for the United States and Great Britain. Although the aerial devastation of Great Britain was appalling, Russia had been invaded, as her two major allies had not. This invasion had cost at least 10 million civilian casualties and heavy property losses in most of the prime industrial and agricultural parts of the Soviet territory. At the end of the war, Stalin was alleged to have said that the British contributed time to the Allied victory, the United States supplied the goods, but Russia paid in blood. Throwing into the common account the heroic British resistance to the Nazis and the massive aid which the United States had furnished, there was no gainsaying that the major part of the German army was destroyed on the Russian steppes.

In demanding at Yalta that the governments of Poland, Czechoslovakia, Hungary, Yugoslavia, Rumania, and Bulgaria be "friendly" governments, Stalin was doing no more than any Western power would have done in similar circumstances; in fact, exactly what they did do in Greece and Italy, where the governments were threatened by Communism. If Stalin and the other Russian representatives at Yalta did not interpret the phrases that were supposed to govern the development of peacetime governments in Eastern Europe very differently from the interpretations of Western statesmen, the Russians were badly outmaneuvered, and sacrificed vital national interests. The other possible explanation of the Russians' acquiescence was that they were so confident of the popularity of Communism that they assumed that any government in Eastern Europe, even though democratically selected, would choose to be a Communist one. Whatever the explanation, Roosevelt and Churchill won an astounding victory at Yalta—too astounding to endure. Among topflight Western statesmen, only Churchill was inclined to be gloomy about the future. His gloom probably came from his superb insight into what was and what was not possible in foreign relations.

Predictably, the good will generated at Yalta lasted scarcely longer than it took the various representatives to return to their countries. Essentially what dashed the high hopes that had been raised was the developments in the liberated countries of Eastern Europe. As Poland, Hungary, Rumania, and Bulgaria were invaded by the Russians and the Nazi-dominated governments driven out, a tripartite Allied control commission was set up in each instance, but weeks before Yalta these commissions were not working as the Western powers felt they should. Within two weeks after Yalta Russian representatives in Rumania charged that the existing cabinet, mainly representing the peasant party, was harboring Fascists, and without consultation with the Control Commission the Russians forced the Radescu government out by an ultimatum and replaced it by a Communist-dominated one. The Lublin government organized by the Russians in Poland had been thoroughly Communist from its inception, and despite the Yalta promises no democratic additions were made, nor were the Western representatives of the Control Commission consulted or even permitted to observe what was being done outside of Warsaw. But it should be pointed out that simultaneously American and British representatives in Italy, although disputing among themselves about the nature of the new central government, were carefully, if subtly, excluding Communists from participation in it. In Greece Western domination was neither careful nor subtle. There a great portion of the countryside and a good part of Athens were controlled by native Communists. Supplied with arms from Yugoslavia, Albania, and Bulgaria, the Communists threatened to overturn the weak British-sponsored government and dominate the country. They were stopped by British troops in a pitched battle in Athens, and afterwards sixty thousand British troops joined in a nationwide campaign against the Communists.

Both the American and the British government protested vigorously against the developments in Rumania and especially in Poland. Roosevelt pointed out to Stalin that the Yalta agreement was "breaking down." Stalin admitted the deadlock, but charged that the two Western powers had equally violated the agreement in Italy and Greece. By the time of the Potsdam Conference of the three powers, in July 1945, on the question of Eastern Europe, the deadlock was complete. In Potsdam Churchill made his famous charge that the Soviets had placed an "iron fence" around the British and American representatives in Eastern Europe, a remark which eventually was to pass into the vocabulary of the Western world as the "Iron Curtain" separating the East from the West, Communism from democracy, autocracy from freedom. It was also at Potsdam that the Russians, showing an increasing appetite for territory, as well as a lack of appreciation of the rising storm in Asia and Africa against Western imperialism, demanded a share of the Italian colonies. The demand was sidestepped but perhaps should have been granted. Russia's seizure of a part of Africa might have done much to destroy the myth that she was the only friend of the Afro-Asians in their struggle to free themselves from the West.

The term "cold war" was not used until 1947, but its antecedents actually began before the Potsdam Conference. During the last few weeks of his life, Roosevelt was exasperated with Russia's actions in Eastern Europe and more so by Stalin's veiled accusation that he and Churchill were seeking to make a separate peace with Germany. Stalin was equally irritated by the Western criticism of his Eastern European policy. For a time Russia refused to send Molotov to the scheduled San Francisco Conference, where it was hoped that all the nations allied against Germany would organize a world organization based on the agreements made at Dumbarton Oaks. The tension between the Western allies and Russia rapidly increased after Roosevelt's death. In major part this was due to the diverging and perhaps irreconcilable interests of the former alliance partners; in part it was also due to the conditions surrounding Harry Truman's succession to the Presidency.

Neither Roosevelt nor Congressional leaders had ever seriously expected that Harry Truman could achieve the Presidency. By no means without ability, Truman in his previous political career in Missouri and in the United States Senate had been successful but not outstanding. His nomination as a candidate for the Vice-Presidency had been compounded of compromise and expediency. When Southerners and conservatives objected to renomination of Henry Wallace in 1944, a combination of big-city machine

Democrats, ardent New Dealers, and labor leaders, who were running the convention for Roosevelt, found in Truman the almost-perfect candidate to recement the quarrelling factions. No politician in either party disliked the jaunty and friendly Senator from Missouri. He was a convivial fellow without personal complexities, always ready to help a colleague of either party when he could, and never known to take an extreme stand or to offend anyone, save on the stump or on the floor of the Senate when debating a party issue. By family he had Southern connections, and his rise in politics had come largely through the support of the Pendergast machine in Kansas City. In his early career he had been conservative on economic issues, but he was such a good organization Democrat that his voting record in the Senate was almost straight New Deal. Roosevelt's opinion of Truman was indicated by the fact that he rarely saw the Vice-President and seldom asked his counsel. And what Harry Truman thought of himself is obvious from his statement, when he first learned of Roosevelt's death, that "the moon, the stars, and all the planets" had fallen on him.

Truman rapidly gained a measure of self-confidence. But in the summer and fall of 1945, without experience or first-hand knowledge of many of the great foreign problems confronting the nation, he very naturally relied upon his advisers in the State Department, where Russian policy was largely determined by the information sent by the American representatives from Moscow. There Ambassador W. Averill Harriman and his most trusted adviser, George F. Kennan, had come to the conclusion that Russia wanted to dominate not only Eastern Europe but as much of the remainder of the world as possible, and that any hope for American cooperation with the Soviets was futile. On his first day in office, Truman later recalled, he was presented with a policy paper by the State Department which conveyed this attitude, and within a week the new President had come to the conclusion that American dealings with the Russians had been a "one-way street," and he made up his mind that the pattern "could not continue." At the Potsdam Conference in August 1945, and afterward, the President apparently accepted the thesis that by the terms of the Yalta agreements the United States and Britain were entitled to act unilaterally in Greece and Italy, whereas Russia was bound by her word to obtain Western consent for the reinstitution of civil governments in Eastern Europe. When the Soviets ignored the West in their dealings with Rumania and Poland, Truman concluded that the Russians were "not serious about the peace" and "were planning world conquest." The President was a remarkably stubborn man and a highly partisan one. Once having taken a position in domestic politics, he was rarely inclined to back down and accept a compromise. His favorite way of meeting opposition was to attack it head on, and so he did with the Russians. On the reconstruction of Southern European governments after Potsdam there was little or no consultation with Russian representatives. Immediately after the defeat of Japan American lend-lease shipments to Russia were stopped abruptly, whereas those to Western European countries continued. Prior to the summer of 1945 there had been extended discussions in Washington about the possibility of American aid in the repair of Russian war damage. Nothing was done, whereas a large loan was made to Britain. On the basis of experience in Poland and Rumania, Truman decided that he would not allow the Russians any part in the control of Japan. Although the term was not yet current, the "cold war" had been declared. Each side distrusted the motives of the other and each sought to profit at the expense of the other.

In the meantime Russia was hastening to communize all the governments of Eastern Europe, and through native Communist parties sought to subvert Western democratic regimes. In the United Nations it attempted, by consistent use of the veto, to thwart all efforts to revitalize economic life in Europe and the Middle East. An unreconstructed Lublin regime became the official Communist government of Poland, which, by a unilateral agreement with Russia, was given all the former German territory east of the Oder River. Since Russian troops occupied Eastern Germany, the communizing process went on there faster than in the so-called independent states. The Czechoslovakian government, which up to June 1948 still contained remnants of democratic parties, was remodelled under Russian pressure. In early March Jan Masaryk had either committed suicide or been murdered, and this ominous event was followed on June 10 by President Eduard Beneš' resignation, whereupon the unalloyed Communist government of Klement Gottwald was instituted. On May 30, 1947, the Hungarian Communists, supported by the threat of Russian arms, removed Premier Ferenc Nagy from office, and the usual one-party dictatorship followed. As early as 1945 Josip Broz (Tito) had instituted his own form of Communism in Yugoslavia, and in Rumania all chance of opposing the ruling Communist regime was dissipated by the abdication of King Michael on December 30, 1947. In Greece the government had been able to survive against armed Communist bands only by massive British support. The Greek Communists, a United Nations investigating committee reported, were being regularly supplied from the neighboring Communist countries of Bulgaria, Yugoslavia, and Albania. With British support, the tottering Turkish government was just able to stave off Russian pressure against the Straits. And in Iran a Russian scheme to set up a separate Communist state in the province of Azerbaijan was foiled by a United Nations' threat to investigate and by severe American pressure.

Future Russian policy was clearly indicated as early as February 1946, when an ominous shift took place in both military and economic planning. Demobilization of the army was abruptly stopped, and the emphasis in the current five-year plan was changed from consumers' goods to armaments. In the spring of 1946, when the American army was hard put to find adequate personnel for the occupying forces in Japan and Germany, the Russian army numbered at least 4 million men. A year later the Cominform was organized to take the place of the old Comintern as an international weapon of propaganda and subversion. The elaborate Russian spy system was further enlarged, and in every country where Communists were numerous strikes were called for obvious political purposes. At the diplomatic bargaining table Soviet strategy consisted of repeating the arguments supporting its case ad infinitum. At numerous foreign ministers' meetings provided for by the Potsdam Conference, peace treaties with Italy, Bulgaria, Hungary, and Rumania were finally accepted, the first on mostly pro-Western terms, the rest on those of Russia. But on the problems of German borders, German reparations, and the ultimate nature of the German state no agreement was possible. Similar deadlocks were encountered in the Security Council of the United Nations, where Russia could impose a veto. In the General Assembly the Soviets resorted to a walkout when the debate was critical of Russian policy or the vote on important matters seemed likely to go against them.

By 1946 and 1947 the nature of Russian foreign policy had become clear. First, the Soviets had foreclosed any hopes they may once have had of advancing international Communism by cooperating with the West. They had decided that little could be obtained by international conferences dominated by a majority vote, and that they could use such meetings only to score propaganda successes. Second, in view of the United States atomic monopoly they considered a direct military challenge too risky. Internal subversion was therefore the only effective weapon left to them in advancing Communism. Favoring this traditional Communist technique were the flourishing state of Communist parties in most Western countries and the deplorable condition of the Western European economies.

Despite American credits, loans, and outright gifts of $11 billion to rehabilitate the economic life of Western Europe, deprivation and want was the normal state of millions in the Low Countries, Western Germany, France, Italy, the Balkans, and the Middle East. Throughout Europe, millions of refugees were seeking new homes. Millions more returning to their old homes found nothing but destruction. Children were without families and women without men. Because of the catastrophic destruction of productive and transportation facilities, hunger was the normal lot—a condition which, of course, led to severe erosion of whatever social and personal ethics had survived the war. Even in Britain the destruction of material and spiritual resources had been so great that both the ability and the inclination to rebuild society were at a perilous minimum. As Winston Churchill observed, Europe was "a rubble heap, a charnel house, a breeding-ground of pestilence and hate." This condition, he might have added, constituted an almost perfect culture for the rapid growth of Communism. Assaulted by the enormous power of Russia on its perimeter and by steady social decay in its interior, Europe was almost helpless. The only possible source of aid against either or both of these threats was the United States.

After the war American policy was premised upon the assumption that after an initial period of short duration Europe would be able to rebuild its own economy. American troops might have to remain in Germany for some time, but apparently no American leader seriously thought that either American arms or American financial aid would be necessary in the period of reconstruction. In discussing the shape of postwar Greece Roosevelt declared that that nation was a British problem and added that he was opposed to involving the United States in any postwar European commitments. Consequently the demobilization of America's troops went on with almost indecent haste as both soldiers and their families at home put pressure on Congress for their speedy return. By 1946 American armed strength had dwindled to a minimum of 2,200,000 men, which was scarcely enough to provide adequately for the occupation forces in Germany and Japan. It was at this juncture that American leadership began to perceive the enormity of its past miscalculations. Soviet cooperation was not forthcoming. Russia had recovered far more rapidly than had been thought possible. Europe was not able to reconstruct itself, and the obvious reluctance of the United States to use the atomic bomb, save for defense, cancelled out a great portion of the power inherent in its exclusive possession. Moreover, against the Russian-stimulated process of internal subversion in Western Europe, the bomb was a weapon without a sting.

During the perilous years of 1946 and 1947, Harry Truman became President in fact, as well as in title. Few men in the history of the United States have been confronted with such awesome problems with so little preparation for them. And few men have risen to meet the occasion so fully as the one-time haberdasher from Independence, Missouri. Repeatedly the President asked Congress for a new selective service act, a request distinctly not popular in the postwar climate of opinion. Congress first responded with a limited one-year extension of the wartime act. In 1947, acknowledging the rising tensions, it reluctantly passed a much stronger measure. But the most drastic changes in American policy were still to come. They were sparked by Russia's growing militancy and by Europe's utter inadequacy to meet either the exterior challenge of Soviet force or the interior threat of Communist subversion.

Washington was, of course, informed about the mounting peril to Europe. But the full extent of the impending disaster was not recognized until Britain told the United States, in early 1947, that because of her critical domestic situation she would have to recall all of her troops from Greece and stop whatever aid she had been giving to Turkey. The probable result, the British note intimated, was that the governments of both countries would collapse before the Communist thrust. With the lend-lease program of 1941 as a model the President, on March 12, asked Congress for a $400 million appropriation with which to supply the two endangered countries with economic and military aid. But this step, revolutionary in itself, was just a beginning. Speaking at Harvard College on June 5, Secretary of State George Marshall called for a massive aid program for the harassed European democracies with the purpose not of relief but of rebuilding Europe's productive resources. Any government willing to assist in the task of reconstruction, Marshall promised, would be welcome.

Neither aid to Greece and Turkey nor the proposed $17 billion reconstruction program for Western Europe went through Congress without stiff opposition from a variety of sources. Led by Henry Wallace and Senators Pepper of Florida and Taylor of Idaho, a left group saw in the so-called Marshall Plan a scheme to wreck all chances of cooperation with Soviet Russia and to establish a new type of American imperialism. Labelling it a "martial plan," Wallace warned it might well lead to war. Supported by domestic Communists, some pacifists, and other leftists, this group attacked the "reactionary" nature of the Turkish and

Greek governments and argued that any such aid should be channelled through the United Nations. On the right a group of Republican Senators led by Robert Taft of Ohio, Kenneth Wherry of Nebraska, and George W. Malone of Nevada argued that the revolutionary scheme would lead either to war or to national bankruptcy. The new Republican House of Representatives elected in 1946, the first since 1928, was especially sensitive to economic arguments. After fifteen years of New Deal and wartime deficit financing, it was eager to balance the national budget and reduce taxes. In view of the pent-up domestic demand for goods, it was argued, a further drain-off by Europe would produce unmanageable inflation. An extreme nationalist note was sounded to the effect that if the plan were a failure, it would be pouring money down a rat hole, but if successful, it would build up in Europe competitors for American foreign trade. Still another bloc deplored the exclusive concentration on Europe and insisted that stopping Communism in Asia was just as important, if not more so.

Most of the Republican Congressional exponents of these arguments came from either the isolationist or the unilateral nationalist pre-Pearl Harbor traditions. These groups, stemming in large part from the trans-Appalachian West, had been defeated in the 1940 Republican National Convention by the internationalist-minded and for the most part Eastern Republicans. Again in 1944, when the issue was more sharply drawn, they were thwarted by the nomination of Thomas E. Dewey. But they still had substantial strength throughout the country and probably even more in the newly elected Republican Congress. Had it not been for the leadership of Senator Arthur H. Vandenberg of Michigan, both Greek and Turkish aid and the Marshall Plan might have been lost. A leading conservative and noninterventionist in the prewar years, he had, as late as 1943, supported the isolationist position at a meeting of the Republican National Committee. Nevertheless, showing a rare capacity to change his mind, Vandenberg supported aid to Turkey and Greece and led the fight for the adoption of the Marshall Plan. After insisting on a survey of American resources to see what burdens could safely be carried on a one-and-a-half-billion-dollar reduction in the amount to be appropriated the first year, and on an amendment that would permit future Congresses to determine yearly the specific sum to be appropriated, Vandenberg pledged the support of the Republican organization in the Senate. In one of the most important speeches ever made from the Senate floor, he stated that the plan sought "peace and stability" for over 270 million people of the stock that had made America. The United States would be less than true to its heritage or to its own self-interest if it permitted "this vast friendly segment of the earth" to collapse before internal decay or Russian aggression.

After six weeks of debate Congress, which had already voted aid to Greece and Turkey, passed the European Recovery Program. By 1955 over $13 billion had been spent under its provisions. The results of the plan, which the *Economist* described as "the most straight-forwardly generous thing that any country has ever done for others," were remarkable. The Western European transportation system was restored, agriculture was mechanized, new mines were dug, and hydroelectric dams and factories were built. By 1950 Western European industrial production had increased by 60 to 70 per cent, that of agriculture by 25 per cent. Within five more years the per capita production of the area exceeded the prewar level, an event that set the stage for a subsequent wave of prosperity exceeding even that of the palmy days of 1928 and 1929. Under the Truman aid program Greece and Turkey were strengthened and saved from Communist aggrandizement. By 1960 Western Europe had been so invigorated that it was challenging the United States for economic and political leadership of the free world. The Marshall Plan had succeeded beyond the wildest expectations anticipated for it.

Even while the Marshall Plan was being debated, two other schemes for the strengthening of free Europe were vigorously supported by the United States. The first envisioned the unification of Germany as a step toward the restoration of self-government and industrial productivity. The second, much more radical and daring in scope, looked toward a unified free Europe bound together by both economic and defense agreements. Unquestionably the industrial heart of prewar Europe had been Germany. Thus, Western European economic recovery could never be complete unless it included a revitalized Germany. This objective could not be achieved as long as the conquered country was divided into four occupation zones.

American policy in 1946 was pointed toward the objective of the unification of Germany, its industrial restoration and its reintegration in the economic life of Western Europe. This was an exceedingly touchy problem. The British had not forgotten or forgiven the German bombings, and the French fear of a revitalized Germany was understandable. But the greatest obstacle was Russia, whose fear of a united Germany was and remained almost pathological. Many times approached on the subject, the Russians demanded as a price for their agreement a major voice in the control of the new state and in the future development of the Ruhr Valley, which contained the great iron and coal complex basic to the economy of Western Europe. Significantly, the Russians did not offer the Western Allies a share in the control of the Silesian coal and iron district which lay in the Russian sector.

Since Communist intervention in Western Germany and the Ruhr was too high a price to pay, the Western countries, in February 1948, agreed to unite their three zones of Germany without Russian cooperation. Subsequently a German constitution was adopted, and in May 1949 the German Federal Republic was recognized and included in the scope of the Marshall Plan. Russian reaction to this *démarche* was quick. Throughout Eastern Europe the Communist parties launched a campaign to eliminate all opposition elements. The Czechoslovakian government was completely dominated by the Communists. In Hungary bourgeois and peasant parties were declared illegal, and so much pressure was brought on Yugoslavia to follow the Russian line that Marshal Tito severed relations with the Soviets. To culminate the counterattack Western Berlin was blockaded and the East German Peoples' Republic organized. Had the Russians been able to force the Western allies out of Berlin, the results might have been catastrophic for the Western position in Europe, as well as in Asia and Africa.

Although there had been much diplomatic bickering and angry invective between Russia and the West up to April 1, 1948, neither side had used force to win territory that had been occupied by the armed forces of the other at the end of the war. But Russia broke that uneasy stalemate in April 1948 by curtailing the overland traffic between West Germany and Berlin, where two million people were threatened with the alternatives of starvation or a dependence upon Communist supplies, which would mean eventual Communist domination. Militarily the Western position in Berlin was a poor one since neither at Yalta nor at Potsdam had the West obtained guarantees of land transit across Russian-occupied Germany, and an attempt to force a passage would bring the onus of starting a war. On the other hand, to write off Berlin meant acquiescence before a Russian show of force and the transfer of 2 million free people to a dictatorship. President Truman's decision to fly supplies to Berlin by an airlift, supported by force if necessary, through air space guaranteed to the West, was inspired not only by a determination to save West Berlin but also by a desire to indicate America's readiness to fight for freedom anywhere in the world. Although both the American and British air commands had warned their governments that the feat was impossible, the airlift actually increased the quantity of Berlin's supplies throughout the following winter.

Russia's lifting of the blockade in May 1949 without challenging the airlift was a capitulation of enormous benefit to the West. It heartened the forces of freedom everywhere and gave impetus to the Truman policy for a united defense of Western Europe. Months prior to the Berlin blockade, the United States had encouraged Western Europe to combine in a mutual defense pact providing for a common army. But to implement the agreement the United States had to promise that she would join and support the united effort. As a result the President announced, on March 18, 1949, the ratification of the North Atlantic Treaty, by which Canada and the United States, in association with ten Western European countries, agreed to create a common army for the defense of Europe. The North Atlantic Treaty Organization was as much a revolutionary step for the United States as it was for the participating European countries. In pledging the United States to help resist aggression against any member state, it violated long-cherished foreign policy doctrines, and the pact was not accepted without violent protest from Congressional traditionalists. Again, as in domestic policy, the roll of the protestants indicated their rural and inland backgrounds. Thirteen votes were cast against the pact, only one of which, that of Oregon's Guy Cordon, came from a state with an ocean border, and one, that of Ralph E. Flanders of Vermont, from a state east of the Appalachians.

In a subsequent debate in 1951 over the President's ordering of four army divisions to Europe, Senator Taft of Ohio led the attack by questioning the constitutionality of the act, which was executed without the consent of Congress and which committed forces to a command over which the Chief Executive had no definite control. Taft also doubted the wisdom of placing any major land forces on a foreign continent in peace or war, because he maintained that America's power was limited and the country did not have the resources to control the world's "air and the sea and also the land." Conceding, however, that the old isolationism was a thing of the past, the Senator accepted the necessity for protecting "the island democracies" if attacked and if victory were possible.

As a counterproposal to the North Atlantic Treaty, Senator Taft and ex-President Hoover argued for a massive air and naval build-up on the North American continent. In case of Communist aggression, this force might be utilized if the facts warranted. The Taft-Hoover doctrine, variously called "continentalism," "fortress America," and "the principle of the free hand," attracted the support of a rapidly developing neo-isolationist–unilateralist group in the Republican Party, as well as that of the so-called Asia Firsters. The latter group was not isolationist but advocated using America's strength in Asia rather than in Europe. Despite all criticisms the North Atlantic Treaty was approved by the Senate by a vote of 82–13, and the United States had merged its future security for an indefinite period of years with that of Western Europe.

Although many of the ideas behind the revolutionary Truman foreign policy came from a variety of advisers, the ultimate responsibility for all of them belonged to the President, who before he succeeded to the office had apparently been little concerned with affairs outside of the nation. Yet in its totality the Truman program contained almost every controlling principle characterizing American policy in Europe through at least the succeeding Eisenhower and Kennedy-Johnson administrations. In essence it was an aggressive policy of defending every Western European state either from direct challenge from Russia or from the subtler menace of internal subversion. It further sought to increase the power of the West by organizing a unified Europe, both militarily and economically. Although militant in its defense of free Europe, the Truman policy never sought by force to convert once-held Communist lands to a non-Communist life. It was essentially a policy of "containment"—a word first used by George Kennan in 1947—a policy that recognized in fact, if not by oral profession, the settlement made at the end of the war by the occupying armies. Western political and economic institutions were to dominate the western and southern parts of Europe, while Soviet institutions were to dominate the East. Measured by its real aims as distinguished from its hopes, the Truman policy was eminently successful. Nothing had been lost from the European territory occupied by Western troops in May and June of 1945; nothing had been gained. Without any official treaties or agreement a European settlement that was to last for a considerable period had been made by tacit understanding. When serious rebellions broke out in Poland, Eastern Germany, and Hungary, the West did nothing to aid the rebels in their attempts to overthrow Communist institutions. Likewise Russia, except in Berlin, never openly challenged the hold Western institutions had upon the lands west of the Iron Curtain. A kind of precarious peace thus came to Europe, a peace that provided the time desperately needed to reconstruct political and economic institutions necessary for vigorous social life. Although many of the details of American postwar European policy could be criticized, in its larger design it was eminently sound, both in formulation and in execution.

If a measure of peace and stability had been won for Western institutions in Europe by the Truman policy, as much cannot be said for Asia. In the Orient the cards were ever so much more stacked against free government. For centuries Asia had been characterized by overpopulation, hunger, and autocratic government. Great portions of the continent in the nineteenth century had to submit to Western imperialism, an imperialism which extracted both the wealth and the self-pride of the native population, at the same time introducing them to the sight but not the possession of Western technology. During World War II the myth of Western supremacy had been shattered by the Japanese. At the end of the war, it was doubtful whether the once-great European nations were any longer powerful enough to hold their Asian empires. Consequently, a nationalism evolved, closely identified with a racial mystique born of resentment against the West and fed by the expectation of an economic and technological development sufficient to provide something better than the marginal life most of the continent's population had experienced in the past. Compounding the Asian confusion at the end of the war was the rapid destruction of old political units and the rise of innumerable new ones, unstable by nature and even explosive.

With the defeat of Japan and the increasing withdrawal of British, French, and Dutch power, one of the few familiar native prewar governments with a chance of exercising enough authority to continue its existence was that of Chiang Kai-shek's Nationalist regime in China. But even Chiang's government was in danger of falling before the explosive fury of one of the new forces sweeping the continent. Whether because of its upper-class origins or because it had been continually attacked by Western imperialism, foreign foes, and native warlords, Chiang's Nationalist movement had scarcely made a dent in China's massive problems. Consequently, out of the continuing chaos Communism had grown rapidly before and during the Japanese war. By 1943 the Communists had established a government in Yenan and from that point were fighting both the Japanese and the Nationalist forces. So threatening had they become that by 1944 Chiang was using almost half a million of his troops against them.

Prior to 1945 American policy had been directed toward getting the two Chinese factions to cooperate in fighting the Japanese. Both of President Roosevelt's representatives to Chiang, General Patrick J. Hurley and Henry Wallace, exerted themselves to this end. In Asia as in Europe the immediate military problem took precedence over long-run political objectives. But after numerous attempts to win an agreement between Chiang and the Communists had proved futile, a bitter dispute broke out among American advisers in China and Washington. Some of the military, exasperated at Chiang's use of arms against the Communists instead of the Japanese, and appalled at the corruption, inefficiency, and weakness that characterized the Chungking regime, argued that the Nationalist government was impossible to deal with. They were joined by a substantial section of the diplomatic advisers on China, especially after a group of American journalists returned from the Yenan Communist headquarters with glowing reports of the contrasting honesty, efficiency, and singleness of purpose that they found there. The Yenan group won further American support when it was described in State Department reports as not being really Communist in nature but only "agrarian." This conclusion seemed to be supported by Stalin's repeated assurances that he was not interested in their future since they were "pseudo-Communists." Despite this growing disposition to look upon the Yenan Communists with favor, Roosevelt concentrated all American support behind the Nationalists, and at the end of the war Chiang's forces were excellently equipped with American arms.

By December 1945 the Yenan Communists also had gained much strength. They had shared in the prestige won by the victory over the Japanese. More importantly, Russian armies operating in Manchuria had turned over to them armaments captured from the defeated Japanese. In the opinion of the American commander in China, General Albert G. Wedemeyer, Chiang's government and army were no match for the Communists without substantial American help. Wedemeyer further insisted that a victory for the Yenan group would be a victory for world Communism and would imperil America's position in the Orient. The United States was faced with three alternatives: (1) to extend major aid to Chiang and possibly participate in the civil war to insure a Communist defeat, (2) to attempt to get an armistice agreement between the two warring factions and organize a coalition government with representatives of both sides participating, (3) to retire from the field completely and permit the issue to be settled by the continuing civil war.

After much discussion Washington decided upon the middle course, at the same time maintaining a sizable aid program amounting to $700 million in two years for the Nationalists. In December 1945 General Marshall went to China to try to secure peace and establish a coalition government. For almost thirteen months he worked assiduously at his task and at one time actually arranged a cease fire, as well as an agreement for a coalition government pending a constitutional convention elected by democratic means. But a lack of good faith on both sides wrecked the agreement, and in January 1947 Marshall quit China for good and returned to Washington as the new Secretary of State, angrily denouncing both the Communists and the Nationalists. After Marshall's return to the United States and the evacuation of American forces, the Nationalist position steadily deteriorated. Although superior in equipment and numbers, the Nationalists were no match for the zealous Communist armies. In a few months the battle for China had become a rout, whole Nationalist divisions, many of them supplied with American equipment, deserting to the Reds. By October 1949 Chiang Kai-shek had fled to Formosa, and the red flag of Communism waved over all China. Immediately after their victory the Chinese "agrarian Communists" began a crusade to eliminate all Americans and American influence from East Asia, meanwhile boasting of their fidelity to Marxian Leninism and to Moscow.

The Chinese Communist victory was probably the greatest diplomatic defeat in the history of the United States. More than a few reasons made it an especially bitter dose for many

Americans to take. For years China had been a favorite arena for American missionary efforts. Although the traditional diplomatic policy toward China contained many elements of commercial self-interest, it had been consistently pointed toward the preservation of that country. During the war Roosevelt worked toward the construction of a powerful postwar China, in the hope that it would offset both Japanese and Russian power in Asia. At the Cairo and Teheran Conferences, China was granted the rather unwarranted status of membership in the big-four powers who, in Roosevelt's thinking, were to police the world in the future. Now, despite all these efforts, the United States had, instead of a major friend in Asia, a most powerful foe.

Red China, possessing a major portion of the world's land surface and population, was potentially the greatest power in the Orient. Additionally, she could call upon the help of millions of Chinese living throughout South Asia and the Pacific. By using race, color, and Western imperialism she could brew an explosive anti-Western mixture, one difficult for the West to neutralize. With such advantages the Communist appeal to the uneducated and impoverished Asiatic masses was considerably enhanced and that of Western ideology diminished. Considering the serious issues at stake and the advantages the United States had had in China at the end of the war, it is small wonder that many Americans, and especially the Republican opposition in Congress, felt that the China policy had been characterized either by colossal stupidity or by a criminal Communist conspiracy or possibly both.

What had gone wrong? Many factors were involved: inexperience, misjudgment, insistence upon immediate military gains irrespective of future political developments, and finally the reluctance of the American people to become involved again in a major Asiatic war. American inexperience in dealing with the Orient had tended to overemphasize the corruption of Chiang Kai-shek's regime, which was undeniably intense by Western standards but apparently average for the Orient. A part of the difficulty came also from the American attempt to operate democratically in an essentially undemocratic country. The assumption made by a group of diplomats, journalists, and generals that the Yenan Communists were simple agrarian radicals rather than Marxian revolutionists was one of the most invalid in recent history. The pursuit of military values at the expense of political ones was exhibited again in the American insistence that Chiang stop fighting the Yenan group and cooperate with it instead. From the vantage point of futile hindsight it seems reasonably clear that the only possible chance, and that a slim one, to have saved China was to offer Chiang massive aid, insisting on the reformation of the Nationalist government, and to cooperate in the defeat of the Yenan Communists. This program in all probability would have required the commitment of American armies as well as funds and supplies. And precisely at the time when American resources were being marshalled to stop the march of Communism in Europe, an Asiatic war was the last thing wanted by any Congressional group save for the most ardent Asia Firsters.

The predictable consequences of the Chinese debacle were soon apparent. Less than a year after the Communist victory, the Red campaign against French Indochina was intensified. And on June 25, 1950, a well-equipped North Korean Communist army invaded South Korea. The attack on South Korea was undoubtedly related to Russia's successful development of an atomic bomb in late 1949. It was also probably inspired by Secretary of State Dean Acheson's policy statement that the United States would protect Japan and the Philippines from aggression but that it could not be expected to defend Korea, Formosa, or the East Asia mainland.

The Korean War was far more extensive than a "police action," as it was first described. By the time the war ended in the armistice of July 1953, it had cost the United States over 35,000 dead and missing soldiers, over 100,000 wounded, and expenditures of over $22 billion. Save for the expenditures, these figures were dwarfed by the South Korean military and civilian casualties. The events surrounding the Korean War were not totally bleak. Due to a temporary Russian boycott of the United Nations, the Security Council was able to act without the inevitable

Soviet veto. On June 25, one day after the invasion of South
Korea, the Security Council unanimously branded the North
Korean attack as aggression and demanded that the Communist
troops be recalled. President Truman's announcement twenty-
four hours later that American land and naval forces would be
sent to Korea did not have official Congressional sanction, but it
was convincing evidence to the world's dictators that in the
future they could not count on the traditional slow response of
democracies. The Security Council's adoption of the American
resolution calling on all member states to contribute forces to
repel the aggression was a vast step forward by the family of nations in the long and stumbling pursuit of security against un-
provoked attacks. By the end of the Korean War sixteen nations
were contributing token amounts of men and supplies to an international army. For the first time in history such an international assembly was paying out blood and money for a cause
unrelated to any immediate hopes for gain of territory or loot.

The international character of the Korean hostilities was not
without its disadvantages. After the Chinese Communists entered
the war, a grave question divided the nations: whether to attack
Communist China and thus involve the United States and cooperating nations in a major war that could turn into a world
war, even an atomic one, if Russia chose to come to the aid of her
Communist partner. With both the Marshall Plan and the North
Atlantic Alliance just being established in Europe, Britain and
France, faced by millions of Russian soldiers east of the Iron
Curtain, were determined to localize the conflict. General Douglas MacArthur wanted nothing short of complete victory. During
his triumphant march up the Korean peninsula in the autumn of
1950 MacArthur repeatedly asserted, despite Communist warn-
ings to the contrary, that the danger of Chinese participation was
minimal. The Chinese action not only proved him dead wrong,
but also demolished his promise to end the war by Christmas.
The disastrous retreat of the United Nations forces into South
Korea was a blight upon MacArthur's brilliant military record,
and during the wearisome campaign to regain lost ground his
hopes for victory were again abruptly curtailed, this time by the

United Nations and by his own government. Fear of full-scale Chinese participation and eventual Russian support led to an agreement between the United States and its allies that the Chinese bases across the Yalu River from the North Korean border were not to be bombed and that the United Nations troops were not to proceed beyond the thirty-eighth parallel, the prewar boundary separating the two Koreas. MacArthur protested vigorously. But in making his objections public and relaying them in writing to a Republican Congressman who later read them from the floor of the House, he was guilty of insubordination to his Commander in Chief, the President. The general also had challenged one of the basic safeguards of democratic government, that of civilian control of the military. There was little else that a strong President could do but to relieve the general of his command.

The dismissal of MacArthur brought to a climax all the furies of partisanship. The loss of China, the less-than-enthusiastic European contributions to the war, and the United Nations' intent to limit the war to Korea had already aroused Republican tempers in Congress to such an intense pitch that in the resulting welter of charges of incompetence, subversion, and conspiracy the nation almost lost its poise. For a time it seemed as if Americans were more willing to attack other Americans than they were to unite their energies against the foreign foe. Still, the Republicans had good grounds for bitter complaint. As Senator Vandenberg repeatedly remarked, the bipartisan Truman foreign policy was largely confined to Europe. On Oriental affairs Republican Congressional leaders were rarely consulted. This was poor repayment indeed since the Republican majorities in Congress from 1947 to 1949 had loyally supported the President's revolutionary European policy. Although many Republicans were extraordinarily inconsistent in signing the Taft-Hoover manifesto on continentalism at one moment and in the next indicting the Administration for losing Asia, the Truman-Acheson policy in the Far East did nevertheless appear to sacrifice much of Asia in order to save the gains made in Western Europe. The rapid development of the Asia First, anti-United Nations, go-it-alone groups of Republicans was a natural evolution, and the Administration's Asia policy a splendid target. The recall of General MacArthur supplied emotional fuel to an already inflamed cause consisting of zealous patriotism and intense partisanship.

Douglas MacArthur was one of the ablest and most imposing generals of World War II. Tall, handsome, and theatrical in act and speech, he had run the military occupation of Japan with a sure and majestic hand. Among the professional politicians it was known that he had been a receptive Republican Presidential candidate in 1948. If he could be depicted now as a martyr to an inefficient, corrupt, and possibly subverted Democratic Administration, he appeared a natural winner for 1952. As a nationalist, an opponent of the United Nations, and an Oriental expert, he was an inevitable center of support for many embittered Republican groups. MacArthur was as much of a proconsul as the United States has possibly ever had, and his return to the United States and appearance before Congress was something of a Roman triumph. But the Potomac was not the Rubicon. The man from Missouri in the White House stood his ground, and the nation accepted his decision. However, though the President had won his personal battle, the Administration's Oriental policy helped at least to lose a Presidential campaign. Dwight Eisenhower might have been elected regardless of the Asia question, but it certainly did him and his party no harm.

The uncertain struggle in the Republican Party for the 1952 Presidential nomination threatened for a time to make for a real shift in American foreign policy, and the Eisenhower campaign against the Democratic nominee, Adlai Stevenson, sounded at times as if this might indeed come about. Before the Republican National Convention, most of the conservative and nationalist elements in the Republican party had rallied around the candidacy of Senator Robert Taft. Supporting the Ohio Senator were the continentalists and fortress-America groups, the old isolationists, the "go-it-aloners," anti-United Nations people, the Asia Firsters, and the extreme, Red-baiting nationalists, who for one reason or another preferred to spend their energies catching domestic Communists rather than confronting grave international problems. It was a formidable if paradoxical group, but Eisenhower was the perfect riposte to the Taft coalition. Supporting him in the party were the followers of the Willkie-Dewey-Vandenberg tradition, and although a good many other elements entered into the decision, Eisenhower's first-ballot nomination and subsequent election constituted a major step in committing the Republican party to internationalist principles. At times during the campaign General Eisenhower, in his assault on the Truman policy, sounded as if he were something less than a fervent supporter of the international viewpoint. But his flirtation with the Asia Firsters, Senator Joseph McCarthy, and the Taft supporters was only an affair of reasonable political expediency and never a commitment to marriage. After Eisenhower's well-publicized New York "harmony" meeting with Taft, the Ohio senator admitted that "differences" still existed between the two in the area of foreign affairs. Eisenhower's appointment of John Foster Dulles as Secretary of State was testimony to his persistent international viewpoint.

Few men have ever had Dulles' training and experience before coming to the State Department. And few Secretaries of State have had such a wavering record on foreign policy. Though he had been a Wilson internationalist, Dulles was a convinced non-interventionist by 1940. He contributed to the America First Committee. But after America's entrance into World War II he again became an internationalist. During Truman's Administration he negotiated the Japanese peace treaty for the State Department, and he acted as Dewey's foreign policy adviser in the campaign of 1948.

As Secretary of State, Dulles was given almost a free hand by Eisenhower, and at times it appeared as if he were radically reshaping the nation's foreign policy. His attack against the Acheson "containment" philosophy and his promises of liberation for the Russian-dominated states of Eastern Europe threatened the unwritten agreement between the West and the Soviet supporting the territorial *status quo* along the Iron Curtain. Dulles' threat to engage in an "agonizing reappraisal" of American commitments in Europe was aimed at France and the other

NATO members reluctant to contribute their promised share of mutual-defense costs. His critical speeches on Indian, Yugoslavian, and Egyptian neutralism added up to the old maxim that those who were not for us were against us. And his references to "massive retaliation" and of "going to the brink of war," as well as his advocacy of armed American intervention in French Indochina, were redolent of the anti-United Nations and Asia-First factions in the Republican party.

But in actuality the Eisenhower-Dulles foreign policy was something far different from what Dulles' oratory implied. The new Administration made some slight modifications, some minor changes in emphasis, in the inherited policy. To the chagrin of radicals and liberals Fascist Spain was made an ally and given extensive economic and military aid. With the signing of the Southeast Asia Treaty more but not too effective emphasis was placed upon saving what was left of non-Communist East Asia. By the abortive Middle Eastern Treaty the Secretary of State unsuccessfully attempted to force the noncommitted Arab states into an anti-Communist alliance, ancillary to NATO. But that was about the total of major changes in the Truman policy. During the anti-Communist rebellions in East Germany, Poland, and Hungary the United States offered no help save verbal encouragement to the courageous Eastern European rebels and thus perpetuated the existing division of Europe. Despite Senator William Knowland's charge that Eisenhower had negotiated a Korean peace "without honor," the armistice commission finally agreed upon a territorial *status quo ante* along the thirty-eighth parallel, exactly what Truman's actions in limiting MacArthur had foreshadowed. What the United States settled for in Korea was containment, not liberation. It also settled for two Koreas, as Truman had settled for two Berlins and two Europes. With the signing of the Korean armistice there was relief in America, but no exaltation.

Not even full containment was achieved in Indochina. After a series of disastrous French reversals, Dulles argued for armed American intervention, even if unsupported by her free-world allies. But in the end Eisenhower, out of approximately the same considerations that moved Truman to avoid a major war with Red China, decided against the commitment of American forces. As a result, at the Geneva Conference of April 1954 Indochina was divided after the fashion of Korea between Communist and non-Communist states. Out of deference to Secretary of State Dulles' sensibilities the United States did not lend her consent to the accord, but by undertaking not to overturn the agreement the Eisenhower Administration had for all practical purposes participated in enlarging Communist-held territory as well as in extending the two-world policy.

Secretary Dulles' subsequent negotiation of the Southeast Asia Treaty, resulting in an organization promptly labelled SEATO, was not, in strength at least, analogous to NATO. No military organization was formed, and indeed, India, Ceylon, Burma, and Indonesia refused to join even this largely consultative organization. The growing Red pressures in South Asia, plus America's increasing propensity to intervene there, were among the considerations that led to the calling of the Bandung Conference of April 1955.

Bandung was a milestone in the evolution of the tortured postwar world. Gathered there were twenty-nine nonwhite representatives from Asian and African nations, including delegates from Red China, for the purpose of discussing the future of the non-European world. Neither the United States nor the European nations nor the Soviet Union had been invited. Predictably, therefore, the keynote of the Bandung Conference was an attack upon colonialism. But the most important development was the formulation of the doctrine of "neutralism," an affirmation that a large part of Asia and Africa would not ally itself with either side in the cold war and that its major aim was to liberate the underdeveloped nations of the world from dependence upon the economically advanced nations. Incorporated in the neutralist doctrine were demands upon the rest of the world for political liberation, for the recognition of racial equality, and for massive economic and technological aid to assure the Orient and Africa a living standard approaching that of the West. Also implied in the Bandung doctrine was the intention of playing the two major power groups off against each other. After Bandung, the going price for Asian support was to appreciate rapidly.

From Asia, neutralism spread rapidly to the Middle East and Africa. Since Egypt and adjacent regions had long been dominated by the British and French, and since American money had to a large degree been responsible for the astonishing rise of Israel, neutralism came naturally to Egypt's young dictator, Gamal Abdel Nasser, as it did for the heads of other Arab states, who could use the doctrine additionally for prying more returns out of the Western companies exploiting the fabulous oil basins scattered around the Persian Gulf. Denied the lucrative oil revenues of the southern Arab states and beset with mass poverty and a calamitously rising birth rate, Nasser sought a solution for Egypt in the construction of a gigantic dam and irrigation works along the Nile, to be engineered and financed, he hoped, with Western skill and money. A treaty granting Egypt the necessary credit was on the point of being ratified in 1956 when Secretary Dulles publicly denounced the agreement because of Nasser's refusal to reduce his purchases of Russian arms.

In an angry protest, Nasser secured a promise of funds and technical assistance for the construction of the Aswan High Dam from the Soviets and subsequently nationalized the Suez Canal, the majority of whose shares were held by France and Britain. He then struck out against British and French colonialism in both Asia and Africa. In response to the rapid Egyptian rearmament with Russian supplies, the seizure of the Suez Canal, and the Egyptian encouragement to such diverse African movements as the Mau Mau uprising in Kenya and the long and bloody Algerian rebellion, Israel, France, and Britain came to a secret understanding. On October 29, 1956, as Israel invaded the Sinai peninsula, France and Britain attempted, with lamentable preparation and execrable execution, to overthrow the Nasser regime and retake the Suez Canal.

These surprising developments threatened utterly to destroy American policy in the Middle East, which had as its major aims (1) the exclusion of Communism from the area, (2) the protection of the gigantic American oil concessions, and (3) the maintenance of Israel as an independent state. Prior to the Suez explosion, the United States had attempted to rationalize its complex Middle Eastern policy by supporting the *status quo* between Israel and the Arab states. But in November 1956 the British-French action in the Suez forced the United States to make a choice between the continuation of that policy and the alienation of Britain and France. To support the Western allies might antagonize the Arabs to the point of endangering American oil concessions and possibly pushing Nasser into the hands of the Russians for protection. Egypt certainly would have become a Russian client. Involved also were the anticolonial sensibilities of the uncommitted nations of Africa and Asia. Support for Nasser and Egypt, on the other hand, meant a deep rupture in and possible collapse of the Western European Defense Community, encouragement of further Arab seizure of foreign property, and the loss of thousands of Jewish votes for the incumbent Administration. Since the USSR had threatened the Western partners with rockets if they did not retire from Egypt, American pressure against its allies might be interpreted by the Kremlin as an indication that the United States would not risk open conflict with the Soviets and thus might invite further Russian expansion. It was a difficult choice, and one that might have been avoided if the American policy prior to the Suez Canal seizure had been more enterprising and imaginative, more energetic and more definite. But the choice had to be made among the thorny alternatives, and Eisenhower and Dulles forced Britain, France, and Israel to retire from Egypt.

The baneful results of the Suez fiasco quickly became apparent. Throughout the Middle East and Africa Nasser's prestige soared, and Dulles' attempt to organize a Middle Eastern Treaty Organization to ward off Soviet pressures was shattered. The explosive Arab nationalist and neutralist movement propelled Syria into a short-lived union with Egypt, the pro-Western government of Iraq was overturned in a violent revolution, and only the landing of United States troops at Beirut stopped a radical Lebanese revolution. The Suez incident also gave impetus to the independence movement in Africa and strengthened the bloody

Algerian campaign for independence, a campaign that in the summer of 1958 helped destroy what remained of the reeling Fourth French Republic and on the threat of an armed rebellion brought Charles de Gaulle to near-dictatorial power in France. Although de Gaulle was far from being a neutralist, he was not an ardent supporter of American-European policy, and the Suez affair impelled him toward a policy of substituting French for American leadership in Europe.

In its eight years the Eisenhower government strongly supported the inherited policy of encouraging Western European unity both politically and economically. The objections of France to the rearmament of West Germany were overcome by persistent efforts, and in October 1954 the seven NATO members agreed to accept Germany into their defense community. The addition of West Germany to Western defense, the armament of East Germany by the Soviets, and particularly the death of Joseph Stalin in March 1953 were new and important counters in the grim struggle for the future of Europe. For a time the succession of Nikita S. Khrushchev, dictator of Russia, appeared to portend a radical change in Communist policy. Khrushchev's denunciation of Stalin, his cordial spirit at the Geneva summit conference with Eisenhower in July 1955, and his apparently tolerant attitude toward developments in the client Communist states, particularly with reference to the establishment of the regime of Wladislaw Gomulka in Poland, all indicated that the Russian temper had changed. But the bloody suppression of the Hungarian anti-Russian uprising in October-November 1956, occurring simultaneously with the Suez crisis, clearly indicated that though Russian leadership had changed, Russian objectives had not. Although Khrushchev reiterated his desire for "peaceful coexistence," he was also candid in his estimate of how a period of coexistence would terminate. His blunt threat to the United States, "We will bury you," clearly conveyed the warning that while the period of coexistence might be relatively peaceful, it would in no sense be convivial. The subsequent competition between the two power blocs in the Congo, Southeast Asia, Berlin, and Cuba revealed just how dangerous to civilization a period of "coexistence" could be.

The reluctance of the Eisenhower Administration to aid the Hungarians in their revolt, as well as Khrushchev's formula for coexistence, is explained by the so-called "balance of terror," Churchill's apt phrase. By 1955 and 1956, Russia and the West realized that each possessed enough atomic armaments to destroy the other, and perhaps the rest of the civilized world as well. On November 1, 1952, the United States had exploded the first hydrogen bomb, a weapon of incalculable power even when contrasted with the awful force of the atomic bomb. Russia countered with one of its own in August of the following year. This situation, unparalleled in human history, was frightful enough to cause even the most impetuous statesman to pause. The further development of intercontinental rockets and of world-girdling satellites capable of carrying atomic warheads intensified the deadlock. Although Russia scored firsts with both rockets and satellites, successes permitted perhaps by the cutting back of United States defense funds, the developments in the two countries were so parallel that neither could be certain which had the scientific advantage. The alternatives to mutual destruction were either an increase in the pace of development of technological achievement and competition in the hope of securing a margin of destruction, or an attempt to abolish the possibility of atomic war by the renunciation of such weapons under an international agreement. But whether within or outside the structure of the United Nations, the two powers, both repeatedly declaring their desire to abolish the awful weapons, failed to agree on exactly how that end was to be achieved. By the early 1960's talk of atomic disarmament was almost academic. Britain and France had joined the atomic club, and Red China was soon to achieve membership. The bomb had become an international status symbol, replacing imperialism and colonialism.

Measured by its promises, the Eisenhower-Dulles policy had not been very successful. It had not achieved a roll-back of Communist power, and in many areas it had even failed to contain the Communists. During Eisenhower's administration Communism had taken over a good part of Indochina and through the Cuban revolution had even penetrated into the Western Hemisphere. Russian arms were scattered lavishly throughout the Middle East by 1960, although Arab nationalism and neutralism were inclined somewhat more toward the West than toward Moscow. Only in Europe and Africa had the Communist ambitions been largely thwarted.

Eisenhower's lack of success in reducing Communist power was understandable. Whereas before 1949 the United States had had an atomic monopoly, after that date the Russian bomb violently shifted the balance of world power. Moreover, the growing Chinese threat in the Orient spread American resources ever more thinly around the perimeter of an enlarged Communist-dominated world. By the middle fifties neither the United States nor Russia had the degree of control they once held within their respective orbits. The growth of Asian and African neutralism, the rise of China, and the resurgence of France, Germany, and Japan marked the end of the period dominated by the two great superpowers. Just as the Soviet was experiencing increasing difficulties in its relations with even small satellites like Rumania, the United States was troubled by a Communist-inclined Cuba and by a balance of international payments problem brought on by her foreign aid program. Although the Chinese-Russian clash and the French-American conflict over European leadership tended to reduce the strain between the two principal nations, the movement toward fragmentation of world political power seemed hardly reversible. And if the past was any guide to the future, the growing multiplicity of claimants for leadership meant more turmoil rather than less. By 1960, when the balance of atomic terror demanded peaceful coexistence, the prospect of a world diplomatic revolution with accompanying conflict seemed imminent.

The failure of Republican leadership to regain America's slipping world power and to stop the growth of Communism had noticeable effects upon public opinion. Congress showed a growing disposition to question the efficacy of foreign aid, either of a development or of a military character. Of particular significance for both party and world politics was the increasing reluctance of southern Democratic representatives, once pillars of internationalism, to supply funds for foreign activities. Among the general public there were also indications of a sense of disillusionment with a world that stubbornly refused to conform to the pattern America expected of it. Beginning to arise from this maldisposition was a public inclination to turn inward and a frustrated demand for stronger action abroad uncomplicated by the desires of America's allies. Often irrationally combined, the two conflicting sentiments expressed themselves in demands for quitting the United Nations, abolition of all foreign aid, and, if necessary, the use of force to stop Communist encroachment.

Such feelings were not confined to the advocates of either party, but since the proposed program had obvious appeal to the once solidly Democratic South and Southwest and was very close to the program supported by the embittered Western Republicans of the Taft tradition, it seemed certain in 1960 that the normal patterns of domestic politics would be shaken.

7

Prosperity and Pessimism

MODERN WAR makes more drastic changes in society than any other social phenomenon aside from revolution. In many instances such changes become permanent. Within the two years after Pearl Harbor the compulsions of war had remade American society as the New Deal had not done in six. Unemployment had practically disappeared, total production, as measured by the gross national product, had increased by over 60 per cent, the customary rights and privileges of most individuals had been seriously altered, and taxes and the national debt had risen as they never had in the years from 1933 to 1938.

Among the more permanent changes that the war wrought on society was a massive uprooting of people from their traditional homes. Over 15 million servicemen were moved to military camps located mostly in the southern, eastern, and western parts of the country, where climate and locale were better suited to training and to embarkation, a hegira perhaps not unrelated to the perceptible postwar movement of Americans from the colder interior of the country to the more equable climates along the coasts. A similar migration was made by civilians attracted to the fantastic multiplication of ship and airplane construction facilities, identically situated. Other war-born industries, and the increasing tempo of conventional production, meanwhile triggered an equally important movement of people from the countryside and the small towns to the larger cities. During the war years almost a million Negroes moved North to locate in the large industrial complexes where wages were high and opportunities for a better life appeared greater. No reliable statistics are available for the white workers who left land and village to become industrial workers. But the increasing urbanization of the nation, which had slowed almost to a stop in depression days, again picked up speed during the war and postwar years. Whereas the percentage of urban population had increased by only .3 per cent from 1930 to 1940, the comparable figure, according to one 1950 census index, showed 2.5 per cent, and according to another, 7.5 per cent. Meanwhile the total farm population had diminished by over a million people. Obviously the war and its immediate consequences had contributed to a vast urbanization of the nation's people, which would in turn eventually make important changes in their social and political attitudes. In addition, the war materially affected the relationship between government and corporations, as well as contributing to significant changes inside corporate structures.

Government expenditures during World War II made the New Deal's pump-priming efforts look puny and archaic by comparison. By 1944 approximately one-half of the nation's production went directly into the war effort, and during the following year Federal expenditures amounted to more than $100 billion compared to the largest New Deal amount of about $8.5 billion. From 1941 to 1946 the government became the direct or indirect employer of most of the nation's working force and the owner of over $16 billion worth of industrial facilities and of millions of tons of strategic raw materials. In large part the facilities were leased to private operators, and after the war most of these were sold outright to private concerns.

For a short time after the end of the war government expenditures were cut back sharply. But then the cold war, the Korean War, mammoth foreign aid programs, the multibillion dollar missile, and the space efforts made the Federal government again the country's prime purchaser. In 1962 Federal, state, and local governmental expenditures amounted to about $170 million, a figure representing almost one-third of the total gross national product. Since over half of this amount was spent by the Federal government, simply by the size of its disbursements it remained the major force influencing the economy.

Had Federal purchasing been spread evenly over the national industrial plant the results of the spending would not have been so marked on either the government or on the private sector of the economy. But a preponderant share of the vast amounts went for direct or indirect military programs, many of which dealt with intricate atomic and space problems. By 1960 the immediate donor of most such funds was the military bureaucracy in Washington, the immediate grantees a few hundred firms commanding enough technical facilities and research intelligence to deliver what was wanted. Just before leaving the White House President Eisenhower warned the nation of the peril involved in the ever-increasing identity of interest between the opulent military patrons and their industrial suppliers. Two years later a knowledgeable journalist published a book entitled *The Warfare State,* in which he argued that the main support for the postwar American economy had been the enormous annual defense expenditures. He also contended that it was of direct interest to the military as well as their chief suppliers and subcontractors to maintain the huge military program which now included within its ranks many of the nation's topflight scientists and engineers. Since expenditures of the postwar magnitude could not be defended in a relatively peaceful world, the danger was obvious that the series of sustaining international crises might become institutionalized as necessary to the existing economy.

The amount of Federal expenditure, as well as the extent of governmental control over capital, labor, and the general public from 1940 to 1960, were roughly measured by the degree of foreign peril, either real or fancied. During the war the countless agencies headed by the War Production Board not only decided what should or should not be produced, but also rationed raw materials, transportation, labor, and many articles of general consumption. They set prices and controlled rents, and more indirectly attempted to determine wage scales and profit rates. Since little opposition to the war existed, little effort was needed to regulate men's minds. But had there been widespread opposition, the government undoubtedly would have coerced agreement. The removal of the Japanese-Americans from their West Coast homes to interior camps, even though their record of loyalty throughout the war was almost unimpeachable, indicated what might have been done with any large group of dissenters.

Immediately after the war a reaction similar to that of 1919 and 1920 took place against governmental intervention in the normal private activities of citizens. But while many powers were wrested from Washington by an insistent Congress and a militant citizenry, the series of international crises in the forties and fifties activated the pendulum to swing in the opposite direction. During the Korean War the controls of World War II were partially re-established. To stop one crippling railway strike President Truman temporarily nationalized the railroads, but his attempt to do the same with the steel industry was thwarted by the Federal courts. In the midst of his 1960 Presidential campaign Vice-President Nixon brought official pressure upon the steel industry to assure the workers a wage raise. Through stockpiling of strategic materials and by the continuing agricultural marketing controls the government was also a major force in determining prices for a long list of commodities and raw materials that ranged from structural steel to sugar beets, from platinum to peanuts.

Government was only one of several major forces in the postwar period contributing to a centralized economic life. The changing structure of both organized industry and organized labor substantially contributed to the process. In 1941 45 per cent of all defense contracts had been given to just six corporations. Although the vast volume of war orders and subcontracting led to spreading the orders among many more companies, the percentage of contracts given to the hundred largest corporations increased. Only with peace and reconversion, the War Production Board told a Senate committee, would it be possible to alter the wartime policy of "big companies first." But as peace never really came, the policy of the "big first" continued despite the efforts of the Smaller War Plants Corporation and numerous House and Senate committees. A web of subcontracting kept many small competitors alive, but it also placed the small companies in a permanently unequal relationship with the industrial giants.

The new postwar technology gave further impetus to the growth of industrial gigantism. With the development of faster-than-sound air transportation, atomic power, and intercontinental and interplanetary missiles, the costs of research, retooling, and development became enormous, and often quite beyond the means of the smaller firms. The enormous distance that industry had spanned in a half century, as well as the scientific, managerial and capital demands made upon it, is illustrated by a comparison of the Wright brothers' airplane assembled in a bicycle shop (1903) with the intricacies of the supersonic jet plane of 1960. In 1962 the one-time radical economist Stuart Chase and Roger Blough, of the United States Steel Corporation, completely agreed on the proposition that an even further development of gigantism was needed if technological growth were to continue.

By 1960 approximately five hundred corporations accounted for two-thirds of the industrial production. Consequently, the character of their controlling bureaucracies was of utmost importance to the nation. As Adolf Berle noted in *The Fictions of American Capitalism: Power Without Property* (1960), the corporate trends already evident during the twenties had now matured. The old owner-manager of the large corporation had practically disappeared. Corporations were now headed by a new professional managerial class, many of whom were college-educated. Although few managers owned any significant number of the corporation shares, they possessed enormous power. Since most of the new capital they required was generated internally from profits and depreciation accounts, they were no longer dependent upon banks, insurance companies, or individual investors. Thus finance capital and Wall Street control of the major corporations, as well as the power of stockholders, tended to wither away. The publicly held securities of the average large corporation amounted to such vast sums that ownership was extremely diffuse. The capital structure of the American Telephone and Telegraph Company, for example, was so great that no individual owned as much as 2 per cent of the voting stock. The remainder was spread among 200,000 investors, whose very numbers made effective control impossible. Consequently, the top managerial group tended to become a self-perpetuating directorate which, though not owning, controlled. They were in a fashion trustees, but trustees remarkably free from formal restraints.

David Dubinsky, one of the more enlightened labor leaders, observed in 1950 that "trade unionism needs capitalism like a fish needs water." He might also have added that as the character of water determines the quality of marine life so does the structure of capitalism influence the nature of unions. During the war union and corporate development took much the same direction and for approximately the same reasons. A flood of war orders created an unnatural demand for labor, and the ability of corporations to charge back rising costs to the government dissipated executive hostility to rising wage scales and union organization. In this benign climate union membership rose rapidly. As growth continued after the war, total membership in 1955 amounted to 17 million, or about one-quarter of the total work force. With ample membership fees and pension funds union bureaucracy grew larger, and power steadily drifted from the shop and the city federation to the national headquarters, from the constituent unions to the national federation. Local strikebreaking by national labor organizations was not unknown. And a precedent was set in 1953 when the President of the A.F. of L. refused to back down before the threat of the Carpenters Union to disaffiliate. After a previous failure to unite, the A.F. of L. and the C.I.O. finally merged in 1955.

As unions grew larger and their power more centralized, their relations with business and government underwent a marked change. During the war years labor policy was controlled in Washington by labor leaders who dealt directly with the government and with the many corporation executives on the wartime boards. The advantages of the arrangement were apparent to the participating partners, and in a postwar period characterized by administered prices at home and a succession of foreign crises abroad the tendency to settle major labor disputes on a national basis became almost habitual. Involved in many such settlements were considerations of internal politics, national security, and the eventual costs to consumers. Increasingly labor policy became a part of national policy, far removed from the shop and the control of the members.

As the American economy in the postwar period became more tightly controlled by relatively small groups in government, the great corporations, and the labor unions, it also became and remained, at least for almost two decades, incredibly productive. Many reasons were advanced for the continuation of the great boom or the surge to abundance. Initially it was triggered by the $150 billion saved by individuals during the war, savings that constituted a deep pool of deferred purchasing power. Thereafter, huge defense expenditures arising from the cold war and the Korean War became a permanent prop to the economy. From 1947 to 1957 security costs of the government, not including veterans' payments, totalled $325 billion, a sum that exceeded the amount spent by private industry for new plants and equipment. In one sense, defense expenditures could be considered a peculiar type of national dole. They resulted in a vast augmentation of purchasing power without an increase in the production of useful goods and an actual decrease in useful labor. Millenniums before, the Pharaonic pyramid construction must have had similar effects upon the Egyptian economy.

A high birth rate, which was to diminish in the sixties, further stimulated industrial growth. Government policy of easy credit rates and almost yearly budget deficits pumped additional purchasing power and inflationary pressure into the economy. The relation of the more-or-less controlled inflationary policy to the continuation of economic growth was evident in the early sixties when a short-lived deflationary period brought lower industrial indices and sharply increased unemployment. Of importance second only perhaps to the government's multifarious activities was the adoption by industry of Henry Ford's formula of the twenties. The triadic gospel of mass production, low unit prices, and high wages was not accepted by either capital or labor in as voluntary a fashion as has been suggested. Business was eager for mass production, but numerous government indictments for price fixing seemed to indicate a willingness of many industries to charge as much as they could. Though labor supported high wage standards, it fought the introduction of labor-saving devices, and when defeated encouraged "featherbedding," or the maintenance of useless positions. But because of the thrusts and counterthrusts of organized labor, capital, and government, because of competitive elements still operating in the economy, and because of the new character of corporate management, production sales and wages mounted and prices, despite the inflationary trend of the years, were maintained at a reasonably low level.

As reflected in the 1960 census statistics, the gross results of this great "surge to abundance" were scarcely believable. By 1955 the American economy, with about 6 per cent of the world's population, was producing almost 50 per cent of the world's goods, a ratio that was substantially reduced after that date by the renewed prosperity of western Europe and Japan. The median family income rose from $3,083 in 1949 to $5,657 in 1959, a rise which, when corrected for inflation, still amounted to 48 per cent. Accompanying this rise in income and the consequent torrent of consumers' goods there was much talk about "a classless society." But despite all of the bounteous wealth, the census figures reported that over 13 per cent of families had an income of less than $2,000, a figure far below the subsistence standard. The greater portion of these unfortunates was made up of nonwhites, the national median for such family groups being only 54 per cent of the yearly income of white families. By 1960 other trouble spots had appeared in the economy. One of the most ominous during the early sixties was persistent unemployment of the unskilled and overemployment of the highly trained. While an estimated 5 to 6 per cent of the labor force in 1960 was unemployed, 7 per cent of the available work was done on overtime. The widespread introduction of automated factories and offices, inspired by high wage costs and a decreasing need for unskilled labor in a sophisticated technology, partially explained the continuing unemployment. As basic, perhaps, was the fact that industry and business were probably faced with the more fundamental problem of overabundance that had dogged agriculture for decades. Economists noted elements of "consumer satiety" among the more fortunate groups.

Probably no other capitalist society has been as resourceful in employing men, machines, and materials for the production of what are essentially nonsaleable goods. Millions of man hours and dollars were poured into surplus agricultural production, surplus armaments, surplus capital, and consumer goods. The agricultural items were either downgraded (e.g., potatoes used for fertilizer) or sent abroad at ridiculously low prices subsidized by the government, armaments were prodigally scattered among so-called friendly powers, and industrial goods and whole factories were given to underdeveloped nations. Simultaneously, the fraction of the labor force in the total population was reduced. The ratio of the old and the retired increased as longevity rates rose and pension plans multiplied; that of the nonworking young was raised by the maintenance of relatively large military establishments and by a sharp increase in the number of students attending institutions of higher education.

In this age of the "affluent society" the care and feeding of the consumer was a continual preoccupation of the business world. He was daily cajoled by advertising, frequently consulted as to his wishes by market surveys, and his future inclinations to buy or not to buy intently studied by research organizations. A marginal decline in his purchasing expectations was often enough to curtail inventories and cause the stock market to waver. Stimulated by the government's easy-money policy, the consumer was furthermore flooded with credit. The extent to which purchasing on credit had become universal in American life was dramatized by the announcement in 1960 that the largest retail concern in the country, Sears Roebuck, had over 10 million credit accounts on its books, or one for every five American families. Credit cards valid throughout the world were issued in abundance, and a lien on future earnings was utilized for such transient items as holiday travel. During the fifties private debts rose from $73 billion to $196 billion. By 1960 eighteen cents of every dollar earned after taxes went to pay back previously contracted installment and mortgage debts. But despite all these devices, unemployment refused to decrease measurably, and this factor, plus the rising burden of private debts, perhaps indicated a maldistribution of income which might eventually imperil the continued efficient functioning of the economy.

Whatever the future of the economy, its record was an astonishing one. Both foreign and domestic commentators reached far for adjectives to describe the new productive machine. "Neocapitalism," "welfare capitalism," and "democratic capitalism," were some of the results. But if "democratic" implied control from below, it missed the mark entirely. Most of the population was supplied and some groups even inundated with a deluge of goods. But the classic competitive process, as admitted by many influential economists, had virtually disappeared. So had any sustained effective control of the great corporations by their legal owners, the stockholders. The individual consumer had about as much effective power in the market place as the small manufacturer or a solitary worker attempting to influence the actions of his union. Economic policy had, on the whole, become national policy determined by the bargaining of governmental, corporate, and to a lesser extent labor elites. Only when the masses were moved to concerted action, in mass buying or mass refusal to buy, was there a profound impulse from below. Generally that sort of impulse came in moments of either euphoria or fright generated by the actions or the words of the controlling elite.

Many significant changes in social patterns took place during the postwar years, some the result of long-time trends in American society, some arising from more recent ones. The shift from the farm to the city continued, and by 1960 fewer than a third of the population lived in towns, villages, and on the farms, some rural counties, like Lecker County, Kentucky, losing a quarter of their population in less than ten years. The traditional mobility of the nation was accelerated by shifting populations within cities. As the newcomers, many of them Negroes, Puerto Ricans, or Mexicans, moved to the cities, a large fraction of the previous urban population went to the suburbs. This two-way traffic created the great sprawling "rurban" districts or "slurbs," as the most unlovely of them were sometimes called, and at the same time, a multitude of problems for the new metropolitan complexes. To the new suburbia went a good proportion of the young, active, and trained part of what had once been the population of the cities. Following them were many commercial and cultural institutions that had given the city its urbanity. What this "brain drain" and the possible creation of a new "rurban squirearchy" meant for American life and politics only the future could answer. Simultaneously, the process of interior decay was already visible in the heart of many metropolitan places. Into these decaying central cores of the cities a new kind of proletariat was possibly developing, with few attachments to traditional American values, whether of upper or of laboring class origin. Since many of them were nonwhites, their cultural heritage was vastly different from the aspiring middle and upper classes. Because large numbers of them were without steady employment they had few attachments to the laboring classes. Due to abundant relief and social service activities, they were relatively well fed and dressed—"the world's best-dressed poor," as they were called. But possibly because they were able to contribute so little to society they were increasingly detached from it, developing a separate mentality and a distinct way of life characterized by either sullen compliance or occasional blazing resistance to the social demands of the majority.

The national population shift from the colder to the warmer climates of the country was responsible for the sharp growth of the Pacific Coast, the Southwest, and Florida. Often overlooked as a vital factor in the changing folkways was the vast amount of American travel abroad. The millions of soldiers transplanted abroad during the war, the continuing shifting of government personnel during the cold war, and the annual swarms of tourists to Europe and Asia added up to an impressive number of Americans who encountered foreign cultures. Social parochialism along with political isolation appeared to be things of the past.

Major movements took place within the employment structure. The reduction of common laborers, from 11 million in 1900 to 6 million in 1950, was speeded up by automation. Feminization of the nation's working forces continued. By 1960 more than one-third of the women of working age were either employed or looking for work. And within some age groups as high as 28 per cent of the married women were working for wages. But perhaps of much more importance in indicating the future social drift was the movement of a major portion of the working force away from the actual production of goods and into the so-called service, amusement, and leisure industries. Despite the great increase in production, by 1960 fewer people were employed in manufacturing establishments than in 1945. By the latter date more than half of the nation's employees were engaged in nonindustrial pursuits. According to the census, the greatest increases had occurred in sales, distributive, advertising, and secretarial services, and in amusement and leisure enterprises. Thus, the number of people involved in actual production was contracting at a rather rapid rate. What psychological change would come from the shift of the majority away from the actual production of things to effecting their movement, their enumeration, or their sale is impossible at present even to surmise intelligently. But in this new mass-consumption society the old equation of man confronting materials and making something new of them had been changed to man confronting man and persuading him to act. A latter-day Emerson might have written: man was in the saddle and rode mankind.

Advertising was one of the basic supports of postwar mass culture. In *The Affluent Society,* John Galbraith, one of the nation's leading economists, commented that the volume of goods needed to ward off mass unemployment and a possible racking depression was only sustained by a "synthesis of desire" which was "sold" to the public principally through the medium of advertising. Advertising's main objective, as one of its leading devotees admitted, was to make the consumer unhappy with what he had and to consider it "obsolete." Long before 1960 the advertiser and his colleague, the public relations expert, had moved into the field of manipulating public opinion about more important matters than consumer goods. The campaign of 1960 and 1961 of the American Medical Association to defeat the Medicare proposal, a scheme to subsidize medical care for the aged, was directed by a skilled public relations organization. Almost every Federal department or commission of consequence had its own staff. In the 1952 Presidential election the Eisenhower organization was advised by one of the leading public relations firms on how to secure a proper public "image" for their candidate, which presumably they could not secure by traditional means. By 1962 even gubernatorial and senatorial candidates had attached public relations experts to their staffs, and the word "image" became a political as well as a business stereotype. What was sought, of course, was not a true or mirror image, but a synthetic one that would hide blemishes and project hidden or nonexistent virtues. Whether in business or politics the objective was to manipulate the public mind.

A rapidly growing monopoly movement in the daily press also contributed to the specter of a managed electorate. As cities became ever larger many of the same forces that produced concentration in industry tended toward the creation of a press monopoly. Whereas in 1910 practically all cities had two or more competing newspapers, the Hutchins Commission report revealed that by 1955, 40 per cent of the large dailies held a local monopoly and that in ten states not a single city possessed rival newspapers. As Irving Dilliard has shown with documentation, the distortion and suppression of news was not exceptional. The average editor showed an increasing propensity to include in his paper so-called "news" material that had been prepared by advertisers. A study of one large Sunday paper indicated that more than half of its reading material had been supplied as "hand-outs" by advertisers and promotional organizations.

Television, which in 1960 was in 87 per cent of American homes, mitigated to some extent the drying up of diverse opinions in the daily press. Federal regulation requiring equal time for political candidates and containing a vague injunction to pursue the public interest kept the expression of opinion on television somewhat freer than in the press. But in some ways television was organized in a more concentrated fashion than the press. Since national programs were so extensive and advertising receipts depended upon the number of viewers, its operators concentrated upon securing the largest possible audience. Although both sides of questions supported by major groups were invariably presented, marginal opinion, minority taste, and strange ideologies were rarely reflected upon the screen. A toleration to acceptable variance was shown, but social heresy was either avoided or depicted so as to make it repugnant. When exhorting the public to consume, television certainly outstripped the newspaper in irrationality and in untruth. Some of its national quiz shows were rigged, most of the applause of its live audiences was contrived, and the utter nonsense, insidious deception and bare-faced falsity of much of its advertising material were obvious. Although television's potential in raising the nation's cultural level was enormous, the great bulk of its programs were trivial and banal.

The Federal government's action in reserving some very-high-frequency transmitting bands for educational television stations promised some improvement. The radio and the movies, two traditional panderers to mass tastes, strangely enough offered another avenue to quality. Since the competition of television had driven much of the profit out of both media, each sought to preserve itself by appealing to specialized audiences, radio to local audiences and the movies occasionally to intellectuals and other fringe groups. By this fragmentation of what had once been a monolithic mass market, low-budget adult movies were sometimes produced, and some nonprofit radio stations, supported by subscription, were able to broadcast programs of superior cultural value.

"No art form, no body of knowledge, no system of ethics is strong enough to withstand vulgarization," one critic of America's mass culture despairingly wrote in 1958. In as pessimistic a mood other commentators noted the nation's aspiration for conformity, which demanded a similarity not only in dress, food, housing, and automobiles but in ideology and philosophy as well. A plethora of books with titles such as *The Organization Man* and *The Man in the Grey Flannel Suit* played variations on the theme. Most such volumes were inclined to link this compelling desire for likeness to basic economic institutions. But at least two authors found deeper reasons for the alleged fear of individualism. David Riesman suggested that under the impact of modern urban and industrial culture the average American had changed his character from "inner-directed," responding to a cluster of internal personal values, to "other-directed," or responding to the mass values held by his neighbors. Erich Fromm, the noted psychiatrist, attributed the sheeplike character of the masses to an impelling desire to escape from the painful necessity of making choices and a resulting willingness to accept the values imposed by the group. In other words, the urge was to escape from individualism and freedom to the security and regimentation of the herd.

Probably most critics overemphasized both the uniformity of the day and the individualism of the past, or of other cultures. The Methodist-Baptist code of nineteenth-century agrarian America was hardly one to inspire much variance in conduct. The upper strata of American social classes, like those abroad, had always worn a uniform of some kind, whether of knee breeches or grey flannel suits was scarcely important. What had changed most in America, as also in Europe, was man's attitude toward man and his individual place in society and in the universe. Nowhere was this more clearly defined than by the creative artists, particularly those engaged in the creation of literature. This re-estimation of man and his place in the universe started not at midcentury but rather during the twenties and the thirties.

In *A Farewell to Arms,* one of Ernest Hemingway's characters observes that the world breaks almost everyone, and those that it cannot break, it kills. "It kills the very good, the very gentle, and the very brave impartially. If you are none of these you can be sure it will kill you too, but there will be no special hurry." This terrifying and sardonic statement, imputing to either society or nature or both a basic malevolence toward the good, the gentle, and the strong, was written some ten years after World War I, and before the Great Depression. It was the comment of a young man who had been through the desperate days following the debacle of Italian arms at Caporetto. But the author was a man who had lived through the relatively peaceful and lush days of the 1920's and who had already acquired a considerable reputation as a novelist. Yet its statement about man and his relation to his fellows and to the universe can be taken with some modification as a reasonable reflection of the sentiment of most other gifted non-Marxian American writers of the twenties and the thirties. From Sherwood Anderson's tales of an Ohio town, published in 1919, to John Steinbeck's novel (1939) of the depression-born migrants from Oklahoma, the writer's general image of man and that of the human condition is almost a constant. If there were individual exceptions, like Robert Frost, writing from a slightly more optimistic angle of vision, there were many who disagreed with Hemingway solely on the possibility of finding much goodness, gentleness, or bravery in the human race. If one looks at Anderson's aberrant rustics, Fitzgerald's glittering, brittle youth, Dos Passos' lost urbanites, Eugene O'Neill's Freudian cast, Faulkner's Southern monsters, and Nathanael West's shrouded characters from a planetary insane asylum, the sum is a frightening, even terrifying one. As John Steinbeck's Okies move west from a dust-covered, poverty-stricken Oklahoma, a turtle crosses the road of their migration. Two automobile drivers turn to avoid the animal, but a third swerves deliberately to crush it. That is one of the more optimistic statements about humanity made by the quality novel during a twenty-year period.

In the world view of America's major novelists human virtue was a rare commodity; in part, perhaps, because it did not pay. In F. Scott Fitzgerald's short story "Dalyrimple Goes Wrong," a young, idealistic war hero comes home to great cheers and a pitiful clerkship. His honesty leads from one trouble to another, until he determines to cast his moral restraints aside. He commits a robbery, becomes a solid citizen, and as the story ends is elected a State Senator. Much the same point but with a significant variation toward irrationalism is made by Faulkner in *Sanctuary*. By the false witness of the nonvirtuous heroine, Temple Drake, an honest bootlegger is killed by a mob while the real gangster, Popeye, dies at the hands of organized justice for a crime he does not commit. In Faulkner's later works, while the good and the bad seem to be punished impartially in the end, in the short run at least victory almost always resides with the most repugnant characters. As the few families with long-developed codes of behavior steadily disintegrate, the South is taken over by an incredible swarm of the barbarous, amoral, avid Snopeses. Of them, one perceptive villager charitably remarks: "There's some things even a Snopes won't do. I don't know just exactly what they are, but they's some, somewhere."

According to most of these authors very little could be done to stop the triumph of evil. There seemed to be, beyond man's power to reverse, a grim and remorseless tide running toward pain, tragedy, and death. Free will was an eschatological fantasy. Hemingway's heroes were men to whom things were done, and as one of his characters remarked, "Madam, there is no remedy for anything in life." This pattern of the hero-victim became so standard in American literature that the hero as a victor practically disappeared.

In that modern equivalent of the morality play, the radio and television horse opera, even the most hideous villains are permitted to enjoy a few small triumphs before they fall under the unerring gun of a virtuous sheriff. But even transitory victory is denied some of the heroes of modern literature. In seeking to make his fortune, Nathanael West's Lemuel Pitkin loses one thumb, one eye, one leg, all of his teeth, his scalp, and his money. He is imprisoned twice, kidnapped twice, and finally loses his life. The only thing Sisyphus had on Pitkin was endurance.

Some critics have used the term "determinism" to explain the growth of the tragic factor in the modern novel. One could just as well explain it as the result of a chaotic society in an anarchistic universe governed by incomprehensible forces, unpredictable and unordered. As Stahr, the movie-producing hero of Fitzgerald's unfinished novel, observed, even the most critical of executive decisions were not based upon logical premises but were guesses tied to a hope. Making a decision was often like choosing a path over a rough, unknown country. One chose a way for little reason at all or because one mountain peak was colored an attractive pink or a valley was a deeper blue. "Man," Doc Barton remarked in Steinbeck's *In Dubious Battle,* "is engaged in a blind and fearful struggle out of a past he can't remember into a future he can't foresee or understand."

The world of the 1920–1930 novel was an irrational one where bad not only flowed from bad, but good often produced the future evil. Seldom, however, was the reverse true of evil producing a positive good. Much more often the pattern was like that in Nathanael West's *Miss Lonelyhearts,* in which the hero, who realized he was a spiritual cripple, finally believed he had found the wholeness and the truth he was seeking in God. Under the illusion that he could then act as a mediator between God and man, he sought to help a real physical cripple, who, fearing that Lonelyhearts was seeking to attack his wife, shot him. The wages of compassion were death.

Whether this fictional world was subject to an overriding determinism or to a pervasive irrationalism, one is forced to conclude in any case that unless the wheels of the cosmic machine were fixed against man, the law of statistical averages was being outraged. Two other explanations are possible. One lies in the old Calvinist belief in predestination based upon the inherent evilness of man, a conclusion which Faulkner admitted. "Since the fall," he wrote in his short story "The Bear," "no man is ever really free and probably could not stand it if he were." The other possible explanation is that man in his present stage of development has evolved into a creature so disharmonious either with his own fundamental character or with some implacable characteristic of the universe that he is subject to automatic penalties. In either case, he is doomed.

Post-World War II literature continued, with some variations, the pessimistic, irrational, and tragic themes of before the war. Writers found society just as inimical to man. It was some "strange sentient organism," John O'Hara wrote, "with a dull implacable hostility" to the individual. The institutions composing it were of the same genus. Created by man, they had become his master. The new machine techniques, Norman Mailer's General Cummings observed, demanded that a master class rule with an iron hand so that the masses be made "subservient to the machine." Both the natural and social worlds were irrational, and what looked like the good and safe course of human action often turned out to be the bad and disastrous. In his novels James G. Cozzens reiterated that human freedom was "the knowledge of necessity," but the "necessary" was often impossible to detect even by his most rational heroes. Men were buffeted, according to Cozzens, by a never-ending series of unreasonable, relentless, inexorable forces; there was no exit save death. "The victor was, of course, the vanquisher of all men, those forces ever victorious of circumstances."

With such conceptions of man's relation to the world, it was not surprising that many writers departed from the existing formal literary structures of the past. The slice-of-life pattern invaded the novel and the play, and much modern poetry was written with as little regard for rhythm and cadence as for intelligibility. The author no longer attempted to order the world for his audience; that would have been an exercise in superstition. Instead, he often retreated into his own very private realm of fantasy, where there were few if any symbols of common understanding. Heroes, or rather, antiheroes, rarely struck out at the world as Hemingway's characters had. Instead, they were often shadowy and passive, tossed here and there like chips on a wild stream. Sometimes they acted scarcely at all either on their fellows or on nature; they simply talked. When the characters of modern literature did act, it was seldom in the traditional pattern of high effort and high passions, but more often in the vein of sustained nastiness, as in Katherine Anne Porter's *Ship of Fools*. Action was often limited to the field of sex, where, casting aside human understanding and dignity, the characters sought to decimate their victims to gain another meaningless trophy for their transient desires.

The literature of the twenties contained some satire—a note of hope, since one does not ridicule the inevitable. But the persistent note of the fifties was pity, pity for man's loneliness and for his inability to communicate with his fellows, and basically, an involved self-pity of the author. There was also pity for man's limited resources—"the corrupted unsound mind in the unsound body, both unnerved by aging,"—and pity for the odds against which he fought. The reiterated plaint was that man got a very raw deal in life in a universe which might have been put together "by some idiot." One way out was to stop being a man. Across the Atlantic, Samuel Beckett's degraded tramp observed without passion, "I have been a man long enough, I shall not put up with it anymore." Characters in American literature who either committed suicide or who seriously thought about it were numerous. This mass withdrawal from life was the ultimate vote of no confidence in man, his beliefs, and the structure of his society.

Social critics were almost as gloomy in their estimate of man and his institutions as were the creative writers. As in creative literature the rapid decay of the earlier optimism had started in the twenties. The sharply changing views of Walter Lippmann and Reinhold Niebuhr may perhaps best illuminate this remarkable intellectual transit over the years. For fifteen years after the Peace of Versailles, Lippmann served consecutively as an assistant editor of the radical *New Republic,* as editor-in-chief of the liberal and literate *New York World,* and as a distinguished columnist for the conservative and influential *New York Herald Tribune.* Journalistically he had moved from the advanced democratic left to the sober right, and one might suppose that his intellectual cloth had been cut to the pattern supplied by his employers. Nothing could have been further from the truth. Lippmann's moves toward journalistic conservatism followed the changes in his thought over a period of some years. As a young man in 1914, Lippmann contended that science offered society the possibility of substituting controlled change for disordered growth. Eleven years later, in *Phantom Public,* he seriously questioned the possibility of progress and wondered whether man could ever really know his environment well enough to control it. It was a mark of his maturity to recognize "the vast indifference of the universe to his own fate." By 1929, in discussing the limits of the attainable for humanity, he adopted an even more stoical position. Since man could no longer achieve what he desired, "he must want what he can possess." In *Phantom Public* he examined traditional liberal democratic aspirations and clearly exposed his disbelief in the ability and fitness of the masses to rule.

Liberalism, he ruefully remarked, had been an instrument of the universal conscience for the freeing of men, but it had not been, and probably could never be, an effective instrument of control once the masses were enfranchised. When freed, the masses easily sloughed off their devotion to liberalism and left to the devout and principled liberal only "the sour reflection that they had forged a weapon of release but not a way of life." After the Scopes antievolution trial in Tennessee, he wrote in 1926 that it was "no longer possible to doubt that the dogma of majority rule contains within it some sort of deep and destructive confusion." His dreary conclusion to *Men of Destiny*, published in the same year, was to the effect that eighteenth-century democratic theory was in permanent eclipse. "Its assumptions no longer explain the facts of the modern world, and its ideals are no longer congenial to modern man." By 1929 he had started his long search for instruments to control the enfranchised masses and to mitigate their excesses.

One of the major difficulties, he later wrote, in seeking controlling sanctions was that most of the traditional principles or "the great fictions" of the past had been eroded by "the acids of modernity." In the search for viable substitutes he discounted traditional religion on two scores. First, the great religions of the past all had in them certain aristocratic principles that would make them unacceptable to modern democracy. Second, modern man found it almost impossible to conceive of a God that he could worship, since science had dissolved the old relationship of the destiny of each individual to the destiny of the universe. In *A Preface to Morals* (1929) he could only produce as a possible substitute for the old discarded myths a "High Religion," basically humanistic in nature, the controlling principle of which was disinterestedness. Later, but before 1941, he suggested the possibility of the formation of a new cultural and political elite, and still later, a reformulation of the eighteenth-century principles of natural law.

From 1915 to 1928 Reinhold Niebuhr occupied a Detroit pastorate, after which he became a faculty member of the Union Theological Seminary. He had been an ardent member of the

social gospel movement, believing intensely in the innate goodness of man. But during the twenties he began to shift the
grounds of his theological and philosophical speculations. In
Does Civilization Need Religion? (1928), he was still persuaded
that the chief function of religion was to assert "the dignity and
worth of human personality in defiance of nature's indifference
and contempt." Even earlier he had recorded his belief that in
some measure the present social misery and discord were due to
"the perversity of the individual." In an article entitled "The
Confessions of a Tired Reformer" (1928), he questioned whether
racial prejudice was not more the result of the universal characteristic of man than, as the liberals thought, of the viciousness of
particular individuals or groups. From then his flight from theological liberalism was at full gallop. By 1932, after the onslaught
of the Depression, he observed that the very best that could be
expected of man was a wise rather than "a stupid self-interest,"
and referred to history as a "perennial tragedy." Six years later
he extended the latter phrase by commenting that human history
was not so much "a chronicle of the progressive victory of good
over evil, of cosmos over chaos, as the story of an ever-increasing
cosmos, creating ever-increasing possibilities of chaos." By then
he was also striking at one of the central doctrines of religious
liberalism or modernism by denying that it was possible to find
a solution to the multiple crises threatening modern man through
the use of rationalism. Reason, he contended, remained a menial
servant of man's passions and of nature's caprices, and the way
back to a relatively peaceful and humane society could be found
only through the use of what he called the "ultrarational" faculties. To save itself humanity had to rely not on *Homo sapiens,* but
rather on *Homo ludens,* the myth maker. A much more comprehensive statement of his ultrarational views (which many of
his opponents called irrational) are to be found in his 1941 Gif-
ford Lectures at the University of Edinburgh, entitled *The Nature
and Destiny of Man.* By some mental alchemy Niebuhr remained
a political radical and a reformer. But his theological views in the
space of some ten years made a one hundred and eighty degree
transit from religious liberalism to a neo-orthodoxy, from the

rational to the ultra or irrational, from engendering hope about the immediate future of the world to a dark and deep pessimism.

It is fascinating to speculate why this massive and profound shift in the thinking of American creative writers and intellectuals took place at the time it did. Most historians concerned only with its immediate political nature and unmindful of the philosophic depth of the change have ascribed it to the disillusionment resulting from the war, America's failure to join the League of Nations, and the triumph of reactionary and materialist politics during the Harding and Coolidge Administrations. Others have explained it as an accumulating response to the series of crises suffered by American society from 1917 to the present, an explanation which does not account for the sharp intensity and the wide latitude of the shift before 1929. Some have tried to relate it to the doctrines of Sigmund Freud and to the new scientific theories of indeterminacy, emanating mostly from biology and physics, which challenged the assuring and comforting nineteenth-century mechanistic explanation of the universe. Still others have seen it as a tidal reaction against the business culture of the twenties. Thus A. M. Schlesinger, Jr., has recently written: "The business culture wanted nothing from the intellectual, had no use for him, gave him no sustenance." Schlesinger further argues that the American intellectual became more of a radical than he had been, more of a friend of the working masses in the factory and the farmer in the field, and a putative New Dealer awaiting 1932.

All of these forces were undoubtedly operative. But what few historians have mentioned as a major cause of the shift in attitudes is the intellectual's deep antipathy to the rising masses and the rapid evolution of modern mass culture. The early 1920's was precisely the time when the vast crowd of lower-middle- and working-class people made their first appreciable impact upon democratic industrial and urban life. The ultimate requirement of mass production made the consumer king, and the tastes and distastes of the buying millions soon dictated the form, the design, the content, and levels of quality not only of consumer goods, but also of many cultural, intellectual, and political institutions.

As early as 1915 Randolph Bourne, the little hunchback intellectual of Washington Square, perceived what was coming. He was gleeful at the demise of the so-called genteel culture of the nineteenth century presided over by millionaires and academicians, but he was not at all happy with what was being substituted for it, a "low-brow snobbery" of the masses which was just as "tyrannical and arrogant" as the aristocratic spirit that had preceded it. "It looks," Bourne concluded, "as if we should have to resist the stale culture of the masses as we resist the stale culture of the aristocrats." But even Bourne, who died during World War I, might have been shocked had he experienced the full impact of the masses on educational and cultural institutions and on national standards of taste. It required H. L. Mencken to register the soaring temperature of indignation. "The American people," he wrote in one heated but not atypical outburst, "taken one with another, constitute the most timorous, snivelling, poltroonish, ignominious mob of serfs and goose-steppers ever gathered under one flag in Christendom since the end of the Middle Ages." Mencken has often been described as a sport, an exceptional nihilist, or simply as a bad boy sticking his tongue out, whose opinions represented no one but himself. If that were so, one is hard-pressed to account for similar phrases uttered by scores of other writers, critics, artists. One has only to look through the first volume of the *Saturday Review of Literature,* founded in 1925, to comprehend how widespread such contemptuous feelings were. Following are some phrases taken from the first year of that journal: "this vulgar society," "the bee swarm of the average," "pervasive mediocrity," "submerged in a sea of the second rate," etc. From other sources come similar ones: "tide of vulgarity" by H. S. Canby; "the unthinking herd," Ludwig Lewisohn; "a herd life," Van Wyck Brooks; "the apotheosis of the average," Ellen Glasgow; "the cult of the second best," Lippmann; "dissolution in the horde," Matthew Josephson; "the well-fed indifferent masses," Rollo W. Brown; "the uprising of the serfs," by a future editor of the *Reader's Digest.*

The evidence clearly suggests that Mencken was not alone in his attack upon the "booboisie." Every one of these phrases, it should be remarked, was written years before Ortega y Gasset's *Revolt of the Masses* appeared in the United States.

From these various strands of contempt for and fear of the masses, of doubts about democracy and progress, and of pessimism about the ultimate destiny of man, one might have expected the weaving of a rather thoroughgoing cultural and philosophical conservatism. As a matter of fact, many of America's intellectuals found other ways of release from their anxiety and frustration. Some fled to London and Paris as a way of revealing their disenchantment with their own culture. Others burned their candle at both ends, indulging in a feverish hedonism. Some found a retreat in extreme aestheticism. George Jean Nathan, cofounder with Mencken of the *American Mercury,* announced that social and political problems did not bother him one iota. What concerned him alone was art, himself, and a few close friends. "For all I care," he concluded, "the rest of the world may go to hell at today's sunset." Still others were attracted by the Russian experiment. Max Eastman, John Dos Passos, and Edmund Wilson all experienced something of a left shift in their political sentiments. From the vantage point of the present, one might well ask whether they were going to the social left or to the right. Is it possible that in the dictatorship of the proletariat they saw the possibility of the cultured becoming the commissars? In the early 1920's, when Edmund Wilson was discussing the way out for the alienated intellectual, he suggested that only two directions were open, either an embarkment on a sea of private fantasy or a retreat into a land where "modern manufacturing methods and modern democratic institutions . . . haven't arrived yet."

The difficulty that most of the intelligentsia faced in outwardly embracing conservatism during the twenties was that hitherto most of them had been ardent radicals. For years before 1920 they had been rebelling against a culture dominated by the post-Civil War millionaires. In that fight their chief ally had been the economic and political radical. To expect them to say farewell to old friends and to join the enemy across the political spectrum was perhaps asking for too much too soon. Most men require a decent interval and a few way stations to cushion an intellectual jump of that magnitude. But perhaps even more of a barrier was the fact that political conservatism in the United States had been and continued to be dominated during the twenties by a class whose narrow materialist views included an area of colossal ignorance and even a suspicion of high culture. Calvin Coolidge and Henry Ford were the reigning conservative heroes—Coolidge, whose views on culture were either totally obscure or nonexistent, and Ford, who confined his "artistic" efforts to collecting old vehicles and McGuffey Readers. Between the intelligentsia and Coolidge and Ford there was nothing in common except hostility. The antagonism was further strengthened during the subsequent Depression by the Roosevelt Administration's energetic efforts in support of the arts and the conservative attack upon practically all the New Deal's intellectual ventures from the Writers' Project to the Federal Theater. As long as the conservatives continued to view state aid to the creative arts as something akin to subverting the foundations of the republic the chances for even a mild flirtation between the two groups was minimal.

Even though the creative mind on the whole continued to regard the political conservative during the twenties and the thirties as its natural enemy, it had nevertheless established the preconditions for the eventual rise of a new political and social outlook. By questioning the doctrine of progress, the intellectuals were tending to sap the reforming élan. By deflating man's claim to moral excellence, they were casting doubt on the possibility of personal reformation. Their assumption that both nature and human society were subject to powerful irrational and uncontrollable forces questioned the validity of much social planning. And their generally pessimistic estimates of the qualities of the masses bred doubts about the worth of extending democracy.

After World War II, the intellectual's path toward philosophical conservatism was made much easier by a number of factors. The Soviets' nationalist policy and Stalin's insistence that the Russian artists cut their creative ideas to fit the Communist party's measurements disabused most Westerners of the hope for a cultural renaissance under Russian socialism. New Deal reforms had achieved many of the aspirations of the one-time radical intellectuals, and thus their programs for social change had arrived at a dead end. But neither the recently endowed labor unions nor the masses showed the deference expected of them by the intelligentsia. Instead, the masses, increasingly concentrating on consuming the multitude of goods and services produced by postwar industry, appeared to the intellectual as colossally indifferent to truth, quality, liberty, and ethics. "Production, consumption and profit," Edmund Wilson wrote with asperity, "have come to play the role that religion played in our grandfather's generation." Such things could not even be discussed, since "they have taken the place of the book of Genesis and the divinity of Jesus Christ. . . ."

In the postwar years, some one-time militant radicals and liberals took long and strange journeys. Although many continued to support liberal causes, some, like Max Eastman and John Chamberlain, for example, became contributors to the bleakly conservative *National Review,* whose editor had pronounced that "all that is finally important in human experience is behind us. . . ." Edmund Wilson toyed with the idea of selective breeding as an antidote to suffocation by the rising mediocrity. The radical journalist Max Lerner described man as "an animal with bestial impulses that can be multiplied by the multiple cunning of his brain." And that consistent apostle of rationalism, Walter Lippmann, labelled the materialist-worshipping masses as the "new barbarians" who were "in" but not "of" Western culture.

Lippmann summed up these antiliberal and antidemocratic sentiments in *The Public Philosophy* (1955). When mass democracy informed through mass communication ruled, Lippmann wrote, no individual confrontation was possible, and consequently by a sort of Gresham's law the irrational statements drove out the more rational. All so-called truths produced by such a system were "self-centered and self-regarding"; all principles were "the rationalization of some special interest." There were "no public criteria of the truth and the false, of the right and wrong beyond that which the preponderant mass of voters, consumers, readers, listeners happen at the moment to be supposed to want." Where mass opinion so formed dominated the government, Lippmann concluded, nothing could result but a "morbid derangement of the true functions of power."

Punctuating this pessimistic chorus were many proposals from both left and right for the restructuring of society. Some critics, among them Reinhold Niebuhr, saw the need for a return to religion and Judaic-Christian values. Others proposed a reconstitution of natural law and natural rights as antidote to the prevailing materialist relativism. Walter Lippmann and Raymond Moley, among many others, argued for natural overriding principles "to command the will and obedience of man." Max Lerner and other radicals preferred to reach back to humanism and traditional socialism for principles of the proposed social reorganization. A few on the extreme right—John Chamberlain, for example—saw "a self-adjusting" natural order in the free market and free capitalism.

Whether from the political right or the left, most critics of the social order hoped to achieve their reconstruction through the creation of a new hierarchical elite that would presumably replace then-operating business, labor, and governmental groups. The character of the new elite was almost as varied as its sponsors. One, a so-called new Jeffersonian elite, was to be "a creative minority" based upon merit and ability, another to be recruited from cultured families, another from a high income level, and still another to be selected from persons with enough technical knowledge so as "to compel the masses to accept rational solutions necessary for survival." But whatever the character of these new select groups, not one of the proposers explained how they could be forged and how they could elicit from the masses the deference necessary to their dominance. Impractical as these elitists were, their large numbers indicated vast disquiet among the intelligentsia with modern mass materialist and relativist democracy. This flight from traditional liberal-radical values added a massive conservative leavening to postwar society which the character of politics was soon to reveal.

8

The Politics of Statics, 1941–1960

WORLD WAR II tended to mute the more strident tones of domestic politics. The flood of war orders providing work for long-dormant industries and more jobs than there were men to fill them somewhat soothed the dispositions of both capital and labor. The abolition of the Works Progress Administration, the New Deal's virtual refusal to propose radical social measures for the duration of hostilities, and the inclusion of thousands of businessmen on the controlling war boards in Washington also helped to suppress temporarily the rancor existing between the supporters of the New Deal and most of the business community. Farmers, faced with unlimited markets for their produce and a government-set scale that insured them more than parity prices for many commodities, were prosperous. And though price, wage, production, and rent controls irritated many people, the great majority accepted them as necessary if the war were to be won. Patriotism and prosperity thus acted as solvents for some of the bitter quarrels of the past decade, solvents which in time were to change the balance of the parties.

Though tending to suppress political divisions in the country, the war sharpened the already growing conflict between the President and Congress. Wars have invariably offered Presidents an ample opportunity for the assumption of near-dictatorial powers. Roosevelt was not timid in seizing the chance. From 1941 on the President, often by necessity, made critical decisions after consultation with a few executive officers. Less and less were Senators and Congressmen called to White House conferences, and increasingly the President asked Congress for immediate action in a peremptory way reminiscent of his first hundred days in office. In 1942, after waiting four months for Congress to act on a price control bill he had recommended, Roosevelt tartly warned the legislature that if they had not acted by October to remove the threat of economic chaos to the country he would. "In the event that Congress should fail to act and act adequately, I shall accept the responsibility, and I will act. . . ." Eighteen months later the President described a pending Congressional tax bill as entirely unsuited to the spirit and purposes of the times. He demanded a law that would abolish all "unreasonable profits," limit personal incomes to $25,000 a year, and provide $10 billion in additional receipts for the government. When the Democratic-controlled Senate passed a bill supplying only an additional $1 billion and ignored his other requests, Roosevelt replied with a sharply censorious veto, which prompted Senator Alben Barkley, one of the President's most loyal supporters, to resign temporarily his position as the majority leader of the Senate.

The timing of Roosevelt's tax demands in 1944 recalled his "soak the rich" program before the election of 1936. His correlative requests in the annual message to Congress in January 1944 for a postwar bill of economic rights, including the right to a job, a decent home, a good education, adequate medical care, and social insurance, raised the suspicion among his opponents that he was willing to run for a fourth term. These requests also ended the wartime moratorium on the discussion of divisive social issues. Persistently Roosevelt refused to campaign for the renomination. When the well-organized Democratic Party Convention met, however, he was selected on the first ballot. But the growing opposition to Presidential dictation as well as to further reforms was made evident by a rebellion of delegates representing big-city machines and the South. With Roosevelt's half-hearted acquiescence they nominated Harry Truman as the Vice-Presidential candidate instead of the liberal incumbent, Henry Wallace.

From the 1938 elections on Republican prospects had been

steadily improving. Although Wendell Willkie had lost in 1940, Roosevelt's margin in popular votes had been much less than in either 1932 or 1936. Moreover, Republican candidates for Congress had fared extremely well in 1940 considering that the party lost the Presidency. Republican resurgence was further marked in 1942 when the formal Democratic control of the House of Representatives was reduced to a mere five votes. Consequently, there was no lack of would-be Republican candidates in 1944. But after Governor Thomas Dewey of New York defeated Wendell Willkie in the Wisconsin primary, his nomination was almost automatic.

Since Dewey was an internationalist and promised to preserve the major social gains of the New Deal, few issues were debated in the campaign of 1944. In his few speeches Roosevelt scarcely acknowledged that he had a competitor. When he did depart from his subjects of war and peace, he identified the Republican party with Herbert Hoover and the Depression. Once again the outcome was scarcely in doubt, but though the President rolled up his customary huge electoral vote, his margin in popular votes—about 3 million—was the smallest for any Presidential campaign since that of 1916. What might have eventually happened to the fortunes of this political wizard was forestalled by his death in the late spring of 1945. Both the complex problems of the peace and the highly explosive domestic issues surrounding demobilization and reconversion were left in the inexperienced hands of Harry Truman.

Despite the loss of China and the Korean War, the Truman-Marshall-Acheson foreign policy won popular approval from the voters. Republican support of the policy, especially when they controlled Congress, and the fact that little of fundamental importance was added to the Truman principles during the next three administrations, is evidence of its quality. Truman's record on domestic affairs, however, was a horse decidedly of another hue.

Perhaps Harry Truman's greatest liability in 1945 and 1946 lay in the public's low estimate of his abilities. He followed one of the ablest politicians who had ever held the Presidency, a man who commanded almost fanatical adoration of the majority at home, and who by 1945 was a world figure of imposing stature. By almost any concrete measurement Truman shrank by comparison with Roosevelt. Physically inconspicuous, he had neither the personal charm nor the assured, cultivated manner of his great predecessor. By comparison his past record was almost a blank one, and he lacked that almost indefinable charismatic quality that a successful Presidential campaign often confers temporarily upon some of the most ordinary politicians.

Truman's inherited Cabinet thought of him in condescending terms. Consequently, during his first few months in office he was obliged to establish his authority. Few administrations since Jackson's have been punctuated by so many personal quarrels. Henry Wallace, Louis Johnson, and J. Howard McGrath were all dismissed from the Cabinet. Henry Morgenthau, Jr., left in a huff, and later James Byrnes and Harold Ickes made public their differences with the President.

Truman's old companions in the Senate also had considerable doubt as to whether he would measure up to the Presidency, and some were not entirely despondent at the prospect. After fourteen years of submitting to the White House, both the Senate and the House were eager to re-establish their authority. The end of the war, a Southern Democrat declared, provided the opportunity not only for dismantling the huge wartime administration but also for "diminishing Presidential power and increasing that of Congress and of the states." This anti-Presidential mood was intensified by the growing conservative complexion of the Congress and the country. The decline in Democratic Congressional majorities from 1938 on had come largely at the expense of the liberal wing of the party. Rising Republican votes in the East and the Midwest had defeated many reliable New Dealers; death had also taken its toll. With the departure of liberal-minded Northern Democrats, control of the Congressional party by traditionalist Southerners became intensified. At one time during Truman's last four years, the President Pro Tempore of the Senate, the Speaker of the House, and the two party whips were all Southerners. Moreover, the chairmen of eighteen of the Senate's thirty-three standing committees were from the South, a number which included most of the more important committees such as those on appropriations, foreign relations, armed services, and banking and currency. Although the Democratic party commanded a national majority during four of the six Truman years, its controlling group in the national legislature was predominantly from one of the two most rural sections of the country, and one that represented less than a third of the nation's total population, and perhaps no more than a fourth of its total voters.

These same years witnessed a similarly striking change in the composition of the Republican party in Congress. In 1938 the Middle and Far Western Republican Senatorial delegation was studded with names like La Follette, Norris, Borah, Johnson, and Capper. By 1950 death and defeat had removed all of these old symbols of revolt against traditional Republican doctrines. During these years a new type of Republican Senator had appeared in the East (especially in New England)—internationally minded and not irrevocably opposed to the interests of labor and minority groups inhabiting the large industrial cities. But the control of the Congressional party was dominated by Republicans from the West, whose thinking lay much closer to the old Republicanism than it did to that of this new Eastern species. Afer the Republican Congressional victory of 1946 Robert Taft of Ohio became the majority leader of the Senate, Kenneth Wherry of Nebraska the majority whip, Eugene Millikin of Colorado chairman of the Republican caucus, and Styles Bridges of New Hampshire chairman of the Appropriations Committee. All of these men came from nonurban states or those, like Ohio, with a long tradition of conservative control. And though Taft departed from the prevailing traditional patterns of their common thought to support housing legislation, the group as a whole tended overwhelmingly to espouse traditional pre-New Deal economic and social theory.

From 1938 on many Southern Democrats in Congress showed a marked tendency to combine with the Republican minority to stop social and economic legislation favoring mass urban groups. During the postwar period the control of both Congressional parties by groups largely representing the South and the Middle and mountain West facilitated a developing coalition probably animated more by the opposition of its constituent parts to the political desires of the urban masses than by positive common principles. The interior of the nation with almost three-quarters of total rural inhabitants was thus in control of Congress.

Both by birth and associations Harry Truman was closely identified with the controlling Congressional groups in each party. Had he chosen to follow his earlier convictions, his relations with Congress might have been far less stormy. But as a Missouri politician and as a Senator Harry Truman was one man, and as a President another. From his wide reading in political history he had acquired a profound respect for the office of the Presidency as well as a Jacksonian attitude toward it. The President, he wrote later, was the "only lobbyist the whole people had in Washington. Almost every aspect of their welfare and activity falls within the scope of his concern. . . ." As the master politician that he was, Truman might have added that the President and the whole people are intimately concerned with one another at the ballot box. He had not spent years living with the Pendergast machine for nothing, and he recognized that a Democratic candidate could not hope to win the office without preserving in some form the four-times-victorious coalition of farmers, laborers, and urban minority groups that Franklin Roosevelt had fashioned.

During the period before the elections of 1946 it appeared as if the President were bent on shattering the combination of interests and sentiment that had maintained the New Deal in office. But Truman felt pledged to carry out the foreign and domestic policies of his predecessor. He was therefore constrained to ask Congress for the first peacetime universal training law and for higher taxes to meet the expanding costs of his foreign policy. Congress honored neither of these requests, nor did it fully meet Truman's demand for a workable price control law to stop the spiralling inflation. An eventual price control compromise failed either to halt ascending prices or to encourage enough immediate production to meet demand. Consequently, black markets reappeared and housewives found themselves unable to obtain meats at their usual shops. The sharp rise in prices brought about numerous labor demands for wage increases, and in 1946 a national railroad strike was threatened hard on long labor stoppages in the automotive and soft coal industries.

Fearing economic chaos the President seized the railroads, and when labor walked off the job in lieu of accepting a compromise wage scale, the President personally appeared before Congress to demand the proclamation of a national emergency under which he might draft the strikers into the army. Fortunately the strike was settled before Truman finished his speech, and his radical proposals were not needed. The President's proposal to draft strikers into the army alienated organized labor temporarily, and public dissatisfaction with inflation, black markets, and price controls—emphasized skillfully by the Republican slogan of "Had enough?"—produced the almost inevitable result. In the elections of 1946 both houses of Congress went Republican. *Life* magazine hailed the Republican Congressional victory as a "significant shift in the government's center of gravity." Congress, which had for years been a "rubber stamp and whipping boy for the White House," would now, it predicted, assume direction of political life. The returning Republicans attempted that and more. Many of them, in fact, saw the election as the equivalent of the Republican victory of 1920 and rejoiced at the opportunity "to repeal the New Deal." Meeting before the opening of Congress, a conference of Republican leaders agreed upon a program of radical reductions in government expenditures, lower taxes, a return to states' rights in health and welfare measures, and the abandonment of government interference with business and labor.

The new Congressional leadership started out bravely if inconsistently with their announced program. The passage of the Taft-Hartley Act outlawing the closed shop, empowered States to pass right-to-work acts, gave employers more latitude in speaking against unions and in petitioning for shop elections, and gave the President limited powers to enjoin strikes that imperiled the national security. The Act also prohibited the use of union dues in political campaigns and required a non-Communist oath from labor leaders using the facilities of the National Labor Relations Board. The President called the Act "a slave labor measure," but it was promptly passed over his veto. Against Presidential opposition the new Congress also reduced taxes and passed a farm support measure that substituted a flexible scale of price supports for the old rigid formula of 90 per cent parity. It did, however, despite much criticism, support the President's European foreign policy.

But the Eightieth Congress by no means took the play for public attention away from the White House. Starting with his annual message in January 1947, Truman fairly peppered the national legislature with requests for basic social reform. His demands for a broad extension of social security, for a scheme of Federally supported public medicine, for extensive aid to education, for further aid to agriculture, and for the repeal of the Taft-Hartley Act were all ignored by the Republican majority precisely as they would have been had the Democrats controlled Congress. But the President was perhaps not so much interested in securing reform legislation as he was in securing his election in 1948 and a Democratic victory. The President's game, of course, was to place the responsibility for the lack of benefits to farmers, laborers, and minority groups on the Republican majority in Congress and by ignoring the contributions of the Democrats to Congressional inactivity to preserve the victorious coalition.

The Republican convention did its best to defeat the Presidential strategy by denying the nomination to Senator Robert Taft, the man who best represented the principles of the party's officeholders. After General Eisenhower declined to be considered on the grounds that the "wise subordination of military to civil power will be best sustained when life-long professional soldiers abstain from seeking high political office," the prize again went to Governor Dewey of New York, already on record as an internationalist and a supporter of most New Deal reforms.

The party platform also clashed with the professions of its Congressional leaders. It advocated a broad extension of the social security program, Federal aid to housing, a "just" system of price supports for farm products, the abrogation of state poll taxes, and fair employment legislation. Only in the platform's demand for government economy did the convention defer to the principles of its officeholders. But by doing so it cast some doubt upon its zeal for the reforms it had already proposed.

If the Republican managers were less than true to the party's Congressional record in the 1948 convention the Democrats had difficulty in finding many principles which were acceptable to even a bare majority of the party. Aroused by Truman's adamant stand against Russia, extreme left-wing Democrats broke away to organize the Progressive Party, led by Henry Wallace and Senator Glen Taylor of Idaho. The more moderate left, including Americans for Democratic Action, was equally opposed to the President because they believed he had deserted the New Deal by eliminating Wallace, Ickes, and Morgenthau from his cabinet. A civil rights program supported by Hubert Humphrey, mayor of Minneapolis, and by the President resulted in the defection from the convention of over thirty Southern delegates. These "Dixiecrats" later held a convention at Birmingham, formed the States' Rights Democratic Party, and nominated two Southern Governors as their candidates. Even the usually dependable big-city bosses, fearing certain defeat with Truman, attempted without success to interest General Eisenhower in the nomination. Because of the President's threat to enlist the striking miners in the army, organized labor was unenthusiastic about a second term, and the Midwestern farmer, it was freely alleged, had returned to his normal Republican affiliation. Had the chances for a Democratic victory looked better or had an acceptable alternative candidate been available, the Convention might have made another nomination. But since the President insisted upon a renomination, the party gloomily went through the familiar motions and prepared itself for defeat.

The following campaign was one of the most startling in recent history. Since the public opinion polls all showed Dewey as a certain winner, the Republican candidate was rather nonchalant in his electioneering efforts. His relatively few campaign speeches were dignified and almost noncontroversial. Dewey challenged neither the premises of the Administration's European foreign policy nor the basic reforms of the New Deal. As the more stalwart Republicans fumed about the "me too" atmosphere of the campaign, the Republican candidate contented himself with the argument that his party would carry out the existing foreign and domestic programs with far more efficiency and economy than could "the tired, confused, strife-ridden and politically minded" Democrats. Dewey left the vulgar aspects of the campaign to his more partisan colleagues.

The President, however, would not participate in a gentlemanly front-porch campaign redolent of the Harding and McKinley tradition. Almost deserted by the higher-ranking members of his party and lacking the plentiful finances of his opponent, he waged an intensely partisan and astoundingly individual canvass, most of which was aimed at bread-and-butter issues. Calling attention to the social welfare promises of the Republican platform, he recalled Congress into an unprecedented July session, demanding that the Republican-dominated Congress live up to the professions of its official program. When the session adjourned without accomplishment, Truman labelled it as a "do nothing Congress," one of the worst in history. The President followed this partisan ploy with an old-style cross-country campaign in which he repeatedly read a partisan record on the Eightieth Congress. In the cities he called the Taft-Hartley measure a slave labor act and asked labor whether it thought it would be better off under a Republican or a Democratic President. Before recent immigrants he flayed the "anti-Semitic, anti-Catholic" immigration bill passed by the Republican Congress. He reminded Jewish voters of his recent and extremely speedy recognition of the State of Israel. In agricultural regions he asked farmers whether they proposed to vote for the Republican sliding scale of subsidies or for the Democratic 90 per cent plan. And almost everywhere he characterized his opponents as the party of the oil and power lobbies.

In a more positive vein "give-them-hell Harry" Truman elaborated his Fair Deal, a program which contained almost every major social reform seriously proposed at any time. It included programs for extensive public housing, for Federal aid to education, for publicly supported medicine and hospitalization, particularly for the aged, a long range scheme for agricultural price supports, the freeing of labor from the Taft-Hartley measure, the extension of social security, and the passage of a broad civil rights measure insuring "equal status to the Negro and other minority groups." But acute politician that he was, Truman relied mainly for success on the past record instead of on future promises. His political philosophy was summed up in his observation late in the campaign that the farmers and laborers would be "the most ungrateful people in history" if they turned the Democrats out and voted the Republicans in.

To the consternation of the poll takers and the surprise of most politicians Truman won, although by a very small popular majority. Though he lost the densely populated Eastern states of Connecticut, New York, Pennsylvania, New Jersey, Delaware, and Maryland, and four states in the deep South, his victories from Ohio west helped make up the winning total of electoral votes. Unable to explain the results in rational terms—Senator Taft remarked that it defied "all common sense for the country to send that roughneck ward politician back to the White House"—most interpreters regarded the election outcome as just one more victory for the coalition of voters that the New Deal had put together. Enough farmers and laborers and members of minority and fringe groups, they explained, were still letting their memories of the depression-ridden thirties dominate their political thinking. But despite the fact that Truman carried virtually every major city in the country, he won most of them by an extremely small margin: New York by only 300,000, Chicago by 200,000, Los Angeles by 8,000, and Philadelphia by less than 7,000. Obviously the city voter was no longer as enchanted with the Democratic party as he had been since 1932. And had not the Southern racial extremists aided Truman with the Northern Negro community by opposing him, the election might have had a different outcome. Otherwise the Truman victory depended upon the support he received from the normally Republican territory from Ohio to the Pacific.

Although the President regularly throughout the next four years recommended his Fair Deal program to Congress, not even a majority of his own party was inclined to support much of it.

Some expansion of social security was obtained. Modest funds were voted for public housing and slum clearance. By executive measures the civil rights of minorities were somewhat extended. But the conservative coalition of Southern Democrats and Midwestern Republicans blocked most efforts at further reform. Moreover, a series of spectacular developments relating to foreign affairs practically obliterated most domestic issues from the public mind.

In 1949 Russia exploded its first atomic bomb, just after two Americans were charged with cooperating with the Russian espionage system. The rumor gained currency that the rapid Soviet perfection of the bomb had been made possible by secret information leaked from official American sources. Since Alger Hiss, one of those charged with Communist connections, had been a member of the State Department under Roosevelt and Truman, the Hiss perjury trial and the spy trials rapidly assumed an air of partisan politics. Some Republicans who had already charged Truman with being soft on domestic Communists saw in Hiss's conviction proof that the Administration and particularly the State Department was honeycombed with traitors. After the victory of the Communists in China and the beginning of the Korean War, the Republican charge was made repeatedly that subversives in the State Department had planned the American debacle in Asia.

Leading the Republican campaign to tar the Administration with the brush of Communism was Senator Joseph McCarthy of Wisconsin. Defeating the incumbent Senator Robert La Follette, Jr., in 1946, McCarthy was practically unknown until he made the public charge in February 1950 that the State Department was "thoroughly infested with Communists." The Senator added that he had a list of 205 Communists in the State Department, although a month later he reduced this number to "fifty-seven card-carrying members of the Communist party." When asked for specific names, McCarthy was unable to produce one. But he maintained himself in the daily newspaper headlines by completely unverified attacks in the same vein upon a series of important Administration leaders, the most prominent of whom were

Secretary of State Dean Acheson and his predecessor General George Marshall.

The official Democratic reply to the McCarthy charges was made by President Truman. McCarthy's activities, as well as those of the House Committee on un-American Activities and of other Republican Red hunters, he said, were "red herring," designed to win votes and not to protect the country from subversion. The President pointed out that long before McCarthy had taken up the subversion cry the Administration's own loyalty boards had been operating, but operating on the traditional basis that precluded "character assassination" by the widespread publication of rumors and unverified facts. Truman concluded that the desperate Republicans, unable to win by any other means, had descended to the irrational issue of a Communist internal conspiracy and were, by their wild and unfounded accusations, destroying reputations and careers for the sake of winning the next Presidential election. Radicals and liberals also accused the Red hunters of attempting to destroy the New Deal heritage by smearing its proponents and reinstituting conservatism just as they had done before, in the election of 1920. But as an increasing number of respected Republicans approved of the anti-Red campaign and as new revelations of Russian espionage in the United States, as well as in Canada and Great Britain, were published, the voters increasingly tended to believe the charge that an internal subversive threat existed and that the Truman Administration was incapable of dealing with the conspiracy.

The Administration ran into other difficulties before the elections of 1952. The President's firing of General MacArthur was necessary if civilian supremacy over the military was to be preserved. But the general's removal was not popular, and the Administration's continued inability to bring the Korean hostilities to an end also provoked the public. Although a majority probably agreed that a limited war was preferable to an attack on China, with the possibility of Russian atomic retaliation, it was difficult to give up the hope for victory and to support an endless war. Almost as damaging to the Administration's reputation was the revelation of fraud in the Bureau of Internal Revenue and "influence peddling" in other important agencies.

The Democrats probably selected their strongest candidate in nominating Adlai Stevenson. His apparent reluctance to become a candidate and his refusal to see most public questions in black and white terms permitted his opponents to charge him with indecisiveness. His careful prose and cultivated wit also opened him to the charge of being an "intellectual" at a time when that class was under popular suspicion of being at best impractical and at worst of harboring subversives. But Stevenson had been a very able Governor of Illinois, and in appearance, mentality, and political instincts he was far removed from Truman. To a party split between Americans for Democratic Action on one pole and racially minded states' rights Southerners on the other, these qualities were a distinct advantage. Even so, after the Republican nomination almost all chance for a Democratic victory vanished.

The contest for the 1952 Republican nomination emphasized that the party had no more cohesion than its opponents. With the death of Senator Vandenberg, Robert Taft had become the official spokesman of the Congressional party on both domestic and foreign affairs. His consistent anti-New Deal record and his advocacy in January 1951 of an "oceanic" foreign policy, which would have protected the island nations of the Atlantic and the Pacific from Communist aggression but would have stopped short of maintaining an American army on either the European or Asiatic continents, had won the support of a good many Republican officeholders. The Taft formula was the first offered by the party that would have greatly limited American commitments abroad and yet could not be labelled isolationist. Both as a foreign policy statement and as an economy measure it appealed to the Midwest, precisely the section that had supplied most of the victories for the party in the long, lean days since 1932. The Senator was hailed as "Mr. Republican," and during the early months of the nomination campaign a Taft victory seemed inevitable.

The Taft candidacy did not go unchallenged. Liberal Republicans, and especially the internationalists in the party, started a search for alternatives. Led by Dewey, Harold Stassen (then President of the University of Pennsylvania), Senator Henry Cabot Lodge, and Governor Earl Warren of California, these groups had a distinct East and West Coast flavor and were recruited mainly from the non-Congressional elements of the party. Eventually most of the anti-Taft men came to support General Dwight D. Eisenhower, at the time commander of the NATO forces in Europe, who in late 1951 retracted his nonpolitical position of four years before. Eisenhower had many advantages for a divided party whose thirst for victory had been so long unslaked. Except on foreign policy, he was without a political record. Few knew until January 1952, when Lodge announced the fact, that he was even a Republican. Born in a small Texas town and raised in another in Kansas by a family struggling to maintain itself economically, he had much appeal for the old-stock rural Americans. His brilliant military career endeared him to many conservative businessmen and made his patriotism unimpeachable, even to the most ardent nationalist. Moreover, the man exuded integrity, personal warmth, and charm, along with other virtues not ordinarily connected with the military profession—modesty and tolerance. Eisenhower had the common touch, which he came by honestly. Although his first few speeches were marked as much by their lack of platform skill as by their author's unfamiliarity with leading domestic questions, Eisenhower's enormous popularity was well attested to by the public opinion polls. Well before the conventions met, a Gallup poll showed that he would likely defeat either of the leading Democratic candidates, whereas Taft was shown trailing them both. The Taft managers did not help their candidate by attempting to secure votes in the convention by the old political methods. But in the last analysis Eisenhower was selected by a slim margin on the first convention ballot because of the prevailing feeling that he alone of the Republican candidates might win. The bitterness of the Taft supporters was summed up in the remark of his campaign manager characterizing the opposition as the "gang of Eastern internationalist and Republican New Dealers who ganged up to sell the Republican party down the river in 1940, in 1944 and in 1948."

For a time after the convention Taft and many of his regular Republican supporters appeared to be thoroughly alienated, and newspaper stories appeared stating that Taft would not help in the campaign unless he was assured that the candidate would support Republican principles. At Eisenhower's invitation, however, Taft was invited to a September conference in New York, after which he announced that the General and he agreed on all important issues except those on foreign policy. Since after the election Taft immediately placed his own supporters in the most important Congressional committee posts, it is a fair inference, despite the testimony in Eisenhower's *Mandate for Change,* that the two men also agreed that the Senator and not the President would be the real leader of the Congressional Republican party. Eisenhower's patent unwillingness to lead Congress during the remainder of Taft's life was later ascribed to his "Whig" view of the Presidency. But perhaps it would be a more accurate guess to lay his Congressional inactivity to a bargain, perhaps only tacitly struck at the Morningside Heights Conference.

The Republican nominee also courted the favor of other important dissident Republicans. There was to be some retreat from an internationalist foreign policy. But in some ways the comments of Eisenhower and his chief adviser, John Foster Dulles, were much more militant in their foreign interventionism than those of their opponents. On domestic issues the nominee sounded almost as conservative as a Midwestern right winger might hope for. Although he declared that he was for the "broad middle way" and that most of the New Deal's social gains should be preserved, he denounced an excess of government intervention and in almost Taftian tones suggested that "if all that Americans want is security, then they can go to a prison." He supported Senator McCarthy in Wisconsin, commenting that while their methods might differ, their ends were the same. He appeared with the reactionary Senator Jenner in Indiana, and of course he attacked the Truman domestic record with wholehearted enthusiasm as predicted. Eisenhower was elected by an impressive margin, losing in only nine Southern states.

The Eisenhower Cabinet was acclaimed by the party's regulars. Although not, as one of the Administration's critics described it, composed of "nine millionaires and a plumber," it was a very wealthy and conservative group and included at least two strong Taft supporters. The State Department's meek acceptance of McCarthy's demands in 1953 cheered the ultranationalists. And the Taft-sponsored legislative program resulting in a reduction in taxes, the grant of the tidal oil lands to the states, and the reduction in the level of government payments to farmers was meat and drink to the party's conservatives. They were equally pleased by the Administration's refusal to permit the TVA to build and operate a coal-burning power-producing station and by the contracts awarded to private companies for the development of hydroelectric power in Hell's Canyon, on the Snake River.

Despite the President's occasional denunciation of "creeping socialism" and the apparent reversal of the national conservation policy, the record of Eisenhower's first term was not an unmixed one. Especially after Senator Taft's death in 1953, the censuring and deflation of Senator McCarthy, and the Democratic Congressional victory of 1954, the Administration's tendency was away from accepted Midwestern Republican principles. During the 1952 campaign Eisenhower had defined his political attitude as one leaning toward conservatism in economic matters and toward liberalism in social concerns. But during the recessions of 1953 and 1954 the Administration used both fiscal and monetary policies to reinflate the economy and suggested it was ready to resort to broad public spending if necessary to stop a downward plunge. In 1954 the President even boasted that by controlling the economy the government could practically guarantee the continuance of prosperity; "the fear of a paralyzing depression can be safely laid away." No New Dealer had claimed more for governmental intervention.

In his second State of the Union message the President described his goals as "first, to protect the freedom of our peoples; second, to maintain a strong growing economy; third, to concern ourselves with the human problems of the individual citizens." In elaboration of the last point he proposed during the remainder of his first term the extension of social security to workers in small establishments and to the self-employed, extensive increases in funds devoted to public housing and to education, and a highways bill which contemplated the construction of over forty thousand miles of superhighways, financed by both state and Federal funds. Despite Secretary of Agriculture Benson's laissez-faire views, payments to support agricultural prices actually rose during the Eisenhower years. And although the military budget was reduced, total Federal spending increased, largely because of social expenditures.

Not all of the President's recommendations were accepted by Congress, which was as thoroughly dominated by the Southern Democratic–Midwestern Republican coalition as its predecessors had been. Certainly on issues of foreign policy, and to a lesser extent on domestic questions, the President received more Congressional support after the Democratic victory of 1954 than before. At various times, starting with his campaign of 1952, Eisenhower had labelled his brand of politics as "liberal conservatism" and then successively as "dynamic conservatism," "moderate progressivism," and "progressive moderation." The ascending scale of progressive emphasis perhaps revealed the President's growing exasperation with the static approach of most of his fellow Republicans in Congress. Or perhaps it reflected his own evolution toward a more progressive scale of political values along much the same course that Roosevelt and Truman had followed before him.

Well before the Presidential election of 1956 Eisenhower had used the term "new Republicanism," which he later modified to "modern Republicanism." And for a period the President acted as if he were about to give his party strong executive leadership in an effort to remodel it. During 1955 he vetoed a bill that would have freed the producers of natural gas from regulation by the Interstate Commerce Commission, not because, he explained, he disagreed with the principle, but because it had been shown that friends of the bill had used money liberally in winning Congressional support. Under strong pressure the President eventually cancelled the Dixon-Yates contract that had bypassed the TVA and awarded the construction of a power station to a private concern. During the election campaign of 1956 he strenuously supported his proposals for more Federal aid to schools and to public housing, pressed for his highway-building program and for a soil bank which would decrease agricultural production by removing marginal lands from cultivation.

The election results of 1956 were among the most anomalous in history. Eisenhower defeated Stevenson by almost 10 million votes, carrying all but seven states in the South, and, even more surprising, winning a margin in each of the four largest cities of the country. The Eisenhower victory in New York, Chicago, Philadelphia, and Los Angeles, to say nothing of that in traditional Democratic cities like Jersey City, indicated that the longtime alliance between the Democratic party and the minority and laboring groups in the large cities had at least temporarily ended, a major political revolution that unquestionably would be taken into consideration by the party managers four years later. But despite the President's immense popularity, the Republican party failed to win control of either the House or the Senate and lost more Gubernatorial races than it won. For the first time in history a winning President was to be confronted with a hostile Congress during its opening session. Analyzing the results, commentators remarked that the Democrats had been beaten in a popularity contest, but had won an election.

Without the President's personal popularity, the Republican party was still a minority one, a fact that spurred Eisenhower, in vigorous postelection efforts, either to reshape or replace it. Both in his second inaugural address and in a talk to the National Committee he emphasized that the party was doomed unless local and state organizations showed more willingness to adopt the principles of what he called "modern Republicanism," which in effect would moderate its hostility to government intervention in economic life and to reforms appealing to the urban masses. When his appeals to the National Committee for party renovation were ignored, the President for a time thought of founding a new conservative party, but gave up the scheme as impractical.

And as his liberal recommendations to Congress were treated with no more respect by the Republican minority, he gradually lost interest in party reform and turned his major attention, as Roosevelt and Truman had done before him, to foreign affairs. The Congressional elections of 1958 continued the existing pattern of nominal Democratic control with real power located in the Southern and Midwestern coalition, a Democratic-Republican alliance that had frustrated his predecessors in office and was to thwart the plans of his successor.

It was perhaps almost predetermined that Eisenhower would not form a new party or commit drastic surgery on the old one. New parties are usually organized and led by young, extremely energetic, ambitious, and dedicated politicians. The President possessed these qualities in very moderate amounts, if at all. As Presidents go, he was rather old when he took office. During his tenure he had two serious illnesses. Even when feeling well Eisenhower scarcely engrossed himself in the political details of his job. He took frequent vacations, left many of the Presidential chores to his subordinates, and avoided partisan politics and politicians whenever he conveniently could. The truth was that the President did not like his job very much and freely confessed his distaste to his personal friends, who, for the most part, were selected from outside the ranks of professional politicians. Moreover, most of his personal qualities ill-fitted him to engage in partisan rows. Eisenhower was a moderate, kindly, and friendly man, a respecter of people, traditions, and institutions, a conciliator instead of a creator.

But if Eisenhower did not remake the official Republican party, he nevertheless sensibly altered it, certainly modified its public presence, and quite possibly saved it from oblivion. A few more Presidential defeats and the party, dominated by the remaining Adullamites in Congress who had either withdrawn from the modern world or who had never entered it, and committed to hopelessly outdated, anti-New Deal, anti-urban, anti-international principles, might well have disappeared as a vital political force. Eisenhower completed what Senator Vandenberg had started; he severed the connection in the public mind between Republicanism and a narrow nineteenth-century nationalism quite antiquated in the modern world. To a lesser degree he also destroyed the link between Republicanism and a dogmatic hostility to social reform, and to that extent he urbanized the party. True, Republican platforms since 1936 had given lip service to many New Deal reforms, and individual Republicans, mostly from urban areas, had greatly contributed to the enactment of both social and civil rights measures. But most Republicans in the Senate and the House before 1953 denied by vote and voice any relationship with the party's published programs, except possibly for those portions dealing with agriculture. The plaint of an Eastern Republican Congressman as he declined to run for office again illustrated the almost intolerable tension existing between the party's professions and its actions. He could not, he declared, continue to talk conservative enough to be nominated, liberal enough to be elected, and reactionary enough to succeed in his party's permanent organization.

By no means did the Eisenhower alterations come without a struggle. For a time the more parochial Republican members of the Senate threatened to pass the Bricker constitutional amendment and submit it to the states for adoption. Had it been accepted, this brain child of Senator John Bricker of Ohio would have severely limited the Presidential power to manage foreign policy and lodged it in the Senate. The Midwestern Republican and Southern Democratic conservative coalition also curtailed or blocked the President's program of domestic reform. Eisenhower's requests for public housing, aid to education, and highways were drastically cut. His recommendation that the Federal government subsidize medical treatment for the aged was ignored. But the President did secure enough in the areas of social security, housing and slum clearance, aid to education, and especially in civil rights for Negroes, to weaken the previous almost automatic relationship between Republicanism and opposition to social measures.

By 1960 civil rights had become a dominant issue in American politics, and one that threatened once more to disrupt and possibly revolutionize historic party patterns. For historic reasons the Negro vote, until 1932, had been largely Republican. But then the New Deal's relief, Federal work, and social security programs had converted it almost overnight. After World War II the opposition by conservative property owners in the cities to high relief costs and Truman's civil rights policy kept most Negroes in the Democratic ranks. By executive order Truman had abolished segregation in the armed forces, and he twice requested Congress to pass civil rights legislation empowering the Federal government to secure voting rights for Southern Negroes as well as equality of public rights. In both instances Southern resistance had blocked legislation and Southern schisms had threatened the unity of the Democratic party.

The Negro's allegiance to the Democratic party was threatened, however, during the Eisenhower Administration for more positive reasons than Southern Democratic resistance to the granting of rights. Spurred by Presidential requests, Congress passed two civil rights measures, in 1957 and 1960, under which the Attorney General started suits to obtain Negro voting rights. Simultaneously, the Interstate Commerce Commission abolished Jim Crow regulations for interstate travel. Of perhaps more enduring importance was the action of the Supreme Court in 1954. The Court, headed by Chief Justice Earl Warren, an Eisenhower appointee, reversed the fifty-eight-year-old rule permitting school segregation in the South provided the facilities were equal. The Court now ordered all public schools desegregated "with all deliberate speed," a decision that caused a racial explosion, first in the South and then in the North.

Although a few of the border states sought to comply with the Supreme Court ruling, it was met with the most vigorous opposition in the rest of the South. At Little Rock, Arkansas, September 1957, the opposition led by Governor Orval Faubus eventually forced the President to send Federal troops to enforce a court order for the desegregation of the public schools and to protect Negro students from the violence of mobs and of local authorities. In other Southern states the Supreme Court decision was either ignored or the public schools were closed. Five years after the first Civil Rights Act less than a quarter of Southern Negroes had registered to vote, and in the space of nine years after the Court decision only 8 to 10 per cent of Southern Negro children were attending desegregated schools.

Responding to this failure of gradualism, the national Negro population of almost 20 million became militant. In both the North and the South, Negro organizations flourished and organized boycotts, sit-ins, and mass demonstrations to secure an equality of rights that rapidly extended to the abolition of all Jim Crow practices, whether formal or informal, and to equal opportunities for jobs and housing. Although most of the Negro protests were, considering the provocation, models of peaceful, democratic action, violence flared even in the North. World War II had brought another great wave of Negroes north, and the massive migration continued until the Negro constituted a major population group in practically all large Northern cities. They were in the majority in Washington, D.C., and Newark, New Jersey; they were a quarter or more of the population of Chicago, Cleveland, Cincinnati, Detroit, Philadelphia, and St. Louis. By 1960 they were a million strong in New York City.

Because of poverty and white restrictions they usually settled in all-Negro slums, where living conditions were not radically different from the immigrant slums of sixty years before. Consequently, all of the old nineteenth-century tensions that had existed between the new "aliens" and the "old Americans" reappeared. But because of the racial difference, the growing scarcity of jobs for the unskilled, and the increasing militancy of Negro leaders, this latter-day conflict was much intensified. By 1960 the question of equal rights had become a major political and social issue in both the North and the South.

At the end of Eisenhower's second term all indications pointed to the possibility that the nation was headed for a major political reorientation. From 1938 on both major parties and Congress had been dominated by conservative and rural-minded majorities. Essentially the situation had come about because of two special situations. First, historic apportionment had given the rural communities an increasingly disproportionate share of representation in state governments, party machines, and in the Senate of the United States. Second, the dominance of the South in the Democratic party and of the Middle West in the Republican, chiefly because they were safe districts for the incumbent officeholders, led to the control of Congress by an informal but real coalition. At the same time, however, an urban nation was becoming rapidly more so. By 1960 70 per cent of the American people lived in towns or cities, a political fact that showed up regularly every four years in Presidential nominations and elections.

Because the President was elected by popular vote, he was the chief representative of the underrepresented urban majority, and as a consequence the postwar conflict between the White House and the Capitol rapidly increased in intensity. The situation was a major cause for the increased prestige of the President, the Administrative wing of the government, and the Supreme Court in the postwar era. Since the thinking of Congress was not in harmony with that of the majority of the country, many major and necessary adjustments had to come through the action of the Chief Executive or by the judiciary. Very much to the point was the Presidential and judicial lead in matters of civil rights, and, in fact, in the reapportionment of political representation. For the first time in history, shortly after 1960, the Supreme Court intervened in local political affairs and ordered reapportionment of state districts, a move that clearly foreshadowed the future diminution of rural power.

Because the official parties had ceased to represent the majority of the voters in several crucial areas, the parties themselves were rapidly losing prestige and strength, a fact attested to both by the rapidly growing numbers of independent registrations and by the almost unprecedented election of 1956, which produced a President from one party and a Congressional majority from another. The critical struggle over civil rights also betokened a change in the traditional make-up of the parties. Essentially a moral and ethical issue, civil rights was of the stuff that creates new parties or alters old ones, as the history of the country attests. In 1960 both parties stood in a paradoxical relationship to the civil rights issue. The Democrats, whose hopes for victory lay in the minority groups and with labor, were permanently embarrassed by a South apparently determined to maintain as many attributes of white supremacy as possible. As the traditional conservative party, the

Republicans were as perplexed as their rivals. For much of twentieth-century conservative strength lay in the rural regions. The South was a natural ally, and any attempt to base the party on the new urban majorities would *ipso facto* change its fundamental nature. Urbanism and civil rights had thus become the fuelling forces for significant political change.

Tension was also increasing between the proponents of the technical and cultural elite and the passive adherents of a social system, the esthetic, cultural, and scientific standards of which were set by the mechanisms involved in the mass production-consumption society. As the rapid technical evolution demanded an ever more rigorously trained intelligentsia, the chief engines of mass culture, education, and information—the radio, television, and movies, the stage, publishing industry, schools, newspapers, and the periodical press—were under constant pressure to adjust their standards to the tastes and the comprehension of the masses. By 1960 educational reform had excited much talk and some action. But whether the secondary schools and the multi-universities could accommodate themselves to staggering increases in enrollment and still persist in raising their standards to the demands of the new society was still an open question. In 1960 the reorientation of American life was yet a matter for the future, even though the latent forces of change had been accumulating rapidly for twenty years. Partially as a result of rural political overrepresentation, as well as because of urgent foreign problems, little had been accomplished in meeting the manifold and intricate problems created by a burgeoning urban and technical civilization, the geography of which often ignored state boundaries, and the demanding standards of which were frequently beyond the comprehension of the masses. But the static quality that had characterized American politics from 1945 to 1960 could not continue indefinitely. The pressures were too insistent and the stakes were too high. By 1960 significant change seemed to be a necessity if the new and vigorous urban society were to endure. Just as many of the old cherished agrarian social virtues had given way to the new, urban values had to evolve to meet the needs of a new and very much changed nation.

Bibliographical Essay

EXCEPT FOR the textbook writers, few historians have attempted an interpretation of the years fom 1920 to the present. This becomes thoroughly understandable: so much has happened during these years, and so much is coming into print about the events, that to expect even an evaluation of the sources of the period is asking the impossible. The historian of very recent times depends as he must upon the monographic studies produced by fellow scholars, but for the years 1920–1960 the amount of scholarly studies based upon original sources is still minimal. For a variety of obvious reasons, the economic affairs for the entire period have been thoroughly studied. And many good diplomatic monographs, covering the years from 1920 to 1941, have been produced. Increasingly, excellent studies are appearing covering selected aspects of American society in the twenties; and the critical literature devoted to New Deal politics has now assumed an imposing bulk. But for a thousand other important subjects the historian must depend upon a host of magazine, journal, and newspaper articles, and upon polemics and exhortative works, many of which are extremely biased and most of which are incomplete. Because of the uncertain quality of many sources and because of space limitations, this bibliography, confined entirely to books, will be highly selective and tilted toward the particular subjects emphasized in the volume.

I. RISE OF THE URBAN MASS MIND

Although Henry May, *The End of American Innocence* (1959), covers only the period from 1912 to 1917, it is of basic importance to an understanding of some of the mass social movements during the twenties. General in tone and more directly focused upon society during the decade are: Mark Sullivan, *Our Times* (Vol. 6, 1935); F. L. Allen's perceptive *Only Yesterday* (1931); Charles Merz, *The Great American Bandwagon* (1928); and Lloyd Morris, *Not So Long Ago* (1949). Robert and Helen Lynd, *Middletown* (1929), a comprehensive sociological study of Muncie, Indiana, has become a prime historical source; as has The President's Research Committee on Social Trends, *Recent Social Trends in the United States* (1933). For contemporary British views of American Society see George Knoles, *The Jazz Age* (1955). And although W. E. Leuchtenberg, *The Perils of Prosperity* (1958), is a general account of the decade, the chapters on morals and on the second industrial revolution should especially be consulted.

MASS CULTURE. Although more directly pointed toward post-World War II society, Max Lerner's *America as a Civilization* (1957) contains much that is relevant to the rise of the mass society in the twenties. Equally oriented toward the present but with equivalent yields for the twenties are two collections of essays of extremely varying qualities: B. Rosenberg and D. M. White, eds., *Mass Culture* (1957), and Philip Olson, ed., *America as a Mass Society* (1963). A must for all students of recent social movements is Dwight MacDonald's "Masscult and Midcult," which forms the first chapter in the author's *Against the American Grain* (1962), a book largely devoted to social analysis by the way of literary criticism. George E. Mowry, ed., *The Twenties* (1963), contains a selection of sources pointed toward some of the mass social phenomena of the decade.

THE CITY. Lewis Mumford, *The City in History* (1961), is a fascinating interpretation of the place of the city in human society over the past 5,000 years. Blake McKelvey, *The Urbanization of America, 1860–1915* (1963), throws much light on recent urban developments in the United States. Unfortunately, other American historians have up to now spent most of their efforts on the colonial and nineteenth-century cities and have left much of the analysis of contemporary city life to sociologists. Among the more rewarding of these works are Anselm Strauss, ed., *Images of the American City* (1961); R. M. Fisher, ed., *The Metropolis in Modern Life* (1955); J. R. Seeley, R. A. Sun, and E. W. Loosley, *Crestwood Heights: The Culture of Suburban Life* (1956); and Robert C. Weaver, *The Urban Complex* (1962).

ECONOMIC INSTITUTIONS. The best general economic history of the twenties is George Soule, *Prosperity Decade* (1947). But T. C. Cochrane, *The American Business System* (1957), throws light on some long-time trends. Adolf Berle and Gardiner Means, *The Modern Corporation and Private Property* (1932), is by now a classic on the changing nature of the corporate structure. For a blistering contemporary evaluation of social impact of the new business see J. T. Adams, *Our Business Civilization* (1929). J. W. Prothro, *The Dollar Decade: Business Ideas in the 1920's* (1954), illuminates the newer thinking of corporate management, while Irvin Wyllie, *The Self Made Man in America* (1954), sets down the history of an older type of corporate executive. Otis Pease, *The Responsibilities of American Advertising*

(1958), is the first intelligent excursion into an institution that needs much more study than it has hitherto received. A general work on the changing technology is Roger Burlingame, *Engines of Democracy* (1940). But the whole relationship between technology and science and modern society has scarcely been touched by the historian.

Among the many more formal economic studies of the period, perhaps the best in pointing up the relationship between economic institutions and society are Frederic Mills, *Economic Tendencies in the United States* (1932); Charles Bliss, *The Structure of Manufacturing Production* (1946); Arthur Burns, *The Decline of Competition* (1936); and R. G. Tugwell, *Industry's Coming of Age* (1927). For a contemporary conservative viewpoint see T. N. Carver, *The Present Economic Revolution in the United States* (1925). Although prepared for the purposes of on-going policy, the U.S. National Resources Committee, *Technological Trends and National Policy* (1937), is a basic source for the first postwar decade.

MASS TRANSPORTATION AND COMMUNICATION. No scholarly study exists of the thorny but intimate relationship between modern society and the automobile. But for an early, courageous attempt see in *The Annals of the American Academy of Political and Social Science* (Nov. 1924, Vol. CXVI) a study entitled "The Automobile: Its Province and Problems." Allan Nevins and F. E. Hill, *Ford: Expansion and Challenge, 1915–1933* (1957), is the second volume of an impressive work. Alfred D. Chandler, Jr., *Giant Enterprise* (1964), deals with the competitive race between Ford and General Motors. Also see the much more critical Keith Seward, *The Legend of Henry Ford* (1948). The rise of mass consumer-credit so intimately intertwined with the automotive industry has still to find its historian. But Gilbert Seldes, *The Great Audience* (1950) and *The Public Arts* (1956), are creditable general works on the influence of the mass media on culture. For the particular institutions see the standard works: on the tabloids—Frank L. Mott, *American Journalism* (1950), and Simon L. Bessie, *Jazz Journalism* (1938); on the movies—Lewis Jacobs, *The Rise of the American Film* (1929); and on radio—Paul F. Lazarsfield, *People Look at Radio* (1946); Paul Schubert, *The Electric Word* (1928); and The Federal Council of the Churches of Christ in America, *Broadcasting and the Public* (1938).

SOCIAL QUESTIONS. Freda Kirchwey, ed., *Our Changing Morality* (1924), is a collection of pertinent essays by contemporaries. Though containing a lot of sociological jargon, John Serjamaki, *The American Family in the Twentieth Century,* is probably the best scholarly study on the subject. John Higham, *Strangers in the Land* (1955), is excellent on the subject of nativism; while for the Ku Klux Klan, A. S. Rice, *The Ku Klux Klan in American Politics* (1962), may be supplemented by the contemporary J. M. Mecklin, *The Ku Klux Klan* (1924) and by a very fine state study, Emerson

Loucks, *The Ku Klux Klan in Pennsylvania* (1936). On the more important developments in Protestantism as they effected social issues, see D. B. Meyer's excellent *The Protestant Search for Political Realism* (1960) and Robert M. Miller, *American Protestantism and Social Issues, 1919–1939* (1958). Norman Furniss, *The Fundamentalist Controversy, 1918–1931* (1954), is useful. Andrew Sinclair, *Prohibition* (1962), a work of a foreigner, is scholarly and highly interesting; but the older Charles Merz, *The Dry Decade* (1931), should be consulted as well as the good local study, G. M. Ostrander, *The Prohibition Movement in California, 1848–1933* (1957).

II. The Politics of Nostalgia

GENERAL. The most comprehensive treatment of the politics of the twenties is found in John D. Hicks, *Republican Ascendancy, 1921–1933* (1960). Two skillfully written interpretations are A. M. Schlesinger, Jr., *The Age of Roosevelt; The Crisis of The Old Order: 1921–1933* (1957) and the previously mentioned Leuchtenberg, *The Perils of Prosperity*. Generally Schlesinger depicts the decade's mistakes as a background for New Deal heroics, whereas Leuchtenberg is more impartial. Other useful surveys are H. U. Faulkner, *From Versailles to the New Deal* (1950), and the older P. W. Slosson, *The Great Crusade and After* (1930). André Siegfried, *America Comes of Age* (1927), is the work of a perceptive foreigner. One of the few good state studies of recent times is J. J. Huthmacher, *Massachusetts People and Politics, 1919–1933* (1959).

HARDING, COOLIDGE, AND HOOVER. Since none of the personal papers of these three Republican presidents are as yet available, all of the studies pertaining to these men have had to rest upon public and otherwise fragmentary sources. For the election of 1920 and its background W. M. Bagby, *The Road to Normalcy* (1962), and R. K. Murray, *Red Scare* (1955), are best; but the older study, F. L. Paxson, *Postwar Years, 1918–1923* (1948), resting almost entirely upon newspapers and periodical material, should be consulted. No good biography of Harding exists, but for the scandals especially, see S. H. Adams, *Incredible Era: The Life and Times of Warren Gamaliel Harding* (1939). William Allen White, *A Puritan in Babylon* (1938), is a brilliant and devastating interpretative study of Calvin Coolidge; C. M. Fuess, *Calvin Coolidge* (1940), is more comprehensive and sober. Except for an insight into the President's mentality the *Autobiography of Calvin Coolidge* (1929), is worthless as an historical source.

E. A. Moore, *A Catholic Runs for President* (1956) should be supplemented by Oscar Handlin, *Al Smith and His America* (1958), and by R. V. Peel and T. C. Donnelly, *The 1928 Campaign* (1931). Herbert Hoover has not fared well with either journalists or historians.

But H. G. Warren, *Herbert Hoover and the Great Depression* (1959), succeeds better than most writers in being fair to the harassed President. Walter Johnson, *1600 Pennsylvania Avenue* (1960), an interesting study of recent Presidents and their policies, is highly critical of the Depression President. For the purposes of maintaining the luster on his own career Hoover probably should not have written his often splenetic *Memoirs,* in particular *The Great Depression* (Vol. 2, 1952). A comparison of the political philosophy expressed in the *Memoirs,* in his earlier *American Individualism* (1922), and in *The New Day* (1928) campaign speeches, make an interesting study. W. S. Myers, ed., *The State Papers and Other Public Writings of Herbert Hoover* (2 vols., 1934), may be supplemented by several works by or about his cabinet members, none of which are of first importance.

FARM AND LABOR POLITICS. Theodore Saloutos and J. D. Hicks, *Agricultural Discontent in the Middlewest, 1900–1939* (1951), is the most complete survey of the relationship between the farmer and politics; J. H. Shideler, *Farm Crisis, 1919–1923* (1957), the most exclusively devoted to the immediate postwar years. G. C. Fite, *George N. Peek and the Fight for Farm Parity* (1954), is good for the McNary Haugen and export debenture schemes. An excellent volume on labor during the decade is Irving Bernstein, *The Lean Years* (1960); but Philip Taft, *The A.F. of L. from the Death of Gompers to the Merger* (1956), and Selig Perlman and Philip Taft, *History of Labor in the United States, 1896–1932* (1935), should also be consulted. Felix Frankfurter and Nathan Greene, *The Labor Injunction* (1930), is the standard work on labor's relations with the law. For the 1924 attempt to combine the farmer-labor vote in a third party movement, see K. C. MacKay, *The Progressive Movement of 1924* (1947) and B. C. and Fola La Follette, *Robert M. La Follette* (Vol. 2, 1953), a not too critical life of the Wisconsin Senator.

LIBERALS AND CONSERVATIVES. Other aspects of the political struggles during the decade may be obtained from the important Clarke A. Chambers, *Seedtime of Reform* (1963), and from biographies of some of the leading liberal and conservative figures. Among the former are A. T. Mason, *Harlan Fiske Stone* (1956); Harry Barnard, *Independent Man: The Life of Senator James Couzens* (1958); D. J. Humes, *Oswald Garrison Villard* (1960); Howard Zinn, *La Guardia in Congress* (1959); and Arthur Mann, *La Guardia* (1959). Among the better volumes on conservative figures are J. F. Paschall, *Mr. Justice Sutherland* (1951); W. T. Hutchinson, *Lowden of Illinois* (2 vols., 1957); and Morton Keller, *In Defense of Yesterday: James Beck and the Politics of Conservatism* (1958).

DIPLOMACY. A convenient summary is Allan Nevins, *The United States in a Chaotic World* (1950). Additional information may be obtained from an unusually good collection of biographies of the Secretaries of State. Merlo J. Pusey, *Charles Evans Hughes* (2 vols., 1951), is an admiring work which may be balanced with the much shorter but more critical Dexter Perkins, *Charles Evans Hughes and American Democratic Statesmanship* (1956). L. E. Ellis, *Frank B. Kellogg and American Foreign Relations, 1925–1929* (1961), does ample justice to his subject. But also see Robert H. Ferrell, *Frank B. Kellogg—Henry L. Stimson* (1963). Among the more finished biographies of recent years is the sympathtic study of Henry L. Stimson by Elting Morison, *Turmoil and Tradition* (1960), but the student should consult the different view presented in R. C. Current, *Secretary Stimson* (1954).

On the more specific diplomatic problems of the decade, C. Leonard Hoag, *Preface to Preparedness* (1941) and Merz Tate, *The United States and Armaments* (1948), are adequate for disarmament; Harold and Margaret Sprout, *Toward a New Order of Sea Power* (1940) and John C. Vinson, *The Parchment Peace* (1955), for the Washington Treaties; and R. H. Ferrell, *Peace in Their Times* (1952) and J. C. Vinson, *William E. Borah and the Outlawry of War* (1957), for the Kellogg–Briand Pact. As the subject of the League of Nations has not attracted modern scholars, the older and Wilsonian-oriented D. F. Flemming, *The United States and World Organization, 1920–1933* (1938), should be read in relation to the relevant parts of Selig Adler, *The Isolationist Impulse: Its Twentieth Century Reaction* (1957). A. W. Griswold, *The Far Eastern Policy of the United States* (1938), is an excellent study of regional policy. F. R. Dulles, *Forty Years of American Japanese Relations* (1937); Dorothy Berg, *American Policy and the Chinese Revolution* (1947); and J. K. Fairbanks, *The United States and China* (1956), cover the major regions of the Far East. G. F. Kennan, *Soviet-American Relations, 1917–1920* (Vols. 1, 2, 1956–58), are part of a superb study for the background to the decade. William A. Williams, *American Russian Relations, 1781–1947* (1952) and Thomas A. Bailey, *America Faces Russia* (1950), contain widely different approaches to the same subject. E. A. Rice, *The Diplomatic Relations Between the United States and Mexico* (1959) and R. F. Smith, *The United States and Cuba* (1960), are two of the better studies on Latin American countries: the first is keyed more to religious problems; the second, to business penetration. For the beginnings of the good neighbor policy see Bryce Wood, *The Making of the Good Neighbor Policy* (1961) and Alexander De Conde, *Herbert Hoover's Latin American Policy* (1951).

III. The End of Normalcy

THE HOOVER ADMINISTRATION. In addition to the studies of Mr. Hoover and his policies, listed in section II, Charles and Mary

Beard, *America in Midpassage* (2 vols., 1939), contains much relevant information. Thoroughly friendly to the administration are W. S. Myers and W. H. Newton, *The Hoover Administration* (1936); R. L. Wilbur and A. M. Hyde, *The Hoover Policies* (1937); and E. E. Robinson and P. C. Edwards, eds., *The Memoirs of Ray Lyman Wilbur, 1875–1949* (1960). Far more critical are R. G. Tugwell, *Mr. Hoover's Economic Policy* (1932) and G. V. Seldes, *The Years of the Locust* (1933). On the Hawley–Smoot tariff, E. E. Schattschneider, *Politics, Pressures and the Tariff* (1935) and J. M. Jones, *Tariff Retaliation* (1934), are adequate. Sidney Ratner, *American Taxation* (1942), contains material relevant to the entire decade as well as to the Hoover years.

STOCK CRASH AND DEPRESSION. Broadus Mitchell, *Depression Decade* (1947), is a broad survey of the Depression years with a heavy economic emphasis. F. L. Allen, *Since Yesterday* (1940) and Dixon Wecter, *The Age of the Great Depression* (1948), are more socially oriented. The best single account of the stock crash is the perceptive and witty J. K. Galbraith, *The Great Crash* (1955). D. A. Shannon, *The Great Depression* (1960), contains an interesting series of human documents on the period. Murray N. Rothbard, *America's Great Depression* (1963), is the work of a conservative economist who argues that government intervention turned a cyclical down-turn into a lasting depression. For an opposing and more contemporary analysis of the reasons for the debacle see Maurice Levin et al., *America's Capacity to Consume* (1934) and Edwin G. Nourse et al., *America's Capacity to Produce* (1934).

Josephine C. Brown, *Public Relief* (1940), covers the Hoover as well as the Roosevelt years, and W. W. Waters (B. E. F.), *The Whole Story of the Bonus Army* (1933), is an almost contemporary account of this significant incident.

ROOSEVELT AND THE ELECTION OF 1932. The fullest picture of Franklin Roosevelt is to be found in the two multivolume works of A. M. Schlesinger, Jr. and Frank Freidel. Schlesinger's *The Crisis of the Old Order* (1957) contains a brilliant partisan account of Roosevelt and his activities up through the Presidential election of 1932. The second and third volumes by Freidel, *The Ordeal* (1954) and *The Triumph* (1956), are more impartial and give an excellent picture of the Democratic party during the twenties as well as a splendid account of the 1932 election. J. M. Burns Roosevelt, *The Lion and the Fox* (1956), presents still another well-written, full-length scholarly portrait, while shorter studies are to be found in the previously mentioned Walter Johnson, *1600 Pennsylvania Avenue*, and in R. Hofstadter, *The Age of Reform* and *The American Political Tradition*.

Among the innumerable portraits of the President by his close political friends, perhaps the best are: R. G. Tugwell, *The Democratic*

Roosevelt (1937); R. E. Sherwood, *Roosevelt and Hopkins* (1948); Frances Perkins, *The Roosevelt I Knew* (1946); and John Gunther, *Roosevelt in Retrospect* (1950). For anti-Roosevelt material, more or less on the personal side, see J. T. Flynn, *The Roosevelt Myth* (1948), which went through twelve printings, and E. E. Robinson, *The Roosevelt Leadership, 1933–1945* (1955). Bernard Bellush, *Franklin D. Roosevelt as Governor of New York,* is useful, as is R. V. Peel and T. C. Donnelly, *The 1932 Campaign* (1935).

IV. THE NEW DEAL

SOCIETY AND POLITICAL THOUGHT IN THE THIRTIES. For the more important social changes during the thirties see the already mentioned Dixon Wecter, *The Age of the Great Depression,* and especially Robert and Helen Lynd, *Middletown in Transition* (1937). F. L. Allen, *Since Yesterday* (1940), is not as perceptive as the earlier volume on the twenties. William Ogburn, ed., *Social Changes During Depression and Recovery* (1935), and Clarence Enzler, *Some Social Aspects of the Depression* (1939), are two of the better books by sociologists who, until very recently, have done most of the writing about social problems of the decade. For varying ideological bases of the New Deal, as expressed by some of the more philosophical New Dealers, see Rexford Tugwell, *The Battle for Democracy* (1935); Henry Wallace, *New Frontiers* (1934); and Thurmond Arnold, *The Folklore of Capitalism* (1937). The first volume contains the speculations of a left-leaning intellectual, the second of an agriculturally-minded mystic and humanist, and the third by a pragmatic, reforming legal scholar devoted to maintaining the competitive system.

POLITICAL SURVEYS. The best one-volume survey covering both internal and foreign politics of the period is the sparkling W. E. Leuchtenburg, *Franklin D. Roosevelt and the New Deal, 1932–1940* (1963). Both the previously mentioned Schlesinger, *The Politics of Upheaval,* dealing with internal affairs to 1936, and Freidel, *The Triumph,* should be consulted. Among the literally hundreds of other books on the general subject of New Deal politics, a few of the superior ones are Editors of the Economists, *The New Deal: An Analysis and Appraisal* (1937); Dexter Perkins, *The New Age of Franklin Roosevelt;* and D. W. Brogan, *The Era of Franklin Roosevelt* (1950). The last is the work of a British authority on American life and institutions. Carl Degler, *Out of Our Past* (1959), and Mario Einandi, *The Roosevelt Revolution* (1959), are of interest because of their viewpoints; and Daniel Fusfeld, *The Economic Thought of Franklin D. Roosevelt and the Origins of the New Deal* (1956), and Thomas Greer, *What Roosevelt Thought* (1958), because of their special approaches. In addition to the books cited in the previous section, which were centered on Roosevelt himself, Samuel Rosenman, *Working with Roosevelt* (1952) and Grace Tully, *FDR, My Boss* (1949), are valuable personal comments on the President by his speech writer and by his personal secretary.

PRESIDENTIAL LETTERS AND DOCUMENTS. S. I. Rosenman, ed., *The Public Papers and Addresses of Franklin D. Roosevelt* (13 vols., 1938–50), may be supplemented by Elliott Roosevelt, ed., *FDR: His Personal Letters, 1928–1945* (2 vols., 1950) and by the much shorter, Basil Rauch, *Selected Speeches, Messages, Press Conferences and Letters* (1957).

THE NEW DEALERS. Interesting group pictures of the chief New Dealers are presented in Joseph Alsop and Robert Kintner, *Men Around the President* (1939), and in the Unofficial Observer, *The New Dealers* (1934). By now practically every important New Dealer has written some kind of an account of his activities. Among the more important of these works not previously mentioned are: *The Secret Diary of Harold L. Ickes* (3 vols., 1953–54), full of fact, rumor, and fancy, but not charity; John M. Blum, ed., *From the Morganthau Diaries* (1959); and R. L. Moley, *After Seven Years* (1939), the personal statement of an early New Dealer who became critical of the reform movement's direction. New Deal activities and accomplishments in the states can be investigated best in the excellent volume by Robert Burke, *Olson's New Deal for California* (1953), and in Allan Nevins, *Herbert H. Lehman and His Era* (1963). The two best personal statements by confirmed New Deal Congressmen are Maury Maverick, *A Maverick American* (1937), and Jerry Vorhis, *Confessions of a Congressman* (1948).

THE COURT FIGHT AND THE SECOND ADMINISTRATION. J. Alsop and T. Catledge, *The 168 Days* (1938), is a colorful contemporary account of this most heated controversy. D. Pearson and R. S. Allen, *The Nine Old Men* (1936), and Merlo Pusey, *The Supreme Court Crisis* (1937), are others of the same vintage. But the more scholarly A. T. Mason, *The Supreme Court from Taft to Warren* (1958), M. L. Ernst, *The Ultimate Power* (1937), E. S. Corwin, *The Twilight of the Supreme Court* (1934), and by the same author, *Constitutional Revolution* (1946), and C. H. Pritchett, *The Roosevelt Court* (1948), should be consulted. For other aspects of domestic politics after 1936 see John Chamberlain, *The American Stakes* (1940), and J. Alsop and R. Kintner, *Men Around the President* (1939).

THE OPPOSITION. Very few volumes by or about the major conservative opponents of the New Deal have appeared, the most important being Herbert Hoover, *The Challenge to Liberty* (1934) and *Addresses Upon the American Road, 1933–1938* (1938); and George Wolfskill, *The Revolt of the Conservatives* (1962) and *A History of the American Liberty League, 1934–1940* (1962). As yet no good biographies of Landon exist. Allan Sindler, *Huey Long's Louisiana* (1956), and Harriet Kane, *Louisiana Hayride* (1941), are adequate but not definitive on Long. Charles J. Tull, *Father Coughlin and the New Deal* (1965), and E. B. Lee, *The Fine Art of Propaganda* (1939), are concerned with the Michigan priest; and Leo Lowenthal and Norbert Gutterman, *Prophets of Deceit* (1949), covers the rising fascist activities in the country. Donald McCoy, *Angry Voices* (1958), is devoted to the agricultural protest from the left. Abraham Holtzman, *The Townsend Movement* (1963), gives the essential facts. The activities of the socialists and the communists are adequately dealt with in David Shannon, *The Socialist Party of America* (1953), and in Irving Howe and Lewis Coser, *The American Communist Party* (1957).

RELIEF RECOVERY AND REFORM. Various strains of New Deal economic thought are to be found in Seymour Harris, ed., *The New Economics* (1947); Alvin Hansen, *Full Recovery or Stagnation* (1938); and A. Burns and D. Watson, *Government Spending and Economic Expansion* (1940). Pointed directly at the problem of recovery from depression is The Brookings Institution, *The Recovery Problem in the United States* (1936), and Joseph Schumpeter, *Business Cycles* (2 vols., 1939). For a general discussion of economic theories of the decade see Joseph Dorfman, *The Economic Mind in American Civilization* (Vol. 5, 1959).

UNEMPLOYMENT AND RELIEF. E. W. Bakke, *Citizens Without Work* (1940), Donald Howard, *The WPA and Federal Relief Policy* (1943), Grace Adams, *Workers on Relief* (1939), and J. C. Brown, *Public Relief, 1929–1939* (1940), cover most of the phases of unemployment and relief policies. The Social Security Act and its subsequent administration may be followed in Paul Douglas, *Social Security in the United States* (1936), and in E. E. Witte, *Development of the Social Security Act* (1962). The New Deal's interesting experiments with building entirely new agricultural communities, reminiscent of the voluntary efforts of the nineteenth-century utopians, is developed in Paul Conkin, *Tomorrow a New World* (1959).

LABOR. Irving Bernstein, *The New Deal Collective Bargaining Policy* (1950) and M. Derber and E. Young, eds., *Labor and the New Deal* (1957), contain interpretative and perceptive studies of an extremely complicated subject. For a more contemporary and colorful account see R. R. R. Brooks, *Unions of Their Own Choosing* (1940). Philip Taft, *The A. F. of L. from the Death of Gompers to the Merger* (1959), is an able survey of the older craft unions from the twenties to the postwar period. Walter Galenson, *The CIO Challenge to the A. F. of L.* (1960), is best on labor's intermural struggle.

AGRICULTURE—CONSERVATION—*TVA.* Gilbert Fite, *George N. Peek and the Fight for Farm Parity* (1954), and Edwin Nourse et al., *Three Years of the Agricultural Adjustment Act* (1937), cover the early period of agricultural reform; Dean Albertson, *Roosevelt's Farmer* (1961), covers the later New Deal and war years. Murray Benedict and Oscar Stine, *The Agricultural Commodity Programs* (1956), is a more technical study of the basic parts of the price support plans. David Lilienthal, *TVA: Democracy on the March* (1944), is the classic, written by the man who contributed most to the giant project. But C. H. Pritchett, *The Tennessee Valley Authority* (1943), and Joseph Ransmeier, *The Tennessee Valley Authority* (1942), should also be consulted. For most other aspects of the New Deal conservation efforts see Edgar Nixon, ed., *Franklin D. Roosevelt and Conservation, 1911–1946* (1957), a two-volume collection of sources.

NRA AND OTHER BUSINESS POLICIES. No comprehensive scholarly study for the entire NRA exists, but see Sidney Fine, *The Automobile Under the Blue Eagle* (1964), for an excellent detailed study of a particular industry. Hugh Johnson, *The Blue Eagle from Egg to Earth* (1935), and Donald Richberg, *The Rainbow* (1936), are the works of two chief administrators of the agency; Leverett Lyon et al., *The National Recovery Administration* (1935), is a collection of contemporary estimates. A. Bernheim and M. G. Schneider, eds., *The Security Markets* (1935); R. M. Fisher, *20 Years of Public Housing* (1959); C. L. Harriss, *History and Policies of the Home Owners' Loan Corporation* (1951); and Timothy McDonnell (S. J.), *The Wagner Housing Act* (1957)—are all valuable studies of particular New Deal Agencies. On monetary policy see Allan Everest Morganthau, *The New Deal and Silver* (1950), and J. D. Paris, *Monetary Policies of the United States, 1932–1938* (1938).

V. THE TOTALITARIAN CHALLENGE

GENERAL. The best general survey of the complicated American foreign policy during the decade is to be found in R. H. Ferrell, *American Diplomacy in the Great Depression* (1957). But see the impressive William Langer and S. E. Gleason, *The Challenge to Isolation, 1937–1940* (1952), and *The Undeclared War, 1940–1941* (1953), for the later years. Shorter but able works are Donald Drummond, *The Passing of American Neutrality* (1955); Allan Nevins, *The New Deal and World Affairs* (1950); and J. Alsop and R. Kintner, *American White Paper* (1940). Two volumes extremely critical of American policy are Charles Tansill, *Back Door to War* (1952), and Charles A. Beard, *American Foreign Policy in the Making* (1946). Julius W. Pratt, *Cordell Hull, 1933–44* (2 vols., 1964), is good on Hull's contributions to the diplomacy of the thirties. An excellent source are the selected State Department papers published annually by the Council on Foreign Relations, *The United States in World Affairs*, W. Shephardson and W. Scroggs, eds.

THE FAR EAST. Excellent background is to be found in the already cited Griswold, *The Far Eastern Policy of the United States,* and in H. S. Quigley and G. H. Blakeslee, *The Far East, An International Survey* (1938). More directed at Depression diplomacy are Armin Rappaport, *Henry L. Stimson and Japan, 1931–33* (1963); T. A. Bisson, *American Policy in the Far East, 1931–1944* (1944); and C. A. Buss, *War and Diplomacy in Eastern Asia* (1941). For the crises preceding World War II see Herbert Feis, *The Road to Pearl Harbor* (1950); F. C. Jones, *Japan's New Order in East Asia* (1954); Paul Schroeder, *The Axis Alliance and Japanese American Relations, 1941* (1958); Joseph Grew, *Ten Years in Japan* (1944); and Walter Johnson, ed., *Turbulent Era* (2 vols., 1952).

THE HOOVER ADMINISTRATION. William Myers, *The Foreign Policies of Herbert Hoover* (1940), is a friendly general survey. For the Manchurian and Chinese affairs see S. R. Smith, *The Manchurian Crisis, 1931–1932* (1948); H. L. Stimson, *The Far Eastern Crisis* (1936); and Robert Langer, *Seizure of Territory* (1947). Other important works are two biographies of Henry Stimson: Elting Morison, *Turmoil and Tradition* (1960), and Richard Current, *Secretary Stimson* (1954); and the Secretary's own work, in collaboration with McGeorge Bundy, *On Active Service in Peace and War* (1948).

ISOLATION AND NEUTRALITY. The ten-year struggle between isolationists and interventionists is treated in Selig Adler, *The Isolationist Impulse* (1957); Wayne Cole, *America First* (1953); Walter Johnson, *The Battle Against Isolation* (1944); and Dorothy Detzer, *Appointment on the Hill* (1948). The more technical and legislative aspects of neutrality are explored in Elton Atwater, *American Regulation of Arms Exports* (1941); Edwin Borchard and William Lage, *Neutrality for the United States* (1940); and C. G. Fenwick, *American Neutrality, Trial and Failure* (1940).

1940 CAMPAIGN AND PEARL HARBOR. M. E. Dillon, *Wendell Willkie* (1952), covers the early career of Wendell Willkie. Joseph Barnes, *Willkie* (1952); D. B. Johnson, *The Republican Party and Wendell Willkie* (1960); and H. F. Goswell, *Champion Campaigner, Franklin D. Roosevelt* (1952)—are more detailed on the election of

1940. The official explanation of the events leading to Pearl Harbor is given in *Peace and War, United States Foreign Policy, 1931–1941.* A friendly but scholarly gloss on the official statements is found in the already cited Herbert Feis, *The Road to Pearl Harbor.* For two highly critical revisionist works see C. A. Beard, *President Roosevelt and the Coming of the War, 1941* (1948), and R. A. Theobald, *The Final Secret of Pearl Harbor* (1954).

SPECIAL SUBJECTS. Volumes on more detailed and special subjects which may be consulted with profit are Alexander De Conde, *Herbert Hoover's Latin American Policy* (1951); Edward Guerrant, *Roosevelt's Good Neighbor Policy* (1950); Bryce Wood, *The Making of the Good Neighbor Policy* (1961); E. David Cronon, *Josephus Daniels in Mexico* (1960); H. L. Trefousse, *Germany and American Neutrality, 1939–1941* (1951); R. P. Browder, *The Origins of Soviet-American Diplomacy* (1953); and F. J. Taylor, *The United States and the Spanish Civil War* (1956). Useful biographical materials are to be found in F. L. Israel, *Nevada's Key Pittman* (1963); Cordell Hull, *The Memoirs of Cordell Hull* (2 vols., 1947); and Sumner Welles, *The Time for Decision* (1944).

VI. THE DIVIDED WORLD

WAR DIPLOMACY. The best general surveys of diplomacy during the war are Herbert Feis, *Churchill—Roosevelt—Stalin* (1957), and W. H. McNeill, *America, Britain, and Russia* (1953). But the extremely anti-Roosevelt, W. H. Chamberlain, *America's Second Crusade* (1950), and H. E. Barnes, ed., *Perpetual War for Perpetual Peace* (1953), should be consulted. As the most important conference in determining postwar relations, Yalta has brought forth a spate of books. Among the best are J. L. Snell, ed., *The Meaning of Yalta* (1956), and R. F. Fenno, Jr., ed., *The Yalta Conference* (1955). On the Potsdam Conference Herbert Feis, *Between War and Peace* (1960), presents the view of a former State Department member. Among the more important biographical items to be added to those cited in the preceding section are E. R. Stettinius, Jr., *Roosevelt and the Russians* (1949); W. D. Leahy, *I Was There* (1950); J. F. Byrnes, *Speaking Frankly* (1947); and Sumner Welles, *Seven Decisions That Shaped History* (1951).

THE COLD WAR. Good general summaries of the cold war diplomacy may be found in N. A. Graebner, *Cold War Diplomacy, 1945–1960* (1962), and in J. W. Spanier, *American Foreign Policy Since World War Two* (1960). E. F. Goldman, *The Crucial Decade* (1961), and Herbert Agar, *The Price of Power* (1957), devote many pages to the Truman foreign policy. Harry S. Truman, *Memoirs* (2 vols., 1955–56), is of course invaluable. But for a very critical look at the Truman policy see D. F. Flemming, *The Cold War and its Origins, 1917–1960,* (2 vols., 1961). T. A. Bailey, *America Faces Russia* (1950), V. M. Dean, *The United States and Russia* (1948), and A. Z. Carr, *Truman, Stalin and Peace* (1950), examine relations between the two countries.

On the Berlin blockade see W. P. Davison, *The Berlin Blockade* (1958). J. M. Jones, *The Fifteen Weeks* (1955), is a study of the formulation of the Marshall Plan. P. G. Hoffman, *Peace Can Be Won* (1951), is a discussion of the plan by its chief administrator. The development of NATO is discussed in H. L. Hoskins, *The Atlantic Pact* (1949).

Asia. Maurice Zinkin, *Asia and the West* (1953), and H. M. Vinacke, *The United States and the Far East, 1945–1951* (1952), are good general accounts. Herbert Feis, *The China Tangle* (1953), should be balanced with A. C. Wedemeyer, *Wedemeyer Reports* (1958), and with A. J. Kubeck, *How the Far East Was Lost* (1963), on the complicated Chinese situation. The development of American-Japanese relations during the occupation is well covered in E. M. Martin, *The Allied Occupation of Japan* (1948), while southeast Asia and India are treated in R. H. Fifield, *The Diplomacy of Southeast Asia* (1958), and in Chester Bowles, *Ambassador's Report* (1958).

The Korean War. G. M. McCune, *Korea Today* (1950), provides excellent background for the Korean War; McGeorge Bundy, ed., *The Pattern of Responsibility* (1952), is a friendly account of the Acheson policies leading to, and during, the war. Distinctly critical of official policy is R. T. Oliver, *Why War Came to Korea* (1950). For MacArthur's version of the famous dismissal see his already cited *Memoirs* and C. A. Willoughby and John Chamberlain, *MacArthur, 1941–1951* (1954). The Administration's case is given in R. Rovere and A. M. Schlesinger, *The General and the President* (1951). J. W. Spanier, *The Truman–MacArthur Controversy* (1959), is a balanced scholarly account. Important books of a biographical nature covering the Truman period include A. A. Rogow, *James Forrestal* (1963); J. F. Byrnes, *All in One Lifetime* (1958); J. F. Dulles, *War or Peace* (1952); A. H. Vandenberg, *The Private Papers of Senator Vandenberg* (1952); K. M. Schmidt, *Henry A. Wallace* (1960); and R. A. Taft, *A Foreign Policy for Americans* (1951).

Eisenhower. Understandably, little scholarly writing based upon sources has been produced for the Eisenhower years. Most of the available books have been written by participants or partisans, and practically all are consciously or unconsciously slanted. For a general view of both foreign and domestic policy of the first administration, Dwight D. Eisenhower, *Mandate for Change* (1963), is invaluable. This may be supplemented by R. H. Rovere, *Affairs of State* (1956), and by *Public Papers of the Presidents of the United States: Dwight D. Eisenhower, 1953–1961* (8 vols., 1955–61). Devoted to foreign affairs, N. A. Graebner, *The New Isolationism* (1956), is critical of the growing international obligations made without thought to the nation's power to respond. J. R. Beal, *John Foster Dulles* (1957), is a most controversial volume. Other books produced by friends of the administration are T. I. Cook and Malcolm Moos, *Power Through Purpose* (1954), and R. J. Donovan, *Eisenhower: The Inside Story* (1956). More critical are G. F. Kennan, *The Realities of American Foreign Policy* (1954) and *Russia, the Atom and the West* (1958); and Dean Acheson, *Power and Diplomacy* (1958). H. A. Kissenger, *Nuclear Weapons and Foreign Policy* (1957), is an able book by an outstanding student of the subject. David Wise and T. B. Ross, *The U-2 Affair* (1962), reports this incredible incident. M. D. Taylor, *Uncertain Trumpet,* is an analysis of recent strategy by a former Army Chief of Staff.

VII. PROSPERITY AND PESSIMISM

GENERAL. Among the numerous books written on postwar society, the more significant and comprehensive include Max Lerner, *America as a Civilization* (1957), and F. L. Allen, *The Big Change* (1952), both more or less on the optimistic side. J. K. Galbraith, *The Affluent Society* (1958), and W. L. Warner, *American Life: Dream and Reality* (1953), are more critical. Philip Olson, ed., *America as a Mass Society* (1963), and Dwight Macdonald, *Against the American Grain* (1958), the first more sociological, the second more devoted to the arts, are sometimes grim in their estimates. See especially in the Macdonald volume the chapter entitled "Masscult and Midcult" published separately (1961). David Riesman and others, *The Lonely Crowd* (1950) and *Individualism Reconsidered* (1958), study the changes in the American personality; C. W. Mills, *White Collar* (1951), those of the new middle classes.

WAR SOCIETY. The social changes made by war are discussed in W. F. Ogburn, *American Society in Wartime* (1947); Jack Goodman, ed., *While You Were Gone* (1946); and in the relevant chapters of A. R. Buchanan, *The United States and World War II* (2 vols., 1964), which is mainly devoted to military events. Directed specifically toward economic mobilization are the official *Industrial Mobilization for War* (1947) and Donald Nelson, *Arsenal of Democracy* (1946). H. M. Somers, *Presidential Agency* (1950), is a scholarly study of peacetime reconversion as well as mobilization.

ECONOMIC INSTITUTIONS. For the postwar developments in economic institutions, among the best studies are J. K. Galbraith, *American Capitalism* (1952); A. A. Berle, *Power Without Property* (1959); Editors of Fortune, *America in the Sixties* (1958), which, while predictive, contains much material on the fifties; Bernard D. Nossiter, *The Myth Makers* (1964); David Lilienthal, *Big Business* (1957); W. W. Leontief, *Studies in the Structure of the American Economy* (1953); and P. F. Drucker, *The New Society* (1950). A more historically oriented study is T. C. Cochrane, *The American Business System* (1957).

Good for the changing nature of businessmen and their creed are F. X. Sutton, *The American Business Creed* (1956); James Burnham, *The Managerial Revolution* (1940); and C. W. Mills, *The Power Elite* (1956), which examines the practices and principles of governmental and labor leaders as well as those of businessmen. W. H. Whyte, Jr., *The Organization Man* (1956), examines the impact of the new business structure on the individual personality.

The main population changes within the country are discussed in I. B. Taeuber, *The Changing Population of the United States* (1958). The move to suburbia and its results for the people involved as well as for the city are covered in R. C. Wood, *Suburbia* (1959); A. C. Spectorsky, *The Exurbanites* (1955); and in the latter chapters of Lewis Mumford's pathbreaking, *The City in History* (1961).

Other valuable works on the growing problems of the modern city include R. C. Weaver, *The Urban Complex* (1963); C. N. Glaab, *The American City: A Documentary History* (1963); Mitchell Gordon, *Sick Cities* (1961); and Jane Jacobs, *The Death and Life of Great American Cities* (1962).

The new generation of labor leaders and their changing relations with their counterparts in business and government are well described in Eli Ginzburg, *The Labor Leader* (1948); in C. W. Mills, *The New Men of Power* (1948); and in *Labor Today* (1964), by B. J. Widick, one of labor's own men. The state of the persistent poor in the nation is discussed in Michael Harrington, *The Other America* (1962).

For the further development of mass culture see B. Rosenberg and D. M. White, eds., *Mass Culture* (1957), a collection of essays mostly by sociologists. The mass media and their effect on the arts are the subject of two volumes by Gilbert Seldes, *The Great Audience* (1950) and *The Public Arts* (1957). The older book by the same author, *The Lively Arts,* should be consulted in its newer edition (1957). For television see the 1962 *Report* of the Federal Communications Commission. More popular treatments of individual phases of the same subject are to be found in P. F. Laszarfield, *The People Look at Radio* (1946); Hortense Powdermaker, *Hollywood* (1950); and Russell Lynes, *The Tastemakers* (1954).

For the growing pessimism in American society see all the volumes by Walter Lippmann and Reinhold Niebuhr, but especially *The Phantom Public* (1925), *Preface to Morals* (1929), and *The Public Philosophy* (1955) by Lippmann, and *Does Civilization Need Religion?* (1928), *The Nature and Destiny of Man* (1941), and *The Self and the Drama of History* (1955) by Niebuhr. David E. Weingast, *Walter Lippmann* (1949), is an attempt at contemporary biography. On the moods of modern literature no substitute exists for reading the many works of the individual authors. But J. W. Krutch, *The Modern Temper* (1929), Malcolm Cowley, *The Literary Situation* (1954), and Edmund Wilson, *The Shock of Recognition* (1955), are the products of three critics with varying points of view. Among the better biographies of major literary figures are Mark Schorer, *Sinclair Lewis* (1961), C. Bowen, *Curse of the Misbegotten* [O'Neill] (1959), and Elizabeth Nowell, *Thomas Wolfe* (1960).

On the postwar political tempers see A. M. Schlesinger, Jr., *The Vital Center* (1949), for liberal developments; W. F. Buckley, *Up From Liberalism* (1959), on conservatism; and Daniel Bell, *The End of Ideology* (1960), for critical comment on the present state of both traditions.

VIII. THE POLITICS OF STATICS

GENERAL. No good work exists covering all postwar domestic politics. The previously cited Goldman, *The Crucial Decade,* covers the Truman period and some of the first Eisenhower Administration. Truman, *Memoirs,* are confined to his term of office. Eisenhower's own *Mandate for Change* ends in 1956, as does Rovere's *Affairs of State: The Eisenhower Years;* while Samuel Lubell's *The Future of American Politics* was first published on the eve of the 1952 election. Walter Johnson, *1600 Pennsylvania Avenue,* carries the study of the Presidents down through Eisenhower. Scarcely anything in book form has been published about either Congressional or state politics, although Richard Rovere, *The American Establishment* (1962), contains comment upon the Congressional leaders of all three administrations, and Warren Moscow, *Politics in the Empire State* (1948), examines the Dewey years in New York.

THE TRUMAN PERIOD. In addition to the works cited in Section VI, a number of other worthwhile books treat the major domestic issues and incidents of the Truman Presidency. Perhaps the most objective work on the Hiss affair is Alistair Cooke, *A Genera-*

tion on Trial (1952). The books on the more general issue of loyalty are legion. Among the best are: R. S. Brown, Jr., *Loyalty and Security* (1958); J. C. Wahlke, ed., *Loyalty in a Democratic State* (1952); and J. W. Caughey, *In Clear and Present Danger* (1958). On Congressional investigations and McCarthy see R. C. Carr, *The House Committee on Un-American Activities* (1952); Richard Rovere, *Senator Joe McCarthy* (1959); and a defense of the Senator, W. F. Buckley, Jr., and L. B. Bozell, *McCarthy and His Enemies* (1954). D. A. Shannon, *The Decline of American Communism* (1959), discusses the party and the government's campaign to destroy it.

ELECTIONS. For the elections of 1948, Jules Abels, *Out of the Jaws of Victory* (1959), is a journalistic account. W. S. White, *The Taft Story* (1954), Stanley Walker, *Dewey* (1944), and K. M. Schmidt, *Henry A. Wallace* (1960), are all more or less campaign-style approaches to their subjects. For the campaign of 1952, P. T. David et al., *Presidential Nominating Politics in 1952* (1954), is amazingly complete for a contemporary work. K. S. Davis, *A Prophet in His Own Country* (1957), is perhaps the best biography of Stevenson. M. J. Pusey, *Eisenhower the President* (1956) and Marquis Childs, *Eisenhower: Captive Hero* (1958), give two varying interpretations of the General. *Major Campaign Speeches of Adlai E. Stevenson* (1953) is a convenient source.

THE EISENHOWER ADMINISTRATION. Politics is the main theme of Samuel Lubell, *The Revolt of the Moderates* (1956), as is also true of Arthur Larson, *A Republican Looks at His Party* (1956), and Dean Acheson, *A Democrat Looks at His Party* (1955). E. J. Hughes, *The Ordeal of Power* (1963) and Sherman Adams, *First-hand Report* (1961), are by two of the President's official family—the first critical of, and the second favorable to, the Administration. Other not already mentioned memoirs by participating officials are L. L. Strauss, *Men and Decisions* (1962), and J. W. Martin and R. J. Donovan, *My First Fifty Years in Politics* (1960). As a background for the extremely significant racial issue see the classic, Gunnar Myrdal, *An American Dilemma* (2 vols., 1944). On the nature of contemporary Southern society, T. D. Clark, *The Emerging South* (1961), Avery Leiserson, ed., *The American South in the 1960's* (1964), and J. W. Silver, *Mississippi: The Closed Society* (1964), are excellent. B. M. Ziegler, *Desegregation and the Supreme Court* (1958), is concerned with the Court's decision and its aftermath. M. L. King, *Stride Toward Freedom* (1958), is by the Nobel prize-winning Negro leader. Other important books by Negro writers are: James Baldwin, *Nobody Knows My Name* (1961), and L. E. Lomax, *The Negro Revolt*. Dan Wakefield, *Revolt in the South* (1961), is by a liberal white; C. E. Lincoln, *Black Muslims in America* (1961), is an account of the radical Negro organization centered mostly in the northern cities.

Other worthwhile studies on special subjects during the Eisenhower Administration are W. R. Willoughby, *The St. Lawrence Waterway* (1961); E. R. Bartley, *The Tideland's Oil Controversy* (1953); and Aaron Wildavsky, *Dixon–Yates* (1961), concerned with the complicated debate over conservation, the production of electric power, and the TVA.

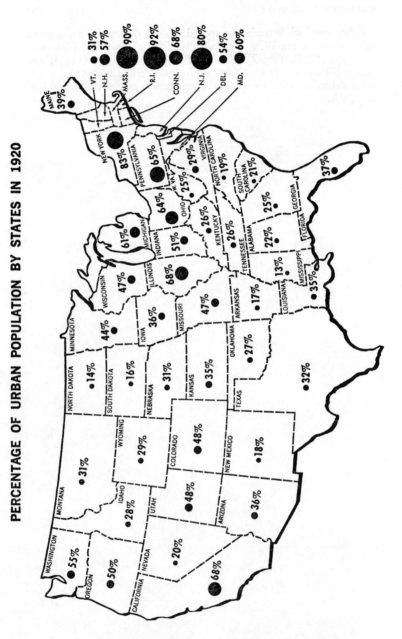

PERCENTAGE OF URBAN POPULATION BY STATES IN 1920

31% 57% 90% 92% 68% 80% 54% 60%
VT. N.H. MASS. R.I. CONN. N.J. DEL. MD.

MAINE 39%

NEW YORK 83%

PENNSYLVANIA 65%

W.VA. 25%

VIRGINIA 29%

NORTH CAROLINA 19%

SOUTH CAROLINA 21%

GEORGIA 25%

FLORIDA 37%

OHIO 64%

MICHIGAN 61%

INDIANA 51%

KENTUCKY 26%

TENNESSEE 26%

ALABAMA 22%

MISSISSIPPI 13%

ILLINOIS 68%

WISCONSIN 47%

IOWA 36%

MISSOURI 47%

ARKANSAS 17%

LOUISIANA 35%

MINNESOTA 44%

NORTH DAKOTA 14%

SOUTH DAKOTA 16%

NEBRASKA 31%

KANSAS 35%

OKLAHOMA 27%

TEXAS 32%

WYOMING 29%

COLORADO 48%

NEW MEXICO 18%

MONTANA 31%

IDAHO 28%

UTAH 48%

ARIZONA 36%

WASHINGTON 55%

OREGON 50%

NEVADA 20%

CALIFORNIA 68%

Source: *Statistical Abstract of the United States, 1964*

PERCENTAGE OF URBAN POPULATION BY STATES IN 1960

VT. 39%
N.H. 58%
MASS. 84%
R.I. 86%
CONN. 78%
N.J. 89%
DEL. 66%
MD. 73%

MAINE 51%
NEW YORK 85%
PENNSYLVANIA 72%
W. VA. 38%
VIRGINIA 56%
NORTH CAROLINA 40%
SOUTH CAROLINA 41%
OHIO 73%
MICHIGAN 73%
INDIANA 62%
KENTUCKY 45%
TENNESSEE 52%
GEORGIA 55%
FLORIDA 74%
ALABAMA 55%
ILLINOIS 81%
WISCONSIN 64%
IOWA 53%
MISSOURI 67%
ARKANSAS 43%
MISSISSIPPI 38%
LOUISIANA 63%
MINNESOTA 62%
NORTH DAKOTA 35%
SOUTH DAKOTA 39%
NEBRASKA 54%
KANSAS 61%
OKLAHOMA 63%
TEXAS 75%
MONTANA 50%
WYOMING 57%
COLORADO 74%
NEW MEXICO 66%
WASHINGTON 68%
OREGON 62%
IDAHO 48%
UTAH 75%
NEVADA 70%
ARIZONA 75%
CALIFORNIA 86%

Index

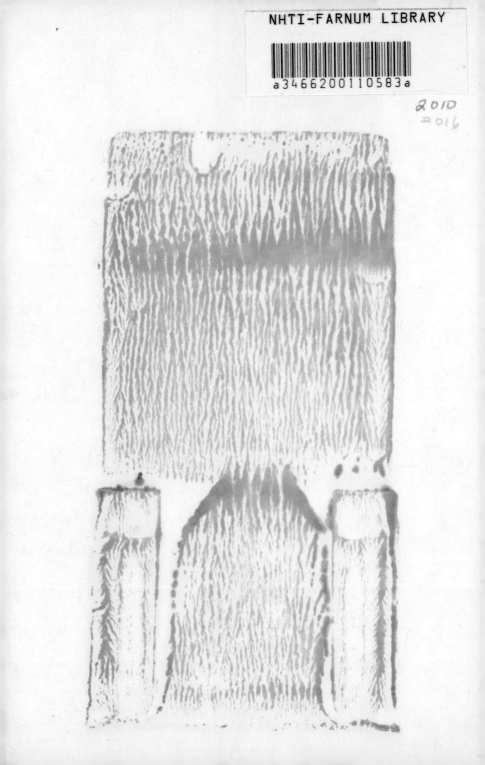

Teach Yourself Accents
The British Isles

Teach Yourself Accents
The British Isles

A Handbook for Young Actors and Speakers

Robert Blumenfeld

An Imprint of Hal Leonard Corporation

Published in 2013 by Limelight Editions
An Imprint of Hal Leonard Corporation
7777 West Bluemound Road
Milwaukee, WI 53213

Trade Book Division Editorial Offices
33 Plymouth St., Montclair, NJ 07042

Due to space constrictions, credits for literary excerpts are listed on pages 125–127, which should be considered an extension of this copyright page.

Printed in the United States of America

Book design by Mark Lerner

Library of Congress Cataloging-in-Publication Data

Blumenfeld, Robert.
 Teach yourself accents : the British Isles : a handbook for young actors and speakers / by Robert Blumenfeld.
     pages cm
 Includes bibliographical references.
 ISBN 978-0-87910-807-6
 1. Acting. 2. English language--Pronunciation by foreign speakers. 3. English language--Dialects--Great Britain--Handbooks, manuals, etc. I. Title.
 PN2071.F6B485 2013
 792.02'8--dc23
                              2013003551

www.limelighteditions.com

With gratitude and inexpressible love to my wonderful, sweet, brilliant parents, Max David Blumenfeld (1911–1994) and Ruth Blumenfeld (b. 1915)

CONTENTS

ACKNOWLEDGMENTS

I would like to thank my many language teachers at Princeton High School and at Rutgers and Columbia Universities. I extend thanks, also, to the staff of the Stella Adler Conservatory; to Mr. Albert Schoemann, Ms. Pamela Hare, and Mr. Mark Zeller at the once-flourishing National Shakespeare Conservatory; and to my students at both of these schools. Very special thanks are due to my wonderful friend Christopher Buck for his love and support, always. I want to express my thanks and gratitude to my friend Mr. Derek Tague for his special contribution in lending me rare books on accents. I would also like to thank my very dear and beloved friends for their unfailing love and support over the many years we have known one another: Albert S. Bennett; Tom and Virginia Smith; Peter Subers and Rob Bauer; Kieran Mulcare and Daniel Vosovic; Michael Mendiola and Scot Anderson; and my family: Nina Koenigsberg, my cousins' cousin; my brother Donald Blumenfeld-Jones, my sister-in-law Kathryn Corbeau Blumenfeld-Jones, and their children, Rebecca and Benjamin; my brother Richard and sister-in-law Ming; my maternal aunt Mrs. Bertha Friedman (1913–2001), and my cousin, her daughter Marjorie Loewer; my maternal uncle, Seymour "Sy" Korn (1920–2010); my paternal cousin, Jonathan Blumenfeld; and my wonderful maternal grandparents from Galicia in the Austro-Hungarian Empire, Morris Korn (1886–1979) and Harriet Korn (1886–1980). I owe a great debt to the authors of the books listed in the

Selected Bibliography, without whose work this book would have been impossible.

I especially want to thank Lon Davis, whose wonderful copy editing of my manuscript has been invaluable; Mark Lerner, for his beautiful design of this book; my wonderful, indefatigable editor, Jessica Burr; and my publisher, the always-encouraging, forthright, and dear friend John Cerullo. Special thanks are due to Mel Zerman (1931–2010), founder and publisher of Limelight Editions, who was not only very helpful throughout the process of getting my first book, *Accents: A Manual for Actors*, published by Limelight in 1998, but was also a kind, charming, and erudite man, one who is greatly missed.

LIST OF PHONETIC SYMBOLS USED IN THIS BOOK

Vowels and Semi-Vowels

ah: like "a" in *father*

a: like "a" in *that*

aw: like "aw" in *law*

ee: like "ee" in *meet*

e: like "e" in *met*

é: a pure vowel similar to the diphthong "ay"; heard in French; lips close together

ih: like "i" in *bit*

o: like "o" in *not*

o: like "o" in *work*

oo: like "oo" in *book*; spelled "u" in *pull*

ooh: like "oo" in *boot*

u: like "u" in *but*

ü: The German umlauted "u" and the French vowel spelled "u" in French; pronounced by saying /ee/ with the lips well protruded, as for /ooh/; heard in some Scottish pronunciations

uh: the schwa; the sound of "e" in *the* before a consonant: *the story*

y: the semi-vowel spelled "y" in *yes*

w: the semi-vowel spelled "w" in *wear* and *we* and "o" in *one*

Diphthongs

ay: the diphthong composed of /e/, which is the stressed half of the diphthong, and /ee/; spelled "ay" in *say*

I: the diphthong composed of /ah/, which is the stressed half of the diphthong, and /ee/; spelled "i" in *fight*

oh: the diphthong composed of /u/, which is the stressed half of the diphthong, and /ooh/ in American English; of the schwa /uh/ and /ooh/ in British English; spelled "o" in *home*

ow: the diphthong composed of /a/, which is the stressed half of the diphthong, and /ooh/; spelled "ow" in *how* and "ou" in *house*

oy: the diphthong composed of /aw/, which is the stressed half of the diphthong, and /ee/; spelled "oy" in *boy*

yooh: the diphthong composed of the semi-vowel /y/ and the vowel /ooh/, which is the stressed half of the diphthong; spelled *you*. This diphthong is the name of the letter "u" in the English alphabet.

Consonants

The consonants /b/, /d/, /f/, /g/ as in *get*, /k/, /h/, /l/, /m/, /n/, /p/, /r/, /s/, /t/, /v/, and /z/ have the standard phonetic values of General American English or British RP. The following additional symbols are used:

ch: like "ch" in *church*; a combination of the sounds /t/ and /sh/

j: like "dg" in *edge* or "j" in *just*

kh: like "ch" in Scottish *loch*; a guttural consonant in Arabic, Hebrew, Yiddish, and German

ng: like "ng" in *thing*

nk: like "nk" in *think*

sh: like "sh" in *show*

th: voiced, as in *this*

th: voiceless, as in *thing*

ts: like "ts" in *sets*

zh: like "s" in *measure, pleasure*

?: glottal stop, which replaces the sound of /t/ in certain words in some accents

Pronunciations are enclosed in forward slash marks: / /.

Stressed syllables in pronunciations are in capital letters.

Introduction
Teach Yourself Accents: The Elements

What Is an Accent?

An accent is a systematic pattern of pronunciation: the prototypical, inseparable combination of sounds, rhythm, and intonation with which a language is spoken. Nearly everyone who grows up in a specific region and social milieu pronounces the language in a similar way, so we can usually tell from someone's accent where that person is from, and to what socioeconomic class an individual belongs.

In show business, we use the words *accent* and *dialect* interchangeably, as in the title "dialect coach" for someone who teaches accents to actors, but, technically, they are not the same thing. A dialect is a complete version or variety of a language, with its grammar and vocabulary, as well as the particular accent or accents with which it is spoken.

Like every language, English has its dialects, including those known as Standard British English and Standard American English. Although mutually comprehensible, these dialects are dissimilar in many ways: An English person is "meant" to do something; an American is "supposed" to do it. In London, people live in flats; in New York, they live in apartments. An English person who wants to visit you may "knock you up," but don't say that to an American! As George Bernard Shaw quipped, "England and America are two countries separated by a common language." Then there are Standard Scottish English (SSE), Australian

English (AusE), and many other varieties, each with its own accents, idioms, and colorful slang. In Sydney, if you're thirsty, you might want to whip over on the knocker (immediately) to the bottle-shop (liquor store) for some cold tinnies of amber (beer). But in Glasgow you would go to an *offie*, a shortening of the UK term "off license," a store where you buy alcoholic beverages to be consumed off the premises. Go get a carry-out before the offie shuts!

There are two kinds of accents: those native to a language, and foreign accents, used by people with a different mother tongue who have learned a language. The two principal standard native accents of English—markedly different from each other—are known as British RP ("Received Pronunciation"), the accent with which Standard British English is spoken; and General American, the most widely used accent of Standard American English.

The muscular habits you have learned automatically and unconsciously—the way you form and utter sounds using the lips, tongue, and resonating chamber that is the inside of the mouth—are so ingrained that it is often difficult to learn the new muscular habits required when you learn another language. Sounds that are similar in the new language to the sounds you already know are, therefore, formed using the old habits. And there are always sounds in the new language that do not exist in the old, and that some people have great difficulty learning to pronounce correctly, such as the /th / *th*/ sounds of English. These are two of the factors that account for the existence of a foreign accent, easily heard as foreign by native speakers. There are also people who learn to speak English or any other language with virtually no discernible foreign accent.

If you are going to do a foreign accent, it's essential to learn some of the language. You will then have a feeling for the muscular habits, for how the lips and tongue are positioned and used during speech. And you will use this basic positioning or placement of the muscles when speaking English. This will automatically give you at least the beginning of the accent.

Sometimes this general positioning is all that is required, perhaps with a couple of specific vowel or consonant sounds added to it.

Native accents include a widely accepted, standard, non-regional accent alongside regional pronunciations. You unconsciously learn your accent from the people you go to school with and who surround you, even more than you do from your parents. If your parents speak with a foreign accent, for instance, you will nevertheless speak with the native accent that you hear constantly, at least if you have been born in a place, or arrived there when you were not yet twelve.

Accents, like languages, disappear when the last speaker dies. There are now only a relatively few upper-class Americans who speak as President Franklin D. Roosevelt did in 1941. The British accents recorded on Edison's wax cylinders by Florence Nightingale; by the poet Alfred, Lord Tennyson; and by actors of the late Victorian period, performing the works of Gilbert and Sullivan, no longer exist. And the native New York City accents of the 1920s and 1930s, preserved in films of the period, such as *Dead End* (1937), are largely a thing of the past, though still well remembered, but the American stage diction of the late nineteenth century as recorded by Edwin Booth in 1890 is something nobody now recalls, and it is different from the recorded British stage diction of the same period. Should you need to use one of these historic accents, you have ample recorded material to listen to.

Whether foreign or native, every accent contains four elements, each of which can be studied separately, but all of which work together simultaneously to form the accent:

1. General positioning, placement, and use of the mouth muscles (lips, tongue) during speech;
2. Rhythm, determined by stress patterns;
3. Music, determined by pitch and intonation patterns;
4. Phonetics, the specific sounds of vowels and consonants, the nature of those sounds being conditioned by the positioning of the mouth muscles, which differs—however slightly—from accent to accent.

Begin your work by reading the summary of the most important information about the accent, and by seeing how it differs from yours, comparing its features with those of your own accent. How do you naturally speak? How do use the muscles of the mouth when you speak? How does this use differ when you do an accent?

Your goal as an actor is to internalize and assimilate the accent so that it becomes your natural, habitual way of speaking, so that it is simply part of you, and not put on. The one exception is when the character is deliberately pretending to be someone with an accent, often a bad, comical one that they intend to be convincing, like several Viennese characters posing as either French or Hungarian aristocrats in Johann Strauss's operetta *Die Fledermaus* (The Bat).

How the Muscles of the Mouth Are Used

The first thing to study when learning an accent is the way the muscles of the mouth are used when you speak. The musculature of the vocal apparatus is used in a different way in every language or accent; and a priori in a different way from what you are accustomed to in your own accent when you are learning a new one. There are, perhaps, only a few such basic placements or positions, but they condition the way vowels and consonants sound, and give each accent its own particular resonance and linguistic flavor.

To create an authentic-sounding light native or foreign accent it is sometimes sufficient to have the vocal apparatus positioned as it would be by someone who really speaks with that accent. The accent may then be thickened by adding certain phonetic changes. The general position of the vocal apparatus during speech is determined by four things: the place of articulation of the consonants (see later in this chapter); the positioning of the tongue when forming vowels; how much the lips are protruded; and how tight or loose the muscles are at the corners of the mouth.

Rhythm: Stress Patterns

Rhythm is created by the stress patterns of an accent. *Stress* indicates which syllables in a word are emphasized or are most prominent. Stressed syllables are usually longer (and louder, and spoken on a pitch differentiating them from adjacent pitches) than the shorter unstressed syllables, just as a half note is longer than a quarter note.

In English, every word has its own particular unvarying primary stress, and there is secondary stressing in longer words. However, in British RP and General American, words may be stressed differently. An example is the word *controversy*: in British RP it is pronounced /kuhn TRO vuh see/; in General American, /KAHN truh VOR see/. Unless you have grown up speaking English, and thus learned English stress patterns automatically and unconsciously, you have to make an effort to learn the stress for every word. Stress in English is called "random": words could be stressed on any syllable, and you don't know where the stress is unless you have learned it.

In English, whichever word is stressed is the one that gives a sentence its meaning, not to be understood out of context. Take, for instance, the sentence "I never said he stole my money." Stressing a different word changes the meaning of the sentence; each meaning in parentheses indicates only one of several possibilities:

1. *I* never said he stole my money. (Maybe somebody else said it.)
2. I *never* said he stole my money. (You made that up!)
3. I never *said* he stole my money. (That doesn't mean I didn't think it.)
4. I never said *he* stole my money. (I said somebody else stole it.)
5. I never said he *stole* my money. (I gave it to him.)
6. I never said he stole *my* money. (It belonged to somebody else.)
7. I never said he stole my *money*. (He stole my keys.)

There are languages in which the first syllable of every word is always stressed, and other languages in which stress is always on the last syllable.

Languages in which a particular syllable is always stressed are said to have "uniform" stress. You always know how to stress words correctly even if you have no idea what they mean. This information is very important in creating a foreign accent, as such automatic habits can carry over into English.

The rhythmic stress patterns of a native language are often difficult to break, as they are so ingrained. They tend to carry over into English, although the correct random English stress patterns can be and often are learned. But the French accent, with its tendency to stress the last syllables of phrases, or the Hungarian accent, with its tendency to stress the first syllables of words, show how difficult it is to unlearn habits related to linguistic stress patterns.

Music: Intonation Patterns

Every accent has its own characteristic music, which is made up of a series of pitch or intonation patterns. Intonation means the pattern of pitch changes in connected speech—that is, in a sentence, phrase, or general utterance. All languages communicate by using a combination of pitch and stress, and the pitch and stress patterns are different in different languages. When you learn an accent, you must study these patterns along with the accent's phonetic aspects.

The pitch patterns (intonation patterns) in English express and convey emotion and meaning in ways we have automatically learned. We can choose to emphasize any word by saying it on a different pitch, higher or lower, from the surrounding pitches.

It is very difficult to describe the intonation patterns of any language, but every language has a distinctive intonation pattern, or systematic way of using pitches to express emotion. You simply have to hear them, and to learn what they mean.

Phonetics

You will make the actual sounds of an accent by learning how to do them physically. First, ask yourself how you make the vowel and consonant sounds of your own natural accent. Close your eyes and observe how those sounds "feel" in the mouth, and where they are placed. You can compare them to the new sounds of the accent. If you are an American doing a British RP accent, for instance, the sounds will feel more forward in the mouth than they do in your own accent, and the consonants will be more strongly articulated; that is, whatever muscle or part of the mouth presses against another part—the two lips, for instance, when saying /b/ or /p/—will be stronger in an upper-class British accent than in a General American accent.

Vowels, Semi-Vowels, and Diphthongs

A *vowel* is a single sound made by passing air through the vibrating vocal cords and then through the vocal cavity without the flow of air being stopped. The shape of the vocal cavity changes with each vowel: the tongue is higher or lower, the vocal cavity is more open or more closed, and the lips are relaxed or protruded or retracted, rounded or unrounded. The stream of air is directed up and either primarily to the back or middle or front of the palate (the "sounding board" of the mouth), and this is called the focal point, or what I mean by the point of resonance. Hence we refer, as I have said, to back and front vowels, which can be open or closed, rounded or unrounded. The vowel /ah/ in *father*, for example, is an open back unrounded vowel. There are also, as in French and Portuguese, nasal vowels, pronounced by lowering the soft palate at the back of the mouth and allowing some air to flow through the nasal cavity just above it, as when articulating the consonants /m/ and /n/.

A *semi-vowel* is a vowel during the pronunciation of which the flow of air is beginning to be stopped by the action of tongue or lips. It therefore has almost a consonantal quality. The two semi-vowels in English are /w/, during which the lips are beginning to close and are slightly rounded, and /y/, during which the sides of the tongue move up toward the roof of the mouth, touching it very lightly. They can interchangeably be called either semi-consonants or semi-vowels. Both /y/ and /w/ combine with vowels to form diphthongs: /yah/, /ye/, /yee/, /yoh/, /yoo/, /wah/, /we/, /wee/, /woh/, /woo/.

A *diphthong* consists of two vowels, or a vowel and a semi-vowel spoken in one breath. One of the vowels is always stressed. The unstressed half of the diphthong is always very short. An example is /I/, a combination of the /ah/ in *father* and the /ee/ in *meet*; /ah/ is stressed. In the case of diphthongs formed from a semi-vowel and a vowel, the vowel is always stressed: an example is the name of the letter "u" or the word *you*, formed with the semi-vowel /y/ and the vowel /ooh/ as in the word *boot*: /yOOH/. A diphthong occurs when the jaw relaxes slightly immediately after the pronunciation of a vowel and while sound is still issuing from the vocal cords. The tongue "glides" to a different position, changing the shape of the interior of the mouth, and we hear a diphthong.

Consonants

A *consonant* is a sound in which the flow of air is impeded or hindered by the action of tongue, lips, or teeth. Each consonant has a "point, or place, of articulation." The word *articulation* means how parts of the vocal apparatus touch each other to form a sound. For instance, to form a /t/, the tongue touches the palate (the roof of the mouth) just where it starts to curve upward, behind the front teeth—that is its point of articulation. The tongue may apply more or less pressure, and this changes the quality of the sound, making the /t/ hard or soft. In British RP, the /t/ is hard, as it is in the phrase *a cup of tea*. In General American, the /t/ is soft; that is, the pressure made by the tongue is not very strong. Say *a cup of tea* to yourself in both accents, and see how different they "feel" in the mouth.

Every language has its own consonant system, its own "inventory" of consonants. In English there are two versions of certain consonants: "voiced," in which there is sound from the vocal cords, and "voiceless" (or "unvoiced"), in which there is no vibration of the vocal cords. The pairs are, voiced and voiceless respectively: /b/ and /p/, /d/ and /t/, /j/ (/dg/) as in *edge* and /ch/ (/tsh/) as in *church*, /v/ and /f/, /g/ and /k/, /z/, and /s/, /zh/ as in *pleasure* and /sh/ as in *sure*, voiced /th/ as in *there* and voiceless /th/ as in *think*.

A letter is used in spelling to indicate what is actually a range of sounds. For example, the /t/ at the beginning of a word is actually a different sound from the /t/ in the middle of a word, different yet again from the sound at the end of a word: e.g., *tip, matter, pit*. In the more heavily "aspirated" version of /t/—that is, with breath added to the sound—sometimes heard in the middle of a word like *matter*, the tongue hardly touches the gum ridge and more air is forced through the vocal cavity; this is called a "tapped t." The "tapped /d/," heard as a substitute for voiced /th/ in some native and foreign accents in words like *other* and in some native accents in words like *whatever,* is also very important in accent work.

For all accents, native and foreign, always look at the consonants /l/, /r/, and /th / th/. These consonants are called "continuants," because their sounds can be continued as long as the speaker has breath. The /r/ sounds are especially important in any accent:

1. **Rhotic sounds:** Rhotic sounds are the voiced consonants spelled with the letter /r/. (The word *rhotic* comes from the name of a Greek letter of the alphabet, *rho*.) The sound associated with this letter in another language is often carried into English in a foreign accent. Is "r" after a vowel—"post-vocalic"—pronounced, or is it as silent as the "b" in *lamb*? When post-vocalic letter "r" is pronounced, the accent is "rhotic"—as in a General American or Scottish accent. When post-vocalic "r" is not pronounced, the accent is "non-rhotic"—as in

a British RP accent. One of the first questions to ask when studying any accent is whether it is rhotic or non-rhotic.

2. **Native accents:** In English, /r/ is a "retroflex" consonant; that is, the tip of the tongue curls upward so that the bottom of the tongue is toward the palate when the sound is articulated. The hardness or softness of the sound depends on whether or not the back of the tongue is relaxed. For instance, in U.S. Midwestern accents it is slightly tensed, and in British RP it is relaxed. In accents native to English, if /r/ is not pronounced it still often influences the vowel which precedes it, because the tongue is beginning to curl upward as if to articulate an /r/, thus giving an impression of the letter /r/. Therefore, we speak of "r-influenced" vowels. In upper-class British English, post-vocalic /r/ is silent, with some exceptions. In General American, post-vocalic /r/ is pronounced, but it is silent in certain regional accents of the U.S., such as New York or some areas of the East Coast of the South. In some accents, among them British RP, Scottish, or certain Irish accents, a lightly trilled or tapped /r/ is sometimes heard.

3. **Foreign accents:** Is the /r/ in a foreign language trilled frontally, as in Italian or Spanish? Is /r/ pronounced from the back of the throat (a "uvular r"), as in French or German? Is /r/ pronounced in the middle of the mouth, with the tip of the tongue curving upward slightly so that the bottom of the tongue is toward the palate, as it is in General American or Mandarin?

4. **The trilled /r/:** To pronounce a trilled /r/ (with one or more taps or flaps) heard in many other languages, including Spanish, Italian, Swedish, Finnish, Basque, Portuguese, Polish, Russian, and Czech, begin by saying a tapped /d/: the tongue makes a minimal, quick pressure when the /d/ is articulated, as in the famous phrase *FuggeDabouDit*. Then say the word *very* with a /d/ instead of an /r/. Draw the tip of the tongue back a very little bit and drop your tongue slightly until you have the impression of saying /r/. Do not curl the bottom of your tongue toward the roof of the mouth. The tip of the

tongue should be just at the opening of the palate in back of the gum ridge. Alternatively, you may begin a trilled /r/ by saying *hurrah* and shortening the vowel in the first syllable until it is entirely eliminated, leaving you with a very breathy sound: /hr/. Continue tapping the tip of the tongue lightly against the opening of the palate, hardly touching it at all. You can then eliminate the /h/.

5. **The uvular /r/:** To pronounce the uvular or guttural voiced /r/ heard in various versions in French, German, Yiddish, Dutch, Danish, Norwegian, and Hebrew, first lower the tip of the tongue so it touches the back of the lower front teeth, then raise the back of the tongue so the uvula vibrates against it, as in gargling, or as in articulating its voiceless version, the /kh/ sound heard in Scottish *loch* or German *Ach!* This consonant is, in fact, the voiceless one in the pair /kh/ and uvular /r/, which is a voiced consonant.

Some Questions to Ask Yourself

Select the accent to suit the character and make it your own by constant repetition and drilling. Whether you do a real or comically distorted accent, it must be organic and, therefore, internal to the character.

1. Is the accent rhotic or non-rhotic? In a foreign accent, does the native /r/ carry over into the accent in English?
2. How is /l/ pronounced— with the back of the tongue raised, as in Russian, or with the tip of the tongue well forward, as in French?
3. How are /th / *th*/ sounds pronounced—correctly, or are substitute sounds such as /d/ and /t/ used?
4. How do the vowels and diphthongs differ from your own accent?
5. What is the character's social and educational background? For instance, there are U.K. accents native to English associated with social classes.

6. If a character is from a foreign linguistic background, how did he or she learn English? A professor of physics who learned English at his European, African, or Asian university may speak with a more upper-class accent in English than a laborer who learned English on the streets of an English or American city. Did the character learn English at school or on the streets of New York or London or Sydney or Johannesburg?

7. How well and how grammatically does the character speak the English language, as indicated in the script? This will often tell you how heavy the accent should be, whether it is native or foreign.

8. How thick or heavy or light is the accent? We sometimes hear such a slight accent that we cannot quite identify it. As an actor you may wish to create such an accent, or you may want to do an accent that is just a bit more identifiable to an audience. People can also be inconsistent within their own accent, and will sometimes pronounce /r/ or /th/ correctly, and sometimes not. As an actor, you should make sure that any accent you do is clearly understood, however thick the original may be in real life.

9. At what age did the person learn English? Below the age of twelve a heavy foreign accent is very rare, if indeed any exists at all. I know people who learned English as a second language, and grew up in New York City. They sound like New Yorkers speaking General American, and have not even a trace of the accent associated with their first language, which they also continue to speak. But even such brilliant people as Einstein and Freud, both of whom learned English comparatively late in life, spoke with very thick German and Viennese accents, respectively. Einstein even had to be subtitled in newsreels.

10. Where can I find actual examples of the accent, used by real people? You want to listen to and, if possible, record these examples. Embassies, consulates, recordings, movies, and restaurants with personnel who come from the country provide some excellent source material. Listening to a good dialect coach is all very well, but you want to find

actual examples and do the work yourself of analyzing what you are hearing.

An Exercise for Teaching Yourself Any Accent

You can use this exercise for studying the practice exercises and monologues at the end of each chapter.

When you know what the sounds of the accent are, and how they "shift" from the sounds you usually make, go through a script you are working on, a book you are reading, or any material you like, and select one sound. You might select /th / *th*/ substitutes, for instance, or a diphthong shift to a pure vowel, such as /oh/ to /aw/. Mark the sounds in some way, then go through the material again, speaking aloud and pronouncing only those sounds.

Do this for all the sound shifts, adding one each time. Do each new sound together with the ones you did previously. Eventually, you will have all the required sounds in place. Also, as you do this, be aware of exactly what the muscles of the mouth are doing, and you will concentrate on the correct positioning or placement of the lips, tongue, and the opening of the mouth, wider or more closed as required.

You will thus become aware of how the whole accent that you have gradually built up feels in the mouth, and you can then make all of that into a habit.

When you have finished this part of the exercise, continue by writing out your own pronunciation using the list of phonetic symbols in this book, or the International Phonetic Alphabet (IPA), if you are familiar with it. Record yourself and listen carefully until you are satisfied that you have achieved the desired sound.

You will then be able to pick up any material and read it with the accent. Once you can do this, you have mastered the accent and it is now part of your actor's toolkit.

1
Standard Upper- and Middle-Class British Accents

British RP (Received Pronunciation) is the middle- and upper-class accent of Standard British English. This accent is used in the theater and the media, and in the academic, financial, legal, and medical professions. *The Oxford English Dictionary* defines RP as "the pronunciation of that variety of British English widely considered the least regional, being originally that used by educated speakers in southern England," and received by them from previous generations.

There are a number of variations of the evolving RP accent, including:

1. **U-RP (Upper-Class RP):** The precise, well-articulated accent used by the educated and the upper and upper-middle socioeconomic classes, especially members of the older generations, but by many younger speakers as well.
2. **Mainstream RP:** The more widely heard non-regional accent, very close to U-RP but not as precise in its articulation, used by upper- and middle-class people throughout Britain, by many contemporary young actors, and by others of varying socioeconomic backgrounds.
3. **Estuary, also called Thames Estuary:** A very close variant of Mainstream RP used by some upper- and upwardly mobile middle- and working-class people. The accent is influenced by features of the general London accent, discussed in the next chapter, especially the glottal stop on final /t/ (see p. 21).

Everyone speaks with his or her own individual version of the RP accent. Listen, for example, to the following actors in film and television projects, and you will get an object lesson: Diana Rigg, Christopher Lee, Peter Cushing, Joan Plowright, Peter Ustinov, Charles Laughton, Henry Daniell, Ronald Colman, Greer Garson, Vanessa Redgrave, James Mason, Basil Rathbone, George Sanders, Margaret Leighton, Judy Parfitt, Claude Rains, Derek Jacobi, Jim Broadbent, Emily Watson, Tom Wilkinson, Hugh Grant, Malcolm McDowell, and Gary Oldman.

Be sure not to miss Trevor Howard and Celia Johnson in Noël Coward's *Brief Encounter* (1945). Listen to Margaret Rutherford as Miss Marple in such films as *Murder She Said* (1961) and as Miss Prism in Oscar Wilde's *The Importance of Being Earnest* (1952), with Edith Evans as Lady Bracknell and Michael Redgrave as Jack. (See Redgrave also in the 1951 film adaptation of Terence Rattigan's play *The Browning Version*.) Sir Alec Guinness is always brilliant, and his diction superb: See him in *The Ladykillers* (1955), with the sweet, genteel Katie Johnson, whose accent features very clear diction; and in *The Man in the White Suit* (1951), with Cecil Parker. (Parker is hilariously befuddled in Danny Kaye's film *The Court Jester* [1955].) And don't miss *I'm All Right Jack* (1959), with Ian Carmichael, Richard Attenborough, John Le Mesurier, and the inimitable Terry-Thomas. *Goodbye, Mr. Chips* (1939) and *The Winslow Boy* (1948) star Robert Donat, noted for his wonderful diction. And see *The Servant* (1963) with Dirk Bogarde, Sarah Miles, and James Fox (whose accent is always very plummy and upper-class); and *The Chalk Garden* (1964), with John Mills, Hayley Mills, Deborah Kerr, Edith Evans, and Felix Aylmer. (Aylmer is also excellent as Polonius in Laurence Olivier's 1948 film version of *Hamlet*, with Jean Simmons and Eileen Herlie.) See Olivier's *Richard III* (1955) with Claire Bloom, John Gielgud, and Ralph Richardson. And see *The Great Gilbert and Sullivan* (1953), with Robert Morley, Maurice Evans, Peter Finch, and Martyn Green, and listen to Green on the series of Gilbert and Sullivan recordings made in the late 1940s and early 1950s.

Newer films and television programs include *Gosford Park* (2001) with Maggie Smith, Jeremy Northam, James Wilby, and Kristin Scott Thomas;

and *The Queen* (2006) with Helen Mirren as Elizabeth II and Michael Sheen as Tony Blair. And see *Her Majesty, Mrs. Brown* (1997), with Judi Dench as Queen Victoria and Antony Sher as Disraeli. (Sher is from South Africa, but sounds perfectly English in that particular role.) Among the other great actors in the film are Geoffrey Palmer, Richard Pasco, and David Westhead. And listen to Edward Fox in the mini-series of George Eliot's *Daniel Deronda* (2002) for the poshest, plummiest accent you've ever heard. The satirical television series *Yes, Minister* (1980–1984) and *Yes, Prime Minister* (1986–1987), with Paul Eddington and Nigel Hawthorne, are hilarious. See Hawthorne also as King George III in *The Madness of King George* (1994), with Rupert Everett, Rupert Graves, and Helen Mirren.

In present-day stage and screen productions, the slightly less well-articulated Mainstream RP and Estuary are more usual than U-RP. Listen to the Estuary accent of the brilliant actor and drily witty, understated comedian Ricky Gervais, born in Reading, near London, in his films and television one-man specials, and in such shows as *Extras* (2005–2007) and the original (British) version of *The Office* (2001–2003), both of which he also wrote. For Mainstream RP, listen also to many of the characters in the different British detective series.

Teach Yourself the RP and Estuary Accents

The three most noticeable features of these accents are: (1) They are non-rhotic, so the post-vocalic (after a vowel) /r/ is silent before another consonant and at the end of a word. (2) The broad, open-throated /ah/ sounds are used in words where Americans use the vowel /a/; see the "ask list," later in this chapter. (3) The schwa is substituted for full vowels in unstressed syllables, creating the accent's rhythm.

1. **Positioning, placement, and use of the mouth muscles during speech:** For RP, the mouth is not open wide, the tongue is held up and

forward, the lips are relaxed and slightly protruded, and the muscles at the corners of the mouth are slightly tensed. For Mainstream RP and Estuary, the lips and tongue are more relaxed during speech than they are in the older accent.

In general, the language "feels" as if it is all frontally pronounced, whereas American English often "feels" as if it is in the middle of the mouth. Feel the point where the tongue touches the opening into the palate to form the sound of /d/ (the "point of articulation" of the /d/). It is there that the general resonance of British RP and Estuary lie. Practice by repeating *dah, dah, dah, dooh, dooh, dooh* several times until you get the feeling you can direct the stream of air forward to that point in the mouth, so the language skips and plays about, "trippingly on the tongue," as Hamlet says.

2. **The sound of /r/:** The accents are non-rhotic, so drop /r/ after a vowel and at the end of a word, and drop /r/ before another consonant: The /r/ is not heard following a vowel and preceding a consonant in the middle of words like *first, heard, word, work,* etc. Think of /r/ in this post-vocalic (after a vowel) position as a silent letter, like the "b" in *lamb* or the "gh" in *daughter.*

    At the beginning of a word, /r/ is a retroflex consonant, with the bottom of the tongue curling up not very far toward the roof of the mouth (palate); the back of the tongue is relaxed. The /r/ may sometimes be given one tap or trill, especially when it begins a syllable in the middle of a word, such as *very.* In British RP, the lips are slightly protruded when pronouncing the initial /r/.

    An "intrusive r" is occasionally (but by no means always) heard where there is none in the actual word: Words like *drawing* are pronounced /DRAW rihng/ and phrases like *Diana and I* are said as /dI A nuh ruhnd I/. The "intrusive r" is heard more often in the Estuary or sometimes in Mainstream RP than in the U-RP accent, where it is generally best to avoid it.

A "linking r" is often used, where a usually silent /r/ at the end of a word is linked to a vowel at the beginning of the following word, as in the phrase *father and I* /FAH thuh ruhn dI/. The "linking r" is sometimes given one tap, particularly in RP, but in Mainstream / Estuary it is pronounced with the usual retroflex sound.

3. **The schwa /uh/:** Use schwas in many unstressed syllables, instead of the full vowel. The rhythm of the language is determined by the use of the schwa, which combines with the pitches to create a type of music different from that of American English. See the section on the schwa later in this chapter.

4. **The broad open /ah/ sound:** See the section on the "ask list" for words which shift from American /a/ in *that* to the British /ah/ in *father*.

5. **Other consonants:** The consonants, especially for U-RP, are harder than in American English; that is, they are articulated more strongly, so the pressure of the tongue is harder. Repeat the following phrase several times as an exercise, keeping your eyes closed and concentrating on how the sounds feel in the mouth: *a cup of tea*. You should feel everything moving in a forward, closed position.

   a. **The sound of /l/:** Learn and use a correct British /l/. This consonant feels more forward in the mouth than in General American English. The tongue is higher than in an American /l/. In articulating /l/, the tip of the tongue touches the upper gum ridge behind the front teeth lightly for an American /l/, and is pressed against the gum ridge more firmly for the British /l/. Practice with the sound *lah, lah, lah, lah, lah, lah* and the repeated phrase *let go*. Close your eyes and feel the placement of the tip of the tongue and the generally forward feeling of the consonant.

6. **Other vowels and diphthongs:**

   a. **The long /aw/:** This vowel, pronounced with the lips fairly closed and well protruded, can be quite long in such words as *all, daughter,* *law*, *talk*, *taught*, and *water* /AWL/, /DAW tuh/, /LAW/, /TAWK/, /TAWT/, /WAW tuh/.

b. **The short /o/:** Use the British short closed vowel /o/ in *hot*, *not*, and *got*.

c. **The diphthong /oh/:** Learn and use the British version of the diphthong /oh/: it is a combination of the schwa /uh/ and the long vowel /ooh/; the /uh/ half of the diphthong is stressed: /UHooh/. Practice with the words *go, going, home, roam, know, slow, though*, and *although*. You should find that your lips are quite protruded as you say these words.

d. **The diphthong /yooh/:** The long sound in *duke* and *tune* is a diphthong combining the semi-vowel /y/ with /ooh/ in *boot*. The full diphthong is almost always pronounced in *duke, tune, flute, lure, lute, institution, constitution, delusion, illusion, lunatic, Tuesday, newspaper*, etc.

   To drop the sound of /y/ can be satirical in the upper classes: e.g., *dook*; it was an affectation of the 1920s and 1930s, along with dropping the /g/ in "-ing" endings, discussed at the opening of this chapter.

   There are some words in which a simple consonant is pronounced without adulteration before /ooh/; for example, the /d/ in *graduate* does not sound like /j/ in *edge*, nor the "x" in *sexual* like /ksh/ as in General American. The British say /GRA dyooh uht (noun); GRA dyooh ayt (verb)/ and /SEKS yooh uhl (alternatively, SEK shuhl)/, but note that this is two syllables, unlike American /SEK shooh uhl/.

   A contemporary trend in Estuary is the dropping of /y/ after /l/ and /s/, so that *lute* /LYOOHT/ becomes /looht/ and *super* /SYOOH puh/ becomes /SOOH puh/.

The Mainstream / Estuary Phonetic Variations

In addition to the details above, you will need to know the following phonetic information for the Estuary accent:

1. **The glottal stop /?/:** A glottal stop is a brief catch in the throat: the glottis closes for a split second to replace the consonant /t/. Like the general London accent, Estuary uses the glottal stop /?/, which, in this accent, often replaces a /t/ at the end of such words as *what, it, that, bit,* and *can't,* but only when they are in the middle of an utterance, rarely when they are at the end: *that really hurts* /tha? REE lee HOTS/; *it was that* /ih? wuhz THAT/. In Estuary, as opposed to London lower-class accents, the glottal stop is not used in the middle of such words as *bottle* and *battle.* In Mainstream RP, the glottal stop replacing a final /t/ is occasionally heard as well, but less often than in Estuary.

2. **Consonants:** In general, consonants are less hard and, therefore, not as strongly articulated as in U-RP. An intrusive /r/ is not uncommon; see above.

3. **The sounds of /ooh/:** In both Mainstream RP and Estuary, some people also insert the semi-vowel /y/ in the words *too* and *do* /TYOOH/, /DYOOH/, lightly pronounced, and almost like a French /ü/; or the sound is heard as a long /ee/ in such words as *intrude* /ihn TREED/. The lips are protruded less than for a pure /ooh/ sound.

4. **The shift from /OOHuh/ to /aw/:** Another change heard in both Mainstream RP and Estuary is the shift from /OOHuh/ to /aw/ in certain words such as *poor*: /POOHuh/ shifts to /PAW/, and *sure* /SHOOHuh/ shifts to /SHAW/.

5. **Syllable-dropping:** In both Mainstream RP and Estuary, unstressed syllables are often eliminated in such words as *believe* and *police,* pronounced as if they were one-syllable words: /BLEEV/, /PLEES/.

The Ask List

This is a partial list of words that are pronounced in Southern and some Northern British Isles accents, by all social classes, with the /ah/ in *father* in stressed syllables, as opposed to the usual American pronunciation of these words with the /a/ in *that.* You will see that the list includes many commonly used words, such as *can't* and *dance.* Note that the word *fancy* is always pronounced with the /a/ in *cat*; many Americans make the mistake of saying it with the /ah/ in *father*. When you practice these words, feel the air against the back of your throat, and open it wide. You will then have the British version of /ah/, the most open-throated vowel of any in English. In the usual American version of /ah/, the throat is not as open.

advantage, after (and words beginning and ending with "after": *afternoon, afterwards, hereafter*, etc.), *answer, ask, aunt, banana, basket, bastard, bath, blast, branch, brass, broadcast, calf, can't, cask, casket, cast, caste, castle, chance, chancellor, chant, clasp, class* (and words beginning with "class": *classmate, classroom, classy*, etc.), *command, countermand, daft, dance, demand, disaster, downcast, draft, enchant, entrance* (verb), *example, fast, fasten, gala, ghastly, glance, glass, graft, grant,* words ending in "-graph" (sometimes, however, pronounced /GRAPH/): *photograph, telegraph*, etc. (but note that the word *graphic* is pronounced /GRA fik/; words ending in "-graphic" are pronounced /GRA fik/; words ending in "-graphical," such as *geographical*, are pronounced /GRA fi kuhl/), *grasp, grass, half, lance, last, lather, laugh, mask, mast, master, nasty, outcast, pass, passing, past, pastor, pastoral, path, perchance, plant, plaster, prance, raft, rascal, rasp, raspberry* /RAHZ bree/, *rather, reprimand, salve, sample, shaft, shan't, slander, slant, staff, stanch, task, tomato, trance, transcript, transport* (and other words beginning with the prefix "trans-" [also heard with /a/, however]), *vast, waft, wrath*

Notes: (1) The letter "a" in *potato* is pronounced /ay/, as it is in General American. (2) The letter "a" in the words *fancy, gas, glacier,* and *mass* is pronounced /a/, as in the word *that*. The word *glacier* sounds like "glassier," with the /r/ dropped; but note that *glacial* is pronounced /GLAY shuhl/.

The Schwa and the Rhythm (Stress Patterns) and Music (Pitch Patterns) of the Accents

The use of the schwa is one of the most important keys to the accents. The schwa—phonetic symbol /uh/—is the brief vowel sound, spelled "e" in the word *the* before a consonant, as in the phrase *the story* /thuh STAW ree/. This sound is often substituted for a longer vowel in unstressed syllables, shortening the syllable. The schwa is much more widely used in British than in American English.

The word *for*—when not stressed—is often (though not always) pronounced with a schwa, /fuh/, before a consonant or a semi-vowel, as in *for you* or *for me* /fuh YOOH/, /fuh MEE/. *For* is pronounced /fuhr/ before a vowel, when the final "r" in *for* is linked to the vowel, as in *for us* /fuh RUS/, or *for instance* /fuh RIHN stuhns (alternatively, FRIHN stuhns)/.

The word *to* is almost always pronounced with a schwa, /tuh/, before the semi-vowel /y/ or before a consonant, as in *to you* or *to be* /tuh YOOH/, /tuh BEE/. *To* is pronounced /tooh/ before a vowel, as in *to act* /tooh AKT/.

The most important stressed syllable in any utterance—from the speaker's point of view—is called the *nuclear tone*, because it is the *nucleus* of the sentence: It makes the speaker's point. The nuclear tone is usually spoken on a longer, stronger, and often higher pitch. The schwas in British RP in the unstressed syllables lead the speaker to the desired emphasis as quickly as he or she wishes, without necessarily rushing to make a point. This gives the sentence a characteristic British rhythm. In the usual rhythm of American speech, vowels in unstressed syllables are given a full value; they literally take more time to utter, and the nuclear tone stands out less than it does in British speech.

For example, in the sentence *The boundaries of the territory were secure*, Americans would usually say /thuh BOWN dreez uhv thuh TE rih TAW ree WOR sih KYOOHR/, whereas the British might say /thuh BOWN dreez uhv thuh TE ruh tree (alternatively, TE ruh tuh ree) wo suh KYOOuh/. The stress on the syllable /TAW/ and the word *were* in the American sentence makes all the difference in the rhythm of the speech, which is slower than in the British utterance. Americans stress all the important words in an utterance; the British stress only the most important words. Notice the use of schwas and the stress pattern (rhythm) in the

RP pronunciation of the sentence *Will there be anything else?* /WIHL thuh bee e nuh *thi*hng ELS/.

A Note on RP Pronunciations

In addition to the words on the "ask list" and in the section on the schwa, numerous words are pronounced differently in British English than in American English. Two excellent sources are Daniel Jones's *An English Pronouncing Dictionary* (Cambridge University Press, 1997) and the *BBC Pronouncing Dictionary of British Names* (Oxford University Press, 1990). The latter includes English, Scottish, Irish, and Welsh names of people and places.

Some Comparative British and American English Pronunciations

1. The past participle *been*: British /BEEN/, rhymes with *bean*; American /BIHN/.

2. Stress: Many words are stressed differently in the two accents. For instance, such words as *secondary*, *secretary*, *ordinary*, *extraordinary*, or *library* lose the secondary stress they have in American English on the "or" or "ar" syllables, which are pronounced in British English with a schwa, or which even disappear entirely: /SEK uhn duh ree (alternatively, SEK uhn dree)/, /SEK ruh tuh ree (alternatively, SEK ruh tree)/, /AW duh nuh ree (alternatively, AW dnree)/, /ek STRAW duh nuh ree (alternatively, ek STRAW dnree)/, /LI bruh ree (alternatively, LI bree)/.

3. Words ending in "-day": For days of the week, in British English, the last syllable is often pronounced /dee/; in American English, the last syllable is always pronounced /day/. *Birthday*: British /BOTH dee/ when the word is not stressed, and /BOTH day/ when the word stands out or is stressed; American always /BORTH day/. *Today*: British and American both always /tuh DAY/. *Yesterday*: British /YES tuh dee/; American /YES tuhr DAY/. *It's my birthday today*: British /ihts mI BOTH dee tuh DAY/ (but *it's my birthday* alone would be pronounced /ihts mI BOTH day/); American /ihts MI BORTH day tuh DAY/.

4. Words with "-ile" endings: These are pronounced /IL/ in British English; /uhl/ in American English. For example, *hostile* /HOS tIl; HOS tuhl/, *missile* /MIH sIl; MIH suhl/, *projectile* /pruh JEK tIl; pruh JEK tuhl/.

5. Words with "-ization" (or "-isation") endings: Often words ending in "-ization" are pronounced in British English with the diphthong "I" instead of the schwa one might expect: *civilization* /sih vuh lI ZAY shuhn (alternatively, shn)/, *organization* /aw guh nI ZAY shuhn (alternatively, shn)/, *realization* /REEuh lI ZAY shuhn (alternatively, shn)/, and so forth.

6. Second-syllable stress: Whereas the British stress the second syllables of *dictate*, *dictator*, *narrate*, and *narrator*, Americans stress the first syllables.

7. *Almost*: British /AWL muhst/ when the word is not stressed; American, and British when the word is stressed /AWL MOHST/.

8. *Always*: British /AWL wuhz/ when the word is not stressed; American, and British when the word is stressed /AWL wayz/.

9. *Anything*: British /E nuh THIHNG/; American /E nee THIHNG/.

10. *Circumstance*: British /SO kuhm stuhnts; SO kuhm STAHNTS; SO kuhm STANTS/; American /SOR kuhm STANTS/.

11. *Clerk*: British /KLAHK/; American /KLORK/.

12. *Controversy*: British /kuhn TRO vuh see/; American /KON truh VOR see/.

13. *Discriminatory*: British /dihs krih mih NAY tuh ree/; American /dihs KRIHM ihn uh TAW ree/.

14. *Ecumenical*: British /EE kyooh ME nih kuhl/; American /E kyooh ME nih kuhl/.

15. *Everything*: British /E vruh THIHNG/; American /E vree THIHNG/.

16. *Figure*: British /FIH guh/; American /FI gyuhr/.

17. *Garage*: British /GA ruhj/; American /guh RAHZH/.

18. *Laboratory*: British /luh BO ruh tree (alternatively, luh BO ruh tuh ree)/; American /LA bruh TAW ree/.

19. *Lieutenant*: British /luhf TE nuhnt/; American /loo TE nuhnt (alternatively, lyooh TE nuhnt)/.

20. *Mandatory*: British /man DAY tuh ree (alternatively, MAN duh tuh ree)/; American /MAN duh TAW ree/.

21. *Medicine*: British /MED sihn/; American /ME dih sihn/.

22. *Migraine*: British /MEE grayn/; American /MI grayn/.

23. *Necessary*: British /NE suh sree (alternatively, NE suh suh ree)/; American /NE suh SE ree/.

24. *Nephew*: British /NE vyooh/; American /NE fyooh/.

25. *Predecessor*: British /PREE duh SE suh/; American /PRE duh SE suhr/.

26. *Privacy*: British /PRIH vuh see/; American /PRI vuh see/.

27. *Process*: British /PROH ses/; American /PRAH ses/.

28. *Schedule*: British /SHE dyuhl/; American /SKED jooh uhl (alternatively, SKED jool)/.

29. *Sexual*: British /SEK syooh uhl/; American /SEK shooh uhl/.

30. *Suggest, suggestion*: British /suh JEST/, /suh JES chuhn/; American /suhg JEST/, /suhg JES chuhn/.

31. *Upon*: British /uh PUHN/ when the word is not stressed—*Once upon a time* /WUNS uh PUHN uh TIM/—British /uh PON/ when the word is stressed—*upon my word* /uh PON mI WOD/; American /uh PAHN; uh PON/.

32. *Vitamins*: British /VIH tuh mihnz/; American /VI tuh mihnz/.

More RP Accent Variations

In the 1920s, some members of the English upper classes adopted a particular affectation: They dropped the final /g/ in "-ing" endings, and were always "goin' huntin', shootin', and fishin'"; the "-in'" ending was distinctly pronounced /ihn/ or, sometimes, /een/. This affectation, ably done by Ian Carmichael as Lord Peter Wimsey in the British television series based on Dorothy Sayers's novels, soon disappeared from aristocratic pronunciation, but it was and is a natural, unaffected feature of working-class speech.

And it is a useful thing to know if you are doing an English play set in the 1920s or 1930s.

Then there are those drawling, affected, character-specific accents in which /r/ is pronounced either as /v/ (veally tvue), or as /w/ (weally twue). Those who speak this way also sometimes pronounce *really* as /RAY lee/, at least when they are actually pronouncing the /r/ as /r/. You might hear /RAY lee tvooh/. A few members of the upper classes sometimes drop /r/ in the middle of a word, so that *very* is pronounced either /ve/ or /vay/, and *very true* may sound like /vay TROOH/, /vay TVOOH/, /vay TWOOH/, or /VAY trooh/. It may be that the people who pronounce /r/ in these ways simply have difficulty pronouncing the sound correctly. Still, this is all rather *twee*, don't you think? (*Twee* is fairly recent British slang for "cloyingly sweet," derived from baby talk for *sweet*.)

Another variation is the very "swallowed" accent, full of the all-important unstressed schwas. This variation is associated in plays and films with the character of ex-colonial officers serving the empire in the days of imperialism, and the accent has been much caricatured. When these characters speak, you sometimes seem to hear nothing but consonants. For good examples of this type of aristocratic and / or military character, see Ballard Berkeley as Major Gowen in the television series *Fawlty Towers* (1975–1979); he exaggerates superbly. Listen as well to John Cleese and Prunella Scales as Mr. and Mrs. Fawlty, with her Mainstream RP accent. She can also be heard doing very upscale U-RP as Lady Markby in *An Ideal Husband* (2000). And observe the accent of the general played by Sir Alec Guinness in *Kind Hearts and Coronets* (1949), in which Guinness plays eight victims. (Dennis Price, as their murderer, has the plummiest of put-on U-RP accents, as does Joan Greenwood as his inamorata; and listen to Valerie Hobson and Miles Malleson as well.) Another perfect example of such a character is the bluff, good-hearted Colonel Julyan, expertly played by C. Aubrey Smith, in Alfred Hitchcock's first American film, an adaptation of Daphne du Maurier's novel *Rebecca* (1940). In that same film, Laurence Olivier is Maxim de Winter, an English aristocrat; George

Sanders (another wonderful plummy accent) is Rebecca's unctuous cousin Favell; and the superb, Australian-born actress Judith Anderson sounds absolutely English as the villainous Mrs. Danvers.

There is still another variant of upper-class accents known as "Sloane Ranger." Making its appearance at the beginning of the 1980s, this accent took its name from the trendy area around Sloane Square and South Kensington, where the well-to-do scions of aristocratic families, called Sloane Rangers, live and play. They go downtown /DIN TIN/ to purchase Spode /SPAYD/ china; and they speak through smiling, closed /KLAYZD/ lips. They probably wouldn't be caught dead having afternoon tea at Fortnum and Mason's—too bourgeois—and, needless to say, they would never have "high tea," which is the term for a working-class evening meal—bangers and mash (sausages and mashed potatoes), and so on. The Sloane Rangers considered themselves and the way they spoke very "posh."

Intonation and Stress: The Music and Rhythm of the Accents

As discussed above, the use of the schwa in unstressed syllables, the stressing of the nuclear tone, the lengthening of its vowel or diphthong, and speaking it on a differentiated pitch give the accent its characteristic rhythm. Stressed syllables may also be spoken on more than one pitch, with a rising or falling tone. Because of the prevalence of diphthongs in English it is easy to use falling and rising tones; one half of the diphthong is at one end of the rise or fall and the other half is at the other end.

At the end of a simple declarative sentence the pitch is lowered slightly, although it may also be raised for emphasis.

At the end of a question the pitch rises, but this pattern may change in certain circumstances. For example, if the word *are* is stressed in *How are you?*, it is also often spoken on an upper pitch and *you* on a lower one.

An imperative, or a command, is usually spoken with a falling tone at the end.

Emotional utterances, such as expletives, may add several pitches to the pattern. Anger is expressed with raised pitches and at a louder volume, but also—and this can be very effective for actors—in low, even tones, with the anger seething underneath.

Listen for pitch patterns to the many examples of films suggested above. In all the RP accents, the intonation patterns are fairly "level" or "flat"; that is, the pitches do not vary much. Still, more musical notes are used than in General American.

Practice Exercises

1. *Were you going there today, if I may ask?*

```
                          /da-
          going there to-        \y,          ask?
     Were you                         if I may
```

Emphasizing the word *there* changes the pattern:

```
                                          ask?
                              day, if I
                  /there to-          may
     Were you going
```

or

```
     Were you going                      ask?
                    \there        if I may
                       today,
     /wo yooh GOH ihng THEuh tuh DAY ihf I may AHSK/
```

Notes: The forward slash represents a rising pitch; the backward slash, a falling pitch. Together with the nuclear tone described above, they give this question a typical rhythm as well as its music.

2. *I don't want to intrude on your studies. You're probably brilliant.*
U-RP: /I dohnt WAWNT tooh ihn TROOHD on yaw STU deez / YAW PRO buh blee BRIHL yuhnt/
Estuary: /I dohn? WAW nooh ihn TREED on yaw STU deez / YAW PRO blee BRIHL yuhn?/

Notes: In the Estuary pronunciation, notice the dropping of the second syllable in the word *probably*. The /n/ in the syllable /yuhn?/ is barely heard, as the lips are not closed to form the full /n/ sound.

3. From Lewis Carroll's *Through the Looking Glass* (1871), chapter V, "Wool and Water"

> Alice carefully released the brush, and did her best to get the hair into order. "Come, you look rather better now!" she said, after altering most of the pins. "But really you should have a lady's maid!"
>
> "I'm sure I'll take you with pleasure!" the Queen said. "Twopence [/TU puhnts/] a week, and jam every other day."
>
> Alice couldn't help laughing, as she said, "I don't want you to hire *me*—and I don't care for jam."
>
> "It's very good jam," said the Queen.
>
> "Well, I don't want any *today*, at any rate."
>
> "You couldn't have it if you *did* want it," the Queen said. "The rule is, jam tomorrow and jam yesterday—but never jam to-day."
>
> "It *must* come sometimes to 'jam to-day,'" Alice objected.
>
> "No, it can't," said the Queen. "It's jam every *other* day: today isn't any *other* day, you know."

4. From *The Posthumous Papers of the Pickwick Club* (1837), chapter XXXIV: "Is wholly devoted to a full and faithful Report of the memorable Trial of Bardell against Pickwick"

"Some time before his death, he [Mr. Bardell, /bah DEL/] had stamped his likeness upon a little boy. With this little boy, the only pledge of her departed exciseman, Mrs. Bardell shrank from the world, and courted the retirement and tranquillity of Goswell [/GOZ wuhl/] Street; and here she placed in her front parlour window a written placard, bearing this inscription—'Apartments furnished for a single gentleman. Inquire within.'" Here Serjeant Buzfuz paused, while several gentlemen of the jury took a note of the document.

"There is no date to that, is there, sir?" inquired a juror.

"There is no date, gentlemen," replied Serjeant Buzfuz; "but I am instructed to say that it was put in the plaintiff's parlour window just this time three years. I entreat the attention of the jury to the wording of this document—'Apartments furnished for a single gentleman'! Mrs. Bardell's opinions of the opposite sex, gentlemen, were derived from a long contemplation of the inestimable qualities of her lost husband. She had no fear—she had no distrust—she had no suspicion—all was confidence and reliance. 'Mr. Bardell,' said the widow; 'Mr. Bardell was a man of honour—Mr. Bardell was a man of his word—Mr. Bardell was no deceiver—Mr. Bardell was once a single gentleman himself; to single gentlemen I look for protection, for assistance, for comfort, and for consolation—*in* single gentlemen I shall perpetually see something to remind me of what Mr. Bardell was when he first won my young and untried affections; to a single gentleman, then, shall my lodgings be let.' Actuated by this beautiful and touching impulse (among the best impulses of our imperfect nature, gentlemen), the lonely and desolate widow dried her tears, furnished her first floor, caught her innocent boy to her maternal bosom, and put the bill up in her parlour window. Did it remain there long? No. The serpent was on the watch, the train was laid, the mine was preparing, the sapper and miner was at work. Before the bill had been in the parlour window three days—three days, gentlemen—a being, erect upon two legs, and bearing all the outward semblance of a man, and not of a monster, knocked at the door of Mrs. Bardell's house. He inquired within; he took the lodgings; and on the very next day he entered into possession of them. This man was Pickwick—Pickwick, the defendant [/duh FEN duhnt/]."

Notes: Known for his public readings from his own works, Dickens's reading of this trial scene was one of his most effective and appreciated performances. Charles Kent tells us in *Charles Dickens as a Reader* (Chapman & Hall, 1872) that it was greeted with "peals of laughter" and that "there was something eminently absurd in the Serjeant's extraordinarily precise, almost mincing pronunciation." In the 1952 film *The Pickwick Papers*, Sir Donald Wolfit is an orotund, vicious Serjeant Buzfuz.

Monologues

1. From George Bernard Shaw's *Man and Superman: A Comedy and a Philosophy* (1903), Act 1

The theme of this play is the eternal battle of the sexes, and the insidiousness of sexism and male chauvinism. Here is an excerpt from Shaw's description of his young leading man, John "Jack" Tanner, meant by Shaw to be a modern Don Juan: "He is too young to be described simply as a big man with a beard. But it is already plain that middle life will find him in that category . . . He is prodigiously fluent of speech, restless, excitable (mark the snorting nostril and the restless blue eye, just the thirty-secondth of an inch too wide open), possibly a little mad . . ."

> TANNER. But you, Tavy [/TAY vee/], are an artist: that is, you have a purpose as absorbing and as unscrupulous as a woman's purpose. [OCTAVIUS. Not unscrupulous.]
> TANNER. Quite unscrupulous. The true artist will let his wife starve, his children go barefoot, his mother drudge for his living at seventy, sooner than work at anything but his art. To women

he is half vivisector, half vampire. He gets into intimate relations with them to study them, to strip the mask of convention from them, to surprise their inmost secrets, knowing that they have the power to rouse his deepest creative energies, to rescue him from his cold reason, to make him see visions and dream dreams, to inspire him, as he calls it. He persuades women that they may do this for their own purpose whilst he really means them to do it for his. He steals the mother's milk and blackens it to make printer's ink to scoff at her and glorify ideal women with. He pretends to spare her the pangs of childbearing so that he may have for himself the tenderness and fostering that belong of right to her children. Since marriage began, the great artist has been known as a bad husband. But he is worse: he is a child-robber, a bloodsucker, a hypocrite and a cheat. Perish the race and wither a thousand women if only the sacrifice of them enable him to act Hamlet better, to paint a finer picture, to write a deeper poem, a greater play, a profounder philosophy! For mark you, Tavy, the artist's work is to show us ourselves as we really are. Our minds are nothing but this knowledge of ourselves; and he who adds a jot to such knowledge creates new mind as surely as any woman creates new men. In the rage of that creation he is as ruthless as the woman, as dangerous to her as she to him, and as horribly fascinating. Of all human struggles there is none so treacherous and remorseless as the struggle between the artist man and the mother woman. Which shall use up the other? that is the issue between them. And it is all the deadlier because, in your romanticist cant [/KANT/, as opposed to *can't* /KAHNT/], they love one another.

2. From George Bernard Shaw's *Major Barbara* (1905), Act 3

This play is a searing anti-war indictment of the arms industry that will sell to both sides in a war simply for profit, and of the blindness inculcated in the populace by religion and its emphasis on an afterlife, and not on improving life as it is lived here and now. Major Barbara, the daughter of international arms dealer Sir Andrew Undershaft, thinks she is doing good, when in reality she is helping to shore up an evil system. For Shaw, the Salvation Army was a symbol of do-gooder hypocrisy.

BARBARA. (*hypnotized*) Before I joined the Salvation Army, I was in my own power; and the consequence was that I never knew what to do with myself. When I joined it, I had not time enough for all the things I had to do.

[UNDERSHAFT. (*approvingly*) Just so. And why was that, do you suppose?]

BARBARA. Yesterday I should have said, it was because I was in the power of God. (*She resumes her self-possession, withdrawing her hands from his with a power equal to his own.*) But you came and showed me that I was in the power of Bodger and Undershaft. Today I feel—oh! how can I put it into words? Sarah: do you remember the earthquake at Cannes, when we were little children?—how little the surprise of the first shock mattered compared to the dread and horror of waiting for the second? That is how I feel in this place today. I stood on the rock I thought eternal; and without a word of warning it reeled and crumbled under me. I was safe with an infinite wisdom watching me, an army marching to Salvation with me; and in a moment, at a stroke of your pen in a cheque book, I stood alone; and the heavens were empty. That was the first shock of the earthquake: I am waiting for the second.

3. From Caryl Churchill's *Top Girls* (1982), Act 2, Scene 3

The characters in *Top Girls*, an innovative play with a non-linear, non-traditional structure, are professional women, young and ambitious. The play has had several revivals over the last decade, including one at the Manhattan Theatre Club in 2007–2008, and most recently, in 2011, at the Chichester Theater Festival. It centers on Marlene, a young woman from a poor background, who leaves her child (born out of wedlock) with her sister in order to pursue a career. Here, another of the women, Win, tells her own story to a young lady, Angie. Estuary would be the appropriate accent for this excerpt, although RP would not be out of place.

WIN. Oh, yes, all that, and a science degree funnily enough. I started out doing medical research [/ruh SOCH/], but there's no money in it. I thought I'd go abroad. Did you know they sell Coca-Cola in Russia and Pepsi-Cola in China? You don't have to be qualified as much as you might think. Men are awful bullshitters, they like to make out jobs are harder than they are. Any job I ever did I started doing it better than the rest of the crowd and they didn't like it. So I'd get unpopular and I'd have a drink to cheer myself up. I lived with a fella and supported him for four years, he couldn't get work. After that I went to California. I like the sunshine. Americans know how to live. Then I went to Mexico, still in sales, but it's no country for a single lady. I came home, went bonkers for a bit, thought I was five different people, got over that all right, the psychiatrist said I was perfectly sane and highly intelligent. Got married in a moment of weakness, and he's inside now, been inside for four years, and I've not been to see him too much this last year. I like this better than sales. I'm not really that aggressive. I started thinking sales was a good job if you want to meet people, but you're meeting people that don't want to meet you. It's no good if you like being liked. Here your clients want to meet you because you're the one doing them some good. They hope.

ANGIE *has fallen asleep.*

4. From Bernard Kops's *Playing Sinatra* (1992), Act 1, Scene 2

Born in London's East End (which was a largely Jewish neighborhood through the 1960s), Bernard Kops is, along with Arnold Wesker and John Osborne, one of the exemplars of modern British "New Wave" Kitchen Sink realism.

A play with a surprise ending, *Playing Sinatra*, last revived in 2010 by the Archway Theatre Company in Horley, Surrey, takes place in the south London childhood home of Norman and Sandra, a middle-aged brother and sister. Although the house is falling apart, they live contentedly, surrounded by memorabilia of their childhood idol, Frank Sinatra. But Sandra falls in love with young Philip de Groot, a con-man. Kops describes him as an attractive, charming man with a ready smile and a soft, soothing voice. He listens carefully to others and does not interrupt them—one of his prime techniques for learning about his potential victims.

De Groot /duh GROHT/ is a Dutch aristocratic name; the pronunciation given here is anglicized. The French phrases *Que sommes-nous? Où allons-nous?* /kuh sum NOOH / ooh a lawn NOOH/ mean "What are we? Where are we going?" The /n/ at the end of "allons" is nasalized; that is, the tongue does not make a pressure on the upper front palate to complete the articulation of the consonant, but remains lowered as /n/ is pronounced.

Before the exchange below, Norman has asked Philip on his first visit to the house to say something about himself and his work.

> PHILIP. [. . .] I used to be an architect. Not bad. Mainly hack work; the exigencies of modern life. The realities. The compromises one has to make. Then, one day, whilst walking in China—I was walking along the Great Wall—I had a kind of mystical experience. It was, if you like, my Road to Damascus. An inner voice boomed, Philip de Groot! What are you doing with your life? What was I doing indeed? From that moment on I was plagued with inner doubt. What is the meaning of me? What is the meaning of existence? Is there a meaning? Should there be a meaning? Que sommes-nous?

Où allons-nous? The book is the person indeed. But my binding fell away. I was terrified. I almost fell apart.

[SANDRA. In that case, have a biscuit. (*She hands him a biscuit.*)]

PHILIP. Ginger nuts. How very nice. How did you know these were my favorites? Anyway, I survived that greatest crisis in my life. And I chucked it all in. I dabbled in many things, trying to find my new self. I've traveled extensively in India. Did voluntary work amongst the bereft of Africa. All the time questioning, surviving. You see me as I am, a seeker. I believe we are the stuff that dreams are made of but we, man, humankind, is in terrible danger. I have a modest income. A legacy. I am content, yet not complacent. I am still searching for my true vocation.

2
London Accents

London in the twentieth century saw the rise of an increasingly diverse population made up not only of native Britons of European descent, but also of a great number of South Asian (Indian, Pakistani, Sri Lankan), African, and Caribbean immigrants and their descendants. The younger generation born in Britain speaks not with the accents of their immigrant parents, but with the accents they were surrounded with in the street when growing up and going through the educational system, so their accents include RP, Estuary, and London middle- and working-class. The contemporary theater reflects this diversity with plays like Roy Williams's *The Gift*, Kwame Kwei-Nkrumah's *Elmina's Kitchen*, and Joe Penhall's *Blue / Orange*.

As an actor, you will want to be familiar with old-fashioned and contemporary working- and middle-class London and Cockney accents, required in so many films, plays, and musicals. Often set in London as well are plays by celebrated contemporary British playwrights, among them Alan Bennett, Alan Ayckbourn, Harold Pinter, Bernard Kops, Simon Gray, Simon Stephens, Caryl Churchill, and Tom Stoppard.

For authentic examples of old London accents, listen to Michael Caine, who does a middle-class version in many of his films, such as *The Wrong Box* (1966), and a lower-class London accent in *Alfie* (1966); and to London-born Stanley Holloway as Alec Guinness's partner in crime in *The Lavender Hill Mob* (1951), as the Station Master in Coward's *Brief Encounter* (1945), and as Alfred Doolittle in *My Fair Lady* (1964). The television series *EastEnders* provides a variety of authentic London Cockney accents to listen to. *I'm All Right Jack* (1959) with Irene Handl, whose Cockney accent is perfect, and with Peter Sellers also doing a superb working-class accent with a pretentious air, is another excellent source. And listen to the music hall comedian Frankie Howerd as the fruit vendor in Alec Guinness's *The Ladykillers* (1955). Films about the London underworld of gangsters and criminals include *Love, Honor, and Obey* (2000), with Londoner Jude Law, whose accent work is always impeccable. And see the television series *Call the Midwife* (2012), made in Britain and set in London's East End.

Teach Yourself the London Cockney, Working- and Middle-Class Accents

1. **The positioning, placement, and use of the muscles of the mouth during speech:** Keep the jaw slightly dropped and the general "feeling" of the accent forward in the mouth. Drop your jaw and say /ah/. This gives you the general position of the vocal apparatus for this accent. The jaws are held loosely and the lips are a bit protruded. The language sometimes sounds a bit swallowed, especially as many initial and final consonants are dropped, as in the phrase *that's right*, variously pronounced /AS roy?/, /DAS roy?/, and /VAS royt/. Vowels and diphthongs are open; that is, the throat and vocal cavity are more open than in either General American or British RP. A clearer middle-class London accent would restore dropped consonants, such as the /l/ in *milk* and would eliminate glottal stops, pronouncing /t/ almost too distinctly. Vowels and diphthong substitutions would be very much as in Cockney, but the jaw muscles would be held more tightly, thus shortening and closing the vowels and diphthongs.

2. **Drop initial /h/:** This is one of the most well-known traits of the accent. But initial /h/ would often be pronounced in middle-class speech.

3. **The sounds of /r/:** In this non-rhotic accent, the sounds of /r/ are the same as in RP; see pp. 18–19. Drop /r/ after a vowel and before another consonant. A "linking r" is common. The "intrusive r" is heard often in this accent: Notice, for instance, the /r/ intruded into the word *jawing* (with the final "g" dropped) in Bill's speech from *Major Barbara*, p. 45: /JAW rihn/.

4. **The all-important diphthong shifts:**

   a. The /ay/ as in the word *say* shifts to /I/: /SI/.

   b. The /I/ as in the word *right* shifts to /oy/: /ROY? (alternatively, ROYT)/.

   c. The /oh/ in *home* shifts to /ow/: /OWM/.

5. **Other consonants:** Consonants are hard; that is, strongly articulated. For instance, the point of articulation and the pressure applied to form /d/ and /t/ are the same as for British RP, with the tip of the tongue slightly forward of its position in General American. But /d/ and /t/ are also sometimes "dentalized"; that is, they are pronounced with the tongue right behind the upper front teeth, so that they sound respectively like /dz/ and /ts/.

   a. **Final /g/:** Drop final /g/ in "-ing" endings for working-class accents. Retain them for middle-class accents.

   b. **The glottal stop /?/:** The glottal stop is a brief catch in the throat: the glottis closes for a split second to replace the consonant /t/ in the middle of words: *bottle* /BO? l/; and at the ends of words: *what* /WAH?/. This is very common in working-class speech, but in a middle-class London accent is heard less often.

   c. **Other dropped final consonants:** Drop final consonants in consonant clusters for a working-class accent; the word *last* is pronounced /LAHS/, for instance.

   d. **Dropped /l/:** The sound of /l/ is sometimes dropped in the middle of a word, especially in Cockney pronunciation, and replaced by /ooh/: milk /MEEoohk/; shelf /SHEoohf/.

e. **The sounds of /th/ and /th/:** Often, /d/ and /t/, or alternatively /v/ and /f/, are substituted for voiced /th/ and voiceless /th/: *the last thing I thought of* is pronounced by Cockneys as /vuh LAHS fihng oy FAW? uv/; middle-class Londoners would say /thuh LAHS thihng oy THAW dahv/, with the /d/ tapped, instead of hard and strongly articulated, and no glottal stop.

6. The past participle *been* usually rhymes with *bean*, but is sometimes heard as rhyming with *bin*.

Intonation and Stress: The Music and Rhythm of the Accents

The London and Cockney accents use more pitches than RP or Estuary. Listen carefully for the intonation in the examples given below. The stress patterns are determined by the use of the schwa and the emphasis on the nuclear tone; see p. 23.

Practice Exercises

1. *I'll have a nice cup of tea with a little bit of milk and sugar.*
/ah WEV uh noys KU puh tsee wihf uh LIH? ooh bih? uh MEEoohk en SHOO gah/

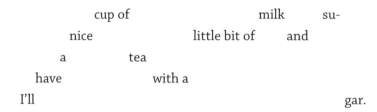

Notes: The pitch pattern suggests some of the music of the accent. Note the dentalized /t/ in the word *tea*, not uncommon in this accent; the tongue articulates the /t/ where /s/ is articulated, right behind the upper front teeth, hence the term "dentalized consonant." The /n/ sound in the word *and* is slightly nasalized.

2. *"Well, I never," I says. "Of course not, of course you never," he says. "Right, I don't think!" He didn't believe me, you see! But I saw her and she was all tarted up, dear! Of course he wouldn't believe it, now would he?*
/WEL oy NE vah roy SEZ (alternatively, NE vroy SEZ) / uh KAWS no? uh KAWS yooh NE vree SEZ / ROY? oy down fihnk / ee DIH? n (alternatively, DIHN?) BLEEV mee yuh see / buh doy SAW ruh an (alternatively, ruh ran) shee wuhz awl TAH ?ih DUP (alternatively, TAW tih DAHP), DEEuh / uh KAWS ee WOO? n (alternatively, WOON; WOOM) BLEEV ih? na WOO dee/

Notes: Notice how many consonants in consonant clusters are dropped. Notice the "linking r" sounds. Notice the glottal stops. Pay special attention to the diphthongs, which are lengthened. In the phrase *but I* the /d/ in the phonetic pronunciation is tapped; that is, the pressure of the tongue when articulating the /d/ is minimal and the tongue comes off it immediately. The /n/ sounds in the words *don't*, *didn't*, and *wouldn't* are slightly nasalized.

3. *Oh! It really is a wery pretty garden*
And Chingford to the Eastward could be seen
Wiv a ladder and some glasses
You could see to Hackney Marshes
If it wasn't for the houses in between . . .
/OW ih? REE lee ihz uh WE ree PRIH? ee GAW dihn
an CHIHNG fuhd tuh thee EEST wuhd koo bee SEEN
wihv uh LA duh an suhm GLAH sihz
yooh koo see tooh AK nee MAW shihz
ihf ih? WAH zn? faw thee OW zeez ihn bee TWEEN/

Note: This verse is from an 1894 Cockney music hall song, "If It Wasn't for the Houses in Between," by Edgar Bateman and George LeBrunn. Notice the "v" substituting for /th/ at the end of "Wiv" (*with*); and the old-fashioned pronunciation of *very*, with an initial "w" that you will also find in the prose of Charles Dickens when he writes dialogue for the Wellers in *The Pickwick Papers*. Notice the dropping of the final "d" in *could*.

4. *I was walking down there the other day and what should I see but the most beautiful girl on the other side of the street, but she was too busy to see me. That's life!*
/oy wuhz WAW kin down VAY uh vee A vuh DI / an WA? shuh doy SEE buh duh mows BEE yooh dee (alternatively, ?ee) foo GOL O nee A vuh SOY duh vuh STREE? / buh? shee wuhz tooh BIH zee duh SEE mee / as LOYF/

Note: In the syllables "doy," "dee," and "duh" in the phonetic pronunciation, the /d/ sounds are tapped. Alternatively, there is a glottal stop on the /d/ in "dee."

Monologues and Scenes for Two

1. From George Bernard Shaw's *Major Barbara* (1905), Act 2

The following scene takes place in the Salvation Army shelter run by Major Barbara. Bill Walker, a rough customer, had attacked and beaten up Jenny Hill, one of the Salvation Army workers, who now wants to forgive him. Note Shaw's writing of the old Cockney accent. Notice the /h/ added to the word "up" in the last line; it is not uncommon to add an /h/ where none exists, almost as a phonetic compensation for dropping so many where they do exist.

BILL. I don't want to be forgive be you, or be ennybody. Wot I did I'll pay for. I tried to get me own jawr broke to settisfaw you . . .
[JENNY. (*distressed*) Oh no . . .]

BILL. (*impatiently*) Tell y'I did: cawn't you listen to wot's bein told you? All I got be it was bein made a sight of in the public street for me pains. Well, if I cawn't settisfaw you one way, I can another. Listen ere! I ad two quid saved agen the frost; an I've a pahnd of it left. A mate n mine last week ad words with the Judy e's goin to marry. E give er wot-for; an e's bin fined fifteen bob. E ad a right to it er because they was goin to be marrid; but I and't no right to it you; so put anather fawv bob on an call it a pahnd's worth. (*He produces a sovereign* [a pound coin].) Ere's the money. Take it; and let's av no more o your forgivin an prayin and your Major jawrin me. Let wot I done be done and paid for; and let there be a end of it. [JENNY. Oh, I couldn't take it, Mr. Walker. But if you would give a shilling or two to poor Rummy Mitchens! you really did hurt her; and she's old.]

BILL. (*contemptuously*) Not likely. I'd give her anather as soon as look at er. Let her av the lawr o me as she threatened! She ain't forgiven me: not mach. Wot I done to er is not on me mawnd—wot she (*indicating Barbara*) might call on me conscience—no more than stickin a pig. It's this Christian game o yours that I won't av played agen me: this bloomin forgivin an noggin an jawrin that makes a man that sore that iz lawf's a burdn to im. I won't av it, I tell you; so take your money and stop throwin your silly bashed face hup agen me.

2. From Harold Pinter's One-Act Play *The Dumb Waiter* (1960)

In a dilapidated basement room, Ben and Gus, two small-time, brutal hit men, wait for the signal that will tell them the job is to be done. There are many long pauses, so characteristic of Pinter's writing that they have come to be called "Pinteresque."

Both characters speak with working-class London accents, and they could be of any ethnic background. "Kaw," pronounced as it is spelled, is typically London, and replaces the word "God." A "lorry" is what Americans call a truck. The expression "Go on!" means here not "Continue," but what Americans mean by "Come on"—you can't be serious.

At the opening, Ben is reading a newspaper, and Gus is in the lavatory. When he re-enters, "scratching his head," Ben slams the newspaper down.

BEN. Kaw!
> *He picks up the paper.*

What about this? Listen to this!
> *He refers to the paper.*

A man of eighty-seven wanted to cross the road. But there was a lot of traffic, see? He couldn't see how he was going to squeeze through. So he crawled under a lorry.
GUS. He what?
BEN. He crawled under a lorry. A stationary lorry.
GUS. No?
BEN. The lorry started and ran over him.
GUS. Go on!
BEN. That's what it says here.
GUS. Get away.
BEN. It's enough to make you want to puke, isn't it?
GUS. Who advised him to do a thing like that?
BEN. A man of eighty-seven crawling under a lorry!
GUS. It's unbelievable.
BEN. It's down here in black and white.
GUS. Incredible.
> *Silence.*
>
> GUS *shakes his head and exits.* BEN *lies back and reads.*
>
> *The lavatory chain is pulled once off left, but the lavatory does not flush.*
>
> BEN *whistles at an item in the paper.*
>
> GUS *re-enters.*

I want to ask you something.

BEN. What are you doing out there?

GUS. Well, I was just—

BEN. What about the tea?

GUS. I'm just going to make it.

BEN. Well, go on, make it.

GUS. Yes, I will. (*He sits in a chair. Ruminatively.*) He's laid on some very nice crockery this time. I'll say that. It's sort of striped. There's a white stripe.

3. From Kevin Hood's *Beached* (1987), Act 1, Scene 3

Maria, the seventeen-year-old daughter of Italian immigrants to London, works as a window-dresser. She speaks with a working-class accent, having been born and raised in Catford, a south London suburb. She is camping out on a deserted beach with her friend Peter, who is from the same neighborhood, and with whom she has run away after his prostitute mother kicked him out. She had arranged for him to rob the shop belonging to her father, Giovanni, but Giovanni had discovered Peter there and chased him away. Here she tells Peter a horrible incident in her life.

Bear in mind that *crisps* is the English word for American potato chips, while *chips* is what Americans call French fries. *Telly* is the British slang for *television*. *Lewisham* /LOO ih shuhm/ is a borough in southeast London. *J-Cloths* are handy-wipes, commercially manufactured rags. *Buona notte, Mariucca—Good night, Mariucca* (an affectionate diminutive for Maria)—is pronounced /BWAW nah NOT te MAH ree ooh kah/. *Giovanni* is pronounced /jo VAHN nee/.

You will readily notice the writing of the accent, which is perfectly accurate. Notice the pronunciation of "me" for "my," which is not only contemporary in certain accents, but is the old-fashioned Victorian pronunciation, heard on recordings of American and British actors of the period.

MARIA. I'll tell you a story, shall I? 'Bout when I was younger. Thirteen. And 'im, on 'is own with me. Me growin' up, 'im wonderin' 'ow I was goin' to turn out. Well . . . every time 'e goes down the pub, 'e locks me in. With me chocolates and me crisps and the portable telly. And at first I can't work it out. And then it dawns. (*Pause.*) What 'e thinks is, first fella I see—I'm on me back with me legs wide open, waitin' for it. That's what 'e thinks.

[PETE. So 'e locks you in.]

MARIA. I don't like that. I ain't 'avin' that. So . . . One night, one Monday night I'm out the winder and leggin' it down Lewisham with some of the naughty girls from school. Disco. (*Pause.*) I mean, what did I expect, eh? Moonlight in me Chianti? Candlelight on me chips? Well, what I got was warm lager, lots and lots of warm lager, and these three fellas, this band, in the back of their van . . . one after the other.

   Silence.

Didn't know what was 'appenin'. Thirteen and pissed, see. (*Pause.*) Long walk 'ome, I tell ya. (*Pause.*) But . . . by the time 'e's openin' the front door, there I am tucked up in bed, all safe and sound. With this 'andful of J-Cloths and ice between my legs. And prayin', oh sweet Maria, prayin' I can 'old off cryin' long enough, 'cause every particle tells me if 'e finds out, 'e's goin' to kill me. I mean really kill me. But it's *all right*. Door opens. "Buona notte, Mariucca." Papa . . . and I almost cry, I almost . . . the thing that saves me is the smell on 'im, beer. That smell. Them fellas. 'Im. (*Pause.*) That was the last of 'im for me. No, Peter, I ain't worried about Giovanni.

4. From Simon Stephens's *Pornography* (2007–2009), "Seven"

First produced in German translation in 2007 with a cast of eight actors, *Pornography* was performed in English at the Edinburgh Festival in 2008, then in London in 2009. The play consists of a series of seven monologues numbered in descending order. These are clearly dialogue-driven scenes, but without specified characters speaking their lines, which are separated by spaces. The characters are not named, but, as the scene proceeds, it becomes clear who each one is. And the play—based on the famous "Seven Ages of Man" speech by Jaques in act 2, scene 7 of Shakespeare's *As You Like It*, "All the world's a stage"—centers on a terrorist who is planning an attack, hence the title: terrorism is obscene, like pornography.

Here we have an excerpt from "Seven"—representing Jaques's first stage, infancy—the opening monologue, for a young, middle-class London mother who could be of any ethnic background. The location is clear from the street names. The concert alluded to was mentioned earlier in the speech. The accent here could be middle-class London, or possibly Estuary.

I push Lenny in his pushchair. He's got one of those three-wheeled pushchairs. It has fabulous suspension. It makes it ideal for city street life. I buy myself a pair of sandals which are pink and they have this golden strap with a little pink flower on. I think in the shops everybody's got the concert on. It's that man I like. He's singing the song about looking at the stars. Look at the stars. See how they shine for you. Maybe today is the most important day that there's ever been. And this is the biggest success of human organization that we've ever known. And everybody should be given a knighthood of some description. There should be some kind of knighthood which is given out to all of the people there. To the people who sell the ice creams even. They should get an ice-cream seller's knighthood. For the important selling of ice cream at a time of organizational urgency. I'd like to watch the Queen knight the boys selling ice cream in Hyde Park today. She wouldn't even need to walk far from her house. She could go on a bike. It would take her five minutes. This is a day of that level of importance.

I'm pushing him so much that he falls to sleep in the end. You bump up and down. I want to walk home. I could duck south of Euston Road. I could head through Bloomsbury. Today is a day for heading through Bloomsbury with a new pair of summer sandals, ideal for the beach, on a Saturday.

I don't.

I start off.

And then I get the bus from Holborn.

And then I get home and Jonathan's not there. He should be there. He should be at home. I don't have the slightest idea where he is. I try not to think about it. The house is quieter without him.

3
English Provincial Accents: The Midlands, Yorkshire

There are more than fifty provincial accents in England, loosely grouped as Southern and Northern accents. The Southern accents include those in the first two chapters of this book: the RP and London accents; the accents of East Anglia, just north of London; and the accents of the Southwest, including those of Bristol, Somerset, Worcestershire, Cornwall, and Devon. The Northern accents include those of Lancashire and the Midlands, with the cities of Manchester and Birmingham; and, northeast of the Midlands, those of Yorkshire, and the "Geordie" accent of Newcastle-Upon-Tyne; and to the northwest, the accent of Liverpool, made famous by the Beatles. We will concentrate on two: the Midlands, especially Manchester, and the Yorkshire accents. For more extensive information on all of the accents mentioned here, see my book *Accents: A Manual for Actors* (Limelight, 2002).

Contemporary recordings of British provincial accents made by linguists show that in the younger generation they are much lighter than they are in older people, and have given way to a more Mainstream RP pronunciation. But they are still heard, and, in many contemporary English plays, you must use the appropriate pronunciations.

The BBC made recordings of some thirty of these accents from villages as close as ten miles distant from each other, and some are very hard to distinguish. You can also hear examples of English provincial accents on the DVD of the television series *The Story of English*, hosted by Robert MacNeil. Listen to the recordings of actor and music-hall monologist

Stanley Holloway; in many of his monologues he uses the Midlands accent. Although born in London, he was able to do the Midlands pronunciation perfectly. And for Northeastern accents, especially Newcastle and Durham, see the television adaptations of Catherine Cookson's novels, among them *The Fifteen Streets* (1989) and *The Dwelling Place* (1996).

Teach Yourself the Midlands Accents

The Midlands accents are those of Britain's industrial heartland, well to the north of London. Birmingham—the British pronunciation is /BO ming uhm/, unlike the city in Alabama /BOR ming HAM/ in General American, and /BOY ming ham/ to some people from Alabama and older New Yorkers—and Manchester /MAN chuh stuh/ are thriving metropolitan centers, with a population of several millions. In the television drama *Breaking the Code* (now available on DVD), starring Derek Jacobi as Alan Turing, the man who broke the German Enigma code in World War II, you have perfect examples of the Midlands accent, as you do in the comedy series *Keeping Up Appearances* (1990–1995), shot on location in the West Midlands, and starring Patricia Routledge as Hyacinth Bucket ("It's Bouquet! B-U-C-K-E-T!"), and Geoffrey Hughes, who is hilarious as her slobbish brother-in-law, Onslow.

The first third of the twentieth century saw the rise of a number of realist playwrights in Manchester, all of whom were independent of the all-powerful London theater scene. They became known as the Manchester School, and included Stanley Houghton, best known for his play about an illicit love affair, *Hindle Wakes* (1910), which was considered daring and controversial when it was first produced; the *Manchester Guardian* editor and drama critic Allan Monkhouse, one of whose plays, *The Conquering Hero* (1923), is a World War I classic; and Harold Brighouse, author of the famous comedy *Hobson's Choice* (1916), which is set in Lancashire. The 1954 film version starring Charles Laughton is a delight, and some of the actors, notably John Mills, do the accent authentically.

For a light Midlands accent, all you need to do is to use British RP with two major variations: the shift from /u/ to /oo/, and the shift from /ah/ to /a/, both detailed below.

1. **Positioning, placement, and use of the mouth muscles during speech:** Say *book, book, book* several times and you will have the correct general position. The jaw muscles are looser than they are in RP, but not so loose as in London accents. The lips are half open, half closed, much as in General American.

2. **Vowels and diphthongs:** Follow the information in chapter 1 for British RP, with the addition of the vowel shift from /u/ to /oo/. The upper class and businesspeople usually have accents very close to RP, but with the vowel shifts just mentioned. The following vowels and diphthongs are also important:

   a. **The sounds of /ah/ and /a/:** The sounds of words with /ah/ in British RP on the "ask list" found in chapter 1 are pronounced with /a/ in such words as *can't, grass, command,* etc.

   b. **The sound of /I/:** In rural areas, this diphthong is often pronounced /oy/, with the lips held tight, so it does not have the open quality of the same shift in Cockney accents.

   c. **The sound of /o/:** In such words as *work* and *first,* /o/ shifts to a lengthened /e/: /WEK/, /FEST/. Notice that the /r/ is dropped.

   d. **The sound of /oh/:** The diphthong /oh/ is pronounced /Oooh/, as opposed to RP /UHooh/.

   e. **The sound of /ow/:** Instead of the sound in either General American or British RP, the sound made in the Midlands, especially in rural areas, is the diphthong /oh/. Thus, *how* and *out* are pronounced /HOH/ and /OHT/.

   f. **The shift of /u/ to /oo/:** There is a ubiquitous, very important shift in both the Midlands and Yorkshire from the standard British /u/ in such words as *but* and *love* to the /oo/ in *book: but* is pronounced /BOOT/, *love* /LOOV/, and so forth. This sound is sometimes heard as a schwa /uh/: /BUHT/, /LUHV/ in unstressed syllables. The word *under* is /OON duh (alternatively, dah)/; *thunder* is /THOON duh/.

g. **The sound of /yooh/:** There is a shift in this sound, especially in the countryside, to /EEooh/, so *news* is pronounced /NEE oohz/ and *duke* /DEE oohk/—but quickly, so that the first half of the diphthong is not lengthened. This is considered in Britain to be a very rural, peasanty accent.

3. **Consonants**: Aside from the information given below, there are no shifts in consonants from RP.

a. **The sound of the letter /r/:** As with RP, the Midlands accents largely drop post-vocalic (after a vowel) /r/ before another consonant and at the ends of words, and are non-rhotic in urban areas, such as the Midlands cities of Manchester and Birmingham. But /r/ in those phonetic positions is pronounced in rural areas, where the accent is often rhotic. The back of the tongue is slightly tensed.

b. **Dropping of initial /h/ and /g/ in "-ing" endings:** In the Midlands, the initial /h/ is often dropped, particularly in working-class accents. The /g/ at the end of such words as *working* and *wedding* is often dropped. The remaining /ihn/ is often pronounced /EEN/.

4. The past participle *been* rhymes with *bean*.

Intonation and Stress: The Music and Rhythm of the Accents

The same level intonation patterns noted in chapter 1 for RP apply to these provincial accents. There are no special variations in stressing English words differently from RP. Pitch patterns are somewhat "flat"; that is, they are less musical than the Southern British accents, but there is sometimes a tendency to rise at the end of a declarative sentence, making it sound like a question (this is also true of Liverpool or Northern Ireland accents). The pattern must not be overused when doing this accent.

Practice Exercises

1. *Now look here, but that's not what I told you to do, now is it? You've got to work harder. It doesn't do to be a slacker.*

Urban: /no look EE yuh (alternatively, EE yah) boot THATS not wuht I TOHLD yooh tuh DOOH no IH ziht / YOOV GO tuh WEK AH duh (alternatively, dah) / ih DUHZ n DOOH duh bee uh SLA kuh/

Rural: /no look EE uhr boot THATS not wat I TOL ee (alternatively, EEoo) tuh dooh no IH ziht / yoov GO tuh WERK AHR duhr / ih DOOZ n DOOH duh bee uh SLA kuhr/

Note: In the rural pronunciation, all the vowels are lengthened, and post-vocalic (after a vowel) /r/ is pronounced strongly. The /d/ in the word *to* in the last sentence is tapped.

2. *Manchester is a lovely city.*
/MAN chuh stuh ihz (alternatively, rihz) uh LOOV lee SIH tee/

3. *We're not far from Liverpool and not far from Leeds. But we're not too near London.*
/WEEuh not FAH froom LIH vah poohl and not FAH froom LEEDZ / boot WEEuh not tooh NEEuh LOON duhn/

4. Practice words for the shift from /u/ to /oo/: *but, put, butt, buck, book, luck, look, above, love, dove, rough, tough, bluff, muck.*

Monologues

1. From John Osborne's *Look Back in Anger* (1956), Act 1

John Osborne's seminal, iconoclastic, realist play, which takes place entirely in "the Porters' one-room flat in the Midlands," caused a sensation when it was first produced. It exploded the myths of a complacent, self-satisfied postwar British society. And it gave rise to the social and playwriting movement of the Angry Young Men typified by Osborne:

disaffected, angry with society, and wanting reform but hardly knowing which way to turn.

The play's hero—or anti-hero—is Jimmy Porter, a bad trumpet player who "browbeats his flatmate [Cliff], terrorizes his wife [Alison], and is not above sleeping with her best friend [Helena], who loathes Jimmy almost as much as he loathes himself." Osborne describes Jimmy as "a tall, thin young man about twenty-five, wearing a very worn tweed jacket and flannels. Clouds of smoke fill the room from the pipe he is smoking. He is a disconcerting mixture of sincerity and cheerful malice, of tenderness and freebooting cruelty, restless, importunate, full of pride . . ." Cliff is "the same age, short, dark, big boned . . . He is easy and relaxed, almost to lethargy, with the rather sad, natural intelligence of the self-taught." In this monologue, Jimmy addresses Cliff, who wants a cigarette.

JIMMY. I thought the doctor said no cigarettes?
[CLIFF. Oh, why doesn't he shut up?]
JIMMY. All right. They're your ulcers. Go ahead, and have a belly-ache, if that's what you want. I give up. I give up. I'm sick of doing things for people. And all for what?

    ALISON *gives* CLIFF *a cigarette. They both light up, and she goes on with her ironing.*

Nobody thinks, nobody cares. No beliefs, no convictions and no enthusiasm. Just another Sunday evening.

    CLIFF *sits down again in his pullover and shorts.*

Perhaps there's a concert on. (*Picks up* Radio Times) Ah. (*Nudges* CLIFF *with his foot.*) Make some more tea.

    CLIFF *groans. He is reading again.*

Oh, yes. There's a Vaughan Williams. Well, that's something, anyway. Something strong, something simple, something English. I suppose people like me aren't supposed to be very patriotic [/PA tree O tihk/]. Somebody said—what was it?—we get our cooking from Paris (that's a laugh), our politics from Moscow, and our morals from Port Said. Something like that, anyway. Who was it? (*Pause.*) Well, you wouldn't know anyway. I hate to admit it, but I think I can understand how her Daddy must have felt when he came back from India, after all those years away. The old Edwardian brigade do make their little world look pretty tempting. All homemade cakes and croquet, bright ideas, bright uniforms: Always the same picture: high summer, the long days in the sun, slim volumes of verse, crisp linen, the smell of starch. What a romantic picture. Phoney, too, of course. It must have rained sometimes. Still, even I regret it somehow, phoney or not. If you've no world of your own, it's rather pleasant to regret the passing of someone else's. I must be getting sentimental. But I must say it's pretty dreary living in the American Age—unless you're an American of course. Perhaps all our children will be Americans. That's a thought isn't it?

HE *gives* CLIFF *a kick, and shouts at him.*

I said that's a thought!

2. From Charlotte Keatley's *My Mother Said I Never Should* (1987)

This play has had several revivals, the most recent being in 2009 at the Watford Palace Theatre in Watford and in 2010 at the Duke's Theatre in Lancaster. It explores the difficult relationships between mothers and daughters, exploring four generations, from 1905 to 1987. One of the characters, Jackie, a young woman in her thirties, runs an art gallery in Manchester. Although she is outwardly successful, she is actually consumed with guilt and unhappiness. She had given birth to her daughter, Rosie, out of wedlock, and, not being able to cope with motherhood and the abandonment by her married boyfriend, Graham, she gave the responsibility of raising the child to her parents. At this point in the play, Rosie, now a teenager, has just reproached her; not wanting to give Jackie the second chance at motherhood she craves, Rosie has accused her of valuing her own life more than her daughter's. Jackie has vehemently denied this, declaring that she loved and wanted Rosie from the beginning but had no support from those she loved. Here Jackie recalls her struggles as a new single mother and reveals how, after seeing Graham with his wife and their children, she tried to reach out to him one last time before turning to her own mother with her baby in desperation.

JACKIE. [. . .] I took you to Lyme Park one day, I saw them together, across the lake, he was buying them ice creams, his wife was taking a photo, I think they live in Leeds now, I saw his name in the *Guardian* last year, an article about his photographs . . . (*Pause.*) It was a very cold winter after you were born. There were power cuts, I couldn't keep the room warm; there were no lights in the tower blocks; I knew he had an open fire, it was trendy; so we took a bus to Didsbury, big gardens, pine kitchens, made a change from concrete. I rang the bell. (*Stops.*) A Punjabi man answered, said he was sorry . . . they'd moved. By the time we got back to Mosside it was dark, the lift wasn't working— (*Stops.*) That was the night I phoned Mummy. (*Difficult.*) Asked her. (*Pause.*) I tried! I couldn't do it, Rosie. (*Pause.*) It doesn't matter how much you succeed afterwards, if you've failed once. (*Pause.*) After you'd gone . . . I kept waking in the night to feed you. A week . . . in the flat . . . Then I went back to art school. Sandra and Hugh thought I was inhuman. I remember the books that came out that winter—how to succeed as a single working mother—fairy tales! (*Pause.*) Sandra and Hugh have a family now. Quite a few of my friends do. (*Pause.*) I could give you everything now. Rosie? . . .

Teach Yourself the Yorkshire Accent

"The language of South Yorkshire to me has a rhythm and poetry to it, which cuts corners and is full of alliteration," says Richard Cameron in his introduction to *Plays: I* (Methuen, 1998). For good examples of Yorkshire accents, watch DVDs of the television series *All Creatures Great and Small* (1978–1990), based on the book by veterinarian James Herriot. It was filmed on location in North Yorkshire. And do see *James Herriot's Yorkshire: The Film* (1993) and *Young James Herriot* (2012). You can hear authentic accents from the mining country around Leeds in the film *Billy Elliot* (2000), on which Sir Elton John's West End and Broadway hit musical is based, and don't miss *The Full Monty* (1997), which takes place in Sheffield, South Yorkshire.

1. **Positioning, placement, and use of the mouth muscles during speech:** To attain the correct position, in which the lower lip is thrust a bit forward and the jaw is tightly held, say *you, you, you* several times, drawing the sound out.

2. **Consonants:**

   a. **/h/-dropping and dropping /g/ in "-ing" endings:** The consonant /h/ is regularly dropped in Yorkshire and most rural Northern accents. The /g/ in "-ing" endings is often dropped, but not always, particularly when a speaker is being careful.

   b. **The sounds of /r/:** Post-vocalic (after a vowel) /r/, especially before another consonant, is usually but not always silent: *Yorkshire* is pronounced /YAWK shuh/, with a lengthened vowel in the first syllable. As the tongue is curled upwards, the back of the tongue is slightly tensed. In rural areas, the accent is often rhotic, with post-vocalic /r/ heavily pronounced.

   c. **The sound of /th/:** Before a vowel, especially in older accents, the /th/, as in the word *the*, often shifts to a /t/, so *the other* is pronounced /TUH duhr/.

   d. **Voiced and voiceless consonants:** There is a tendency to shift voiced consonants to voiceless before a voiceless consonant beginning another word or syllable, particularly in rural, isolated areas:

for example, the phrase *cloud passes* becomes /KLOHT PA sihz/. The phrase *told to me* would be pronounced /TAWLT (alternatively, TAWL) tuh mee/.

 e. **The glottal stop /?/:** As with Scottish and London accents, a glottal stop sometimes replaces a /t/ at the end of such words as *hot* and *not*: /HO?/, /NO?/.

3. **Vowels and diphthongs:** Vowels are generally longer than in the Southern English accents, and fewer schwas are heard. The shifts mentioned at the beginning of the chapter apply here, with the following additions:

 a. **The sounds of /ah/ and /a/:** These vowels are often reversed, so *can't* is pronounced /KANT/ and *that* is pronounced /THAHT/. The sounds of words with /ah/ in British RP on the "ask list" found in chapter 1 are pronounced with /a/ in such words as *ask, grass, command*, etc.

 b. **The sound of /ay/:** This diphthong usually shifts to a single lengthened vowel /e/, so *say* is pronounced /SE/.

 c. **The sound of /oh/:** This diphthong is usually shifted to the single vowel /aw/ in *law*, so *go home* is pronounced /GAW HAWM/.

 d. **The sound of /ow/:** In Yorkshire, as in much of the North, this diphthong is regularly heard as the sound of /ooh/. The words *cow, cloud, loud, how*, and *now* are all pronounced with /ooh/: /KOOH/, /KLOOHD (alternatively, KLOOHT)/, /LOOHD/, /HOOH/, /NOOH/.

 e. **The shift of /u/ to /oo/:** There is a ubiquitous, very important shift in both the Midlands and Yorkshire from the standard British /u/ in such words as *but* and *love* to the /oo/ in *book*: *but* is pronounced /BOOT/, *love* /LOOV/, and so forth. This sound is sometimes heard as a schwa /uh/: /BUHT/, /LUHV/ in unstressed syllables. The word *under* is /OON duh (alternatively, dah)/; *thunder* is /THOON duh/.

f. **Diphthongization of vowels:** A schwa is sometimes inserted after a pure vowel or a diphthong, so a word like *daily* is pronounced /DEUH lee/.

4. The past participle *been* rhymes with *bean*.

Intonation and Stress: The Music and Rhythm of the Accent

The information given above for the Midlands also applies to Yorkshire. A stressed syllable with its long vowel is spoken on a higher pitch than those surrounding it, which gives a certain rising pattern to the intonation. Listen to the actors in *Billy Elliot*, for example, and you will hear this occasional pattern.

Practice Exercises

1. *But as I say, do you see that cloud passing overhead? That means rain, that does, before the afternoon is out. No, it's not over yet, this rainy season.*
/buh raz oy SE / juh see THA KLOOHT PA sin awv RED / thah MEENZ REN tha DOOZ bee FAW TAH fta NOOHN ih ZOOT / NAW SNAW OOH vah yet / thihs RE nee SEE zuhn/

Note: Notice the /r/ replacing the /t/ in the syllable /raz/—also typical of Newcastle and Durham pronunciations; the /r/ should be given one trill. Pay special attention to the dropping of the final /t/ in *that*. The /t/ is not replaced by a glottal stop. Take note, also, of the lengthened vowels in general, as in the words *say* and *rain*.

2. From the dialogue of Joseph, the old Yorkshire servant in *Wuthering Heights* (1847) by Emily Brontë

"What are ye for? T'maister's down i' t' fowld. Go round by th' end ot' laith if ye went to spake to him. . . . There's nobbut t'missis; and shoo'll not oppen't an ye mak yer flaysome dins till neeght. . . . Nor-ne me! I'll hae no hend wi't . . ."

/wo TAHR yuh FAWR / TMAY stuhrz down iht FOWLD / gaw ROWND
bih TENT ot LAYTH ihf yuh wen tuh SPAYK tihm / thuhrz NAW biht
TMIHS ihs / uhn SHOOHL nawt U pihnt uhn yuh MAHK yuhr FLAY
(alternatively, FLE) suhm DIHNZ tihl NIHKHT / NAWR nuh MEE / ahl
HE naw HEND weet/

Translation: What are you meaning to do? The master's down in the fold.
Go round by the end of the fence if you want to speak to him . . . There's
nobody but the mistress; and she won't open it if you make your fearsomely
loud noises till night . . . Nor I! I'll have no hand in it!

Notes: This is a historic Yorkshire dialect. Notice the similarity to Scots
accents, with the use of the word *hae* for "have" and *neeght* for "night,"
for example. The /r/ may be a trilled /r/, instead of the standard retroflex
consonant. In a Yorkshire accent the word *wuthering* (fiercely blowing,
as with winds on the heights) would be pronounced /WOO thuh rihng/.

3. *I think it was at eight o'clock or so that he came down the street on his own
bicycle, must have been.*
/oy THIHNK (alternatively, TIHNK) twuhz DAY duh KLAHK uhr saw thuh
dee KAYM DEoohn DSTRAYT awn eez awn BOY skuhl MOOST uh BEEN/

Notes: The /d/ sounds in /DAY/ and /dee/ in the phonetic pronunciation
are both tapped; that is, the tongue lightly articulates the consonant and
immediately comes off the gum ridge, and there is extra air in the /d/ as
well. The /d/ in /DSTRAYT/ is barely heard. Notice the dropping of /h/
in the word *he.*

4. *There was not another person to be seen for near two miles round.*
/THUHR wuhz naw duh NOO THUHR POR sn dbee seen fuhr NEE uhr
TEEooh MOYLZ REoohnd/

Notes: In the syllable /duh/ in the phonetic pronunciation, the /d/ is tapped. The /d/ in /dbee/ is barely heard.

A Scene for Two and a Monologue

1. From Lee Hall's Screenplay of *Billy Elliot* (2000)

Billy Elliot, a boy from a working-class family in the mining country near Leeds in Yorkshire, wants only to dance. First, however, he must overcome the provincial preconceptions of masculinity, as defined by men like his hard-working father. Sports and labor are acceptable pursuits for a male, so the thinking goes, but certainly not dance. As author Lee Hall tells us in his introduction, dance is considered "high art," and therefore "desiccated, pretentious, irrelevant bullshit."

The following scene takes place one morning in the Elliots' kitchen.

> BILLY *is sitting at the end of the table.* DAD *is sitting at the other staring at* BILLY. GRANDMA *is in the middle, eating pork pie, savoring it as if it was the most delicious meal in the world. A long staring match.* DAD *is expecting* BILLY *to apologize.*
>
> DAD. Ballet.
>
> BILLY. What's wrong with ballet?
>
> DAD. What's wrong with ballet?
>
> BILLY. It's perfectly normal.
>
> DAD. Perfectly normal!
>
> GRANDMA. I used to go to ballet.
>
> BILLY. See.
>
> DAD. Aye, for your Nana. For girls. Not for lads, Billy. Lads do football or boxing or . . . wrestling. Not friggin' ballet.
>
> BILLY. What lads do wrestling?
>
> DAD. Don't start, Billy.
>
> BILLY. I don't see what's wrong with it.
>
> DAD. You know perfectly well what's wrong with it.

BILLY. No, I don't.

DAD. Yes, you do.

BILLY. No, I don't.

DAD. Yes, you bloody well do. What do you think I am? You know quite nicely.

BILLY. What? What are you trying to say?

DAD. You're asking for a hiding.

BILLY. No, I'm not. Honest.

DAD. You are, Billy, Billy!

BILLY. It's not just poofs, Dad. Some ballet dancers are as fit as athletes. What about Wayne Sleep? He was a ballet dancer.

DAD. Wayne Sleep?

BILLY. Aye!

DAD. Listen, son, from now on you can forget about the fucking ballet. You can forget the fucking boxing as well. I've been busting my arse for those fifty pences. From now on you'll stay here and look after your Nana. Got it? Good.

GRANDMA. They used to say I should be a professional dancer.

DAD. Will you shut up?

BILLY. I hate you. You're a bastard.

DAD. Get off! Billy! Billy!

2. From Richard Cameron's *Can't Stand Up for Falling Down* (1991)

The play, written as a series of monologues, is set in a small mining town in South Yorkshire. It tells the story of Lynette, Ruby, and Jodie, three young women whose lives are linked together by their relationships, long in the past, with one of the villagers, Royce Boland. Lynette, a twenty-two-year-old working-class woman, had finally married this town bully, a violent drunkard who abuses her, physically and mentally. She wants to escape, but like many women in her predicament, dares only to protest in the most limited way, and tries to take steps to save herself.

LYNETTE. Royce has now moved into the back bedroom, thank God. It's been a bit of a time, these last few weeks. I got a knife on the bedroom door lock and managed to get the paint off so it works, I can lock it at night now. Makes it a bit safer. I just don't know what he might do next, after the things he's said to me. Coming in, throwing things. Spoiling things in the house. What's the point of trying to keep things nice? I keep my room clean. I make my own meals when he's out. It's like a pigsty down there.

I used to clean it up after he'd pulled everything out of the kitchen cupboard and smashed it, but I cut my hand quite bad on a bit of glass from the sauce bottle, I think it was, and I had to leave it. I should have had stitches really. It's funny. I thought it was tomato ketchup.

"Serves you fucking right," he says. "Cleaning up. You're always cleaning up. Leave it. FUCKING LEAVE IT!" and something's exploded in my head and he must have hit my ear. My hand's full of blood but it's my ear that hurts. "Don't you swear in this house! You stop saying your foul language to me, I won't have it. Don't swear!" and I'm hanging on to the edge of the sink to stop from falling over, I'm going dizzy. It makes me ill to hear bad words said before God and he knows it and he says it all the more, over and over, and my hand's under the tap and my head's swimming and ringing loud and the water turns red.

That night I mend the door lock with one hand, while my other hand is throbbing through the cloth, and I hear him hammering and sawing in the shed in the yard, like it's been for days now into the night, but I don't care any more about what he's doing, I don't care, and I don't care if God doesn't want me to say it, I wish he were dead, I wish he were dead.

4
Scottish Accents

Scottish accents can be divided roughly into three large groups:

1. The Northern accents of the Highlands and Islands (Skye, the Hebrides);
2. Central Scotland, Ayrshire, the Scottish Midlands, which is Robert Burns country;
3. The Southern Border and Lothian accents of the Lowlands, including those of Edinburgh and Glasgow.

We will cover the upper- and middle-class Edinburgh accent, as well as some useful Edinburgh working-class and Scottish Midlands / Highlands variations.

Standard Scottish English (SSE), spoken by the professional and middle classes, includes Scots vocabulary and grammatical features. If you are doing a Scottish accent, you need to familiarize yourself with them. Christine Robinson and Carol Ann Crawford's *Scotspeak: A Guide to the Pronunciation of Modern Urban Scots (Scotspeak Book and CD)* (Luath Press Limited, 2001) is a thorough handbook, meant for actors.

Scots, spoken by many members of the working classes, is the closest of any language to English—so close, in fact, that it is sometimes thought of as a dialect. In the Highlands, SSE and Scots gradually replaced Scottish Gaelic /GA lihk/, a Celtic language related to Irish Gaelic and still spoken in the Highlands.

Scots vocabulary includes such words as *gloaming* (twilight), *greet* (weep), *wean* /WEE uhn/ ("wee one," child, kid), and *bairn* /BERN/ (child), and negative verbs such as *dinnae* or *dinna* /DIH nay/, /DIH nah/ (does not, do not)—the first pronunciation is typical of Edinburgh. A Scots speaker will say, "I dinna ken," while a speaker of SSE will say, "I don't know." Such Scots words as *bonny* (pretty, beautiful), *dirk* (dagger), *lad* and *laddie* (boy), *lass* and *lassie* (girl), and *wee* (little) have become a part of English vocabulary.

Authentic Scottish accents can be heard in such masterpieces as two of Bill Forsyth's films, *Local Hero* (1983) and the wry and charming *Gregory's Girl* (1981). Avoid the imitation accents in so many versions of Robert Louis Stevenson's *Kidnapped*, but do see the 1978 TV miniseries (available on DVD, but only in the British format), starring Glasgow-born David McCallum. Gordon Jackson, also born in Glasgow, has a wonderfully light Scottish brogue in *The Prime of Miss Jean Brodie* (1969). Maggie Smith, in the title role, does an excellent Edinburgh accent, as does Celia Johnson in the role of Miss McKay. See Gordon Jackson, also, as the butler Hudson in the British television series *Upstairs, Downstairs*.

Edinburgh-born Sean Connery, perhaps Scotland's most famous contemporary actor, occasionally uses his real accent, as he does in *The Rock* (1996), although in the James Bond films he sounded deliberately English. In older films, listen to Edinburgh-born Finlay Currie as Magwitch in David Lean's film of Charles Dickens's *Great Expectations* (1946) and as Queen Victoria's Scottish retainer John Brown in *The Mudlark* (1950). In *Her Majesty Mrs. Brown* (1997), the Scottish comedian and actor Billy Connolly plays John Brown, giving us a totally different portrait from that of Finlay Currie. Gerard Butler as John's brother, Archie Brown, and Jimmy Chisholm and Elaine Collins as Mr. and Mrs. Grant, also speak with authentic accents. Sir Alec Guinness stars as Major Jock Sinclair in *Tunes of Glory* (1960), about a Scottish regiment; this film co-stars Duncan Macrae, among other Scottish actors. For working-class Edinburgh accents, see Danny Boyle's film *Trainspotting* (1996), starring Robert Carlyle and Ewan McGregor and set in the underground Edinburgh drug scene. Dougray Scott, in Tom Cruise's *Mission: Impossible II* (2000), speaks with a clear Fife accent.

Teach Yourself the Scottish Accents

1. **Positioning, placement, and use of the mouth muscles during speech:** The general position of the lips is relaxed and slightly forward. For Edinburgh accents, the tongue is up and held slightly back. The muscles at the corners of the mouth are not tensed or held tightly. The accent generally "feels" as if the air flow is directed to the gum ridge opening up into the palate.

2. **The sounds of the letter /r/:** All Scottish accents are rhotic. For Edinburgh, pronounce /r/ in the usual retroflex fashion, almost as in General American, but with the tongue not curled as far back and without touching the tongue to the opening of the palate; or you may give the /r/ one light tap or flap only, but this sound is rarely heard. The back of the tongue is relaxed. Pronounce post-vocalic (after a vowel) /r/ before another consonant—for example, in the middle of such words as *first* and *work*. For a heavy Highlands accent, you may pronounce a very lightly trilled or tapped /r/, also sometimes called an /r/ with a burr, at the beginning of a word or syllable, as well as at the end of a word.

3. **Other consonants:**
   a. **The glottal stop /?/:** The glottal stop is a brief catch in the throat: the glottis closes for a split second to replace the consonant /t/, in the middle of such words as *bottle* /BO ?l/ and at the end of such words as *what* /WAH?/; this vocal pattern is ubiquitous in working-class Edinburgh accents and in the Scottish Midlands / Highlands.
   b. **Dropped consonants:** Certain consonants are regularly dropped, such as the /f/ in *yourself*, pronounced /yawr, or yoohr SEL/. The

voiceless consonant /*th*/ in a final position is often dropped, as in the word *with*: *wi'* /WIH, or WEE/.

c. **/h/ and /wh/:** Scots pronounce initial /h/. Words beginning with the spelling /wh/ are often pronounced with /hw/, so a word like *where* is pronounced /HWER/, with the vowel lengthened. In working-class speech, the distinction is often eliminated, and only initial /w/ is heard: /WER/.

d. **The sounds of /l/:** In initial position in SSE, a "dark" /l/ is usual; it is pronounced with the back of the tongue raised. Practice this /l/ with the words *please* and *middle* /PLEEZ/, /MIH dl/. In Edinburgh, a "liquid" /l/ is also heard: The blade of the tongue is not thickened, and the tip of the tongue is not pressed and held against the upper gum ridge. This /l/ is sometimes heard in initial position, but is more usual after another consonant. In working-class speech, final /l/ is often dropped in the middle or at the end of such words as *all*, *call*, *careful*, and *salt*: /AW, or AH/, /KAW, or KAH/, /KAYR fooh/, /SAWT/. In the Highlands, /l/ is pronounced with the tip of the tongue more forwardly placed behind the upper front teeth and the blade of the tongue thickened.

e. **The voiceless consonant /kh/:** The sound of /kh/ is the same as in German *Ach!*, and is made by vibrating the back of the tongue against the uvula, as if you were about to spit. It occurs in place names like *Loch* (Lake) *Lomond* and in expressions like *Ach!* and *Och!* Heard in Highlands accents, the sound often shifts to /k/ in Edinburgh working-class speech, so *loch* is pronounce /LOK/.

f. **Devoiced consonants:** In some older Highland speech, certain consonants are devoiced, notably /j/ and /zh/, so the words *gentleman* and *pleasure* are pronounced /SHEN tl muhn/ and /PLE shuhr/.

3. **Vowels and diphthongs:** Vowels are always lengthened slightly before /r/. The schwa is much less in evidence than it is south of the border in England, and full, if short, vowels appear in every syllable in

more careful Scottish speech, but not always in working-class speech. The vowels /ih/ and /ee/ are pronounced as in RP, but /ee/ is sometimes diphthongized by adding a slight schwa at the end of the vowel.

a. **The sounds of /ah/ and /a/:** In the words on the "ask list" in chapter 1, such as *ask*, *answer*, *bath*, *can't*, *father*, and *grass*, this sound is close to American *that*, rather than RP *father*. The /a/ in *cat*, *that*, etc., is pronounced much like /ah/ in General American *father*, but is not as open. Note that the Scots pronunciation of *father* is /FAY thuhr/.

b. **The sound of /ay/:** Such words as *date*, *hate*, and *late* are not pronounced with the diphthong /ay/, but with a lengthened /e/: /DET/, /HET/, /LET/. Practice sentence: *I hate to tell you, but you're late for our date* /ah HE tuh TEL yuh bih? yoohr LET fur ahr DE?/.

c. **The sounds of /e/, /o/, /o/, /oh/, and /u/:** The pure vowel /e/ is open in words like *dress*, *perfect* /PAYR fekt/ as an adjective, /payr FEKT/ as a verb, and *heard* is pronounced /HERD/. As far as many Scots are concerned, words like *fern*, *fur*, and *fir* do not rhyme, as they do in General American English /FURN/, /FUR/, /FUR/, but have two different vowels. In Scotland they are pronounced, respectively: /FERN/, FUR/, and /FUR/. Note that in Edinburgh *coat*, *cot*, and *caught* all rhyme, and are pronounced with a lengthened pure /o/ close to the /aw/ in *law*: /KOT/. The sound of /o/ in such words as *deserted* and *work* shifts to /er/: /duh ZER ted (alternatively, tuhd)/. Note that the diphthong /oh/ in such words as *coat* and *know* are pronounced not with a diphthong, a lengthened pure /o/ close to the /aw/ in *law*: /KOT/, /NAW/.

d. **The shift from /ih/ to /e/ and from /e/ to /ih/:** In some words, the sound of /ih/ is pronounced /e/, as in the word *impossible*: /em PAW sih buhl/. In some words, /e/ shifts to /ih/, as in the word *never*: /NIH vuhr/.

e. **The sound of the diphthong /I/:** In Edinburgh the diphthong /I/ is usually pronounced with a very short /oy/, or is flattened in some words to a long /ay/ diphthong, as in the word *say*; so, for instance, the word *price* is pronounced /PRAYS/. The pronoun *I*, however, often drops the second part of the diphthong before a consonant, so *I* is pronounced /AH/. In the Highlands, /I/ is often pronounced like /ee/ in *wee* (except for the pronoun, which is pronounced /AH/); so, for instance, the word *Highlands* becomes /HEE luhnz/; spelled in Scots "Hielands."

f. **The sound of the short pure vowel /o/:** In such words as *not, got,* and *hot* this vowel is lengthened, so it is a bit like the /aw/ in *law*.

g. **The vowels /oo/ and /ooh/:** There is no long /ooh/ vowel where one might expect it, in such words as *boot*. Instead, the vowel /oo/ in *book* is heard, so that *food* is pronounced /FOOD/ instead of /FOOHD/; *pool* rhymes with *pull, brooding* with *pudding, wool* with *tool*, etc. In the Highlands, the French "u" (pronounced by saying /ee/ with the lips strongly protruded /ü/) is often heard in words like *to, do, foot, book,* and *true* /TÜ/, /DÜ/, /FÜT/, /BÜK/, /TRÜ/, in which word it is also sometimes lengthened and preceded by a very short /ee/, i.e., /TREEü/.

h. **The sound of the diphthong /oh/:** In Edinburgh, the diphthong /oh/ is heard in words like *no, go,* and *home* in educated speech as the pure vowel /aw/: /NAW/, /GAW/, /HAWM/. In the Highlands, this diphthong /oh/ shifts to the /ay/ in *say*. So, "No, go home," spelled in SSE and Scots "nae, gae hame," is pronounced /NAY GAY HAYM/. The lips are not rounded and protruded as they are in the British or American versions of this sound. In both accents, however, the lips may be protruded, and /oh/ is sometimes heard as the pure vowel /ooh/: /NOOH GOOH HOOHM/.

i. **The sound of the diphthong /ow/:** The diphthong /ow/, in such words as *about, house, how, mouth,* and *round*, is pronounced in Edinburgh like the /ooh/ in *boot* in RP and General American: /uh BOOHT/, /HOOHS/, /HOOH/, /MOOHTH/, /ROOHND/. In the Highlands, /ow/ is often heard with the same sound as the French

/ü/ as the second half of the diphthong, so *house* is pronounced /HAÜS/. Practice phrase: *Round about the house* /ROOHND uh BOO? thuh HOOS/.

j. **The sound of the vowel /u/:** The "u" in *but*, also spelled with an "o" in words like *above*, *love*, *mother*, etc., is sometimes pronounced in Edinburgh like a very short /o/ in *work* /uh BOV/, /BOT/, /MOTHER/. In the Highlands, you might hear "u" pronounced like a short /ih/: /u BIHV/, /LIHV/, /MIH thuhr/.

4. The past participle *been* rhymes with *bean*, as in British RP.

Intonation and Stress: The Music and Rhythm of the Accents

In Edinburgh, pitch and intonation are fairly even, with the usual drop at the end of a declarative sentence, and a rise in pitch at the end of a question. But indignation or anger give rise to more pitches. And younger speakers tend to raise the volume at the beginning of an utterance, giving a kind of staccato feeling to the stress patterns. The lengthening of vowels and diphthongs before /r/ also gives the accent its characteristic rhythm.

In the Highlands, intonation patterns are more "musical," and more notes are used than in the Lowlands.

Practice Exercises

1. *Birds on a fir tree or in the ferns certainly don't wear fur coats. I caught him on the cot wearing my coat, and I pulled him off and threw him in the pool.* /BURDZ awn uh FUR TREE awr ihn thuh FERNZ SER tuhn lee DAWNT WER FUR KOTS / I KOT him awn the KOT WE rihng mI KOT / and I POOLD hihm OF and *THROOH* hihm ihn thuh POOL/

Notes: Remember that in SSE, words spelled with "i" and "u," such as *fir* and *fur*, are pronounced with /u/ as in *but*; and words spelled with "e," such as *fern*, pronounced with /e/ as in *met*. There is no distinction between the vowels in *cot*, *caught*, and *coat*, all pronounced with a lengthened pure

/o/ close to the /aw/ in *law*; or between *pull* and *pool*, pronounced with the /oo/ in *book*.

2. From Robert Burns's *The Braes O' Killiecrankie* /thuh BRAYZ uh KIH lee KRAHN kee/

> *Whare hae ye been sae braw, lad?*
> *Whare hae ye been sae brankie, O?*
> *Whare hae ye been sae braw, lad?*
> *Cam ye by Killiecrankie, O?*

/HWER hay yee BEEN say BRAW lad / HWER hay yee BEEN say BRAN kee AW / . . . /KAM yee bah KIH lee KRAHN kee AW /

Translation: Where have you been so bravely, lad? Where have you been so proudly [also, finely] dressed, oh? . . . Did you go by Killiecrankie, oh?

Notes: A *brae* is a steep hillside, or a rising riverbank.

The battle of Killiecrankie ("aspen wood" in Gaelic) was fought in 1689 in the hills at the Pass of Killiecrankie, near the village of the same name, and was part of the first Jacobite Uprising supporting the Stuart claim to the throne of England. There were two more such uprisings, in 1715 and 1745, when the cause was lost for good.

3. From an old Scottish ballad

> Rob Roy is frae the Hielands come,
>   Down to the Lowland border;
> And he has stolen that lady away,
>   To haud his house in order.
>
> He set her on a milk-white steed,
>   Of nane he stood in awe;

Until they reached the Hieland hills,
   Aboon the Balmaha.

Notes: The meaning of the Scots words: *frae* /FRAY/ means "from," *haud* /HAWD/ means "hold," *nane* /NAYN/ means "none," *aboon* /uh BOOHN/ means "about" or "near to." One of the entrances to the Highlands, the Balmaha /BAHL muh HAH/ is a pass on the western side of Loch Lomond.

Rob Roy MacGregor (1671–1734), the Scottish Robin Hood, was an outlaw and a rebel, and a colorful hero to many in the Highlands. He fought in the first Jacobite Risings of 1689 and 1715. His life has been fictionalized a number of times: in Sir Walter Scott's popular novel *Rob Roy* (1817); on stage in Reginald de Koven and Harry B. Smith's operetta *Rob Roy* (1894)—in honor of which the cocktail of the same name was invented; and in two films, Walt Disney's *Rob Roy, the Highland Rogue* (1953) and *Rob Roy* (1995).

4. From Robert Louis Stevenson's *Kidnapped* (1886), chapter xvi, "The Lad with the Silver Button: Across Morven"

"I am seeking somebody," said I, "and it comes in my mind that you will have news of him. Alan Breck Stewart is his name." And very foolishly, instead of showing him the button [given to David Balfour by the well-loved Alan Breck Stewart as a token by which David might be recognized as a friend of Alan in the dangerous Highlands], I sought to pass a shilling in his hand.

At this he drew back. "I am very much affronted," he said; "and this is not the way that one shentleman should behave to another at all. The man you ask for is in France; but if he was in my sporran," says he, "and your belly full of shillings, I would not hurt a hair upon his body."

I saw I had gone the wrong way to work, and without wasting time upon apologies, showed him the button lying in the hollow of my palm.

"Aweel, aweel," said Neil; "and I think ye might have begun with that end of the stick, whatever! But if ye are the lad with the silver [/SIH luhr/] button, all is well, and I have the word to see that ye come safe. But if ye will pardon me to speak plainly," says he, "there is a name that you should never take into your mouth, and that is the name of Alan Breck; and there is a thing that ye would never do, and that is to offer your dirty money to a Hieland shentleman."

It was not very easy to apologize; for I could scarce tell him (what was the truth) that I had never dreamed he would set up to be a gentleman until he told me so. Neil on his part had no wish to prolong his dealings with me, only to fulfill his orders and be done with it; and he made haste to give me my route. This was to lie the night in Kinlochaline [/KIHN lokh AH lihn/] in the public inn; to cross Morven [/MAWR ven/] the next day to Ardgour [/AHRD GOWR, or GOWuhR/], and lie the night in the house of one John of the Claymore, who was warned that I might come; the third day, to be set across one loch at Corran [/KO ruhn/] and another at Balachulish [/ba luh KHOOH lihsh/], and then ask my way to the house of James of the Glens, at Aucharn [/AW khuhrn, or khahrn/] in Duror [/DYOOH ror, or DOO ror/] of Appin [/A pihn/].

Notes: *Kidnapped* takes place in 1751, several years after the abortive 1745 uprising, led by Bonnie Prince Charlie (Charles Edward Stuart, claimant to the English throne). One of the novel's themes is the ongoing conflict between the Lowlanders, who supported the Hanoverian monarchy, and the Jacobite Highlanders, who supported the Stuart cause. The narrator is David Balfour, a Lowlander and an anti-Jacobite. For the most venal of reasons, his uncle Ebenezer has David kidnapped aboard a ship bound for the Carolinas. This chapter takes place soon after the ship is wrecked off the coast of Scotland. David has survived and made his way to the mainland. Shortly before the shipwreck, the captain had rescued the Jacobite supporter Alan Breck Stewart from a small boat, and then tried to rob him. David had helped the grateful Alan fend off his attackers.

Note the difference between David's Lowlands accent, and that of Neil Roy, the "Hieland shentleman" whose native language is clearly Gaelic and not English. Stevenson keeps his accent indications to a minimum, enough to give us a flavor of Highland speech. Notice the devoicing of the initial /j/ sound in *gentleman*, typical of this western Highlands Gaelic accent. A *claymore* is a short sword, much used in the Highlands at this period. The Gaelic prefix "kin-" means "at the head of": *Kinlochaline* means "at the head of Loch Aline."

Monologues

1. From Robert Louis Stevenson and W. E. Henley's Five-Act Melodrama *Deacon Brodie, or The Double Life* (1880; first performed, 1882), Act 1, Scene 9

Set in Edinburgh in the 1780s, Stevenson's rarely performed *Deacon Brodie* is the story of cabinet-maker and locksmith William Brodie, deacon of the trade guild of Wrights and Masons. He was a town councilor and respected citizen by day, while by night he was a womanizer and gambler, always in debt, and the head of a gang of burglars. In 1786, he was caught, tried, and hanged. It was rumored that he had had a surgeon friend design a special metal collar that would prevent the hanging from being fatal. After the execution, his body was taken to the surgeon's house. He was revived, and escaped to the continent, where he was sighted in various cities, so legend has it. When his grave was later opened, his coffin was empty. Nobody knows to this day if he actually died by hanging, or if he survived.

This story inspired Stevenson not only to write his play, but also his more famous tale *The Strange Case of Dr. Jekyll and Mr. Hyde*.

In a 1997 film, *Deacon Brodie* (not based on Stevenson and Henley's play), Billy Connolly stars in the title role, along with an excellent cast. Listen to the authentic accents, the intonation and the specific pronunciations, including the constant dropping of "g" in "-ing" endings. You will hear, for instance, the following:

1. The preposition "to" before a vowel /TEE/: *to apply* /tee uh PLI/;
2. *Father* /FAY thuhr/;
3. *Whore* /HÜR/;
4. The phrase *out of my way* /AÜT uh mah WAY/;
5. *Old* /AWLD/;
6. *Would nae* (would not) /WOOD nay/;
7. *Careful* /KEER fooh/;
8. *Soldier* /SOH juhr/;
9. The name *William* /WU lyuhm/; and the nickname *Willie* /WU lee/.

In this monologue from the play, we see Brodie alone in his room, preparing to go out. He has just told his sister he was going to bed and that he was too busy to listen to the news of her forthcoming engagement.

BRODIE. (*He closes, locks, and double-bolts the doors.*) Now for one of the Deacon's headaches! Rogues all, rogues all! (*Goes to clothes-press and proceeds to change his coat.*) On with the new coat and into the new life! Down with the Deacon and up with the robber! (*Changing neck-band and ruffles.*) Eh God! how still the house is! There's something in hypocrisy after all. If we were as good as we seem, what would the world be? The city has its vizard on, and we—at night we are our naked selves. Trysts are keeping, bottles cracking, knives are stripping; and here is Deacon Brodie flaming forth the man of men he is!—How still it is! . . . My father and Mary—Well! the day for them, the night for me; the grimy cynical night that makes all cats grey, and all honesties of one complexion. Shall a man not have half a life of his own?—not eight hours out of twenty-four? (Eight shall he have should he dare the pit of

Tophet.) (*Takes out money.*) Where's the blunt? I must be cool to-night, or . . . steady, Deacon, you must win; damn you, you must! You must win back the dowry that you've stolen, and marry your sister, and pay your debts, and gull the world a little longer! (*As he blows out the lights.*) The Deacon's going to bed—the poor sick Deacon! Allons! (*Throws up the window and looks out.*) Only the stars to see me! (*Addressing the bed.*) Lie there, Deacon! Sleep and be well tomorrow. As for me, I'm a man once more till morning. (*Gets out of the window.*)

Note: The pit of Tophet ("burning place") in the Bible is presumably in or near Jerusalem. The Canaanites practiced child sacrifice there. By extension, Tophet stands for Hell.

2. Two Monologues from Duncan McLean's *Blackden: A Play in Eight Monologues* (1999)

Mounted to great acclaim in Glasgow in 1997, *Blackden* is a powerful, up-setting, gripping play by one of Scotland's greatest contemporary writers. With ominous political overtones in the Brechtian manner, it is an experiment in the use of monologues, as McLean tells us in his introduction to *Plays: I* (Methuen, 1999). Each of the play's eight scenes has a name that reflects its theme.

The play is set in the fictitious village of Blackden, not far from Aberdeen. Through four characters we learn the story of the iconoclastic, troubled, desperate Patrick "Paddy" Hunter, who never appears in the play, but is imitated by some of the other characters. Patrick has apparently left Blackden, and gone nobody knows where. Everyone tries to figure out why he left, what drove him away. By the end of the play, it is clear that he has fled what he considered a claustrophobic, strangling environment that offered him nothing except a parochial, narrow existence that he no longer wanted.

A. From Scene 2: "While I'm Alive I Intend to Live"

Shona Findlay, twenty-two years old, is the chef at the village pub. She has known Patrick more than she lets on at first. As she enters in her cook's uniform, she is, so McLean tells us, a "mixture of reluctance and defiance." The characters begin by telling us their names, almost as if they were testifying in court. Here is the beginning of what Shona has to tell us, in her rural accent. The Highlands variations would be appropriate for this character.

> SHONA. Shona Findlay. The Caravan, Corse Woods. But . . .
> (*Pause.*) I don't . . . I don't ken him really. Well, I ken who he *is*,
> like. Fuck's sake, round here you ken who aabody [everybody]
> is—aye, and every bastard kens you! And it's true I was speak-
> ing to him on Friday, just. But—it's not like I chum around with
> him or anything, just. It's not like, ken, anything was *happen-*
> *ing* between us. It's his sister I'm friendly with, really. Helen.
> (*Shrugs.*) Well, even there you see: I haven't heard from *her* for
> ages either. This time last year since I saw her. She went away
> to uni [university], see, and that . . . pissed me off. (*A nervous*
> *laugh.*) I ken it's daft now, but—I was just a bairn then. I mean,
> this was . . . three years ago. There we was, best pals, me and
> Helen, and suddenly she announces she's off to uni in Edinburgh.
> I mean to say, can you just abandon your pals like that? Follow
> your own . . . Ach, forget it.

B. From Scene 3: "I Never Stopped to Listen to the Feelings"

Patrick's aunt, Heather Roberts, a council office worker in her mid-thirties and "the younger sister of Paddy's mother," works in a nearby town. "She is a little bit arty. She is confident and calm, or at least appears so most of the time . . . Her voice is soft and level," as she smokes a cigarette. Her accent is more sophisticated than Shona's, perhaps the middle- to upper-class Edinburgh accent of SSE detailed above.

HEATHER. I blame myself. To an extent. Not that I think I drove him away in any sense. No, it was . . . a whole lot of factors that contributed to that. But I blame myself for not noticing he was on the verge of it. (*Pause.*) Not noticing! Dear, oh dear. I didn't have to notice. I . . . just had to listen. But of course I was too busy *talking* to listen. As per always, as Patrick would say. (*Takes a drag, looks up.*) Sorry. Heather Roberts. Pond Cottage, up by the big house. (*Another drag, then she begins.*) I took a run up to The Strath on Friday night, and he was just away to go out, so I didn't stay long. Moira—that's my sister, his mother—she was away to Edinburgh, a long weekend, visiting Helen at the uni. And just getting away from this place: this time of year's difficult for her. So: I didn't stay: I gave him a lift down the road in fact. (*Thinks. Impersonates Paddy, jumping up with his excitement and irritation.*) "I'm fed up of getting lifts here, there and everywhere . . . everybody jumping down my throat to give me lifts every minute of the day." This is Patrick by the way. "I'm completely *scunnered* with it, Heather! I want to get somewhere under my *own* steam for a change!"

3. From the National Theatre of Scotland's *Black Watch* (2006) by Gregory Burke

Produced numerous times since it premiered at the Edinburgh Festival, *Black Watch*, a play with music, was seen in New York in 2011. The show is based partly on interviews with Scottish soldiers of the world-famous Black Watch regiment serving in Iraq in 2004. The history of the regiment, established in Fife by King George II in 1739, is outlined in one monologue by a soldier, Gammy, who also opens the show.

The play is a gripping, upsetting look at the meaning of being a soldier, of how it feels and what they go through, from illusion to boredom to terror. It is available on a 2008 DVD, in British format only. The soldiers' accents are often very thick working-class Scottish English, full of glottal stops. They are in sharp contrast to the Writer, who is an interviewer speaking

SSE, to English news commentators, Scottish aristocrats speaking RP, an officer reading in RP accents the e-mails he has written to his wife, and the politicians speaking SSE. The accents, which clearly indicate the social class of the characters, tell the story of the patriotic illusions about glory fed to the soldiers, and "exploited by the army," as Gammy says. Later in the play, he tells us with regard to the war in Iraq, ". . . it's no like they're a threat tay you or tay your country, you're no defending your country. We're invading their country and fucking their day up."

You will notice the spelling—"ay" is pronounced /ay/—that is an excellent indication of this working-class accent; and the verbs "didnay" and "cannay," clear indications of Scots element in SSE. There are also glottal stops on nearly all the final "t" sounds. In other places in the script, you can hear the soldiers pronounce /HES tuh ree/ for *history*, /KEOOHTS/ for *Celts*, /MYER/ for *more*, /Ü? SID/ (with the "d" barely pronounced) for *outside*, /POWZ/ for *pals*, /NAY wer/ for *nowhere*, /SOH juhrz/ for *soldiers*, and /TRÜ zuhrz/ for *trousers*.

———————————

A cannon stops the music as a door at one end of the space opens to reveal Gammy dressed in civvies.

———————————

GAMMY. A'right. Welcome to the story of the Black Watch.
   Beat.
At first, I didnay want tay day this.
   Beat.
I didnay want tay have tay explain myself [/tee yeks PLAYN mee SEL/] to people ay.
   Beat.
See, I think people's minds are usually made up about you, if you were in the army [/en thee AHR mee/, with a strongly trilled "r"].
   Beat.

They are though ay?

Beat.

They poor fucking boys. They cannay day anything else. They can-nay get a job. They get exploited by the army.

Beat.

Well I want you to fucking know. I wanted to be in the army. I could have done other stuff. I'm not a fucking knuckle-dragger.

Beat.

And people's minds are made up about the war that's on now ay?

Beat.

They are. It's no right. It's illegal. We're just big bullies.

Beat.

Well, we'll need to get fucking used tay it. Bullying's the fucking job. That's what you have a fucking army for.

5
Welsh Accents

Welsh, a Celtic language, is still spoken by about half a million people as a first language in many parts of rural Wales. It was the native language of the vast majority of the population until the mid-eighteenth century. But even in Shakespeare's day, Welsh people spoke English, like his characters Owen Glendower /GLEN dow wuhr/, or Glendwer (the letter "w" represents the vowel /ooh/ in Welsh orthography), in *The First Part of King Henry IV* and Fluellen /flooh EL uhn/ in *The Life of King Henry V*.

For beautiful Welsh accents, listen to the original recording of Dylan Thomas's *Under Milk Wood*, with Thomas himself as the First Voice; and to his other recordings, all of which are available on CD. In many of their films, Anthony Hopkins and Richard Burton have a touch of their Welsh accents in their usual British RP speech. The film of Emlyn Williams's autobiographical play *The Corn Is Green* (1945) contains good, authentic Welsh accents. The accents are generally less authentic in *How Green Was My Valley* (1941), set in a Welsh mining town. See *On the Black Hill* (1988), about a pair of identical Welsh twins; and the wry comedy *The Englishman Who Went Up a Hill but Came Down a Mountain* (1995), about the whimsical adventures of English cartographers in a Welsh village. Set in the Cardiff club scene in the 1990s, *Human Traffic* (1999) provides examples of contemporary Welsh accents, and of accents from all over Britain. An interesting documentary about this beautiful country is *The Shape of Wales* (2001).

Teach Yourself the Welsh Accents

One of the most important aspects of the Welsh accent is the intonation (pitch) patterns, which give the accent its distinctive music; see more later in this chapter.

1. **Positioning, placement, and use of the mouth muscles during speech:** The general position is with the lips generally slightly closed and a bit forward. The jaw is fairly loose, and the tongue generally low in the mouth during speech.

2. **The sound of /r/:** The back of the tongue is relaxed as its tip curls upward. Post-vocalic (after a vowel) /r/ and /r/ at the end of a word are silent, especially before another consonant. In the middle of a word like *very*, and at the beginning of a syllable the /r/ is sometimes heard as a lightly trilled or tapped sound.

3. **Other consonants:** Consonants are very clearly and strongly articulated, and a Welsh accent is known for its clear, strong liquid /l/.

   a. **Dropped /h/:** This consonant is sometimes dropped in urban Welsh accents, unless the speaker wishes to emphasize a particular word.

   b. **The sound of /j/:** This sound does not exist in older Welsh accents, so its voiceless counterpart /ch/ is often substituted for it, especially in the mountainous north: the word *just* is pronounced /CHUST/. Even Shakespeare in *Henry V* has his Welsh character use this sound. Fluellen says, of the Irish Captain Macmorris in act 3, scene 2, "By Cheshu, he is an ass, as in the world: I will verify as much in his peard."

   c. **The sound of /z/:** This sound does not exist in Welsh. As a result, particularly in the north of Wales, an /s/ is substituted, especially in final position, so the word *is* is pronounced /IHS/ instead of /IHZ/.

d. **The sound of /zh/:** This sound does not exist in Welsh. Instead, its voiceless counterpart /sh/ replaces it, so *pleasure* is pronounced /PLE shuhr/.

4. **Vowels and diphthongs:** Every vowel and diphthong is clearly pronounced, except in past-participle verb endings like "-ed" (as in the words *unstressed* and *lengthened*) and usually follows the phonetic value of the letter representing it. The name *Margaret*, for instance, is pronounced with all its syllables: /MAH gah ret/. Diphthongs are long. Vowels in the middle of a word are lengthened slightly. In one-syllable words vowels are lengthened, and they are lengthened also before the dropped /r/ in stressed syllables.

a. **The schwa /uh/:** There is very little use of the schwa, and all vowels in stressed and unstressed syllables receive their full value. In word endings where we would expect a schwa, as in the word *mother*, a short /ah/ is heard: /MU thah/.

b. **The sound of /ah/:** This vowel is sometimes heard as the /a/ in *that*, or as a less open-throated, more closed vowel than that of RP (see the "ask list" in chapter 1).

c. **The sound of /oh/:** The /oh/ diphthong is sometimes heard as if it were the /ooh/ in *boot*: the word *home* rhymes with *broom*. It is usually the same sound as in the American /oh/, /Oooh/, with a short stressed /o/, as opposed to the RP version /UHooh/, with a stressed schwa as the first part of the diphthong, so *go home* is pronounced /GOooh HOoohm/.

d. **The sound of /u/:** In South Wales, the vowel /u/ in *but* is sometimes heard as a schwa in all words: The word *butter* is pronounced /BUH tah/.

e. **The sound of /y/:** This semi-vowel is often inserted between two vowels. The word *fire* is pronounced /FI yah/. In such words as *news* and *duke* the /y/ is always pronounced after the initial consonant: /NYOOHZ/, /DYOOHK/. On the other hand, in words containing

/l/, such as *regular* and *particular*, a schwa is sometimes heard before the /l/: /RE guh lah/, /pah TIHK uh lah/.

5.   The past participle *been* rhymes with *bean*.

Intonation and Stress: The Music and Rhythm of the Accents

The pitch or musical pattern of Welsh accents is very important, particularly in the old-fashioned village accents, such as those featured in Dylan Thomas's *Under Milk Wood*. A Welsh accent is often said to be lilting because of the prominent rise and fall of pitches, making it less even-toned than British RP or General American. This characteristic should not be exaggerated, but it is true that there is a delicious musicality to a Welsh accent.

Stress patterns are the same as in British RP, and stress is fairly even, but vowels and diphthongs are lengthened for the nuclear tone.

Practice Exercises

1. *The sentence goes down, you see, then up again and so forth, you see.*
/*the* SEN tens gohz DOWN yooh see *then* UP a GEN and soh FAWTH yooh SEE/

One possible pitch pattern:

```
The sentence                        again       forth,
        goes      you see,     up
            down,          then        and so        you see.
```

2. *The investiture of the Prince of Wales at Caernarvon Castle is an ancient ceremony, and a most impressive pageant, gorgeous in colorful uniforms and the castle all draped in flags and banners.*
/thee ihn VES tih tyuh uv thuh PRIHNTS uv WAYLZ at kIr (alternatively, kah) NAH von KAH suhl ihz an AYN chent SE ruh muh nee / and uh MOHST ihm PRE sihv PA jent / GAW jus in KU luh fuhl YOOH nee fawmz and thuh KAH suhl awl DRAYPT ihn FLAGZ and BA nuz/

Notes: This is a South Welsh accent. The /r/ sounds in the word *Caernarvon* can be dropped. Alternatively, a very lightly trilled /r/ may be heard instead of the retroflex /r/ in such words as *Caernarvon, prince,* and *draped.* For a North Welsh accent, devoice the final consonants in the words *is, uniforms, flags,* and *banners*: /ihs/, /YOOH nee fawms/, /FLAKS/, /BA nus/.

3. From Shakespeare's *The History of Henry IV (I Henry IV)*, Act 3, Scene 1

> GLENDWER. Cousin: of many men
> I do not bear these crossings: Give me leave
> To tell you once again, that at my birth
> The front of Heaven was full of fiery shapes,
> The goats ran from the mountains, and the herds
> Were strangely clamorous to the frighted fields.
> These signs have marked me extraordinary,
> And all the courses of my life do show
> I am not in the roll of common men.
> Where is the living, clipped in with the sea,
> That chides the banks of England, Scotland, and Wales,
> Which calls me pupil, or hath read to me?
> And bring him out, that is but woman's son,
> Can trace me in the tedious ways of Art,
> And hold me pace in deep experiments.

4. From "Love and Hate," in *My Neighbors: Stories of the Welsh People* (1920) by the prolific Welsh author Caradoc Evans (1878–1945)

> By living frugally—setting aside a portion of his Civil Service pay and holding all that he got from two butchers whose trade books he kept in proper order—Adam Powell [/POH el/] became possessed of Cartref [/KAH tref/] in which he dwelt and which is in Barnes, and two houses in Thornton East; and one of the houses in Thornton East

he let to his widowed daughter Olwen [/OL oh wen (alternatively, OL wen)/], who carried on a dressmaking business. At the end of his term he retired from his office, his needs being fulfilled by a pension, and his evening eased by the ministrations of his elder daughter Lisbeth.

Soon an inward malady seized him, and in the belief that he would not be rid of it, he called Lisbeth and Olwen, to whom both he pronounced his will.

"The Thornton East property I give you," he said. "Number seven for Lissi and eight for Olwen as she is. It will be pleasant to be next door, and Lissi is not likely to marry at her age which is advanced. Share and share alike of the furniture, and what's left sell with the house and half the proceeds. If you don't fall out in the sharing, you never will again."

At once Lisbeth and Olwen embraced.

"My sister is my best friend," was the testimony of the elder, "we shan't go astray if we follow the example of the dad and mother," was that of the younger.

Monologues

1. From Shakespeare's *Henry V*, Act 4, Scene 7

FLUELLEN. I think it is in Macedon where Alexander is porn. I tell you, Captain, if you look in the maps of the 'orld, I warrant you sall find, in the comparisons between Macedon and Monmouth, that the situations, look you, is both alike. There is a river in Macedon; and there is also moreover a river at Monmouth; it is call'd Wye at Monmouth; but it is out of my prains what is the name of the other river; but 'tis all one, 'tis alike as my fingers is to my fingers, and there is salmons in both. If you mark Alexander's life well, Harry of Monmouth's life is come after it indifferent well; for there is figures in all things. Alexander, God knows, and you know, in his rages, and his furies, and his wraths, and his cholers, and his

moods, and his displeasures, and his indignations, and also being
a little intoxicates in his prains, did, in his ales and his angers, look
you, kill his best friend, Cleitus.
[GOWER. Our King is not like him in that. He never kill'd any of
his friends.]
FLUELLEN. It is not well done, mark you now, to take the tales
out of my mouth, ere it is made and finished. I speak but in the
figures and comparisons of it. As Alexander kill'd his friend Cleitus,
being in his ales and his cups; so also Harry Monmouth, being in
his right wits and his good judgements, turn'd away the fat knight
with the great belly doublet. He was full of jests, and gipes, and
knaveries, and mocks; I have forgot his name.
[GOWER. Sir John Falstaff.]
FLUELLEN. That is he. I'll tell you there is good men porn at Monmouth.

Note: Notice the devoicing of some initial consonants in Fluellen's speech:
He says "prains" instead of "brains," and uses the phrase "look you" a fair
amount, a cliché associated with Welsh speech.

2. From Dylan Thomas's *Under Milk Wood: A Play for Voices* (1952)

This poetic radio and theater piece evokes a Welsh fishing village and all its
inhabitants. It is narrated by the First and Second Voices. The First Voice
was played by Dylan Thomas (1914–1953) himself, and he recorded it; in
the 1972 film version that Thomas had scripted, Richard Burton played
the First Voice. There is no intrinsic reason why the First Voice cannot be
played by a woman. Here is the opening monologue:

FIRST VOICE. (*Very softly*) To begin at the beginning:
It is Spring, moonless night in the small town, starless and
bible-black, the cobblestreets silent and the hunched courters'-
and-rabbits' wood limping invisible down to the sloeblack, slow,

black, crowblack, fishingboat-bobbing sea. The houses are blind as moles (though moles see fine to-night in the shouting, velvet dingles) or blind as Captain Cat there in the muffled middle by the pump and the town clock, the shops in mourning, the Welfare Hall in widows' weeds. And all the people of the lull and dumbfound town are sleeping now.

Hush, the babies are sleeping, the farmers, the fishers, the tradesmen and pensioners, cobbler, schoolteacher, postman and publican, the undertaker and the fancy woman, drunkard, dressmaker, preacher, policeman, the webfoot cocklewoman and the tidy wives. Young girls lie bedded soft or glide in their dreams, with rings and trousseaux, bridesmaided by glowworms down the aisles of the organplaying wood. The boys are dreaming wicked or of the bucking ranches of the night and the jollyrodgered sea. And the anthracite statues of the horses asleep in the fields, and the cows in the byres, and the dogs in the wetnosed yards, and the cats nap in the slant corners or lope sly, streaking and needling on the one cloud of the roofs.

You can hear the dew falling and the hushed town breathing.

Only *your* eyes are unclosed to see the black and folded town fast, and slow, asleep.

3. From Gary Owen's *Crazy Gary's Mobile Disco* (2001), 3: "Don't Die Just Yet"

The innovative, fiery plays of Gary Owen are the jewel of the Welsh theater today, and, indeed, of world theater. His first big hit was *Crazy Gary's Mobile Disco*, really three plays in one, each play being a monologue. In the third play, Russell Markham—*"in him Jimmy Dean lives once again. He wishes"*—tells us about his life, and does various voices and characters. Here, a friend has asked Russell a question.

I don't even attempt an answer. I just make my apology and back slowly away—but he grabs me and says, "Look, you've gotta fucking answer me, OK, because, of course, there is no friend, there is no guy, everything I've been telling you about, it's me, it's my life—I've wasted the last thirty years and now I've got cancer for a skeleton and only the fact that my blood has been replaced with liquid morphine is keeping me from going mad with the pain. And what I need to know is, this girl, this perfect girl who, if you must know, had copper hair like a newly minted penny and eyes as blue as a fiver—if I call her up and tell her my whole empty life has been a tribute to her, no, not even a tribute, it's just been a shell, a mould, a casting around the vacuum where our love should have grown—

—will she laugh at me, or will she think it's beautiful?"

I pull the guy's hands off me, and I say, "What the fuck? What do you mean, you've wasted the last thirty years? You're the same age as me. We were at school together."

"Yeah," he says. "We were at school together."

"But you're fucking fifty," I say to him. "You're fifty years old and you're dying of cancer."

"Yeah," he says.

"And that can't be," I tell him, "'cause you're the same age as I am. And I'm twenty-three."

4. From Gary Owen's *The Drowned World* (2002), Scene 2

This startling, exciting, iconoclastic play in nine scenes was first performed at the Traverse Theatre in Edinburgh. As its director, Vicky Featherstone, says in her introduction, "*The Drowned World* defies much explanation—it is a great play that is visionary in its perception and terrifying in its vision."

TARA (*looks at* DARREN.) He's fine.
 Turns away from him.
He's fine except he can't speak.

His eyes flick open occasionally but they don't focus properly: they focus on empty points in the room. Like he's seeing into another world. Like he's leaving me already.

 Beat.

And I don't know what to do.
We had plans.
He told me a story about the day that involved cutting back the rhododendrons and pruning the roses. It didn't involve
Any of this.
And he's asleep.
He's left me alone.
I hug him and his breath
Sets the hairs of my neck on end
He's wrapped in blankets
Blankets this citizen gave us
He smells of them
He smells like a citizen
I pull them off and bury my head in his chest
I open his shirt so I can taste his skin: and it tastes of blood
I open my eyes and I can see into the cut
I can see
I can see his heart.
The cold of the basement
is freezing it.
I can see ice crystals
Forming inside the cut.
He is freezing from the inside out.

6
Irish Accents

Dublin, capital of Eire /E ruh/, the Republic of Ireland, and Belfast, chief city of Northern Ireland, which is part of the U.K., as well as every one of Ireland's thirty-two counties, have their own accents. We will cover three accents often used in movies and plays: general Northern Irish, including Belfast; Galway on the West Coast of Ireland; and Southeastern accents of Kildare / general Dublin.

The original language of Hibernia, as the Romans called Ireland, was Gaelic /GAY lihk/, and is the main early influence on the accent in English. Gaelic is a Celtic language related to Scottish Gaelic and Welsh. Today it is the first language of an estimated ninety-four thousand people, and is spoken in a number of separated areas of Ireland. The attempt to revive it is ongoing, and perhaps an additional almost two million people speak and read Gaelic as a second language.

There are numerous examples of authentic Irish accents available on film. Listen to the many supporting players in *A Man of No Importance* (1994), set in Dublin, and starring Albert Finney, whose accent is perfect as a man who admires and emulates Anglo-Irish writer Oscar Wilde. Also listen to Milo O'Shea and the other Irish actors in the film of James Joyce's *Ulysses* (1967). Worth hearing as well is Dublin-born Barry Fitzgerald in such Hollywood films as *The Quiet Man* (1952), despite the intentional exaggeration of his accent. See Carol Reed's magnificent film *Odd Man Out* (1947), with James Mason as a hunted Irish rebel leader. *The Crying Game* (1992) with Belfast-born Stephen Rea, is good for Northern accents.

In the Name of the Father (1993) and *The Boxer* (1997) both star Daniel Day-Lewis, whose accent work is always perfect. *Michael Collins* (1996) takes place during the 1916–1921 rebellion, with the always-superb Liam Neeson, born in Ballymena, County Antrim, Northern Ireland, in the title role. And for hilarious comedy, see the late, great Dublin-born David Kelly (1929–2012) as the builder O'Reilly in season 1 (1975), episode 2 of *Fawlty Towers*, "The Builders." He is also charming as Grandpa Joe in *Charlie and the Chocolate Factory* (2005); in all, he appeared in more than one hundred television and film projects, including the aforementioned *A Man of No Importance*. Another great actor from Dublin is Brendan Gleeson, whom you can hear using his own accent in playwright and filmmaker Martin McDonagh's movie *In Bruges* (2008), along with Colin Farrell, also from Dublin. Gleeson also plays Alastor "Mad Eye" Moody in *Harry Potter and the Goblet of Fire* (2005) and *Harry Potter and the Order of the Phoenix* (2007). For Limerick accents, see the moving film *Angela's Ashes* (1999), based on Frank McCourt's wonderful, Pulitzer Prize–winning book. John Huston's last film, *The Dead* (1987), is based on James Joyce's short story in *Dubliners*; the atmosphere of the film and the performances by the Irish cast are superb. Wonderfully acted, *The Wind That Shakes the Barley* (2006), with moving performances by Cillian Murphy, Padraic Delaney, and Liam Cunningham, is a wrenching film about brotherhood and betrayal in the 1920 rebellion.

Documentaries and travel films will give you a vivid impression of Ireland, such as the 1997 documentary *Danny Boy: In Sunshine or in Shadow*. Also excellent are the historical documentaries *The Irish in America* (1995) and *The Irish in America: Long Journey Home* (1998).

For recordings, search Audible.com and you will find books on Irish history, fiction, and drama, many read by Irish authors and actors. The lyrical Dublin accent in Sean O'Casey's readings from his works, such as *Juno and the Paycock*, available as MP3 downloads, is not to be missed. You can also see him interviewed on YouTube. Available from Audible are Siobhán McKenna's readings of Molly Bloom's soliloquy in James Joyce's

Ulysses, *The Collected Stories of Katherine Anne Porter*, *The Poetry of W. B. Yeats* (which includes the voice of Yeats himself), *The Very Best of William Butler Yeats* (also featuring Cyril Cusack and Micheál Mac Liammóir), and Joyce's *Finnegan's Wake*, with the prolific Cyril Cusack, who appears in many films. You can also see Cusack in the Tom Cruise movie *Far and Away* (1992), along with his fellow co-stars Colm Meaney and Niall Toibin. The following CDs are also useful: *John McCormack in Irish Song* (Pearl, Gemm CD 9338, n.d.), in which you not only hear the thrilling voice of the famous tenor singing, but also speaking, on track 20 when he introduces "The Londonderry Air"; *The Irish Songbook: 21 Treasured Irish Songs by Timeless Voices of Yesteryear* (Moidart Music Group, MID CD 006, n.d.); and *"The Minstrel Boy": Irish Singers of Great Renown* (Pearl, Gemm CD 9989, n.d.).

Teach Yourself the Northern Irish and Belfast Accents

The two most noticeable features of the Belfast accent are its music (see later in this chapter); and the fact that the accent is non-rhotic, so post-vocalic (after a vowel) /r/ is usually not heard.

1. **Positioning, placement, and use of the mouth muscles during speech:** The opening of the mouth for Belfast and Northern Irish accents is in between the General American wide and British RP closed positions, just slightly more closed than in General American. The jaw is relaxed.
2. **Consonants:**
   a. **The sound of /h/:** The initial consonant /h/ is pronounced, and in such orthographic combinations as "wh" in *where*, it is pronounced as if the spelling were "hw": /HWER/.
   b. **The sound of /l/:** The consonant /l/ is dark, liquid, and slightly retroflex (the bottom of the tongue curls upward), especially in the South

of Ireland. This /l/, with the tip of the tongue well forward during its pronunciation, is a key to the general placement of the accent.

c. **The sound of /r/:** In the North, generally, and in Belfast, post-vocalic (after a vowel) /r/ is often dropped, or very lightly pronounced; the accent is usually non-rhotic.

3. **Vowels and diphthongs:**

a. **The sounds of /a/ and /ah/:** The /a/ in words like *bad*, *that*, and *cat* is heightened (the tongue is slightly raised), close to the /ah/ in *father*, but not as open: /BAHD/, /THAHT/, /KAHT/. The /ah/ sounds in the "ask list" in chapter 1 are pronounced with the /ah/ in *father*, as in British RP, but less open-throated.

b. **The vowel shift from /aw/ to /ah/:** The vowel /aw/ in such words as *talk* and *law* shifts to /ah/: /TAHK/, /LAH/.

c. **/ay/ to /e/:** In such words as *say,* the diphthong /ay/ shifts to a lengthened pure vowel /e/.

d. **The shift of /e/ to /a/:** The /e/ in words like *met*, *bed*, and *bet* is broadened, close to the /a/ in *bad*: /MAT/, /BAD/, /BAT/. Sometimes, the sound is diphthongized, especially in working-class accents: /MEuhT/, /BEuhD/, /BEuhT/.

e. **The shift from /ih/ to /e/:** The short /ih/ sounds like the short /e/ in *met*, so the word *killed* is pronounced /KELD/, *think* is pronounced /THENK/, and so forth. In some areas of the city of Belfast, there is a shift from /ih/ to the schwa /uh/: *sit* shifts to /SUHT/, and *sit down* is pronounced /SUHT DAHüN/. The word *inward* is pronounced /EN werd (alternatively, EN wed)/.

f. **The sound of /I/:** Importantly, in Belfast and the North, /I/ remains /I/ as in standard varieties of English.

g. **The shift from /oh/ to /aw/:** In such words as *home*, the diphthong /oh/ shifts to a lengthened /aw/.

h. **The shift from /ow/ to /I/:** In Belfast and the North, the diphthong /ow/ shifts often to /I/: The words *round about* are pronounced /RIND uh BIT/.

   i. **The shift from /u/ to /oo/:** The /u/ in *but* is like the /oo/ in *book*.
      It is also sometimes heard as a schwa, particularly in working-
      class accents.
   4. The past participle *been* rhymes with *Ben* or with *bean*.

Intonation and Stress: The Music and Rhythm of the Accents

Two important characteristics of Belfast speech are lengthened vowels,
and its particular musicality: A rising tone which we associate with questions is sometimes heard at the end of a declarative sentence, as in the
example given here:

And that was the sort of thing he wanted to tell me, you see.
/ahn THAT wuhz thuh saw te THENG hee WAN ted tuh tel mee yuh see/

Note: The "t" in *sort of* is very aspirated, almost like a flap with lots of air in
it, instead of being a hard "t." Here is one possible pitch (intonation) pattern:

                                                        me,

        that   you see.

   And   was the sort of thing he wanted to

                                                    tell

Practice Exercises

1. *Like I said to yous, that's really very true, and sure, you'll be after knowing*
the truth of it somewhere along the road anyway.
/lIk I sad tuh yuhz (alternatively, yihz), thats REE lee VA ree TREEOOH
an SHAWR (alternatively, SHOOR) YIHL (alternatively, yoohl) bee AF tuh
NAWN (alternatively, NAW ihn) thuh TREE ooh*th* uhv iht SOOM we uh
ruh LANG thuh RAWD A nee WE/

Note: Notice the lengthened vowel replacing the diphthong in the last syllable of *anyway*.

2. *It's not what you're thinking at all, I can assure you. I'm done with telling you.*
/uhts nawt wuht yuh THANK uhn uh DAL I kin uh SHYOOR (alternatively, SHEER) yooh / ahm DUN wih*th* TAL ihn yuh/

Notes: The /d/ in the syllable /DAL/ is lightly tapped.

3. *We only went to the theater, then he walked me home through the lane. And I met him there anyway.*
/wee AWN lee WAN tuh thuh THEE uh tuh than hee WAKT mee HOHM *th*rooh thuh LEN / nI MAT im THAY uh RA nee WE/

Note: The /ay/ sounds in the word *lane* and the final syllable of *anyway* are considerably lengthened.

4. *You're an idiot to be so jealous. Come to my arms. It's you I love, you know, my darling.*
/yahr (alternatively, yawr) an IH dee iht tih bee saw JAL uhs / KUM tuh mI AHMZ / its yooh I LOOV yuh NAW mI DAH lihng/

Note: The /d/ in the word *idiot* is tapped.

Monologues
1. From Christina Reid's *The Belle of Belfast City* (1986), Act 1, Scene 3
This play tells the story of three generations of women in one dysfunctional Belfast family. Their problems mirror those of the larger socio-political dilemmas engendered by the Anglo-Irish Agreement of 1985. Some of the characters naïvely and nostalgically reminisce about a supposedly idyllic

past, and it is the contrast between the glorified past and the truth of the present—with its bigotry, fears, and prejudices—that form the core of the play.

Jack is married to Janet, to whom the following speech is addressed.

> JACK. (*Quoting from St. Paul*) It is good for a man not to marry. But since there is so much immorality each man should have his own wife and each woman her own husband. The husband should fulfill his marital duty to his wife, and likewise the wife to her husband. The wife's body does not belong to her alone, but also to the husband. In the same way, the husband's body does not belong to himself alone, but also to his wife. Do not deprive each other except by mutual consent. Then come together again so that Satan will not tempt you because of your lack of self-control. I say this as a concession, not as a command. I wish that all men were as I am . . . I love you. Come back to me.

2. From Brian Friel's *Dancing at Lughnasa* (1990), Act 1

In Brian Friel's great "memory" play *Dancing at Lughnasa* (/LOOH nah sah/—"gh" is often silent in Irish orthography), set in a fictitious town in the Northern county of Donegal, Michael reminisces about his childhood, and the people he knew in the small village where he was born.

For a Donegal accent, bear the following specific phonetic information in mind:

1. In initial position a lightly tapped /r/ is often heard.
2. The voiceless /th/ in words like *think* is pronounced /t/: /TIHNK/.
3. Final "g" in "-ing" endings is often dropped: *nothing* is pronounced /NUT en/.

This monologue is by Michael's aunt Maggie.

MAGGIE. When I was sixteen I remember slipping out one Sunday night—it was this time of year, the beginning of August—and Bernie and I met at the gate of the workhouse and the pair of us off to a dance in Ardstraw. [. . .]

And at the end of the night there was a competition for the best Military Two-step. And it was down to three couples: the local pair from Ardstraw; wee Timmy and myself—he was up to there on me; and Brian and Bernie . . .

And they were just so beautiful together, so stylish; you couldn't take your eyes off them. People just stopped dancing and gazed at them . . .

And when the judges announced the winners—they were probably blind drunk—naturally the local couple came first; and Timmy and myself came second; and Brian and Bernie came third.

Poor Bernie was stunned. She couldn't believe it. Couldn't talk. Wouldn't speak to any of us for the rest of the night. Wouldn't even cycle home with us. She was right, too: they should have won; they were just so beautiful together . . .

And that's the last time I saw Brian McGuinness—remember Brian with the . . . ? And the next thing I heard he had left for Australia . . .

She was right to be angry, Bernie. I know it wasn't fair—it wasn't fair at all. I mean they must have been blind drunk, those judges, whoever they were . . .

Teach Yourself the (West Coast) Galway Accent

1. **Positioning, placement, and use of the mouth muscles during speech:** For Galway, similarly to Belfast, the mouth is less open than

in General American and open wider than the British RP positions. The jaw is relaxed.

2. **Consonants:**

   a. **The sound of /h/:** The initial consonant /h/ is pronounced, and in such orthographic combinations as "wh" in *where*, it is pronounced as if the spelling were "hw": /HWER/.

   b. **The sound of /l/:** The consonant /l/ is dark, liquid, and slightly retroflex (the bottom of the tongue curls upward), especially in the South. This /l/, with the tip of the tongue well forward during its pronunciation, is a key to the general placement of the accent.

   c. **The sound of /r/:** The accent is rhotic with very heavy post-vocalic (after a vowel) /r/ sounds; a trilled /r/ is sometimes heard at the beginning or end of a word. The back of the tongue is tensed slightly as its tip curls far up.

   d. **The sounds of /th/:** Voiced /th/ is pronounced /d/. Voiceless /th/ is pronounced /t/: *I think that's so* /oy TIHNK dats saw/.

3. **Vowels and diphthongs:**

   a. **The sound of /a/:** The vowel /a/, slightly more open-mouthed than the General American version, is used where British RP uses /ah/; see the "ask list" in chapter 1.

   b. **The vowel shift from /aw/ to /ah/:** The vowel /aw/ in such words as *talk* and *law* shifts to /ah/: /TAHK/, /LAH/.

   c. **The shift from /ay/ to /e/:** In such words as *say* the /ay/ shifts to a lengthened /e/.

   d. **/I/ shifts to /oy/.**

   e. **The shift from /oh/ to /aw/:** In such words as *home*, the diphthong /oh/ shifts to a lengthened /aw/.

   f. **The shift from /ow/ to /ay/:** The /ow/ diphthong is often pronounced /ay/, so *about* is pronounced /uh BAYT/.

   g. **The sound of /yooh/:** This diphthong is pronounced in such words as *lute* and *new*: /LYOOHT/, /NYOOH/. In the orthographic combination "du," a /j/ is added, so the sound is pronounced /jooh/: the word *duty* is pronounced /JOOH tee/. The phrase *the Duke of Westmoreland* is heard as /duh JOOHK v west MOOHR luhnd/.

4. The past participle *been* rhymes with *Ben* and sometimes with *bean*.

Intonation and Stress: The Music and Rhythm of the Accent

The lengthened vowels, especially before /r/, give the accent its rhythmic pattern. Strong emotion is often expressed by a high pitch on the important, stressed syllable. Otherwise, the usual intonation patterns prevail of raising the tone at the end of a question, and dropping it at the end of a declarative sentence.

Practice Exercises

1. *Like I said to yous, that's really very true, and sure, you'll be after knowing the truth of it somewhere along the road anyway.*
/loyk I SIHD tuh yuhz dats RAY lee VE ree TROOH an shoohr yuhl bee AF tthuhr NAWN duh TROOHT uhv iht SOOM wee uhr uh LANG duh RAWD IH nee WE/

Notes: The /r/ sounds at the end of *sure* and in *road* may be trilled. Notice the lengthened vowel replacing the diphthong in the last syllable of *anyway*.

2. *It's not what you're thinking at all, I can assure you. I'm through with telling you.*
/its NAT WAT chuhr TIHNK ihn uh TAHL I kuhn uh SHOOHR yuh / Im TTHROOH wit TEL uhn yuh/

3. *We only went to the theater, then he walked me home through the lane. And I met him there anyway.*
/wee AWN lee WIHNT tuh duh TAY tthuhr / dihn hee WAHKT mee HAWM tthrooh duh LEN / uhn I MIHT hihm DER IH nee WE/

Notes: The vowel in the word *lane* is short, but the same vowel at the end of the word *anyway* is lengthened. The /r/ sounds may be trilled or given one tap.

4. *You're an idiot to be so jealous. Come to my arms. It's you I love, you know, my darling.*
/yuhr an IH juht tuh bay saw JEL uhs / KOOM tuh mI ARMZ / ihtsh yooh oy LOOV yuh NAW mI DAHR luhn/

Note: The /t/ at the end of the word *idiot* should be given one light, aspirated tap.

A Scene for Two and a Monologue
1. From Seumas O'Brien's One-Act Comedy *Matchmakers*

This charming play by an almost-forgotten author was produced in 1916 at the Abbey Theatre in Dublin. Mr. and Mrs. Corcoran are farmers, as is Denis Delahunty. The Corcorans have one daughter, Kitty. You will notice the wonderful slang epithets and the spirited manner of all the characters.

The play takes place on "an island off the West coast of Ireland" in the days before Irish independence for most of the island; and the scene is the "interior of Donal Corcoran's house. Donal and his wife are seated in two comfortable armchairs by the parlour fire. The parlour is well furnished, and Kitty is busy dusting, as visitors are expected. Donal is a man of about fifty-six years, and his wife is a little younger. Donal is reading a copy of the *Galway Examiner*, and his wife is knitting a stocking."

From the newspaper, Donal Corcoran learns to his astonishment that his neighbor Mr. Delahunty is to be ennobled. He reads, "Baronetcy for the chairman of the Innismore Board of Guardians. His Majesty the King has been pleased to confer a Royal favour on the worthy and exemplary Denis Delahunty, who in future will be known as Sir Denis Delahunty, Bart., in recognition of his services to the people of Innismore. It was with a feelin' of pride and admiration that . . ."

This is a scene for Kitty and her father, with some interruptions from her mother, and deals with the growing issue of marrying for love versus arranged marriages, which are quite common in many cultures.

KITTY. (*Takes the paper and smiles. Falls on a chair nearly overcome with laughter. The parents look on in amazement*) Sir Denis Delahunty! (*Laughs heartily.*)

DONAL. What are you laughin' at? You impudent hussy!

KITTY. (*still laughing*) Sir Denis Delahunty, Bart., my dear!

DONAL. Yes, yes, Sir Denis Delahunty. And what about it?

KITTY. Dinny Delahunty, the old caubogue, a baronet, and no less! (*Laughs.*)

DONAL. I'll have no more of this laughin', I say. What at all, are you amused at, I'd like to know?

KITTY. Oh, father, sure 'tis a blessing that some one has a sense of humour, like myself and the King. And 'twas the great laugh he must have had to himself, when he made a baronet of Dinny Delahunty. Not to mention all the other shoneens and huxters, from here to Bantry.

DONAL. How dare you speak to me like that, miss, when 'tis yourself that will be Lady Delahunty one of these fine days. Dinny, I mean, Sir Denis himself, is comin' here to-night to make a match with his son, Finbarr.

KITTY. Wisha, indeed, now! And who told you I am going to wed Finbarr Delahunty? And he a more miserable shoneen than his old crawthumping humbug of a father.

DONAL. If you'll speak as disrespectfully as that again about any of my friends you'll be sorry for it. 'Tis I'm tellin' you that you are to wed Finbarr Delahunty and that's information enough for you, my damsel.

KITTY. I'll spare you the trouble of picking a man for me, father.

MRS. CORCORAN. Don't be disobedient, Kitty. You must remember that I never laid eyes on your father until the mornin' I met him at the altar rails.

KITTY. You should be ashamed to acknowledge the like, mother.

DONAL. Ashamed of me, is it? The father that rared and schooled you!

KITTY. I have said nothing at all to offend you, father. But I have already told you that I am going to pick a husband for myself.

DONAL. You are goin' to pick a husband for yourself! Are you, indeed? Ah, sure 'tis the stubbornness of your mother's people that's in you.

2. From Martin McDonagh's *The Beauty Queen of Leenane* (1996), Scene 4

This is the first play of the Leenane Trilogy, the other two being *A Skull in Connemara* and *The Lonesome West*.

A brutal portrayal of a horribly dysfunctional relationship between a mother and daughter, the play ends with Maureen, the daughter and "beauty queen" of the title, murdering Mag, her mother, in a fit of passion.

The play takes place in "the living room / kitchen in a small house in the west of Ireland." As McDonagh tells us, Mag Folan is "a smallish woman in her early seventies with short, lightly permed gray hair and a mouth that gapes slightly." Maureen is "a plain, slim woman of about forty."

In this speech, Maureen talks to her mother and her new friend Pato, who is about her age. Pato has spent the night, and has just come into the room, putting on a shirt. Mag is dumbfounded, and Maureen is standing around in her underwear, having found romance at long last. She talks about a nervous breakdown she had.

You will notice the typical Irishism of saying "me" for "my," which was also the general nineteenth century pronunciation of "my," as recordings show. "Fecking" is an Irish pronunciation, and "shite" /SHIT/ is an Irish pronunciation of the word *shit*. The word *oul* means "old" in this accent. Connemara is name of the West-Coast Irish district, often meaning all of Galway.

The accents, which were very thick in the Broadway production that was brought over from the U.K., should be carefully and clearly worked on.

> MAUREEN. In England I was, this happened. Cleaning work. When I was twenty-five. Me first time over. Me only time over. Me sister had just got married, me other sister just about to. Over in Leeds I was, cleaning offices. Bogs. A whole group of us, only them were all English. "Ya oul backward Paddy fecking . . . The fecking pig's-backside face on ya." The first time out of Connemara this was I'd been. "Get back to that backward fecking bog of yours or whatever hole it was you drug yourself out of." Half of the swearing I didn't even understand. I had to have a black woman explain it to me. Trinidad she was from. They'd have a go at her too, but she'd just laugh. This big face she had, this big oul smile. And photos of Trinidad she'd show me, and "What the hell have you left there for?" I'd say. "To come to this place, cleaning shite?" And a calendar with a picture of Connemara on I showed her one day, and "What the hell have you left there for?" she said back to me. "To come to this place . . ." (*Pause.*) But she moved to London then, her husband was dying. And after that it all just got to me.

Teach Yourself the Kildare / Dublin (Southern Irish) Accents

These accents are very strongly rhotic, except among those individuals who imitate British speech. There are class differences in Dublin accents; see the Sean O'Casey monologues later in this chapter.

1. **Positioning, placement, and use of the mouth muscles during speech:** For Southern Irish accents, such as Dublin / Kildare, the jaw is fairly loose and the mouth more open than in General American,

but not as widely open as in London accents. Practice the Irish /l/ (see below), with the tongue well forward, to get the general position.

2. **Consonants:** Consonants are generally the same as in standard varieties of English. Take note of the following important changes, however:

   a. **The sound of /h/:** The initial consonant /h/ is pronounced; in the orthographic combination "wh" in *where*, it is pronounced as if the spelling were "hw": /HWER/.

   b. **The sound of /l/:** The consonant /l/ is dark, liquid, and slightly retroflex (the bottom of the tongue curls upward). This /l/, with the tip of the tongue well forward during its pronunciation, is a key to the general placement of the accent.

   c. **The sound of /r/:** The accent is rhotic, and the heavily retroflex post-vocalic (after a vowel) /r/ is pronounced with the tongue curled farther back than in General American, so that the sides of the bottom of the tongue really touch the inner sides of the upper gum ridge. The back of the tongue is relaxed. In educated Dublin speech, the /r/ is very lightly pronounced. It is harder in working-class speech.

   d. **The sounds of /th/:** These sounds are often substituted by /d/ for the voiced, and /t/ for the voiceless sounds, but by no means is this always the case. In Dublin, /th/ before /r/ is often heard as /t/ or even /ts/, as in the word *through* /TSROOH/, in working-class but not in educated speech.

3. **Vowels and diphthongs:** The shifts in vowels and diphthongs are listed at the beginning of this chapter. Add the following sounds:

   a. **The sound of /a/:** The vowel /a/, slightly more open-mouthed than the General American version, is used where British RP uses /ah/. See the "ask list" in chapter 1.

   b. **The vowel shift from /aw/ to /ah/:** The vowel /aw/ in such words as *talk* and *law* shifts to /ah/: /TAHK/, /LAH/.

c. **/ay/ to /e/:** In working-class speech especially, the long /ay/ diphthong often shifts to a lengthened pure vowel /e/, so *tea* is pronounced /TAY/. See the first practice exercise later in this chapter.

d. **/e/ to /ay/:** The long /ee/ in words like *tea* is often pronounced /ay/ in *say*: /TAY/, especially in working-class speech.

   Practice words for the shift from /ee/ to /ay/: *tea, meat, Jesus, leave, here* (rhymes with hair), *beer, teach, reach, believe* /TAY/, /MAYT/, /JAY zuhs/, /LAYV/, /HAYR/, /BAYR/, /TAYCH/, /RAYCH/, /buh LAYV/.

e. **The schwa /uh/ inserted before or after /r/ and after consonants:** Particular to Dublin speech, especially working-class, is a schwa inserted before /r/ in words like *beer, square, floor, pair, horse* /BEEuhR/, /SKWEEuhR/, /FLOOHuhR/, /PAYuhR/, /HOOHuhRS/. Sometimes, a schwa is inserted after a consonant, so *Dublin*, for example, is pronounced /DU (alternatively, DOO) buh lihn/; the word *arm* is pronounced /AH ruhm/.

f. **The sounds of /I/:** This diphthong often loses the schwa that follows it in words like *mile* and *trial*. Sometimes, /I/ shifts to /oy/, especially in working-class speech. The words *mile* (General American pronunciation /MI uhl/) and *trial* (General American pronunciation /TRI uhl/) are pronounced either /MOYL/ and /TROYL/ or /MIL/ and /TRIL/. In Dublin, /I/ ranges from /oy/ to /OOHee/.

g. **The shift from /oh/ to /aw/:** In such words as *home*, the diphthong /oh/ often shifts to a lengthened /aw/.

h. **/oy/ to /I/:** The shift of the /oy/ in words like *boy* to the /I/ diphthong is very marked, especially in working-class speech.

i. **/ o/ to /oo/:** The /o/ in such words as *occur, nurse, work,* and *first* is pronounced like the /oo/ in *book*, and sometimes like /aw/: /uh KOOR/, /NOORS/, /WOORK (alternatively, WAWRK)/, /FOORST (alternatively, FAWRST)/.

j. **/u/ to /oo/:** The vowel /u/, in words like *but*, often (but not always) shifts to /oo/ in words like *book*, particularly when not stressed.

k. **The sound of /yooh/:** Words like *tune* and *duke* are pronounced with the semi-vowel /y/ before the vowel /ooh/ in educated Dublin speech. But in working-class speech (where a word like *true* can be pronounced /TREE yooh/), the /y/ is not added for any consonants, voiced or voiceless, so *tune* is pronounced /CHOOHN/ and *duke* is pronounced /JOOHK/.

4. The past participle *been* usually rhymes with *bean*.

Intonation and Stress: The Music and Rhythm of the Accents

Vowels and diphthongs are sometimes considerably lengthened before /r/ and to make a point generally, giving these accents their characteristic rhythm. There is a lilt to Dublin accents, and the use of more notes than are heard in either British RP or General American. Listen carefully to the suggested recordings and films so you can reproduce these pitch patterns accurately and authentically.

Practice Exercises

1. *Like I said to yous, that's really very true, and sure, you'll be after knowing the truth of it somewhere along the road anyway.*

Kildare / General Dublin: /LIK I sed tuh yuhz thats REE lee VE ree TROOH and SHOOuhR yuhl bee AF tuhr NOH ihn thuh TROOH*TH* uhv iht SUM hweuhr uh LAHNG thuh ROHD E nee WAY/

Inner Dublin: /loyk (alternatively, lIk) oy SED (alternatively, SAD), tuh yuhz dats (alternatively, ats) REE lee VE ree TSROOH an SHAWR yuhl bee af t*her* NAWN duh TSROOHT uhv iht SOOM (alternatively, SUM) weeuhr uh LANG duh RAWD A nee WEE/

2. *It's not what you're thinking at all, I can assure you. I'm done with telling you.*

Kildare / General Dublin: /ihts NOT WUHT yuhr (alternatively, yawr) *TH*IHNK ihng a TAHL I kan uh SHOOHR yooh / Im dun wit*h* TEL ihng yooh/

Inner Dublin: /its NAT WAT yuhr (alternatively, chuhr) THIHNK (alternatively, TIHNK) ihn uh DAHL oy kin uh SHOO uhr yuh / oym DOON (alternatively, DUN), wit TEL (alternatively, TSEL) ihn yuh/

Notes: In the Kildare / General Dublin pronunciation, the /t/ in the syllable /TAHL/ is aspirated and lightly tapped, as is the /d/ in /DAHL/ in the Inner Dublin pronunciation. Notice the forward Irish /l/ sounds in the words *all* and *telling*, in both pronunciations.

3. *We only went to the theater, then he walked me home through the lane. And I met him there anyway.*
Kildare / General Dublin: /wee OHN lee WENT tuh thuh *THEE* uh tuhr then hee WAKT mee HAWM *th*rooh thuh LEN / And I MET hihm THAYR E nee WAY/
Inner Dublin: /wee AWN lee wen tuh duh *THEE* tuhr den hee WAKT me HAWM tsrooh duh LEN / an oy MET hihm DAY uhr (alternatively, DTHAY uhr) E nee WAY/

Notes: In the Kildare / General Dublin pronunciation, the /t/ in the word *theater* is lightly tapped and heavily aspirated, as is the /t/ at the end of the word *met*. The vowel /e/ in /LEN/ is elongated in both pronunciations. In the Inner Dublin pronunciation, the /d/ in the syllable /duh/ is lightly tapped.

4. *You're an idiot to be so jealous. Come to my arms. It's you I love, you know, my darling.*
Kildare / General Dublin: /yawr an IH dee uht tuh bee soh JE luhs / kum tuh mI AHRMZ / ihts yooh I LUV yooh NOH mI DAHR lihng/
Inner Dublin: /yuhr en IH jit (alternatively, dyuht) tuh bee saw JEL uhs / koom tih moy AH ruhmz / its yooh oy LOOV yuh NAW moy DAHR luhn/

Note: In the Kildare / General Dublin pronunciation, the /d/ in the syllable /dee/ is lightly tapped.

Monologues and Scenes from Sean O'Casey's Dublin Trilogy
1. From *The Shadow of a Gunman* (1923), Act 1

This is the first of the three "Dublin plays," the other two being *Juno and the Paycock* and *The Plough and the Stars*. O'Casey was a committed Socialist, and portrayed the Irish working class with stark humor and deep understanding and compassion.

Like all the plays in the trilogy, the setting is a Dublin tenement—a different one in each play. The play unfolds against the background of the Irish independence movement in May 1920. Two men in their thirties, Seumas /SHAY muhs/ Shields and Donal Davoren /DO nuhl da VAW rihn/, are speculating about the contents of a mysterious bag that had just been left in a nearby corner by an IRA soldier named Mr. Maguire. *Gael* is another word for Irish. Knocksedan is an estate of houses in the North of Dublin. In Irish folklore, Balor of the Evil Eye was a king of giants. A *pro-cathedral* is a parish church that has been designated a temporary cathedral. A staunch supporter of Irish independence, James Stephens (1882–1950) was an Irish poet and novelist known for his compilations of Irish folklore. *Dark Rosaleen* is a poem that was well known at the time; it was written by Irish poet James Clarence Mangan (1803–1849), who was much admired by W. B. Yeats and James Joyce. The poem reads, in part, "Oh, my dark Rosaleen, / Do not sigh, do not weep! / The priests are on the ocean green, / They march along the deep."

You can treat Seumas's lines, addressed to Davoren, as a monologue. His accent is middle-class Dublin and, as an educated man, he knows Gaelic, which he used to teach.

> SEUMAS. (*with a gesture of despair*) Oh, this is a hopeless country!
> There's a fellow that thinks that the four cardinal virtues are not
> to be found outside an Irish Republic. I don't want to boast about
> myself—I don't want to boast about meself, and I suppose I could
> call meself as good a Gael as some of those that are knocking about
> now—as good a Gael as some that are knocking about now—but I

remember the time when I taught Irish six nights a week, when in the Irish Republican Brotherhood I paid me rifle levy like a man, an' when the Church refused to have anything to do with James Stephens, I tarred a prayer for the repose of his soul on the steps of the Pro-Cathedral. Now after all me work for Dark Rosaleen, the only answer you can get from a roarin' Republican to a simple question is "goodbye . . . ee." What, in the name o' God, can be bringin' him to Knocksedan?

DAVOREN. Hadn't you better run out and ask him?

SEUMAS. That's right, that's right—make a joke about it! That's the Irish people all over—they treat a joke as a serious thing and a serious thing as a joke. Upon me soul, I'm beginning to believe that the Irish people aren't, never were, an' never will be fit for self-government. They've made Balor of the Evil Eye King of Ireland, an' no signs on it there's neither conscience nor honesty from one end of the country to the other. Well, I hope he'll have a happy day in Knocksedan.

2. From *Juno and the Paycock* (1924), Act 3

This play was one of O'Casey's great successes, and was produced at the Abbey Theatre.

Christopher Murray, in his introduction to the 1998 edition of the Dublin plays, quotes critic James Agate's review of the 1925 London production: "*Juno and the Paycock* is as much a tragedy as *Macbeth*, but it is a tragedy taking place in the Porter's family."

Set in "the living-room of a two-room tenancy occupied by the Boyle family in a tenement house in Dublin," the play tells the story of "Captain" Jack Boyle, the peacock of the title, who gads about Dublin with his friend Joxer, leaving Mrs. Juno Boyle to tend to everything. The title alludes to Roman mythology, in which Juno, the wife of Jupiter, is attended by her favorite bird. Here, the mythological situation is reversed.

The spelling reflects perfectly the working-class accent, as in this speech by Mrs. Boyle from the opening scene of act 3, in which she gives her daughter advice. Mary Boyle is in love with the schoolteacher Charles Bentham: "But you shouldn't be frettin' the way you are; when a woman loses a man, she never knows what she's afther losin', to be sure, but, then, she never knows what she's afther gainin' either. You're not the one girl of a month ago—you like one pinin' away. It's long ago I had a right to bring you to the doctor, instead of waitin' till tonight." And in this speech of Juno's to Mary from act 1, the accent is even more clearly indicated: "If you weren't well yourself you'd like somebody to bring you a dhrink of wather. (*She brings a drink and returns.*) Isn't it terrible to have to be waitin' this way. You'd think he was bringin' twenty poun's a week into the house the way he's going on. He wore out the Health Insurance long ago, he's afther wearin' out the unemployment dole, an', now, he's thryin' to wear out me! An' constantly singin', no less, when he ought always to be on his knees offerin' up a Novena for a job!"

But here Mary Boyle, Jack and Juno's daughter, recites some verses in a more refined accent. She is talking to her friend Jerry Devine, who is in love with her. She likes him but does not feel about him the way she feels about Bentham.

> MARY. Do you remember, Jerry, the verses you read when you gave the lecture in the Socialist room some time ago, on Humanity's Strife with Nature?
> JERRY. The verses—no; I don't remember them.
> MARY. I do. They're runnin' in me head now—
>> An' we felt the power that fashion'd
>> All the lovely things we saw,
>> That created all the murmur
>> Of an everlasting law,
>> Was a hand of force an' beauty,
>> With an eagle's tearin' claw.

Then we saw our globe of beauty
Was an ugly thing as well,
A hymn divine whose chorus
Was an agonizin' yell;
Like the story of a demon
That an angel had to tell;

Like a glowin' picture by a
Hand unsteady, brought to ruin;
Like her craters, if their deadness
Could give life unto the moon;
Like the agonizing horror
Of a violin out of tune [/CHOOHN/].

3. From *The Plough and the Stars* (1926), Act 1

The third play of the Dublin trilogy also takes place in the tenement
house apartment of the Clitheroes /KLIH thuh ROHZ/. It is set against
the background of the fight for Irish independence in 1920–1921. The
hard-working charwoman Mrs. Grogan, as O'Casey tells us, is "a doleful-
looking little woman of forty, insinuating manner and sallow complexion.
She is fidgety and nervous, terribly talkative . . ." At the opening of the
play, Fluther Good, a locksmith and carpenter, is repairing the lock on
one of the doors, while Peter Flynn, uncle of Nora Clitheroe, is sitting
and watching him. When Mrs. Grogan enters, he leaves, annoyed at
what he considers an intrusion. We first hear Mrs. Grogan on the other
side of the door.

The expression "been after" expresses the past tense in this dialect.
With his spelling, O'Casey indicates the Inner Dublin working-class accent very well.

You can do this as a scene, or treat Fluther's lines as parenthetical, and
do it as a monologue.

MRS. GROGAN. (*outside*) Who are you lookin' for, sir? Who? Mrs. Clitheroe? . . . Oh, excuse me. Oh, ay, up this way. She's out, I think: I seen her goin'. Oh, you've somethin' for her; oh, excuse me. You're from Arnott's . . . I see . . . You've a parcel for her . . . righto . . . I'll take it . . . I'll give it to her the minute she comes in . . . It'll be quite safe. Oh, sign that . . . Excuse me . . . Where? . . . Here? . . . No, there; righto. Am I to put Maggie or Mrs.? What is it? You dunno? Oh, excuse me.

(*Mrs. Grogan opens the door and comes in . . . She has a draper's parcel in her hand, the knot of the twine tying it is untied . . .*)

(*Removing the paper and opening the cardboard box it contains*) I wondher what's that now? A hat! (*She takes out a hat, black, with decorations in red and gold.*) God, she's goin' to th' Divil lately for style! That hat, now, cost more than a penny. Such notions of upperosity she's gettin' (*Putting the hat on her head*) Oh, swank, what! (*She replaces it in parcel.*)
FLUTHER. She's a pretty little Judy all the same.
MRS. GROGAN. Ah, she is, and she isn't. There's prettiness an' prettiness in it. I'm always sayin' that her skirts are a little short for a married woman. An' to see her, sometimes of an evenin', in her glad-neck gown would make a body's blood run cold. An' th' way she thries to be polite, with her "Good mornin', Mrs. Grogan," when she's goin' down, an' her "Good evenin', Mrs. Grogan," when she's comin' up. But there's politeness an' politeness in it.
FLUTHER. They seem to get on well together, all th' same.
MRS. GROGAN. An' they do, an' they don't. The pair o' them used to be like two turtle doves always billin' and cooin'. You couldn't come into th' room but you'd feel, instinctive like, that they'd

just been afther kissin' an' cuddlin' each other . . . It often made me shiver, for, afther all, there's kissin' and cuddlin' in it. But I'm thinkin' he's beginnin' to take things more quietly; the mysthery of havin' a woman's mysthery no longer . . . She dhresses herself to keep him with her, but it's no use—afther a month or two, th' wondher of a woman wears off.

SELECTED BIBLIOGRAPHY

Books

Barber, Charles. *The English Language: A Historical Introduction*. Edinburgh: The Edinburgh University Press, 1997.

Blumenfeld, Robert. *Accents: A Manual for Actors*. Revised and Expanded Edition. New York: Limelight Editions, 2002.

Brook, G. I. *Dialects of English*. New York: Oxford University Press, 1967.

———. *Varieties of English*. London: MacMillan and St. Martin's Press, 1973.

Comrie, Bernard, ed. *The World's Major Languages*. New York: Oxford University Press, 1990.

Cruttenden, Alan. *Intonation*. New York: Cambridge University Press, 1986.

Crystal, David. *The Cambridge Encyclopedia of the English Language*. New York: Cambridge University Press, 1995.

Giegerich, Heinz J. *English Phonology*. New York: Cambridge University Press, 1992.

Gimson's Pronunciation of English. 5th edition, revised by Alan Cruttenden. London: Edward Arnold, 1994.

Hughes, Arthur, and Peter Trudgill. *English Accents and Dialects*. 3rd edition. London: Edward Arnold, 1996.

Jones, Daniel. *An English Pronouncing Dictionary*. 15th edition. Edited by Peter Roach and James Hartman. New York: Cambridge University Press, 1997.

———. *The Pronunciation of English*. New York: Cambridge University Press, 1992.

Ladefoged, Peter. *A Course in Phonetics*. 3rd edition. Philadelphia: Harcourt, Brace College Publishers, 1993.

———, and Ian Maddieson. *The Sounds of the World's Languages*. Oxford: Blackwell Publishers, 1996.

McArthur, Tom, ed. *The Oxford Companion to the English Language*. New York: Oxford University Press, 1992.

McCrum, Robert, William Cran, and Robert MacNeil. *The Story of English* (a companion to the PBS series). New York: Elizabeth Sifton Books, Viking, 1986.

Moss, Norman. *British/American Language Dictionary*. Lincolnwood, IL: Passport Books, 1984.

Pointon, G. E., ed. and transcriber. *BBC Pronouncing Dictionary of British Names*. New York: Oxford University Press, 1990. This dictionary includes English, Scottish, Irish, and Welsh names of people and places.

Robinson, Christine, and Carol Ann Crawford. *Scotspeak: A Guide to the Pronunciation of Modern Urban Scots (Scotspeak Book and CD)*. Edinburgh: Luath Press Limited, 2001.

Trudgill, Peter. *The Dialects of England*. Oxford: Blackwell Publishers, 1990.

Upton, Clive, and J. D. A. Widdowson. *An Atlas of English Dialects*. New York: Oxford University Press, 1996.

Wells, J. C. *Accents of English*, in three volumes: (1) *Introduction*; (2) *The British Isles*; (3) *Beyond the British Isles*. New York: Cambridge University Press, 1992. This is the best and most complete series of books on the subject.

Audio Recordings

Accents for Actors: Ireland, Wales, Scotland, and England. Compiled and directed by Christopher Casson, with a commentary by Joseph D. Pheifer. Cassette SAC 1027. New Rochelle, NY: Spoken Arts, Inc., 1983. All accents are with native speakers.

BBC vinyl records: (1) *English with an Accent*. BBC 22166 (23 accents); (2) *English with a Dialect*. BBC 22173 (British Isles accents), n.d. All accents are with native speakers.

ABOUT THE AUTHOR

Robert Blumenfeld is the author of *Accents: A Manual for Actors* (1998; Revised and Expanded Edition, 2002); *Acting with the Voice: The Art of Recording Books* (2004); *Tools and Techniques for Character Interpretation: A Handbook of Psychology for Actors, Writers, and Directors* (2006); *Using the Stanislavsky System: A Practical Guide to Character Creation and Period Styles* (2008); *Blumenfeld's Dictionary of Acting and Show Business* (2009); *Blumenfeld's Dictionary of Musical Theater: Opera, Operetta, Musical Comedy* (2010); *Stagecraft: Stanislavsky and External Acting Technique—A Companion to Using the Stanislavsky System* (2011); and the collaborator with noted teacher, acting coach, and actress Alice Spivak on the writing of her book *How to Rehearse When There Is No Rehearsal: Acting and the Media* (2007)—all published by Limelight. He lives and works as an actor, dialect coach, and writer in New York City, and is a longtime member of Equity, AFTRA, and SAG. He has worked in numerous regional and New York theaters, as well as in television and independent films, and has performed in many comedies and farces. For ACT Seattle he played the title role in Ronald Harwood's *The Dresser*, and he has performed many roles in plays by Shakespeare and Chekhov, as well as doing an Off-Broadway season of six Gilbert and Sullivan comic operas for Dorothy Raedler's American Savoyards (under the name Robert Fields), for which he played the Lord Chancellor in *Iolanthe* and other patter-song roles. In 1994, he performed in Michael John LaChiusa's musical *The Petrified Prince*, directed by Harold

Prince at the New York Shakespeare Festival's Public Theater. For the Mc-Carter Theatre in Princeton, New Jersey, Mr. Blumenfeld performed the role of the First Voice in Dylan Thomas's *Under Milk Wood*. He created the roles of the Marquis of Queensberry and two prosecuting attorneys in Moisés Kaufman's Off-Broadway hit play *Gross Indecency: The Three Trials of Oscar Wilde*, and was also the production's dialect coach, a job that he did as well for the Broadway musicals *Saturday Night Fever* and *The Scarlet Pimpernel* (third version and national tour) and for the New York workshop of David Henry Hwang's rewritten version of Rodgers and Hammerstein's *Flower Drum Song*. At the Manhattan School of Music, he was dialect coach for Dona D. Vaughn's production of Strauss's *Die Fledermaus* (2009) and for Jay Lesenger's production of Weill's *Street Scene* (2008), which he also coached for Mr. Lesenger at the Chautauqua Opera. Mr. Blumenfeld currently records books for Audible, among them *Pale Fire* and *Bend Sinister* by Vladimir Nabokov and *A Modest Proposal* by Jonathan Swift. He has recorded more than 320 Talking Books for the American Foundation for the Blind, including the complete Sherlock Holmes canon (four novels and fifty-six short stories), Victor Hugo's *The Hunchback of Notre-Dame*, Alexandre Dumas' *The Count of Monte Cristo*, a bilingual edition of Rainer Maria Rilke's previously unpublished poetry, and a bilingual edition of Samuel Beckett's *Waiting for Godot*, which he recorded in Beckett's original French and the playwright's own English translation. He received the 1997 Canadian National Institute for the Blind's Torgi Award for the Talking Book of the Year in the Fiction category, for his recording of Pat Conroy's *Beach Music*; and the 1999 Alexander Scourby Talking Book Narrator of the Year Award in the Fiction category. He holds a B.A. in French from Rutgers University and an M.A. from Columbia University in French language and literature. Mr. Blumenfeld speaks French, German, and Italian fluently, and has smatterings of Russian, Spanish, and Yiddish.

CD TRACK LISTING

Tracks 2 through 7 contain the Practice Exercises for each chapter. Track 2 also includes the Ask List (p. 22) and "Some Comparative British and American English Pronunciations" (pp. 24–26).

1. List of Phonetic Symbols Used in This Book (4:20)
2. Chapter 1: Standard Upper- and Middle-Class British Accents (12:48)
3. Chapter 2: London Accents (0:54)
4. Chapter 3: English Provincial Accents: The Midlands, Yorkshire (2:03)
5. Chapter 4: Scottish Accents (2:42)
6. Chapter 5: Welsh Accents (2:47)
7. Chapter 6: Irish Accents (2:55)